DUAL | LIVES

For Celeste,
Thank you so much
for your support.
All my bests
Michael Bell

additional praise for DUAL LIVES

*"In Michael Bell, I found an artist with the rare ability to
render reality in a modern photorealistic style combined with
the creative composition of an old master.*

*When I sought out the cover art for my book, Michael was not only
my first choice as an artist, he was my only choice.*

*In this literary work, realism is rendered, not by color and line, but by the words
of an amazingly talented man, who rose to become an educator, an artist,
and a philanthropist. It is an inspiring story."*
– JOHN A. GOTTI, *Bestselling author of SHADOW OF MY FATHER*

*"No one would accuse Michael Bell of modesty. He is a tough guy with a big
heart who cares deeply and sincerely about the power and importance of art to
bring communities together and to heal deep emotional and psychological
wounds. His connection with and impact on his students is inspirational.
In Dual Lives, a very uplifting story unfolds."*
– ERIC FISCHL, *World-renowned painter, sculptor, and bestselling
author of BAD BOY,* MY LIFE ON AND OFF THE CANVAS

*"A life lived in art comes in many forms. Few people have
combined more than one of these art-inflected lives
into one lifetime like Michael Bell."*
– JERRY SALTZ, *Senior Art Critic,* NEW YORK MAGAZINE

*"An unusual memoir by a professional artist who has become an inspiring and
Award-winning art teacher in public schools full of disadvantaged youth.
It is very different from just about any other teacher memoir I have read."*
– JAY MATHEWS, *Washington Post columnist and New York Times
bestselling author of WORK HARD. BE NICE.*

*"Dual Lives is the exciting story of Michael Bell, artist to America's most
infamous and art teacher to kids who have scooped up millions in awards for
their work. He deftly weaves his poignant personal story with those students
who have thrived under his guidance. Discover the keys to your own creativity
and mentorship in this unique book."*
– DANIEL H. PINK, *New York Times bestselling author of DRIVE
and A WHOLE NEW MIND*

additional praise for DUAL LIVES

"When you think of an artist and creator, you think of Michael Bell.

Being an artist is something you're born with. It's talent one has in their blood that drives itself through the human body and puts a thought or idea on canvas for the world to see.

I'm so proud of my best friend and brother for his accomplishments. Money can't buy talent. It does, however, buy the talents' creations."
– DOMINIC CAPONE, *Actor, producer, and great-nephew of late mob boss AL CAPONE*

"Art is within all. Our life experience shapes art's form and texture as it inversely changes us. Michael Bell knows the power of an artful life better than most. He has helped countless students find their first steps of self-discovery on their own creative paths.

As a mentor, his inspirational approach is made manifest in his protégés as they find something greater within themselves.

Art transforms, and Bell is there as lives are transformed by the challenge of growing in the ageless hands of art—and Michael Bell."
– DAVID J. LEESON, *Pulitzer Prize winning photographer*

"Really great work. I love the way he captures someone, in his art and in his book. He is truly an artist with a vision."
– JOSEPH R. GANNASCOLI, *Vito from THE SOPRANOS, celebrity spokesman and entrepreneur*

"While it is true that boxing is about sport and competition, boxing is also about overcoming, building confidence. This book will truly highlight that."
– PAUL MALIGNAGGI, *2-time world champion fighter, SHOWTIME/CBS boxing analyst*

"Always hang on to what you believe in. Never what you see . . . 'Cause what you see might just be an illusion."
– STEVE MARTORANO, *Celebrity cook, owner of* CAFÉ MARTORANO'S *and the real life ROCKY of South Philly*

MICHAEL BELL

DUAL | LIVES

FROM THE | TO THE
STREETS STUDIO

MMXVII
MBELLART Productions

To Commission Original Artwork by Michael Bell
or for Public Speaking/Workshop Inquiries visit:
www.MBELLART.com

Cover photography by Adia Chaney
Author headshot by Isaiah Foster, ShineInc Photography

Formatting by
www.12on14.us

ISBN-978-0692871003

Published by
MBELLART Productions, LLC
www.MBELLART.com

*For my son, Carmen, may he always believe in himself
as strongly as I do. You will always be my hero
and my one and only true champion.
I love you, pally.*

∞

*For my wife, Lisa, thank you for going on this journey
with me, and for staying on it—doing whatever it takes
to keep our family together. Our love truly is eternal.
Always remember* **480**.

∞

*For my brother, Will, my fellow "Warrior,"
I hope my story will inspire you to share your story
with the world one day too.*

∞

*For both of our families . . . the Bell's and the Molinaro's.
Thank you for always encouraging us to lead
such creative and meaningful lives.
For that, and so much more, I'm forever grateful.*

All my love,

MICHAEL BELL

CONTENTS

PREFACE

Over the course of my storied career, I have worked closely with countless fascinating students, artists, educators, actors, musicians, *gangsters even*. While I couldn't fit everyone's stories into the writing of this book, I do want to thank everyone I've met along my journey and those who contributed to my story.

For all you students and aspiring artists out there . . . keep fighting to be your best, keep fighting to live up to your legacy, and keep fighting to lift one another up. Never let anyone intimidate you along your journey.

There were times while writing this that I may not have been able to recall exact conversations or events with total clarity so I've improvised where I felt it necessary to move the story along. Some information has also been provided by third party sources. There are some identities, time frames, and locations that were changed or omitted.
*Some to protect the **innocent**. Some to protect the **guilty**.*

I also have strong opinions in this book which I do not hesitate to state. They are my own personal convictions which I have the right to express. To make certain, though, Kristy K. Anderson, Esq., General Counsel for MSEA/NEA carefully reviewed this manuscript prior to publishing. I'd like to extend my gratitude to her for her time and legal advice.

I hope you find my memoirs to be inspiring and equally as captivating. This is my life . . . *from the streets to the studio.*

DUAL | LIVES

FOREWORD

BY PETER J. GOTTI

DECEMBER 16, 2014

"Hello Michael, this is Peter Gotti. Please contact me as soon as you possibly can, I have a time sensitive project that I need to come to decision on immediately. Thanks, Michael."

At the time of that phone call, I had no idea that Michael Bell would have such a profound effect on my life, like he would so many others. Up until that moment, I only knew of Michael "the Artist," who, for whatever odd reason, my father, John Gotti, saved and savored a letter from, many years prior.

I had little idea of Michael Bell the teacher, the father, the husband, the inspiration, complex leader, and most important of all, *true friend*. But much of this history you will read about here in his memoir.

History teaches us, though, that everyone has a story. You will learn from Michael that "pictures are also filled with stories, and every one of us has a story to tell." Thus, on that December day, my family and I were blessed enough to have Michael enter our souls, where he will reside until his last breath.

In the fleeting times, and superficial world of today, it is a near impossible feat to come across individuals that embody drive, compassion, undying will and determination to not only succeed at their craft but to commit their entire being into whoever they come across on a daily basis. Michael is one of those individuals. He brings every oozing drop of blood, sweat, and tears into his every encounter, and believe me, it is an extreme roller coaster of actions and emotions that buckles you in for your very own "Ticket to Ride."

In 1971, Michael Bell was born into this world to hard working, hard scrapping, and proud Irish/Italian parents. If one doesn't know, let me inform you, this is a fiery combination of cultures that you, the reader, will encounter at many turns. Very early on in his childhood, it was evident that Michael inherited a gift from his beloved Grandmother Violet—a gift to "capture one's soul through art." This remarkable woman taught him to "draw a line from his life to his art that is straight and clear."

While young Michael was using his pencils, pens, and paintbrushes to "dream it, create it, and become it" he was also coming into the acquaintance of many men and women that have faced and overcome unbelievable adversity in one capacity or another. This ability to adapt and overcome would also assist Michael often in his life—the ability to look anguish and pain in its ugly face, and not allow it to consume your heart. Along the balancing act of exploring the complex mind that Michael is blessed and cursed to have . . . you will meet people of deep, extreme circumstances and situations, that Michael was uniquely able to relate—men and women of darkness and shadows, as well as explosive light. Such encounters and strong personalities taught Michael to dance with the raindrops as if you will never feel the rain again.

Michael takes us on a "visual journal" through these encounters, and the lessons life teaches us along the way. The reader is left to wonder if the perfect storm of unique personalities, characters, family, and steady burning fire inside him contributed to the creation of Michael "the Teacher" and his fascinating and thoroughly impressive record in public education. A record that in the last twenty years has earned him "Teacher of the Year" accolades, "National Art Honor Society Sponsor of the Year" for the entire country and in 2013 a mind blowing trifecta of national awards and achievements that most educators that are tops in their profession will never achieve.

My belief is . . .
Michael hasn't even begun to paint his masterpiece.

IN EDUCATION, words can be impressive, but actions speak volumes. You will learn how Michael built one of the most powerful art programs in the nation, and along the way, mentored his "tribe" to earn over ten million in scholarships the past five years alone.

Michael proves on a daily basis what is possible if you show your students that you truly care and if you are willing to go all the way, commit heart and soul to "entering the student's world" one can and will "make champions." You will also learn about the many innovative programs that Michael and his accomplished team brought to fruition, such as *ArtQuest* and Michael's remarkably inspirational *31 Nights* project.

Throughout his epic journey, Michael will let you take a long, deep look into the window of his soul, his unfiltered thoughts and actions. Michael's trials and tribulations have taught him to never judge another unless you have walked in their shoes. As he reflects, you will learn how sometimes "very good people make very bad decisions," yet they can still go on to make a miraculous difference in others' lives and constantly pay it forward.

So, come ride shotgun with Michael, along with his ravishing "Bonnie to his Clyde" Lisa, his spitfire soulmate. Come into Michael's world, a world that will introduce you to "Lil' C"—a true miracle from God, a miracle child that can inspire mountains to be moved, while willing you to always, always be "BRAVE" no matter what.

You will learn of a remarkably strong, beautiful little girl named Angelina, whom I never met, but often dream of, and will be connected to for the rest of my life, because of the compassion, love, and emotion that Michael instills in us.

I hope you enjoy the ride that so many of us were blessed to be a part of. Michael teaches us that if you can dare dream it, and are willing to work hard for it, anything, and I mean ANYTHING is possible. As Michael reminds us to look in the mirror quite often, one must ask from his teachings . . .

"Are we willing to go after all we dream of?"

Michael makes sure we realize that "it's up to us whether our journey is defined by our origins, or by our maniacal drive to fight our way out of them . . ."

What does your journey map?

ONE

THE TIME IS NOW

Yes, *the time is now . . .*
It's summertime. Friday, 10 A.M. to be exact, and like many of you reading this, I'm also searching for answers. I'm lying down on a deck chair by my pool feeling the warmth of the morning sun as it climbs high over the Chesapeake Bay. Sounds of the garbage trucks rolling through the neighborhood collecting the trash fill the otherwise serene suburban backdrop of my neighborhood. As I stare out at the Bay, I'm pondering my place in the world. And as I sit here, I feel disenfranchised.

I'm unhappy with the direction that the current state of education in our country has taken, and dissatisfied with my place in life as an artist and what I've had to endure to do what it is I was born to do. No matter what I try, I just can't seem to shake these thoughts and enjoy the beautiful sun-baked skies on this seemingly picture perfect summer day.

The signs are everywhere. My senses are heightened. And, as I get up and walk through the same studio doors I've passed through a thousand times to turn my pool filter on, I'm stopped in my tracks by this small, rusted copper sign no larger than an index card mounted to the inside door of my studio that reads, "You're the Captain of this Ship."

Below the signage is a relief sculpture of an actual ship mounted to the door frame. As I stare at it, I imagine the stormy seas I'm about to navigate through in my life. Now, this particular sign has been hanging in this same spot ever since we bought this house eight years ago, but it's the first time I've ever stopped to really read it.

It's like it suddenly spoke to me. Instantly, it made me think of actor Robin Williams, whose students in his famous role as instructor John Keating in *Dead Poet's Society* addressed him as "Oh Captain, my Captain." This is a film I share with my own high school art students as an annual tradition just before kicking off *ArtQuest*, an art exhibition I founded and sponsor, which has become one of the largest and most community inclusive student art exhibitions in the entire country.

If you're an artist—maybe you're still seeking out that magic formula for "how to make it" in the art world or how to get your work out there and land your first big solo show. Perhaps you're just intrigued by the company I keep and want to hear some unique behind-the-scenes stories surrounding how those long-lasting friendships formed. Maybe you want to learn how my paintings were made, or what it's like to be commissioned by the likes of John Gotti and numerous other actors from hit Mob shows like *the Sopranos, Goodfellas, A Bronx Tale* and others . . .

If you're a teacher—you're possibly sitting right where I am now. You're looking for that next bit of inspiration to get you motivated to tackle another year that's upon you. If you're a leader, maybe you want to know how to lead with great vision.

If you're a parent—you could be looking to gain some insight into how to juggle two very complex worlds, like me, while still finding ways to make family your priority. At the end of the day, *your family* is who you're going to make the most important memories with, so they've got to come first.

I will tell you this, the road has never been easy, and you never really *get there.*

I do have numerous recipes for success, and a long-standing, proven track record in both Art and in Education, both of which are careers I've been able to sustain simultaneously for over two decades. Both are also careers considered by most to be two very thankless fields, but for me, I consider them the most rewarding on the planet.

There's always more to go after, always more worth fighting for. And I'm the kind of fighter that believes in bringing the fight to you, leaving my mark in ways that cannot be ignored.

Maybe you'll *be that artist. Be that teacher. Become that change* you want to see in the world; whether it's in your classroom, in your studio, or even in your home. I just know the time is now, and I'm going to lay it all out on the table.

AS I AWOKE this particular morning, before putting pen to paper, it was the background noise from a television infomercial left on from the night before that summoned me to get up. It was a religious sermon, of all things, but it felt like the words were being spoken directly to me. Ever have that happen before? Maybe it's just the artist in me, but whenever I'm really in the flow of creation, or in the midst of something big that's about to happen, I receive signs like this. It's like the universe is showing its face and sharing its secrets with me. These signs often take the shape of songs on the radio, random things people will say to me, people that suddenly come or go in and out of my life. And if you're like me, or if you've ever had anything like this happen to you before, you know exactly what I'm talking about.

As I rubbed my eyes open to see the television, this preacher was barking out the same two words over and over again—"It's time! It's time!" I immediately thought to myself, "He's right." I believe it is time, but not just for me, *for all of us.*

I feel like a revolution is coming. It's in the air. And I say, bring it! Now July is typically *family time* for most people. It's when summer vacation is in full swing. Teachers are digging their heels into the first real weekends of summer and kids are out having the time of their lives, without a care in the world. No more teachers, no more books—*that kind of mentality.* But for me, July is always a busy time.

Every July I teach an inspirational summer art camp for our county's public school system. It's a Gifted and Talented Visual Arts Enrichment Program (GT Program) for the "best of the best" in county that runs for a week in the summer and ten Saturdays over the course of the school year. I first piloted the program all the way back in 2000 and have been teaching it ever since. July has also been when I've typically reflected on the past year and planned for the upcoming one.

But July 2015 was very different. It became both a month and a year that changed everything for me. People I valued disappeared from my life, literally and figuratively. People at the highest levels of a public education system that I once trusted and thought were genuine turned out not to be. And, as an educator who's risen to the highest ranks of what is supposed to be a noble and meaningful profession that's supposed to be about doing what's in the best interests of kids—even I can see the writing that's on the wall.

It's time for serious change.

Systematically, it's time for major changes at the local, district and state levels in education. Problems that initially began with *No Child Left Behind* have taken an even greater turn for the worse with *Race to the Top* and more changes are still coming with the *Every Student Succeeds Act.* And in art, globally, it's time for the real artists to step up and rage against the current hypocrisies surrounding an Art World that's steadily turned into the "Art Market," which speaks volumes to the shift alone.

Education, Art, Politics—they're all becoming big corporate businesses masked behind the guise of "doing what's best for kids, for culture or for the people". And, given the increased numbers of terrorism, the rising hatred surrounding our nation's police, political elections, and educational agendas, this world is in need of serious change. And I'm not talking about "superficial changes." I'm talking about the need for a shift in our mindsets.

For me, the changes hitting my personal life came hard and fast the third week into July and life as I knew it changed forever. Our son Carmen, who just turned eight years old this past April, was officially diagnosed with Autism. *Autism Spectrum Disorder* (ASD), coupled with *Attention Deficit Hyperactivity Disorder* (ADHD). Specifically, with what was once labeled *Asperger's Syndrome*. We researched it heavily and had to come to grips immediately with one major takeaway — *there is no cure.*

So as I sat there, reflecting back on all the good I've done for my art students over the years, how I've helped countless numbers of them earn tens of millions in scholarship offers, averaging two million a year and climbing over the past five years alone, I thought about what all those kids' journeys looked like. How much time and energy it took from me in order to help get them there. How much effort went into helping them earn the most prestigious national awards presented to only the "best of the best" student artists in the entire country, from *Scholastic Art & Writing* National Medalists to *National Art Education Association* Rising Star Award Winners, and we're not just talking once or twice, but for the past seven years in a row.

I thought back on my own journey as an artist, which began as a kid who won his first art show at the age of five and never looked back. I always knew I was meant to be an artist, and I've always gone after my dreams. Always beat to my own drum. I've always been a leader in every sense of the word.

But what about *our son*?

What about *his dreams*? What will *his future look like now*?

Will there be another "me" out there to help him? Another *teacher* out there that cares enough to try and help him realize his dreams the way I've helped so many others realize theirs? Is there someone out there to help him rise about his quirks, his limitations to find his true gifts?

As I reflected on all this and how I might be able to help him, I'm also thinking . . . *why this book — and why now*? And then it hit me. The answer is simple. For me, this is one last valiant effort to create something truly epic for the next generations of artists, teachers, students and parents to read and learn from, and for my son Carmen, so he will truly know my heart, know his story, understand why I do what I do, what my journey has looked like, and how I "made it."

Perhaps this will help him find *his why* as he embarks on his journey through life.

As I present mine to you, I give it to you from someone at the top of their game who is still in the trenches of the classroom, still helping kids rack up millions in scholarships annually, and still in the studio making art for some of the most famous *and infamous* people in the world.

As an artist, as an educator, as a husband, as a father, I leave this book with each of you as inspiration, before leaving it all behind me to focus solely on helping our son make it through the next chapters of his brave journey.

And my journey has been a remarkable one.

I truly hope it will inspire you to do something truly epic with yours.

The time is now . . .

TWO

IF YOU BUILD IT THEY WILL COME

Great teachers . . . and I mean the truly great ones, all have one thing in common—*they know how to read a story.* This is a lesson I learned from rising to the top ranks of the teaching profession, and from being around the very "best of the best," including other national award-winning educators over the course of my career. Guys like Anthony J. Mullen, who said it best in a November 2009 keynote address he delivered while we were selected presenters at the *National Blue Ribbon Schools* ceremony in Washington D.C.

He put it simply, "Great teachers know how to read a child's very incomplete story and script confidence onto their blank pages. They know how to give their story a happier ending than it would have been without our mentorship."

For me, this meant one thing—*showing kids that you truly care.* I believe that's the first thing kids learn about you—*whether you truly care or not.*

How much does our United States government truly care? When Anthony J. Mullen was named 2009 National Teacher of the Year, do you know how much time he was given in the Oval Office with the President?

Just five minutes.

Barely enough time for a photo-op and a handshake.

So it's really up to us. I've always wanted to make a difference in people's lives, particularly my students' lives, because more often than not, they're going off into battle all alone, fighting through day to day circumstances and tragedies beyond comprehension. Some, more tragic than most people would even be able to bear, all the while—*they're still showing up.*

Whether it's showing up for school, showing up for practice, at the gym, at church, or to their jobs, they're still showing up. Whatever your profession is you'll find people like this that keep showing up, no matter what they're going through. So, you want to keep showing up for them and, in turn, you want them to keep showing up for you. You want to hook them. Give them a place to call home, especially if their actual home isn't the sanctuary it really should be.

And, whether we're talking teaching or being an artist, in either job, you can't give a half-hearted effort and assume no-one will notice. At the end of the day, your kids will notice. The art critics will notice. The work you do will speak to the effort you poured into it and you have nobody to fall back on but yourself.

This is why I love the sport of *boxing*.

You can learn a lot about yourself in that "squared circle of truth." My grandfather on my mother's side was a boxer, as were some cousins on my father's side, so it was something that was already ingrained in my blood. But it's become more than that. It's a sport that's all about having absolutely no-one to fall back on but yourself, and having the kind of balls to face your fears head on no matter who steps into the ring with you.

You must fight back. And if you put in the work before the fight, it helps you to develop some margin of control over your circumstances. But, once in the ring, just like when I step in front of a blank canvas to paint, or in front of any class I teach, I have to be able to adjust on the fly, to whatever the circumstances are that present themselves to me.

I do this by *being fearless.*

In the classroom, once those kids enter—*it's on!* And once that school bell rings you have no-one to fall back on but yourself, much the same as the way a fighter is left alone to fight in the ring at the sound of each bell, one round after the next until the fight is over. So you better be prepared, and you better develop some fearlessness in order to survive in the lion's den, especially if you're among other lions.

Now, throughout my career as an artist and as a national award-winning educator, I've learned some important rules to help you survive in the lion's den. These rules can also be applied to almost any career.

The first is—*show up for the process*. Be ever present. In your work and in the lives of those you impact on a daily basis.

But also—*show up ready*. No matter how big or how small the venue or opportunity appears to be, come prepared as if it were the biggest opportunity of your life because you never know where it might lead you, in your career, or on your life's journey.

Lastly—*be prepared for anything.*

So, as I re-assess my journey, it's probably time for you to re-assess yours. It's time to tighten up your circle and only associate with people that are headed in the direction you want to be headed in. Surround yourself only with people that are on the same mission you're on. People that can *lift you up*. People that want it as bad as you do. People you can *learn from* and that are willing to help you.

As I wrote this, *Wanted Dead or Alive* just came on the radio. The lyrics are fitting. It's definitely time to begin again and continue moving forward towards the next chapters of my life, as you are with yours. And within my chapters, you will uncover some great keys. Keys to help you unlock your own creative freedom. Keys to building whatever it is you want to build; whether it's a nationally acclaimed program like mine, or the keys to building your own self-sustaining career as an artist, educator, or leader in your business or community. All are roads I've traveled by venturing off the path. All are roads that have always led me back to the arts.

I believe *creativity is king.*

And I know you'll be able to make personal and emotional connections to my stories. Everyone's connection will be different, but it's up to you to find out what your connection is and why it's speaking to you. So, find these keys I've embedded in this book for you. And once you find them, all you'll need to do is DRIVE.

Drive full steam ahead toward your full potential.

Now, in school, kids are dealing with assaults on their self-esteem daily, and if you're a teacher it's up to you to recognize this. In business, it could be your employees and what they're dealing with. In your art, it's being able to recognize that crucial moment before your painting could literally turn to shit! Whatever the case is, I always recognize these poignant moments, especially when a kid is going through something difficult, only because I've walked in their shoes and I've seen that familiar look on their face every day I stare in the mirror. That's my gift, though. I can literally sense it the moment a kid walks past me what's going on with them. It doesn't have to be some big red flag, or an outburst of disruptive behavior, or even a frown. Sometimes they mask their pain extremely well. *I always just know.*

Growing up, I faced an endless string of lousy teachers, one after the next. None of them went beyond their call of duty to try and get through to me, or even tried and really get to know me, let alone try and help me earn any scholarships to get into college, despite my natural talents in art. Make no mistake about it; I wasn't looking for help back then either. If anything, I pushed people away. My parents could tell you that. Much the same dismissive way your kids will try and push you away to hide what's really going on inside, behind closed doors. I was always busy building walls around me those closest to me couldn't scale.

So, I've made it my mission in my own professional teaching career to do what nobody ever did for me. Maybe it will also become your mission. Or, if you experienced the opposite, maybe you will pay it forward and do for someone what someone else did above and beyond the call of duty for you. This is why I went into teaching in the first place—*to catch kids before they fall.*

Because I will tell you this—*teaching* is the last profession I really ever considered going into. I've always felt more comfortable in a room full of gangsters than teachers, and I always surrounded myself with what society has labeled "the bad guys." I was one of them at one point in my life—*they were my people.*

It wasn't until my junior year in college, after going through some extraordinary circumstances that I truly wouldn't wish on my worst enemy that I fell in love with the art of teaching as a potential profession.

And for the past few years I've had a great run at doing the unprecedented—helping my art students earn MILLIONS in scholarships. The past five years looked like this: $2,047,000 in 2011; $2,255,000 in 2012; $2,124,688 in 2013; $1,336,676 in 2014; $2,445,342 in 2015 and $2,120,720 in 2016. And this is just the financial impact I've had on kids in my profession.

I've also produced seven National Art Education Association (NAEA) Rising Star Award Winners, seven years in a row. This prestigious award is presented annually to just one student artist in the entire nation in art. I share these stats with you not to brag or boast, but so you can get a glimpse of what stats I actually do keep track of. And, with each winner, I've flown these student artists and their families across the country each year to be celebrated for their accomplishments because that's what it's really about—*the experience of it all.*

In addition to my NAEA Rising Star Award Winners traveling the country to receive recognition, I've also produced eight Scholastic Art & Writing National Gold and Silver Medalists in both Painting and Photography the past three years in a row. This is an award presented to just .7% of the nation in art out of over 300,000 applicants annually.

These Gold Medalists are honored and recognized under the bright lights of world famous Carnegie Hall in New York City. In case you're unfamiliar with it, Scholastic is heralded as the nation's largest recognition program for teens in the visual and literary arts in grades 7 - 12, and some very elite company have earned Scholastic Art & Writing Awards while in high school.

And by elite company, I'm talking Andy Warhol, Richard Avedon, Stephen King and Sylvia Plath, just to name a few.

I first heard about Scholastic while attending the NAEA's 2010 Rising Star awards ceremony for my student artist, Katie Emmitt, in Baltimore. I just happened to be seated next to Kat Hendrix, representing the Alliance for Youth Artists and Writers, who was also there to give a presentation for Scholastic.

She leaned over to me after seeing Katie's work and asked, "Did she submit to Scholastic? She definitely would have won something if she did. Her work is phenomenal!"

My response, "No, but tell me more. What's Scholastic, and how do we enter next year?"

When I got back to school, I immediately pitched it to my kids. That very next year, in 2011, I had my first Regional Award Winner in Leigh Rogers, a photographer, who submitted an amazing series of self-portraits from a *31 Nights* project I created to challenge my kids with.

Now, winning anything for Scholastic at the Regional level is a huge deal. It's not a national medal, but it's still a monumental accomplishment. My kids were competing against everyone from Washington D.C. all the way through New York City up to Maine. It's a huge Northeast demographic, and a strong one on the East Coast, so I was really proud of Leigh for earning our program's first Regional Gold Key winning photograph.

That same year, Louis Fratino became my first back-to-back NAEA Rising Star Award Winner. I flew him and his family out to Seattle to receive his national award. Louis would later be recognized with me, along with Katie Emmitt at the U.S. Department of Education in Washington D.C. These students really helped me keep raising the bar for future generations of artists at Southern High.

The year after that, I went from one Regional Award Winner to six in 2012. These six awards were shared by just two students, Tyler Mills and Tommy Taylor, two kids I also hold near and dear to my heart, in the categories of both Painting and Photography respectively. Both were kids from two different sides of the tracks, but both had interesting stories and were battling their own set of demons through their art. Tommy I'd end up helping bail out of jail, and Tyler I'd help earn a massive scholarship to RISD.

In 2013 I went from six to thirteen Regional Awards, doubling the previous years' amount, and doubling the number of students winning Regional Awards. You see the trend here? *You build it, they will come.*

It doesn't happen overnight, but in 2014, after three straight years of promoting the accomplishments of my previous years' Regional Award Winners, the push was really beginning to catch fire throughout the rest of my Art Department. I made a little competition out of it, and this would prove to be the year we broke through, shattering all prior years' winnings as our students earned sixty-seven Regional Awards across the entire department. From thirteen to sixty-seven all I can say is "wow!" Of those sixty-seven Regional Award Winners, I finally earned my first five national medalists in the category of photography.

The way it works goes like this—all the Gold Key winners from across the country at the Regional level get pooled together in the next round of competition for National Medals, and just 1% of the nation earn those. Silver Keys and Honorable Mentions don't get to move on. Out of our twenty-three Gold Key winners, I ended up with our five national medalists. Two Gold and three Silver, respectively in Katharine Milbradt, Hannah Larney, Carley Meredith, Meghan Segreti and Shanna Dunlap.

These five get to be recognized with me at Carnegie Hall in New York City. How cool is it that Scholastic even recognizes National Medalist Teachers and awards them with the same huge Gold and Silver medals that the kids get, along with a nice embossed certificate to hang on your "wall of fame" when you get back home.

It doesn't get any better than this!

My initial thought when getting this great news was, "Why just have these five go to New York City to experience seeing their work at Parsons on exhibit with the best teen artists in the nation? Why not bring ALL of our Regional winners along for the ride?"

This would give our underclassmen something to shoot for next year, and for those that were seniors, it would bless them with one last amazing memory.

After all, while my kids might forget the stats I share with them year after year, they'll never forget the experience of going to New York City. Some of our kids in South County have never even ventured into Annapolis, let alone left the State of Maryland. This would be a memory they'll never forget.

So, I rented us a huge coach bus, took our very first group of National Scholastic Medalists from 2014 and their families, along with our sixty-seven Regional Awards winners, and two of our other art teachers, Marlene Kramer (who has been my right-hand-woman, so to speak, since hiring her back in 2000) and Amanda Hagerman, (a rock star I hired in 2008), in hopes of inspiring them to encourage more kids to apply the following year. The kids that earned Regional awards could also rally around the ones headed into Carnegie Hall with me on the bus, tour New York City, and visit the *Art.Write.Now* Exhibition at Parsons as a group, all the while being able to visualize . . . "One day, this could be me."

Nick Cannon was Scholastic's keynote speaker and he was simply incredible, sharing his journey from being an unruly kid diagnosed with ADHD who went from failing his high school English class, to becoming the youngest staff writer in television history. He talked about how his energy was channeled in the right direction, and how he had teachers that never gave up on him. I can really relate to his inspiring story now, especially since our son's Autism and ADHD diagnosis. He, in my opinion, is still to this day the most inspirational keynote Scholastic has ever had.

That's the one thing that a short-sighted administration simply doesn't get. Kids need to go places to visualize success, and it's our job to put them front and center, smack in the middle of their hopes and dreams. To visually allow them to see what they might be able to achieve one day.

This is how to help kids *visualize success mentally first*.

CARLEY MEREDITH
CLASS OF 2014

"Good or bad, art has always been therapeutic for me. And while I cannot think of anything specifically that I learned in art, because a class with Mr. Bell is not like the average class, I will always remember exactly how being in that room made me feel.

His classroom always felt just like home and the only place that you could really get away from anything. A lot of us found our sense of 'belonging there' and that's where our heart was. We spent most of our days there or found an excuse to visit him. There was always music playing, and a couch to relax on. You could just chill out and create whatever you wanted. Art was the only thing I was grateful to be a part of in school because I felt like I had finally found my place.

Mr. Bell is such an important influence in my life because he believed in and supported me even when I couldn't do that for myself. He made us all feel like we mattered and sometimes that's all someone really needs. What separates him from everyone else is that he always cared about us and always made sure 'we were good.' If something's wrong, he'll try to fix it. If someone's giving you a hard time, he'll put them in their place. If you need someone to talk to, he's all ears. I don't think I'll ever have another teacher like that but that's the kind that kids need.

He helped us realize what we wanted to become and showed us that we could do it. I'll always have so much love and respect for him because he cared about us individually. He gave everyone the push we needed, gave us the drive to do something and a purpose to explore and understand ourselves as well as one another. I went on to become one of five of Southern High's first Scholastic Art National Medalists in photography. I even got to take a bow at Carnegie Hall."

THREE

WE MAKE CHAMPIONS

To kick off the 2014 - 2015 school year, I spray-painted the words "WE MAKE CHAMPIONS" along my G-wing art hallway at Southern High. I had no idea how prophetic it would become for my National Art Honor Society (NAHS) senior officers Mikayla Hennessey, Hannah Larney, Shanna Dunlap, and junior officer Sienna Broglie.

Shanna Dunlap had already accomplished groundbreaking awards the previous spring, becoming Southern High's first photographer to win our annual ArtQuest "Best of Show" award.

Shanna, Mikayla and Hannah would go on to compete for the nation's NAEA Rising Star award, presented annually to just one student artist in the entire country. This would be an award Shanna would win. And then there's Sienna, whom I've taught since she was a 7th grader in the GT Program. She's an incredible painter who also won bigtime awards that particular year.

So, just as I knew it would, the huge class trip to New York City worked as fuel to inspire our kids to come back the following year and try and top what our crew in 2014 accomplished, and they did just that, stepping back up to the plate to win eighty-four Regional Awards out of over three hundred submissions in 2015.

Now, three hundred submissions is a tremendous amount, but when you couple that statistic with the fact we are the smallest, most rural public school at the far end of one of the largest counties in Maryland, with only 1,100 students overall, it speaks even greater volumes to the dedication of our students and our Art Department as a whole. It also speaks volumes that every single student in the past few graduating classes all took at least one or more art classes while students at Southern High.

So how did his magical year begin? With our participating in the nation's first Creative Industry Studios, where these four could engage in hands-on workshops with me and some well-known professional artists, while collaborating with other top NAHS student artists from across the nation. Phil Hansen, famous for his *TED talk* entitled *Embrace the Shake*, gave the keynote, while David Modler and Eric Scott (*the Journal Fodder Junkies*) delivered hands-on workshops. I've known these two guys for years, and still team up with them to give presentations and *Visual Journaling* workshops across the country. Thus far we've hit San Diego, Texas, New Orleans, Chicago, and New York City.

David and I would later create a pipeline for student artists from Shepherd University in West Virginia, where he is an Art Professor, to intern with me at Southern High in Maryland.

Now, getting back to the CIS trip, it was filled with more camaraderie than anything else. Just kids being kids, getting to know one another better and bond as friends, artists, and with me, whom they so affectionately labeled "Art Dad" by the week's end.

Some highlights of our trip together included: museum tours; cutting out on a few to slip away and explore Chinatown together; and then there was the frantic call I got from Shanna around midnight as I sat with Phil, David and Eric having some late-night appetizers at the hotel restaurant. She proceeded to tell me how she was sorry they hadn't checked in with me yet, but they missed their Metro stop and got lost—*but not to worry*—they'd still call me when they got in safe, despite the *really bad neighborhood* they wound up in.

"*These crazy kids!*" I thought to myself.

There were lots of fun photos taken throughout the week to document our adventures, and an infamous *photo booth shoot* they made me take with them at a Gallery Wrap-up Party wearing a pimp hat, crazy sunglasses, beads, you name it.

There were also serious talks among the five of us about making a Documentary Film, chronicling our journey throughout the rest of the year, much like the 2010 film, *The Street Stops Here*, which provided a personal portrait of Bob Hurley, the nation's best high school basketball coach and six of his all-stars from St. Anthony High School in Jersey City. I'd liken his program to ours. While my kids and I never actually ended up shooting the documentary film, we definitely should have.

These four kids went on to do the unthinkable, setting records across the nation and earning scholarships in art that rival most athletes. My three senior stars exceeded over one million dollars between the three of them. Here's how their journeys played out:

MIKAYLA HENNESSEY, 2015 NAHS PRESIDENT

Mikayla had her artwork showcased in four exhibitions across the State of Maryland (Baywoods of Annapolis, MSDE Headquarters, the Captain Avery Museum, and ArtQuest). She won 8 Scholastic Art Regional Awards, including 2 Gold Keys, 3 Silver Keys, and 3 Honorable Mentions. At ArtQuest, she took home 1st Place in Drawing, Best Thematic Series, Best Self Portrait in Drawing, and 1st Place in Visual Journaling. She also won the Community People's Choice and the Unsung Hero Award, totaling $567 in prize money, all in one night at the office. She earned the University of Hartford Art School and Honors Program scholarship totaling $88,000 in scholarship offers.

HANNAH LARNEY, 2015 NAHS VICE PRESIDENT

Hannah began her senior year highly touted nationally, as one of two returning Scholastic Art National Gold Medalists in Photography. This year, not resting on her laurels, she earned ten Scholastic Art Regional Awards (1 Gold Key, 4 Silver Keys, and 5 Honorable Mentions). She also participated in the aforementioned exhibitions that Mikayla participated in, and at ArtQuest she won the Conceptual Achievement Award, 2ⁿᵈ Place in Drawing, Best Mixed-Media Piece, Best Art Historian Award, and the most coveted Grand Prize of all—ArtQuest 2015 "Best of Show", taking home $375 in prize money in one night.

Hannah also became Southern's 2015 "Scholarship for Scholars" winner for the county in art (a $5,000 award), becoming my fourth winner of this prestigious honor. As for her scholarships in art, impressive to say the least: SAIC-$54,000, Pratt Institute-$76,000, MICA-$88,000, Lesley University-$48,000, VCU-$40,000 for a grand total of $311,000 in scholarship offers. Hannah committed to VCU.

SHANNA DUNLAP, 2015 NAHS SECRETARY

Shanna's my half-a-million dollar kid! She's been a record setter since entering my program. Her journey began with her becoming the first sophomore to ever win a Scholastic Art Regional Award. Then she became Southern High's first photographer to ever win the most coveted "Best of Show" award at ArtQuest as a junior. One of her award-winning ArtQuest photos was even selected for a "Big Brother, Big Sister" Auction where it sold for $125. Her AP 2D Photography portfolio earned her a perfect score of a 5, also in just her junior year, joining Hannah Larney and three others to become one of Southern's first five National Scholastic Art Medalists to go to Carnegie Hall.

Her senior year, when I asked Shanna, "How will you top all this?" She came back to win 1ˢᵗ place in the Maryland State Federation for Women's Club Contest, more awards at ArtQuest and she went on to win the nation's most coveted NAEA Rising Star Award, given to just one selected student artist in the entire country. Shanna would become my 6ᵗʰ winner of this prestigious award. All previous winners went on to huge scholarship offers. Shanna's totals her senior year: Marywood's Dean Scholarship-$64,000, University of the Arts-$108,000 (which included the Trustee Scholarship-$88,000 and Dean's Scholarship-$20,000), MICA-$98,000 (which included a Creative Vision Award-$50,000,

Maryland ArtStar prize-$20,000, Fanny B Thalheimer Scholarship-$20,000, and National Art Honor Society Scholarship-$8,000). Pratt Institute awarded her the Presidential Merit Scholarship-$76,000, SAIC-$54,600 Merit Scholarship, VCU-$32,000, and Savannah College of Art and Design (SCAD) came through with $142,100 (which included one Academic Honors Scholarship-$13,200, another Academic Honors Scholarship-$48,000, Federal Pell Grant-$22,900, SCAD Achievement Scholarships-$40,000, SCAD Student Grant-$6,000, and the Student Incentive Scholarship-$12,000). Shanna's Grand total: $574,100 in scholarship offers. Shanna committed to attend SCAD in Savannah, Georgia.

So now you know *what* these incredible student artists accomplished under my tutelage—now I'll show you *how*.

IT WAS THE BIG FIELD TRIP TO NEW YORK CITY that proved to be the lightning rod I thought it would be. It gave our kids the spark they needed to try and "top" the kids from the previous year, *which they did*, earning a whopping eighty-four Scholastic Art Region-at-Large awards, beating the previous years' sixty-seven.

I also had another Scholastic Art Gold and Silver National Medalist in the category of painting in *Sienna Broglie*.

With that momentum behind me, I geared up to take another big crew back to New York City to keep that train rolling. But, this was also the year Southern High ushered in yet another new principal—my tenth in twenty years, to be exact.

Whether it was because he was new and didn't want to ruffle any feathers up the food chain or whether policies actually had suddenly changed this particular year I'll never know, but we were flat out refused our field trip back to Manhattan in 2015.

The reason: "Sorry, no field trips in June."

Short and sweet. *Sad but true.*

Our trip was scheduled for June 2nd, just two days into the month, but none of this seemed to matter. Welcome to the wonderful world of educational bureaucracy. Total bullshit as far as I was concerned, not to mention a total slap in our faces.

Especially when Southern High did, in fact, take an organized bus trip later that June to rally around the baseball team as they went on to compete for the State Championship. *Sadly, none of this seemed to matter.*

The Administration used the fact that the bus to the Baseball State Championship was sponsored by an outside organization, and that the trip was taken after regular school hours to justify it all. Again—*more bureaucracy, more semantics.* Our kids were pissed. But, they're good kids and they didn't buck the system, or cause any major waves, although they easily could have. They eventually cooled their heels and resigned to the fact it was a trip that was just not meant to be.

I tried arguing that since our national award-winning student's painting was scheduled to be on display June 2nd at Scholastic's *Art.Write.Now* Exhibition at Parsons, this trip could also double as a college visit for these kids, which was a legitimate argument, but it all fell on deaf ears and all those kids were going to miss out on the trip of a lifetime.

So, on June 2, 2015, my National Scholastic Medalist, Sienna Broglie, and I traveled solo to the Big Apple, along with my wife Lisa and Sienna's parents. No eighty-four student entourage to cheer her on like the previous year, but we made the most of it.

Her larger-than-life sized self-portrait in oils on canvas entitled *Mould Me* rocked the exhibit on display at Parsons, and she got to take a bow with me in front of a crowd of thousands gathered at New York City's world famous Carnegie Hall. Whoopie Goldberg and Chelsea Clinton were two of the keynote speakers, and Sienna got to rub elbows with each of them.

It's funny sometimes how my dual lives collide. Often, one life fuels the other and vice-versa. When I look back over my career it's almost as if every other year the headlines flip-flop back and forth between both worlds, with one year garnishing more headlines in my art career, and then the next year more headlines in the art education arena as my kids reap the rewards.

I guess that's just how it goes. I ride the tide of whatever wave seems to bring me to the most exciting destinations.

June 2nd proved to be no different. And, while it was unbeknownst to Sienna and her family exactly why I kept getting up and excusing myself to step into the lobby during the ceremony at Carnegie Hall, they never would have guessed in a million years that it was because I was busy taking calls from none other than John A. Gotti (Junior), who knew I was in town and wanted to make plans to get together.

John Junior is the eldest son of John J. Gotti, Sr., who was one of the most powerful crime bosses in America. He was dubbed *the Dapper Don* for his flamboyant style and charisma and later *the Teflon Don* after beating three high-profile trials in the 1980s. And, just like his infamous father, John Junior also was also once branded one of America's most notorious gangsters and head of the Gambino Crime Family. Unlike his father, who was eventually convicted and sentenced to life in prison without parole, where he passed away in 2002, John Junior *survived* four racketeering trials between 2004 and 2009, earning him the moniker *the Teflon Son*. Prosecutors finally announced in 2010 that they would not seek a fifth prosecution. John holds steadfast that he has long since left the world of crime, extortion, loan sharking, racketeering, all things surrounding what is known to us as "the life."

As for me, I've only ever known him as "John", an endearing family figure to our son, dear friend and loyal patron of my art.

My strong friendship with John began back when he first commissioned me to paint a portrait of him and his iconic father for the cover of his own memoir, *Shadow of my Father*, which is being made into a movie entitled: *The Life and Death of John Gotti*, with John Travolta playing the role of his iconic father. I hit it off with John Junior and his younger brother Peter famously over the course of my working on this painting, doing unveilings and spending time with their family around the holidays each year thereafter. We became very close friends and remain so ever since.

So, after several trips to the lobby to take John's phone calls and after Sienna received her national medals and was headed off to have dinner with her family, I headed off with Lisa to meet up with John Junior to have dinner with him.

Originally we were going to meet up in Brooklyn, but traffic was insane, the awards ceremony at Carnegie Hall ran a little longer than expected and there wasn't a cab in sight willing to tackle going from midtown to Brooklyn this time of day.

So, John said, "Wait there, I'm about fifteen minutes out. I'll come pick you up myself."

Only, after twenty minutes or so I didn't spot John anywhere.

But suddenly, my cell phone rings, "Look across the street," the guy said.

There we spot this Italian guy waving to us, flagging us down. We cross, and he opens up the back passenger side door of a double-parked car for my wife, and I hopped in the front.

"I'm Angelo, a friend of John's," he explains in a thick Italian accent. "He's not far. We go. I take you to John."

A few twists and turns later, heading downtown, then turning back around, reminiscent of the car scene on the George Washington Bridge with Michael Corleone, Sollozzo, and McCluskey in *the Godfather*—we finally pulled into a deserted side street off 1st Avenue.

And then, *there he was.*

The man himself—John A. Gotti.

Emerging out from behind a back alley near *Luzzo's*, this quaint old-school Neapolitan Restaurant. It was like something out of a movie. John smiled at us as he approached the car, greeted us with hugs and kisses on the cheek and we all headed inside to a back corner table facing the rest of the restaurant that appeared already reserved just for John. Then we were greeted by Tony D'Aiuto, John's longtime friend, lawyer, and part-owner of *Luzzo's*. We feasted over a huge spread and cocktails. Afterwards, a cigar together and a walk-talk along the High Line.

As we strolled, it was apparent that everyone still knew exactly who John Gotti Junior was, as we were invariably met with countless respectful hellos from everyone walking past us, from tourists to construction workers alike.

"These are Gurkha's, the finest around," John shared with me as we fired up two cigars he had for us.

"Did you know that each cigar is infused with Louis XIII Cognac?" he continued.

It was a magical time, but just like that, a few hours later, it was back to reality. Angelo dropped us off at Penn Station and we headed home. For me it was time to go back to work at Southern.

The following year, Sienna topped her National Scholastic Medals by becoming the nation's 2016 NAEA Rising Star Award Winner, my seventh straight winner of this honor, and she received that prestigious award in Chicago on St. Patrick's Day. And, while she never got the experience of meeting *the Teflon Son*, I did take her out for dinner while in Chicago with *the Windy City's favorite son*, Dominic Capone III (who also just happens to be Al Capone's great nephew). Domo, as I call him, is another dear friend of mine with a notorious lineage whom I did many paintings of over the years. So, with that said, I did get to corrupt poor Sienna just a little bit. She said she had "the time of her life!"

She also went on to more big things. All sparked by the initial fire I lit with that class of 2014 and our field trip to Carnegie Hall. I knew Sienna would follow in the footsteps of the great ones in our program, kicking off her junior year with a feature spread in *The Capital* newspaper, touting her as one of 2015's "most outstanding high school juniors." And, in addition to becoming my sixth Scholastic Art National Gold and Silver Medalist student artist, she also earned 2 Gold keys, 3 Silver Keys and 2 additional Honorable Mentions at the Regional Level. Her National Gold Medal winning painting, *Mould Me*, elucidated a metaphor for the "recipe" today's society has for its youth, "molding us into what society thinks we should look like and become". It was first on exhibit at the Sheila C. Johnson Design Center at Parsons, The New School for Design and the Pratt Manhattan Gallery in New York City, and then it traveled the country.

Later that summer Sienna got the news she passed her AP Drawing Portfolio with a perfect score as a junior, and in 2016, as a senior, and my NAHS President, she also earned a perfect score on her AP 2D Photography Portfolio in addition to becoming my 7th NAEA National Rising Star Award Winner. In 2016 she also earned an additional 5 Scholastic Art Gold, 3 Silver & Honorable Mentions at the Regional level. Her scholarship offers were also incredibly impressive: Pratt Merit-$104,000, RISD Merit-$88,000, MICA- $102,000 (which included the Merit Scholarship for $62,000, Fanny B Thalheimer Scholarship-$26,000 and the National Art Honor Society Scholarship-$8,000). She also won the 2016 Scholarship for Scholars-$6,000, the National Arts and Letters Winston Art Scholarship-$1,200, and the SAIC Merit Scholarship-$89,000. Sienna totaled out at $384,200 in scholarship offers and committed to SAIC in Chicago.

That spring of 2016 I also *three-peated* with Scholastic National Medalists. Two more of my student artists, Nicholas Orsini and Caterina Grandi, earned Silver Medals in Photography and Painting respectively.

And, for a second year straight under a new administration, we were not allowed to take a bus full of kids back to Carnegie Hall under that same guise of "still no field trips in June."

With all this said, I continue to fight the good fight for my kids and for our program. I'm also very proud to say that I've literally built one of the most successful high school art programs, not just in our state, but in the entire nation, while maintaining a thriving and often, very colorful painting career, but not solely on talent—*on a dream and a vision*.

While we definitely make champions, my vision has always been guided by three principles you'll soon get to know very well: *Imagination. Dedication. Hard Work.*

SIENNA BROGLIE
CLASS OF 2016

"I remember sitting on the bench in front of Shaw Memorial in the National Gallery for upwards of an hour, just sitting there talking with Mr. Bell and Shanna about life, swapping dramatic stories and juicy gossip. We were supposed to be sitting in some lecture, but what fun is that?! Out of all the lectures, we were supposed to go to we probably managed to attend one or two. One could say we were the delinquents of the trip. A handful of NAHS Chapter Officers from around the country brought a few members to Washington D.C. for the three-day convention hosted by NAEA. It was called 'Creative Industries Studios.'

Altogether there couldn't have been more than ninety of us, teachers included. Most of the groups were staying in a hotel as Mr. Bell did, but Shanna, Hannah, Mikayla and I decided to save some money and commute by Metro. We only got lost once and to Mr. Bell's dismay, he got a phone call at 11:30 P.M. from Shanna letting him know we had taken the wrong line landing us in the Capitol Heights Metro Station. Getting home late and waking up early every morning was hard, but well worth it. It was that trip that I really got to solidify the mentorship that I have with Mr. Bell today, plus we got tons of free art supplies and plenty of time to peruse D.C.'s wealth of fine eateries.

Mr. Bell would meet us every morning at the hotel with a fresh apple muffin for each of us; he even carried all our backpacks of supplies, landing him with the endearing title of 'Art Dad'. The trip was an opportunity to bond with each other and network with other NAHS Officers from around the country. It was a blast! At the kick-off party, we even got Mr. Bell to go into the photo booth with us. Looking back on that trip I remember the car ride home from the last day in Shanna's small convertible. Hannah and Mikayla stayed in D.C. for a concert, so it was just me, Shanna and Mr. Bell. Again we talked about life and even discussed the idea of making a movie documenting each of our journeys throughout the year. This, like most other whims, faded away with time, but the feeling I had that night never will. I was completely and utterly filled with inspiration, something that has been with me ever since."

FOUR

IMAGINATION—DEDICATION—HARD WORK

These three words are our program's mantra. They were the very first words I ever spray painted on the walls of my studio back in 2011 after coming off an incredible year, earning National Board Certification, which is a rigorous national teacher credential that has been earned by just 3 percent of the nation's teachers. On top of that, one of my students (Katie Emmitt) became my first national NAEA Rising Star Award Winner. I've since created this mantra into black *Art-Strong* wristbands with those three words printed in white lettering, separated by a star in between each word.

Each star symbolizes: the legacy of rock stars in Art from each previous year; the rock star inside themselves they needed to strive to be every day; and the rock star they are yet to become, bright and filled with promise.

This is the steadfast belief that I instill in each of my students, and we hand out these wristbands as a gift to our students across the department annually as a constant reminder of what we believe in. And make no mistake about it, we're not a Visual Arts Magnet School, and we aren't blessed with some inexplicable talent pool smack in the middle of South County, Maryland.

We take kids as they arrive at our doors, and we meet kids where they are talent-wise and bring them up to where they exceed even their own aspirations. Southern High is also the smallest, most rural public school in all of Anne Arundel County, with just eleven hundred students. Yet, despite this, we've built one of the largest departments in the county with five full-time art teachers, which is a far cry from the two-person department I joined in 1994.

All this coming to fruition many, many years after I was named Anne Arundel County Public Schools "Teacher of the Year" back in 2004. I believe in being a man who never rests on his laurels. This is all evidence to support that fact. But our kids will tell you. They'll tell you flat out just like it says on my hallway in big bold letters: *WE MAKE CHAMPIONS.*

They will become a *somebody* because of what they're a part of with us. They will not succumb to what life throws their way. They will not become another statistic, another tragedy, or another dropout. Not our kids. Because it's our job to know how to catch them before they fall. It's our job to learn ways to hook them. Keep them interested. Get them excited about the possibilities ahead of them.

This has been my mission since I began my career in education. Maybe it will become yours, in whatever path you're on in your life. After all, it's not enough to just have talent. It's not enough to just work hard to perfect your craft. It's what you do with it that matters most, in the form of what you give back, how you give it away, that's what is remembered most.

And if you believe in it and if you build it—*they will come.*

The kids, the scholarships, the shows, the local, regional and national acclaim—*your legacy.*

LOUIS FRATINO
CLASS OF 2011

"Our art classroom was the old gym in our high school. I always found that very fitting considering the manner in which Mr. Bell rallied his students to paint with hard work and dedication (a phrase we wore on our wrists, Lance Armstrong style). Notwithstanding the occasional tracksuit, Mr. Bell really was like a coach. Not one that shouted from the sidelines, he painted with us in class. Mr. Bell treated us like a team with a clear goal, to do a good job and to win a lot of scholarship money.

In the art studio, students from all tribes would rub shoulders. I think that was really important for me as a teenager. I was not particularly athletic and I was sometimes painfully aware of how different I was from my male peers. A more typical art class may have reinforced those differences, but Southern championed artists, and Mr. Bell made them as celebrated as our football players. Each year we had a school-wide show called *ArtQuest*, which made me think of a heroic knight gone out to seek the Holy Grail, or $125 cash for being the 'Best of Show.' It may have been better attended than our Homecoming game, which isn't so surprising considering it was the only event designed at our school that invited everyone to perform, which is was what was so amazing about it. Of course, the real die-hard art freaks ran the show but there was always a Pole Vaulter who made an immaculately sculpted ceramic hamburger or some sort of transgression among the clearly defined high school social order.

Our art department leveled the playing field. I was able to show a side of myself I could be really proud of in a way that my peers respected and were amazed by. I know that was only the case because Mr. Bell made the art studio an enviable place to be, which it was. We had the radio going, the door open in warmer months. There was the ring of the more elite 'easel-users', the dingy sofa, and these roundtables that everyone felt compelled to deface in myriad and sometimes beautiful ways. It was a really special place.

Mr. Bell's advice to me has been following me. He noticed something about the drawings in my sketchbooks that he wasn't seeing in my paintings. 'The little drawings in your sketchbook were worth painting,' he said!

I remember feeling like I had just heard the most ludicrous advice ever. I did end up following his advice for that portfolio of work, and I had a lot of fun doing it. Years later, after slowly tightening back up as a sophomore in college, a professor said the same thing, which ended up being a real turning point for me. Still, I am chasing the loose, bright freshness of my drawings as I paint. Mr. Bell saw that early on I think.

I was able to go to Seattle my senior year because of an NAEA Rising Star Award that I won—it was something Mr. Bell really pushed and helped us win. I'll never forget having spent that time in Seattle with my parents, which was my first time on the West coast. The award was cool, but Seattle was such an amazing place. I then realized my work could take me to other places in the world.

I am currently writing this for Mr. Bell while on a *Fulbright* grant for painting right now in Berlin, Germany.

It is an amazing city. I know I wouldn't be here today if I wasn't so lucky to have been a student at Southern while Mr. Bell was there. He helped me build a confidence but also a dedication that is absolutely essential to doing what we do, which is to paint."

FIVE

WELCOME TO HOLLAND

W hen we first received our son's "official Autism diagnosis" I stumbled upon an Autism poem, *Welcome to Holland*, written by Emily Perl Kingsley. The poem was her creative way to try and describe the experience of raising a child with special needs and how it actually felt from her unique perspective.

The poem made me cry when I read it because we, too, just landed in "Holland" and it was then that I suddenly realized we'd now be spending the rest of our lives there. My wife and I used to joke about how "we're just here, living in Carmen's world," but now it took on a whole new meaning. We literally have to live in *Carmen's world*, and it's up to us to learn the new language of this foreign country and the laws of *his land*.

Long before our son's diagnosis of Autism and ADHD, the rough seas and unpredictable days and nights we had been trying to navigate through blindly up until this point definitely took its toll on us, as I'm sure it does for many parents of any special needs children. Whether it be issues with teachers or school, finicky eating habits, or other things most parents take for granted.

Things ranging anywhere from toileting, teaching him how to ride a bike, tie his own shoes, even getting to sleep at a decent hour—these have all been real struggles. It's a diagnosis that has taken us a couple years to finally get, but one that we could also see coming.

Some days it seemed clearer to us than others, but with ASD, *Asperger's* in particular, no child is the same. And while Carmen fit some of the checklist items on the Autism Spectrum, in other areas he didn't fit at all, so it was confusing at times, *baffling even*.

Are these "quirks" things he'll grow out of? Was this just him being a kid? He was our only child, so we had no way of knowing for sure. We just knew he was different from other kids on the playground.

He walked and talked early, though, always had great eye contact, even as a baby, but it was the "other things" we started noticing that became worrisome to us. Things we initially just thought were funny or cute, steadily evolved—from getting over-excited and flapping his hands uncontrollably to "quirks" experts at *the Kennedy Krieger Center for Autism* explained to us were called "stimming", "perseverating" and "echolalia," all terms that were very new to us, but ones we'd learn to understand well. We always just thought it was so cute the way he'd get so excited over his trains at such an early age because he was so freakin' smart!

He knew his alphabet early, could name the fifty states with ease, and he quickly graduated from *Thomas the Tank Engine* to a full blown collection of O gauge and HO scale trains (not an inexpensive hobby either, mind you). We'd take many Saturday afternoon drives to the train store, and every summer it was off to the Strasburg Railroad.

There was also the particular way he'd need to line all of his toys up perfectly, and the obsessive way he'd have to tap the same spot on the wall of our living room before going in or out of the room, which lasted only a few months before evolving into something else. Like how he'd start making these excitable noises which gradually evolved into noises coupled with an uncontrollable wringing of his hands and grimacing facial expressions he makes when he's overstimulated. This seemed to begin while he was watching his trains but it kept going even as he got older, whether its trains or watching *Minecraft* videos on *YouTube* (a game that's also proven to be another obsession).

Lately, he's also become fascinated with Grandfather clocks and goes online to watch videos on how the chimes move and how the clocks are constructed. It's come to the point where I had to log off my *Amazon* account on our *iPad* because he was putting $4,500 cable-driven, triple chime Grandfather clocks in my Shopping Cart! He even discovered what the small letters under the six-hand of this *Howard Miller* wall clock that his Great Aunts Connie and Carmina gave to him stand for. The lettering reads *Western Journey* so he looked that up online and figured out that this particular model had three chimes, *Whittington*, *Westminster* and *St. Michaels*. From there, he located a small switch lever hidden beside the Roman numeral three (after I repeatedly told him there wasn't a switch). Boy was I was wrong on that one!

With all his attention to small details and how stuff works, he will probably become an engineer one day. It's pretty amazing how his mind works actually. While most kids want to go to the mall, he prefers us taking him to an antique clock store to look at all the different clocks and listen to how they chime. The last time we visited *Greco Jewelers & Clock Shop* in Barnegat, New Jersey the clockmaker was so impressed that Carmen knew there had to be eight chime rods to make a triple chime and four to make a single chime that he went back into his workshop and gave Carmen the gift of a *Hermle Mechanical Clock* movement to take back home.

Now, don't ask me what any of this means. But Carmen knows. The old man was smiling so proud.

He told us, "Your son should apply to the Rolex School. He'll be able to write his own ticket. It's a lost art only a few people in the entire United States can master. You should look into it."

I wish his teachers would see the kind of attention to detail he has, instead of simply labeling him because he can't explain back the story behind his reading comprehension homework as easily as the next kid.

Carmen's also a "numbers guy" and can tell you the exact hotel room number we stayed at in Wildwood down the Jersey Shore dating back to our first stay there when he was just five years old. Often, when he remembers something he will tell you about it in such photographic-like detail as if it happened yesterday, and then we'll be completely taken by surprise when I realize he's telling us something from back in, say, 2012.

So, with the diagnosis that has been a long time in the works, it's "officially real" now, for us both and for us as a family. It was a difficult pill for his grandparents on both sides to swallow too because this was all unfamiliar terrain.

And so, what we once simply thought of as cute little quirks, stuff Carmen has since labeled his *whacky stuff*, we now understood it for what it really was. We were beginning to grow concerned with what other people might think. Other kids in particular, because kids can be cruel. This was also something Lisa and I both started to fear long before his diagnosis.

Some days he'd come home and lash out in a rage, as if from out of nowhere, but where it was really stemming from were issues he was internalizing from school. Now, we love our son exactly the way he is. He's the sweetest boy in the whole world and he has a heart of gold and a smile that lights up the room. Charm, charisma, you name it this kid's got it in spades. He's definitely an old soul, with a soft shyness about him that can melt anyone's heart. He's really funny too!

But at school, kids started to notice his *whacky stuff*, because he can't control it. And our battles began with schools back when he was just in Pre-K when his first teacher refused to allow him to bring a *koosh ball* as a fidget tool to help his stimming. This would be our very first of many battles with schools, and with teachers sadly not willing to go above and beyond for our son.

But it was also the first time I truly listened to my gut and reached out for help, which came in the form of a well-respected colleague, Jodi Johnson, then principal of Kennedy Krieger at Southern High School, which was like a school within our school. Jodi offered to observe Carmen while in Pre-K, and she monitored not only his behaviors but how he was being treated by other kids and by his teachers. She helped put us on the right track with initial behavior modifications and also helped get Carmen fast-tracked to *the Kennedy Krieger Center for Autism* in Baltimore, which had a two-year wait list.

While we waited patiently for help, Carmen found a way to make it successfully through Kindergarten and first grade; although it was becoming more apparent he was different than other kids, especially in social settings. He was trying so hard to fit in and make friends, but with all the wrong kids—*kids not as tolerant of his quirks*. Kids that were frankly being flat out mean to him. If myself or my wife ever saw it in action we'd let those kids know right away in front of everyone what we thought of how they were treating Carmen.

We'd tell him, "They're not your friend. Look at how they're treating you. Can't you see it? Stay away from that kid! They don't deserve your friendship."

But he didn't understand any of this. Still doesn't. He simply can't see it. It's part of who he is. It's part of his Autism, not being able to pick up on social cues like most kids are able to . . . like when someone's getting annoyed by you or doesn't want to play with you, stuff that most people can see written all over someone's face or in their body language. This is all stuff that wasn't so easily detectable for Carmen. For him, due to his ASD, he was on sensory overload all the time, and too easily distracted to be able to focus on reading someone.

While we can focus on one thing at a time, and it's inherent for us to piece together someone's expression, gestures, posture, the tone of voice and our brain immediately lets us know what someone else thinks and feels about us, Carmen's brain works differently. While he can see all these things that we see from a physical standpoint, they don't all come together like one big puzzle that forms quickly in our brains. For him, they stay fragmented and don't always make sense, or by the time they finally register, the moment has long passed. Couple that with not being able to filter any outside distractions out, whether it's the tapping of someone else's pencil, to a bird chirping in the distance, to other people's conversations, for him it's exhausting. It's like being in a room where there are all these people talking at once and you can't understand anything any one person is saying.

This, we were now beginning to understand, was becoming physically draining and emotionally exhausting for him. Not to mention, trying to pick up on all the social cues, things like giving other kids more "personal space" or using his "indoor voice." He just wants to fit in with his peers in ways that were so natural for the rest of us. None of it's his fault.

And, once he entered second grade, while he stayed a whiz at Math, finishing up problems other kids struggled with in no time, his struggles with reading comprehension became more and more evident. He was literally beginning to feel the pressures of a public education system that just recently adopted *Common Core Standards*, which is more focused on data-driven instruction than relationship-building. As teachers became more and more focused on being accountable for test scores and simply teaching kids to the test, they ended up covering way too much curriculum in way too short of a time span, so much so they are not able to take the extra time to build great relationships with the kids in their classes. And, if you teach a child with ASD, every child on the Autism Spectrum is so very different, yet they all have one thing in common—they're waiting for you to enter *their world*, not the other way around. It's up to great teachers to find a way in, but for us, our child was beginning to get lost in the shuffle. And for me, as a parent and as an educator—*this was unacceptable.*

So one day, while I was at work talking with one of our custodians, Taricio Simms, about Carmen, mentioning to him how I wanted to get him into some activities, but that the team sports thing just wasn't a good fit, he turned me on to a boxing gym that just opened up in our area. He said I'd hit it off famously with the owner, Tony since he was originally from Brooklyn and also had family in Jersey. He said he was "my kind of people."

"Boxing?" I thought to myself . . . "Hmmmmm . . . that might just be a good fit!"

SIX

LIL' C—THE BUTCHER

One of the greatest fighters of our time was once asked what he believes in. "I believe in me," he said. "I have no other choice." These are the same words I painted on our son's wall in his bedroom the day after receiving his Autism diagnosis.

"**I BELIEVE IN ME**" . . . in big bold letters above his door. It's something my wife Lisa and I remind him every day, because Carmen's fight is much different than the fight most people have to undergo in life.

So, taking my custodian's advice, I called Tony "Ace" Acevedo, owner of the new *Kicked Up Fitness* boxing gym in Annapolis. We immediately hit it off. I explained to Tony how we tried Karate once but it didn't really stick. There were too many distractions and too much lag time in between exercises. But boxing, I figured, was worth the shot. And the more I researched, it seemed boxing could be good for Carmen due to the repetition, and the rituals—from the wrapping of the hands to the repetition of punches, turns, and the way boxing forces your whole brain to think and react in concert with your body.

There's an art to it most people don't realize.

So, at age seven, I signed Carmen and myself up for one-on-one boxing lessons with Autumn Wolf, one of Tony's younger boxing coaches, and Tony agreed to train me himself. After all, I could never expect Carmen to do something I, myself wouldn't do too, much the same way I am in the classroom with those kids. This became our father-son ritual. We'd go to the boxing gym together every Monday, Wednesday, and Friday. This also became more than just training. It was us training for a new way of life: *the life of a fighter.*

From the moment I first stepped foot in that boxing gym I was sold. Carmen loved it immediately too. Everyone treated him great and made him feel like their adopted son. And, to help ease the cost of private lessons between the two of us, which we definitely couldn't afford, Tony agreed that if I paid for Coach Wolf's lessons with "Lil' C", as the guys at the gym began calling him, he'd train me for free in exchange for some art for the gym.

"My time for your time," Tony said. That became our arrangement. So, in the studio, I began pouring in hours on a huge New York City skyline mural as a backdrop for the "East Side" of the boxing ring on *OSB*, and we, in turn, began pouring in hours training after school three times a week.

I unveiled the first of many artworks I'd do for Tony with Lil' C in front of a packed house at a "fight night" where locals competed for Amateur Boxing titles. Arthur Neal, Tony's right-hand man was the Ring Announcer and was the one who introduced me and my son to the crowd. He'd later prove to become one of my dearest friends.

One of the gym's favorites, Sean "Rocky Lights Out" Cormier won in dramatic fashion and became one of our son's big idols in the gym. I took him to every one of Sean's fights and we cheered him on while sitting ringside. Sean would also become more than just another fighter in the gym to our son. He'd also become like family. He'd play with Lil' C, chasing him through the gym every time we'd arrive. It became their ritual to fight one other, Sean on his knees, letting his protégé, Lil' C, get some shots in on him, making him feel every bit the part of a champion every time they are in the gym together. I'd even help Sean by sparring him from time to time with Clint and Neal. Tony would sponsor him when he made his first trip to *the Golden Gloves* in D.C. in 2016, cheering him on, in his corner for every fight. Sean later gave Lil' C the greatest gift of his Golden Gloves necklace. We'd even celebrate Sean's son, Carter's first birthday with him.

This was definitely where we belonged now. I was always more comfortable around street tough guys like John and Peter Gotti, anyways than spending my afternoons on a barstool someplace. So, finding this boxing gym with tough guys like these was a Godsend. And Coach Wolf also became more like an extended member of our family than just his boxing trainer.

From that year on, I'd order every single big Mayweather *Pay-Per-View* fight, cook up a huge spread and invite over Tony, Wolf, Neal, Clint and the rest of the gang from the gym over to watch the fights with me and Lil' C. I'd later begin a second mural for Tony with a Hollywood themed backdrop for the gym's "West Side" in our second year at the gym.

Lil' C "the Butcher", Coach Wolf would further nickname him, is a permanent fixture there now and he's getting really good at this violent craft. It's all thanks to an incredible cast of some of the toughest and most genuinely dedicated guys I've ever met that have given our son a new home, away from the struggles and frustrations he experiences in school. They simply take time out to show him they truly care. It's even helped him develop a newfound confidence he never had before boxing. He not only stands up for himself now with bullies at school, but he even stands up for other kids. I'll never forget the day I picked him up from school and he had this bandage on his hand.

"What happened pal? You get hurt" I asked.

"You won't be mad at me?" he replied tentatively, as he hopped into the back seat, buckling himself into his car seat.

"I promise I won't get mad. What happened?"

"I fell," he said.

"What do you mean—*fell*? In recess?" *Now I'm getting angry.*

"Well, I got tackled, actually."

Now I'm pissed.

"It's okay, it's okay!" he exclaimed.

"And how is that? How is *that* okay?" I yelled.

"Because I hit him!" he smiled.

"You hit him?" *I was thoroughly shocked.*

"Right in the face!" he smiled proudly. *I smiled back.*

I couldn't have been more proud than I was at that very moment—hearing that he stood up for himself like that. But, just to put things into proper perspective, Carmen is a kid who literally doesn't have a mean bone in his body. He's gone through more than most already in his life, and for him to finally stand up for himself . . . let's just say it's been a loooooooong time coming.

"Were you scared? I mean, when you hit him?" I asked.

"Yeah, at first. But it felt good," he said proudly, "You know, sticking up for myself."

Up until this point, Carmen would always be so kind to any kid at school, no matter how badly they treated him. It bothered the shit out of my wife and me when anyone was mean to him. Like I said, he just wants other kids to like him. Accept him for who he is. But kids can be horribly cruel though, and this one kid, in particular, had been giving him a hard time for a while, to the point that Carmen would come home so upset over it I'd have to just hug him and let him get it all out of his system, whether it was in the form of tears *or rage.*

I'd just let him take it out on me and try to calm him down when he'd get to the point of hyperventilating.

It literally gets that bad.

I guess it got to that point on this particular day that his "muscle memory" from all his boxing training finally kicked in and he *just reacted.*

"Did you get caught?" I asked him.

"No, it was at recess. Nobody was watching, so I stuck up for myself like you always tell me to."

"Atta boy!" I said. "I'm not mad at you. I'm *proud* of you!"

"You are?" he smiled, still not completely understanding if he did a good thing or not.

"Sometimes good people have to do bad things. I know this is hard for you to understand. Just know this—you will never be in trouble with me or your mother for standing up for yourself and fighting back. You have my word."

When we got to the gym I had already texted Tony and Wolf, who shared the news with Neal and the rest of the crew as we pulled into our parking spot. They were all lined up waiting to high-five and cheer on Lil' C as he walked into the gym. It was like one of those special moments in his life he'll never forget. Neither of us will. I love those guys for that.

The next day, I picked him up after school and he's got this same little smirk on his face.

"What happened today, pal?" I asked, very curious.

"You're not gonna be mad?" Carmen asked, like yesterday.

"No, I'm not gonna be mad, just tell me."

"I hit him again!" Carmen yelled, smiling proudly.

"What? Are *you* turning into the bully now?"

"No Daddy, he pushed my friend down since he won't go after me anymore, so I ran after him and punched him and told him—*leave my friend alone!*"

"What did he do?" I asked.

"Ran off crying to the teacher," Carmen smiled proudly. "He won't be pushing either of us down anymore."

"I'm proud of you for sticking up for your friend. No more fighting for a while now, okay? Let's try and keep it in the ring."

"Okay, Dad. You're proud of me, though, right?"

"I couldn't be more proud of you, pally."

And with that, off we go to another afternoon at the gym. So, while some consider boxing a barbaric craft, for us, it has literally become a glimmer of hope in our son's life. It's one of those sports where you have no-one to rely on but yourself. To succeed, skill and talent alone are not enough. The will to win is worth much more. It teaches character and resilience. Boxing has also somehow unlocked a part of our son's mind that wouldn't be unlocked otherwise. It's certainly helped him grow stronger physically, but also psychologically and emotionally.

It's building his confidence. And, it's through his newfound confidence that he's inspiring other children to also become fighters. *Autism Speaks*, which is one of the world's leading Autism advocacy organizations, even shared his story in a blog that went viral entitled, "The moment my son with Autism said, I believe in me." So while he's giving others hope, we're in his corner fighting right alongside him.

Former two division world champion Paulie Malignaggi said it best, "Boxing loved me when no-one else would." Our sentiments exactly, champ. While talking further with Paulie he explained to me, "For a kid looking for that missing piece in his life, it does at times hit home in just the right way."

So, with the real life fight now officially hitting home right in front of us, we also began ordering every book on Amazon that Dr. Washington, Psychologist at *the Kennedy Krieger Institute for Autism* recommended. We bought weighted *Aspie Blankets*, which are supposed to help children with ASD and Asperger's find comfort under the weights. It's why, we'd later learn, Carmen always used to ask us to "sit on me." He'd bury himself in tons of pillows on our bed, taking total control over our bed. He liked weighted vests too. We also changed diets, trying to avoid certain foods with gluten, dairy or high in sugar. We literally started trying anything and everything at that point.

So, while the pain of receiving that "official diagnosis" was a different kind of pain, one I've never experienced before, we're fighting back. At first, it felt like a helpless kind of pain that would keep us up nights crying ourselves to sleep, wondering how we're going to help our son. Now it's now just turned into a fight we're both prepared to fight alongside him for the rest of his life. It's all that seems to matter anymore. That's the vow Lisa and I made to one another the day the official verdict came down. We would do anything and everything that could potentially help our son.

Life just became that simple. I even began researching the best breed of dogs for children with Asperger's and Autism. We had just buried our first dog, Rocco earlier that spring and it saddened Carmen, so I thought a new puppy might help.

Rocco was a big black one hundred and fifty pound Rottweiler mix that had been with us for over ten years. A few years after Carmen was born he was so old he couldn't stand up on our hardwood floors anymore, so the last two years of his life he stayed at my in-law's house down the Jersey Shore where he found companionship with my father in-law's hunting dog Bianca. Rocco finally passed away in the summer of 2014. My father-in-law, Bill, buried him in their backyard so Carmen could still visit him whenever he wanted to.

So as I researched, I kept reading how great Newfoundland dogs are with "Aspie children" and stumbled upon a rescue shelter that happened to be having a pet auction. They had a litter of Newfoundland puppies that were just eight weeks old, and I found one that I kept going back to again and again online. He was so freakin' cute. I put in the pet adoption application that very night and the following Monday morning Lisa drove an hour with Carmen while I was teaching our county's annual summer GT Program to try and get him.

When Carmen and Lisa first got there they told them that the puppy we wanted was already taken. Then, just before they were about to leave, one of the organizers from the shelter rushed back over to tell them they mixed up the name tags and the puppy we actually wanted was still there.

"We got it him!" Lisa texted me, coupled with the cutest picture you could ever see of Carmen holding his new big black, fluffy bear-like puppy in his arms.

We named him Nero, *black in Italian*. There was nothing like seeing the smile on my son's face as he hugged his new puppy.

So, I finished out the week of July 13th - 16th teaching the GT Program and once the program concluded I spent another back-to-back weekend skimming through the various books we ordered online that finally arrived. And just like that, it was Monday again, July 20th to be exact.

A date I'll also soon never forget.

SEVEN

ANGELINA

July 20, 2015 was definitely a Monday in every sense of the word. I felt like I was still stuck in neutral. It had only been one week since we received the devastating news about our son's Autism diagnosis, and I felt lost at sea.

Back in April, I met up with my tattoo artist, Ty Pallotta in Baltimore at the Villain Arts Tattoo Convention to get some celebratory birthday ink. I asked him to continue down my *St. Michael, the Archangel* half-sleeve and complete the narrative with a *Daniel in the Lion's Den* full-sleeve just below it, which he completed on me in one long twelve-hour sitting. I didn't realize how prophetic that ink would become. Three months later it was exactly how I felt after receiving our son's diagnosis.

I spent the last three years trying to figure out how to mend the fractured relationship between my own family and me ever since my Grandmother's passing . . . (*more on that later*). And, after coming off of a year that I became completely dissatisfied with the current state of public education in our country and dispassionate about our new administration, I was frantically grasping at anything that might help me figure a way to get through the rest of the summer, not certain what it was going to look like anymore.

Lisa stayed home for the first five years of Carmen's life. Once he finally entered kindergarten she finally went back to work. Five years on one income, not to mention a teacher's salary, can certainly take its toll on your financial situation, but we did what we felt was the right thing to do by our son, no matter what it would cost us, and no matter how much debt it put us in. Carmen's well-being meant more to us than anything else. Knowing he was being raised by "us," being in his mother's care all day long during his formative years, not by a "stranger" in some day care facility was important to us. *These were our values.*

But now, as I'm writing this, and with boxing changing his outlook on life, Carmen was beginning to enjoy school more, in particular—the after-care program (SACC), which seemed to be helping his social skills. The entire staff at SACC is fabulous. They all took an active interest in his life and went out of their way to really get to know him and look out for him. I love each and every one of them for that. Mrs. Brenda, the director, and I would talk about his overcoming struggles in school, about family and our love of the New York Giants. Mrs. Janet and I would talk about my alma mater, Lycoming, where her son ended up playing football. And, with Carmen's newfound confidence from the work he was putting in at the boxing gym he began to gain some *swagger*. Now he gets picked first instead of last in Dodgeball because "he can catch a fifth graders ball!"

So, Monday, July 20, 2015, Lisa was at work and I just dropped Carmen off to play at SACC. When I returned home, it was eerily quiet in the house. I collapsed on my couch, reflecting back on our "new reality" over the past month. I also finally decided to begin journaling everything out in my sketchbook, like the artist in me naturally would—*and then my cell phone rang.*

It was my best friend Louie.

Now I love Louie. I've known him for over twenty years. He's always been like a second brother to me. He comes from a big Italian family with four sisters and they all treated me like one of their own, ever since my college years. Louie was best man in my wedding. Lisa and I also became Godparents to his oldest daughter, Alex, who Louie had while still in high school. Since having Alex, Louie's been married twice, first to Brenda Cordrey, with whom he had two children with (Louis, Jr., and Angelina), and now to Nicole West, with whom he had another child with a couple years ago named Lorenzo.

I was best man at Louie's first wedding with Brenda. His second wedding I barely made the groomsmen's roster, which kinda made me feel like the ugly girl at the dance, but that's just how it goes. Life drifts people apart over time. At the end of the day though, whenever we'd get together, it still always felt like no time had passed. We could still talk like brothers. But this wasn't any ordinary phone call.

This one was about his daughter — Angelina.

She had just turned eleven in April and she'd been fighting one of the rarest forms of Sarcoma cancer for about a year and a half since she was first diagnosed at the age of nine. It started in her stomach. She'd beaten it twice through chemo and surgery and was even allowed back home for a short stretch, but the cancer came back again, *this time with a vengeance.*

Immediately as I answered the phone Louie said, "I need you to come to Philly. Can you meet me at the Children's Hospital?" He sounded desperate and I could hear tears as he was getting choked up and could barely talk.

"Okay," I assured him, "let me just touch base with Lisa and see what time she gets off work to see when we can get up there."

"No, I need you to come *now*. Right now! Cancer is gonna take my baby girl!" he exclaimed.

I literally hung up, grabbed my keys and raced off for Philadelphia that instant. I left a message for Lisa to pick up Carmen from SACC as soon as she got off work, and that "I wasn't sure what time I'd be home, but figured it'd be late."

When I first arrived at *The Children's Hospital of Philadelphia* (CHOP), the doctors gave Angelina anywhere from one to three days to live. This was their prognosis. It didn't look good. And neither did Angelina. She was so frail, just skin and bones, her stomach bloated and filling up with blood and tumors.

She was also hooked up to all these tubes and couldn't get out of the hospital bed except to use the bathroom, and was generally so uncomfortable she'd often scream out in excruciating pain. The doctors said they couldn't perform another surgery, and she was so frail they didn't think her body could take any more chemo. But, despite the prognosis, I tried my best not to think about the negative, and emulated only positive thoughts. Give Louie strength for his daughter as only I knew how to.

Now, I'm the kind of Dad that has always been really close with my son. Inseparable would be a better way to describe our relationship. I was Carmen's first human contact upon coming into the world and was the first one to hold him. Because of our close bond, even to this day, when my son even has a cold or lets out the slightest of coughs it goes through me like nails on a chalkboard. I feel it through my bones. So, I'm sure you can imagine what it felt like to hear Angelina's every scream.

It was going right through me.

I couldn't bear imagining it being Lisa or me in Louie or Brenda's place. But I also knew someone had to be strong. Someone had to be a voice of calm in the midst of all the chaos of the day. So every time Louie started to break down in front of her, I'd get him out of the room, hug him, let him cry on my shoulder, and remind him not to cry in front of her. Big as Louie was, about 6'4" around 240 pounds or so, he'd melt like a little teddy bear when it came to Angelina, much the same way as I remember him melting when I was back in college with anything involving his oldest daughter, Alex.

So I'd tell him, "Don't let her see you giving up. Fight with her. Don't give up hope. Despite what the doctors are saying she's still here. She's still fighting. Only let her see strength from you. You're her Dad—*her hero*. That's who she needs to see. Make her believe there's still hope."

And she fought.

One day rolled into the next. We'd spend hours by her bedside sitting in silence, praying for her as she slept. At other times, we'd race to bring nurses to her aid the moment something appeared to be going wrong. I'd listen to Brenda telling her stories and playing music from Angelina's *iPhone*. Brenda would sing along to her, *You are so Beautiful* and *Daniel's Song*. It made me cry. We'd spend evenings in *the Ronald McDonald House* at the end of the hall, sharing sympathetic glances with other parents of children battling the same battles we were. Many of the families there were of different nationalities, some spoke English, others didn't. It didn't matter. Every look was universally the same. Everyone was there for the same reason. It was that same pain everyone shared on their face, fighting through it to give customary smiles of hellos and goodbyes in passing. I'd also started spending nights doing my laundry since I only came with what I was wearing and each day kept rolling on into the next.

ABOUT A WEEK OR SO IN, Louie must have felt sorry for me and had his sister Carolyn buy me a comfortable pair of sneakers, some sweat socks, and he lent me one of his track suits. It was either that or he felt I was too overdressed to take me seriously anymore in my Italian alligator print dress shoes, see-through socks, and black silk shirt.

Every night I'd *FaceTime*, my wife, and son before they went to bed. I'd do it far away from her room, downstairs in the main lobby near the big clock sculpture they had placed just outside *Ryan Seacrest Studios*.

My son loved seeing that big clock sculpture every night. He was fascinated with how it moved and wanted me to show him its inner workings, so I'd walk him around the colorful array of oversized gears in the backdrop in the expansive lobby as we talked.

He'd ask me, "Daddy, why are you in Philadelphia? We hate Philly, don't we? I mean, I thought we were New York GIANTS fans. Why would you go to *Philly*?"

It made me laugh.

Talking with him took away the pain temporarily before heading back upstairs to Angelina's room.

A few nights turned into a week, so Lisa finally explained to Carmen that Angelina was really sick and Daddy had to stay in Philly to do everything he could to help her and to be by his Uncle Louie's side. One night I let Carmen *FaceTime* with Angelina as she lay in her bed. It was so sweet to watch. Lisa told me they would say prayers for Angelina to get better together every night before going to sleep.

I only told two other people I was in Philly—my new boxing trainer Arthur Neal, and my son's trainer Autumn Wolf. Other than that, there would be no posts about it on Social Media. No "send prayers please" kind of stuff. I just wanted to be there for Louie and focus all my attention on him and Angelina. But I also felt the need to have the kind of tough guys like these in our corner.

While Tony trained me for the better part of our first year at the boxing gym, he recently had the opportunity to train fighters overseas in Japan for six months. So, when Tony left, I picked up my paces with Neal, Tony's second in command. We picked up right where Tony and I left off. Neal turned out to be even harder on me than Tony! He urged me to start putting in some roadwork (jogging) on the weekends and pushed me to train even harder on Fridays.

"Fuck happy hour," he'd say. "*This is our happy hour.* Grinding while the others are out wasting their time and money on shit and people they don't need and don't really matter to them. We're working to be better men," he'd preach to me.

Mr. Neal, as everyone called him, could also see how boxing was helping me release some of my "inner demons" too, finding comfort in this violent craft that came so naturally to us somehow. And with the kind of year I was having, who was I to say no? Boxing was better than any kind of therapy anyway, for me and for my son.

So, when I got the call and raced off to Philly, and as one day started fading into the next, I figured I should at least let Neal and Wolf know where I was. They were used to me showing up with "Lil' C" at the gym to train so religiously that when we stopped coming in due to my abrupt journey to Philly, the guys began to worry. Part of me didn't know how long I'd be in Philly for anymore either. So, I told Neal and Wolf I was at CHOP, and I wasn't sure when we'd be back at the gym. From that day on, Neal became a constant source of strength for me while in Philly.

That was just who he was. He even looked the part of a warrior—a "big ass black dude with muscles for days" is the best way I've heard him described physically. Neal is close to ten years older than me, but for the kind of shape he's in you'd never know it. My son says he looks like a superhero action figure if that gives you any idea how strong the guy is. He also spent some time in Camden, New Jersey, of all places while in the military, so he was familiar with my world. Familiar with street guys who grew up around "the life." We'd always talk about his kids and his relationship with them. How much being around me and Lil' C reminded him of just how much he missed being with all of them.

He even offered to drive up to Philly and be by my side the day I told him where I was. From moment one he was in our corner like I imagined every good boxing trainer should be. After all, he literally was *my corner man*. But this was a different kind of fight. One that none of us couldn't have trained for. One we just had to pray on, keep our shoulders back, chin up and try and leave it in God's hands. And I continued to try and stay strong, at least for Louie and Brenda's sake.

Neal would call and check in on me every night.

I love him for that.

By this point, Brenda's parents, Kathy and Chic arrived and were either sleeping in the hospital in a visitor's room, or in the room with us every night. Louie's mom, Marie, was also sleeping at the hospital some nights. It was an interesting arrangement, to say the least. But we all bonded with each passing night and shared stories night after night. Some nights I'd stay up with Marie swapping war stories about the good old days. Other nights I'd talk art with Brenda's Mom, who is also a very talented artist.

Most nights, though, I'd just be catering to Louie. Whatever I instinctively felt he needed at whatever moment he needed it.

That's what I was really there for. Just to pitch in when I could, make sure he stayed strong and had a familiar face of a dear old friend who had been with him since the beginning.

As for sleeping arrangements, there was Angelina in her hospital bed, Louie's ex-wife Brenda (Angelina's mom) lying next to her on a couch pulled bedside, two air mattresses on the floor where Louie and his wife Nicole would sleep—them on one, me on the other—and a hospital cot for Brenda's Mom to sleep on. Every night we'd take turns staying awake and clicking Angelina's pain medicine button every half hour.

And then, beginning around the eighth night in, we witnessed one of two miracles while at CHOP . . .

MIRACLE NUMBER ONE was when Angelina suddenly woke up and was oddly coherent, talkative even. The pain seemed to subside and she appeared to be doing great! The doctors concurred. They said they couldn't believe she was still here, let alone sitting up in bed talking like she was. It was a special day for everyone. And one, coincidentally or not, she was able to spend surrounded by tons of visitors who decided to come on this particular day. It became a steady flow of countless cousins and close friends of the Miele family flying in from all over the country, as well as Nicole's family and their friends. There had to be well over fifty people visit her on this day. So many that they couldn't accompany all of us in *the Ronald McDonald House* so they opened up another conference room for everybody.

My Goddaughter, Alex, arrived with her newborn baby girl, Addison, who I was so proud to finally hold in my arms for the very first time. One of Louie's friends from Brooklyn then showed up with a suitcase, literally, an actual suitcase filled with Italian cold cuts, stuffed peppers, *fresh mozz'*, *gabagool*; not to mention homemade Italian pastries like *cannoli* and *sfogliatelle*, my personal favorite. She even brought her own cutting board. It felt like I was back home for a split second, and it was suddenly shaping up to be like a Miele family reunion.

This proved to be the only day I was able to get Louie out of the hospital for an hour or so for the first time all week. I felt like he needed a breath of fresh air, and after a couple guys from our old crew (groomsmen from Louie's first wedding) flew in to join us, in the form of Scott Phillips and Tommy Savel, for a second it felt like old times. We even broke his balls and got Louie to laugh a little, joking about, "How does it feel to have that many baby mama's all in the same place at the same time?!" This was us joking with him after Alex's mother Becky's recent arrival. That would be *baby-mama number three*.

We all grabbed a quick drink at a bar around the corner from the hospital, just for a momentary dose of sanity, even though he felt guilty leaving Angelina for even a second. I just wanted him to get out and breathe in some fresh air outside the hospital's sterile walls, and feel the pulse of what locals call "the Fighting City of Philadelphia," made famous from Rocky Balboa's heroics pulsating through the streets like the beating heart of resilience against the backdrop of the city.

And, each new morning, I'd perform my own daily ritual of moving my car in and out of the Penn Parking Garage, which was a few blocks down from CHOP. It was only $5 per day at Penn garage, but if you left it in there longer than 24 hours it went up to $20, so I'd go back and move it each day, drive around the block once and then re-park it back in the garage.

Louie would ask me, "Why don't you just move the car into CHOP's parking garage? I'll validate it for you so you won't have to pay the $20, and then you're right here?"

But I'm superstitious. Angelina was still fighting. So I kept my car at Penn and kept my daily ritual up. Like a coach wearing the same tie while his team is winning. It's superstitious, I know. But it was all about one thing—*anything to keep her fight alive.*

It also became more than that. It enabled me to share Angelina's story with the familiar faces seeing me perform this daily ritual over the past two weeks, like the bus driver, who was this sweet old woman that transported me back and forth from Penn to Children's Hospital after I moved my car each day.

And then there was this unbelievably charming, upbeat kid working behind the ticket booth window in Penn Parking Garage where I went to validate my car each day. Every single day I'd see these same two people. And every day that kid behind the ticket booth would smile at me wide as could be as I arrived at his window to pay my $5. Not a day would go by that he wouldn't ask how Angelina was doing.

He'd say to me, "Every day that I see you is a good day. Because I know she's still here with us, still fighting."

I'll never forget him saying that. I'd smile back at him, feeding off his strength and encouragement. I'd tell him to have a good day too.

He'd be quick to shoot right back with, "I will, as long as I keep seeing you! It's when *I don't see you anymore* it'll be a bad day. Right now, today—*today is good*. Today is a good day."

The bus driver asked about Angelina every day too. It was such a strange energy around the hospitals. There was all this positivity embodying all the upbeat, smiling faces working for the hospital industry, amidst all those *other faces* that became all too familiar. The ones with that look of desperation, in need of hope, the ones in search of a lifeline that might never come.

As an artist, I'm naturally gifted at reading people, reading facial expressions, reading body language. And, as a teacher, this also translated into the natural way I could read a child's story and know what exactly is going on with them, even before they're ready to tell me. So, I also easily read the look that was painted on the faces of every mother and father there at that hospital. It was one I also saw in the mirror every night as I'd wash my face before bed. One I saw in Louie and in every one of his family members.

MIRACLE NUMBER TWO occurred after the crowd of fifty plus family and friends had finally dissipated. After everyone got to take their pics with Angelina, laughed with her, and shared stories with her. It was getting late and only a small flock of us were left sitting in a semi-circle around Angelina's bedside.

I can't remember exactly everyone that was still there, but I do recall Louie, his sisters, and his mother Marie. I also remember the conversation that was shared. It's one I'll never forget. One that confirmed what I already believed about there being *life on the other side.*

Angelina sat straight up in bed as if possessed and said, "I'll give each of you one question to ask Poppy. He's here with us now."

Poppy is Louie's Dad, Lou, Sr. A tough, old school guy, hard as nails. He passed away before Angelina was born, though. I also loved Louie's Dad. While he was hard on Lou growing up, I got along great with the old man. When I lived on campus during my college years at Lycoming where Louie and I first met, his Dad used to bum cigarettes off me when he discovered we smoked the same brand of Camels. He was on an Oxygen tank at night towards the twilight of his life and at that point, he definitely wasn't supposed to be smoking.

But that's just how he was—*stubborn to a fault.*

He'd coax me with, "C'mon Michael. Nobody's gonna know. I'm not gonna tell Marie." I'd laugh and always give him one. Louie's Dad was a good guy. Tough on Louie, being Louie was his only son and his namesake and all, but a good guy deep down.

The first time I met Louie I was with my college roommates, Tommy Navarro and Tony Luci. Navarro grew up in Williamsport with Louie and we met up with him one night at this local nightclub in town. When we entered, Louie already had some low-life by the throat, pinned up against the wall. Apparently, the guy was talking trash about his old man. Something about the Feds busting his old man for illegal poker machines or something like that. You know, the Cherry Masters? The kind of machines bartenders pay out on?

Well, Louie, I found out right away, wouldn't have anyone talking smack about his family, especially not his father, may he rest in peace. Lou, Sr. never would've allowed it either, that's for sure. He once broke a local restaurant owners' jaw over a lot less. So, meeting Louie for the first time as he's choking some guy out, while still making time to greet me with a smile and a handshake with his free hand, I just knew we'd become best of friends.

He was my kind of guy.

When Louie's Dad passed away, I painted a portrait of them together. I did it fast too, which would become a common theme among many other important works I've done over the course of my career. From the portrait I did for Dominic Capone to debut on his reality TV series *The Capones* back in 2013 to the portrait I did for John A. Gotti for the cover of his book *Shadow of my Father* that I completed in December of 2014—these would both prove to be all-nighters. And just like the day I heard Big Lou passed away, I raced right to my canvas with brushes to paint the portrait.

And, as time would go on, back when I was in college, Louie and I became closer and closer. He used to drive through campus in his black Lincoln Navigator to pick me up in front of my dorm room to take me out. Literally, he'd drive right through the campus, nearly running over anyone in his path.

Lycoming College has since put up gates and laid a sidewalk where Louie used to plow right through, due to his tearing up the grounds so badly on the really rainy nights. We'd stay out late when he'd come get me, end up talking all night at a local tavern or at his Dad's warehouse on East 3rd Street. Some nights we'd just sit in his SUV and talk. One of those nights we were parked by a lake and stayed up late talking about his old man. It started to downpour so bad that his SUV got buried in the mud and we had to spend the night in his car until the sun came up to get out.

So, when it came to Louie—*I always just went.*

Louie never had to ask me twice. I'd just be there at a moment's notice. But that's how a real friend is supposed to be.

And, as we sat there, gathered around Angelina, who never actually met Louie's Dad, she was adamant that he was with us that very minute and we were supposed to ask him questions.

So we did.

Louie began recording all this on his cell phone once he realized the magnitude of the miracle that was transpiring before our very eyes.

And she answered every question—questions we couldn't comprehend how she knew. It was as if she was channeling his spirit from the other side. I'd never seen anything like it. For instance, there's no way she'd have known Big Lou smoked, but she asked Marie out of nowhere, "Nonny, how come Poppy is smoking?"

I chuckled and asked Angelina if Big Lou was also drinking *Dewars*. She nodded yes, not stopping to ask what *Dewars actually was*. She also asked Marie how many Grandchildren she had.

When Marie answered, "Twenty," Angelina shot back with, "No you don't. You have twenty-one! How come you don't count the one you had that wasn't born." Marie was beside herself.

"How could she have known I had a miscarriage so many decades ago?" Marie asked us all, bewildered and amazed.

It was all becoming too surreal—Angelina channeling all these departed souls.

She went on to tell Louie that "Poppy wants you to know he's proud of what you've done (with the business). That he never said it, but he's really proud of the man you've become."

The room got quieter conversations like these went on for almost an hour.

It was like we were all given this greatest gift. The gift of knowing that our loved ones were there to greet us on the other side one day. I felt a great comfort in knowing that, having recently lost people closest to me, but also I dreaded the timing of all this.

I silently wondered whether she was making a miraculous recovery, or if this was the beginning of the end.

EIGHT

LET'S PLAY THE LOTTERY

That night Louie and I bought lottery tickets. The reason was two-fold. The first being, we thought miracles were at work here. Everyone in Louie's family had been praying for Poppy to intercede. And, at that point, it looked like he was. The second reason was due to strange events surrounding two purchases we just made downstairs, first in the CVS and then in the hospital gift shop.

I had to get some contact lens solution and a few other things. My total at the CVS came to $10.08. Louie says, "I got this, put your money away" and then he proceeded to pay. As we headed back for the room, just before hitting the elevator Louie forgot something he wanted, so we stopped off at the hospital gift shop right across from the elevators. I grabbed a coffee while Louie gathered some snacks for the room, contemplating whether or not to get Angelina a balloon. Louie's sister Michele had arranged for actress Angelina Jolie to send over this big Tweety Bird balloon, along with a recorded video message to try and cheer her up, so Louie ultimately decided to just stick with snacks.

The total came to $10.08—*again.*

We both looked at each other.

The guy behind the counter immediately asked, "What is it? What's the problem fellas?"

Just then, two bags of potato chips flew right off the rack all by themselves hitting the floor behind us. Literally, no gust of wind, nobody else in the place. Just all by themselves.

"Did you just see that?! What the hell is going on here?!" shrieked the cashier, totally spooked.

"I don't know," Louie shot back with, "but something's definitely up," he went on to explain . . . "We literally just bought stuff at the CVS and the total was $10.08. Same as what just came up here. Look at the receipt! $10.08—again! Look for yourself if you don't believe us . . ."

The guy looked at both receipts, shook his head in disbelief, and then yelled, "Get the hell outta here! You two are freaking me out!"

So, we left and decided to buy lottery tickets. $50 worth.

We played the Pick 4, number 10-08—straight and boxed.

I still remember Louie saying to me, "That number's gotta mean something. Even if we don't know what it is now, it's gotta mean *something*, right?"

The next day everyone wanted that same level of coherence from Angelina as yesterday. Everyone was hoping she'd answer more incomprehensible questions from the other side. Give us more theatrics. *More miracles.*

But things seemed to begin to take turns for the worse. The doctors all began visiting Angelina more and more over the next couple of days. A Priest came by next. Finally, one of the nurses Louie and Brenda became friendly with over the course of Angelina's stays at CHOP came by and brought her flowers, which, if you know hospital protocol—this was definitely a *no-no*.

That scared the shit out of me.

The nurse cried as she gave the flowers to her.

It was then that I realized why she did what she did. It was the nurse's last shift before she was off for a ten-day vacation. She feared it might be the last time she'd see Angelina ever again.

NINE

10:08

I never wish for anyone to have to experience the kind of pain everyone felt on Thursday, July 30, 2015, as we helplessly watched this sweet, innocent child suffer through each last breath she took. Her heart rate skyrocketed while her white blood count dropped off significantly. I'll never forget watching Brenda's Dad, Chic covering his ears as he stood by watching over her because he couldn't stand to hear her gurgling as her lungs began to fill up with fluids.

On this, what would become our last night at CHOP, Louie's cousin Aaron flew in from Arizona. He's an oncologist, so it was great to have him here. It was also perfect timing. He helped get Angelina comfortable and convinced the doctors to do a procedure to free her airway so she wouldn't choke to death.

Towards the end, Louie's sister Angela and I found ourselves alone in the room with just Angelina, Louie, and Brenda. It was just the four of us by ourselves for what felt like the very first time in nearly two weeks. Louie's wife Nicole was off somewhere in the hospital with her daughter, Sabrina. So, Angela looked at me, and I looked at her, as we instantly realized *this was our window* to allow Louie and Brenda to finally be alone with their daughter.

"You two should really have some time alone with Angelina, without anyone else around—*just you and Brenda*. She needs that. You're her parents. Her blood," I told Louie, as Angela nodded, backing me up as we headed for the door to stand guard from the outside, unbeknownst to them we were orchestrating all this so they could have some much-needed alone time with Angelina.

My wife, Lisa told me over the phone that she felt this was one of the reasons Angelina was still holding on for as long as she was. That she didn't have any time alone with just her parents. But, up until this point, it proved nearly impossible to get the two of them alone with her. There was always someone around. Whether it was Louie's wife or one of his family members visiting or nurses popping in, it proved impossible up until this point. So, when we saw the moment, Angela and I seized it for them.

In hindsight, I think Angelina was more worried if Louie and Brenda were going to be okay than she was about her own well-being. She was such an incredible fighter. And, up until this point, she had continued to defy the odds of both logic and medicine. She even survived one last surgery to put a PICC line in to help her get a steady stream of meds without us having to continuously hit the button when we felt she was in pain.

I thought this was a good sign at that time since, initially, the doctors said she might not be able to live through the procedure. But she did, with flying colors. It was Louie, however, that reminded me of the fact that regardless if the PICC line worked they still weren't treating her actual cancer anymore, which meant that her tumors were still spreading and that even if they stopped Angelina from bleeding internally, they still couldn't treat her tumors. She simply couldn't handle another round of chemo. This was just a procedure to make her more comfortable.

I didn't want to hear that. I was still in denial that she'd ever leave us. I thought we had at least one more miracle on the way.

Louie told me later that night that Angelina asked him when they were alone if he still loved her Mom. Angelina even made them kiss. Kids are funny. In the end, I guess she just wanted her family to still be together. *This stuck with me.*

She wanted to know that they were going to be okay—even if she wasn't going to be. I learned a lot from Angelina over the course of those two weeks sleeping by her bedside and watching the family dynamics at play. I think a lot of people did.

This all stayed with me, as I related it to our son and what we were going through with him now, having been handed his official diagnosis just one week prior to getting the call from Louie for me to come to CHOP.

"Nothing would ever steer me away from my family," I vowed to myself. Not after seeing all this. *Our kids need us.* This is one thing I took away from spending over two weeks sleeping at Angelina's bedside.

I'll spare you the horrific details of what it was like to be there in her last hours. What it was like to hold her sweet, innocent little hand while she fought for her last breath as my dear friend squeezed her tighter than ever before, SCREAMING at the top of his lungs how he wanted to go with her.

Then it happened.

We both caught each other's eye and we looked at the clock. It was two minutes past ten, with that ominous number **10:08** printed out on our Lottery Tickets quickly approaching with each tick of the clock.

Finally, at 10:05 Louie couldn't take it anymore and yelled for me to run and get Louis, Angelina's teenage brother, who was down in *the Ronald McDonald House* watching television. I raced down the hall, grabbed him up and told him to hurry!

As we ran back into her room, *the process had begun.*

The clock struck 10:08 P.M. when she first lost consciousness, only to return for a few more baited breaths as Louie screamed for her to not leave! Louie then suddenly came to the realization that *enough was enough.*

And, as much as I know it killed him to let her go, he screamed at the top of his lungs, "GO ANGELINA! GO TO POPPY! Go to him, my sweet Angel!!"

I held her hand as Louie and Brenda clutched onto her . . . until she just—*stopped.*

She suddenly looked at peace. It was like she was sleeping. It took over an hour for us to pry Louie and Brenda off of her sweet, little lifeless body so that the nurses could come in and clean her up in preparation for the next phase of her journey—*her burial.*

A piece of me died in that room with that sweet little girl on that day.

I remember walking down that hallway one last time to collect my laundry. As I approached the last room at the end of the hall, I slowly passed one of the Spanish-speaking mothers of a child being treated there. We were the only two in the hallway.

She must have recognized the anguish in my face and immediately started crying, and then she hugged me tightly.

In her best English, she whispered up into my ear through her sobbing, "I'm sorry. *I'm so, so sorry . . .*"

I imagined she was contemplating what that moment might look like for her with her own child. That much was written all over her face as we held each other in that empty hallway.

I immediately thought of the kid working the ticket booth at Penn Parking garage not seeing me ever again and knowing why.

ONCE THE MADNESS of the better part of over an hour passed, it was now well after midnight, the morning of July 31st.

We suddenly all came to the strange realization we had to leave. Everyone began scrambling to pack their belongings.

It was bizarre.

I only had the shoe box from my new sneakers Louie bought me and a plastic *CVS* bag containing my toiletries. I was invited, like everyone else there, to stay at a friend of Louie's on the outskirts of Philadelphia that night, since it was so late and everyone was planning to drive back to Williamsport to get Angelina's funeral arrangements in order the next day.

But something strange happened. It was another one of those signs that would continue appearing to me as I continued taking everything in with my third eye—*my artist's eye.*

As I reached for my CVS bag, sitting next to it was one of those personalized Coca-Cola cans.

The word "**DAD**" was inscribed on it, glaring back at me, along the side of the can in big bold letters.

I felt like it was the Universe was talking to me again.

"No," I said to Louie, "I'm going home. To my wife and to my son . . . *I'm going home.*"

When I got back into my car for one last trip out of the parking garage late that night I had forgotten all about the fact that the CD I had in my car was a *Mob Hits* album Louie burned for me years ago. The song that blasted as I turned the ignition on my black Caddy was, of course, Louie Prima's hit song, *Angelina, Waitress at the Pizzeria* . . .

It was the song Louie named Angelina after.

I let the song play as I left Philly for home. I cried the whole way back as I thought about everything we just went through. I thought about how broken my family was at this point in my life. From the fractured relationship I had with my parents, to my own marriage, which, due to all the recent turmoil—was *rocky at best*. I thought about the fight we had still ahead of us with our son's battle with Autism.

All of this reminded me what a blessing Carmen was, and how fortunate I was to have a family like my wife and son to go home to. As I thought long and hard about our beautiful son, I imagined what it must be like for Louie, and who he would never be able to head home to again—*his beautiful daughter, Angelina*. Everything was hitting me like a ton of bricks.

The minute I arrived at the door around 4:30 A.M., I didn't even have to turn the key. Lisa was standing there waiting for me. She opened the door to me and I just burst into the most gut-wrenching storm of tears and heartache I've let go of in a long, long time.

"We couldn't save her," I cried. "We did everything we could, but we couldn't save her!"

"It's okay. I know," Lisa tried to console me as she began crying right along with me as she held me there in her arms.

"I tried. We tried so hard, but we couldn't save her. She's— she's . . . *gone*."

All the crying woke our son up and I tried to wipe my tears quick as I could. He ran out from the bedroom and jumped from the step in our living room into my arms. "Daddy's home!!!" he yelled excitedly.

Then he paused as I held him tighter, "Why are you crying, Daddy? Is it Angelina? Is she okay?" he asked.

"She's home son. She's gone home," I said, remembering my own Grandfather's last dying words he spoke to my mother before he passed, and I kissed him over and over again before tucking him back into our bed, climbing in right next to him.

The next day I talked on the phone with Peter Gotti, youngest son of the infamous *Teflon Don*.

I had to explain to Peter why my scheduled trip back to the City to see them that summer wasn't going to pan out. How a lot of things that particular summer didn't quite pan out as I had planned. Peter understood right away. He asked me to text him a picture of Angelina smiling so he'd only imagine her that way.

"Michael, I'm sick to hear this," he told me. "There is no greater injustice or pain than the loss of a child. People that think they have problems don't know what real problems are. Anything that we can do, whatsoever, I'm there. I'm going to be around for a few weeks. One of these nights I'll jump in the car and come for a bite in D.C."

He also shared with me a story about his iconic father, John Gotti, Sr., whom I admired, respected, and painted numerous pictures of over the course of more than a couple decades.

"When my father realized he had Squamous cell cancer," Peter explained, "which is the most violent, aggressive form of cancer he said 'Do not cry one minute for me. Better me than some five-year-old girl.' So, I'm sorry for Angelina. On my children, I swear, if you had called me from the hospital, I would've joined you there. I left my wife and children for six months to be at my father's side for two hours a day. I would've also let a little of me pass with that little girl too," Peter sympathized.

To this day, Peter still keeps the photo I texted him of Angelina smiling, and one of me kissing Angelina's forehead when I was in the hospital by her bedside. He tells me it's a reminder of what's important in life.

That's the kind of guy he is. Not how the media paints him and his family out to be.

The next week leading up to Angelina's funeral, we drove our son three hours down to the Jersey Shore to stay with my in-laws and then we headed another four hours over to Williamsport, Pennsylvania, for Angelina's funeral where I was asked to speak at her Mass.

It wasn't something we wanted our son to see. I also knew it was going to be one of the hardest weekends I'd ever have to be a part of, aside from those eleven excruciating days lying next to Angelina in that hospital room.

THE NIGHT BEFORE HER WAKE, I dreamed of Angelina. I told Louie and Brenda about it when we arrived. I knew nothing I could ever say was going to ever fix what happened or take the pain of losing their daughter away. I know this because of how my own mother became after losing my sister during childbirth, slipping into a lifelong battle with depression. I was worried about Louie and Brenda doing the same. It broke my heart to see them in such pain.

I knew when we left for home at the end of the weekend, life for everyone else would go on, but in a way, Louie and Brenda might feel like my mother once felt, which was stuck in this one strange place as the rest of the world around them moves on.

After all, Angelina became their *sole purpose* for living over the past two years. Every day they literally woke up to fight for Angelina's life, and now she was gone. The fight was over. What are they supposed to do now? But there have always been signs that have been bombarding me from every direction over the course of my life. *There must be a reason for everything.*

So I finally told Louie and Brenda about my dream. It was the only time I've ever dreamed about Angelina in my entire life. Her hair was long and flowy in it, not shaved bald from the chemo. She was smiling and laughing as her long auburn hair blew carelessly in the wind. She was jumping through clouds, transitioning from one to the next while swinging from balloons. From one balloon to the next she flew as if they were placed perfectly in the sky just for her. One hand at a time, just like a gymnast would, she flew through the air, laughing and smiling like the happiest kid in the world, amidst all those balloons.

Louie smiled, as a tear immediately formed in the corner of his eye.

"You're not gonna believe this . . ." Louie's voice now at a whisper, "Just this past week," he explained while gazing up at the skies above us, "the week leading up to the funeral, we set off a bunch of balloons into the air for Angelina from my backyard."

I smiled at him, grabbed him by the back of his neck and gave him a big kiss on the cheek.

"I guess she caught them," I smiled to him, as tears began to roll from our eyes.

AS WE LEFT WILLIAMSPORT, we headed back to the Jersey Shore to pick up our son to celebrate our 19th wedding anniversary in Wildwood with him. August 11th, the day after our anniversary I received a message from three weight division world champion and future hall of fame boxer "Sugar" Shane Mosley. We had been exchanging correspondences (DM's) back and forth through twitter. He was interested in commissioning me to do a painting for him. I shared our son's story with him, along with some video clips of him boxing. What he did next not only surprised me but restored my faith in humanity for the moment. He offered to give me and my son two VIP tickets to see him fight in a rematch against Ricardo Mayorga at a star-studded *Pay-Per-View* bout nearly one month to the date of Angelina's passing, August 29th, at the Forum in Los Angeles.

"I will leave two passes for you. You're a good Dad," he said to me.

I thanked him again and again, "It will be our son's first plane ride across the country. He's going to be so pumped to see you win!"

"So happy to be part of that Michael," he replied.

I explained to Sugar Shane, "My Grandfather was a boxer, so I've always loved the sport. But now, I'm just fighting for our son."

"Wow, that's deep. Maybe you can do that painting for me when you get back," he asked.

"You got it champ. Not a problem."

It turned into the trip of a lifetime, being ringside and in the VIP area with former IBF welterweight world champion "Showtime" Shawn Porter, former WBC welterweight champion Victor Ortiz, rappers 50 Cent and BowWow, and countless other fighters and celebrities sitting ringside to watch the future "Hall of Famer" Shane Mosley get his knockout in dramatic fashion. He definitely gave the fans the fight they were all waiting for.

While Angelina sadly lost her battle with cancer, we will continue to fight our son's battle with Autism.

And we'll do it just like Rocky Balboa says: "One step at a time. One punch at a time. One round at a time."

ALEXANDRA MIELE
OUR GODDAUGHTER

"You could say I had somewhat of a non-traditional upbringing when I was a child, but who doesn't anymore. Due to this, I was not baptized until I was about twelve years old, which might as well be considered a sin in a Catholic family; however, I thought it was pretty neat because it gave me the freedom to pick my own Godparents. Michael Bell and his wonderful wife Lisa were always such caring and loving people, that I knew right away they would be a perfect fit for me.

Michael met my father when he attended Lycoming College in our hometown of Williamsport, Pennsylvania and they formed a friendship that has lasted a lifetime now. Although we live in separate states and can't see each other as much as we all would like to, that has never stopped the Bell family from being there for me and my family when we needed support the most.

When my younger sister became very sick and within a short amount of time began fighting for her life, our family was beyond devastated. We spent countless hours praying and asking God why this could happen to such a young, innocent child.

In her final weeks, my father called Michael and without a second thought he was in his car driving to the hospital in Philly to be with our family, leaving is amazing family to spend the next ten sleepless days and nights with mine, keeping in mind he left so quickly he never even packed an overnight bag.

My family will never forget this, and forever will be indebted to the Bell family for everything they have done for us.

Love you Michael, Lisa, and Carmen."

TEN

BUILDING RELATIONSHIPS

After the summer of 2015, I returned to school and was hired to deliver two back-to-back two and a half hour long workshops to new teachers on "Building Relationships" between teachers and students, administrators and co-workers, families and the community.

Coming off of Angelina's funeral, our son's Autism diagnosis, and one year into what I felt would probably be a short tenure with our new Administration, change was definitely in the air. And, while I wasn't particularly seeing eye-to-eye with the administration, it was now beyond the "no field trips in June." Our program had just been cut for the first time in twenty years.

I wouldn't have been so disheartened if it wasn't for the fact our administration *changed the game on us*, and it adversely impacted our program's numbers in devastating ways. Mandating all incoming 9th graders to take their Tech. Ed. credits all freshman year in order to satisfy graduation requirements sooner left no room in kids' schedules for electives, and it cut our 9th grade enrollment in Art nearly *in half*. Not to mention, the new teacher that was excessed from my Department was one of my own former students I just hired fresh out of college, Douglas Ellmore.

Doug was near and dear to my heart. I taught him since he was a 6th grader in the GT Program. He became an ArtQuest "Best of Show" winner and earned a major scholarship to MICA. Once graduated from MICA I hooked him up with Mark Coates, one of my former mentors to help Doug earn his teaching certificate, and when a position opened up at Southern and I immediately hired him. Then, just like that, one year later under a new administration—*he was excessed*. Thankfully, an elementary school art teacher in our cluster gave me "the heads up" that she was retiring, so I helped Doug land a job teaching there.

So, here I am, hired to inspire new teachers on how to build great relationships, just as the relationship between me and my Administration was quickly eroding. Now, don't get me wrong, I liked our new principal. He was a really nice guy. He even came to one of my art exhibitions in D.C. I just didn't agree with his policy making decisions. But this is the game. A principal can do whatever they want to do. You have to just suck it up and deal with it and support their decisions, whether you agree with them or not. *That's also important.*

It's a lesson this one art teacher I mistakenly hired a few years back (*and one I was just as quick to get rid of as fast as I could*) failed to grasp the concept of. *Your boss is your boss is your boss.*

Like John Gotti once said, "If you think your boss is stupid, remember, you wouldn't have a job if he was any smarter."

Once I found out what an insubordinate miscreant this new teacher was, I convinced my Coordinator to give them an "opportunity elsewhere" (*just so I could get rid of them*). They wound up being *promoted* to Department Chair at another school, which was hilarious. But, I wasn't going to just sit back and watch someone tear down twenty years of my hard work, whether it's an insubordinate underling drilling holes in my boat while others were busy rowing, or a new boss taking the wind out of our sails.

So, while I was busy re-assessing my situation, for many teachers, this particular time of year was also time to re-group. This proved to be a time when, while I struggled with my own relationships, it still never stopped me from being great at my job.

When I'm at work I'm always on my A game. I love my job. And, building strong relationships with students, even with my administration over the course of two decades, is one of the things I had done better than anyone. So, despite everything that was currently going on, I was charged up to give this workshop.

Now, I've delivered this type of a workshop to first, second and third year teachers quite a few times over the course of my career, but this year, given the nature of all that had happened in my life leading up to it, between our son and Angelina, I wanted it to be the very best presentation I've ever delivered. Re-energize everyone, including myself! Give them the inspiration they all need to start their year. Give them what they paid for and more.

And if you're someone who's ever been to one of my artist talks or workshops—*the energy is palpable in the room.*

As the room began to fill, they did exactly as I imagined . . . they perused the visual journals, wondered why they were there, and what they were about to get themselves into.

Someone took a picture of my visual journals sitting in front of her and tweeted: "Not sure what is happening, but I'm excited for this Building Relationships session with @mbellart".

Once everyone arrived, I kicked the day off with my favorite Mickey Hart quote, "Adventures don't begin until you get into the forest, and the first step is an act of faith."

I then asked everyone "Who's ready to get into the forest with me?" Beneath the quote on the big screen behind me was a slide of Van Gogh's prophetic painting, *Wheatfield with Crows*.

I challenged them to "Imagine if Vincent Van Gogh was a child in their class and painted this painting, would they have been able to predict this to be one of his very last paintings . . . before he committed suicide? Would they have been able to read into the narrative he embedded into his work? Would they have been able to prevent it?"

I remind everyone, "There's a narrative to your careers just like there's a narrative to your lives."

Now their interest was piqued, so I shared—*how* I became a great teacher and *what* all great teachers have in common . . .

"It's the ability to read our students' stories," I added, which is what everyone was literally doing with the visual journals I placed in front of them. "There are a lot of things kids bury deep within that private world of those visual journals."

The importance of being able to read a kids' story was something I heard again and again in various different forms over the years while taking part in "Teacher of the Year" banquets and at National Blue Ribbon Schools Conventions from other national award-winning educators.

You never heard any of these incredibly inspiring educators get up and talk about their *classroom management*, how great their *data was*, or about how a certain *technique or lesson* they taught made all the difference in the world. You also never heard about how impressive their skill set was as a mathematician or scientist. What you heard were *stories*.

Personal stories of triumphs against all odds.

Stories about how they were able to turn their kids' lives around despite many circumstances—not through some magic one-size-fits-all formula, but from the strong relationships they formed with their kids.

This is the culture I've established and a legacy that I believe any leader is responsible for creating within their workplace. It's your responsibility to help your students build this same culture for themselves, and towards one another. I treat my class like a coach would treat championship winning teams. I'm their "guide on the side" as opposed to being any kind of "sage on the stage."

Quoting one of my former students, Erika Ellis, who so eloquently posted this on *Instagram* for all my future art stars to see: "Mr. Bell *only* makes champions."

And, whether a kid is planning to go to art school or not, it's my job to prepare them with the necessary skills to do whatever it is they want to do in life. Now, my kids learn a lot in my classes, but it's never a lot about "techniques." They learn by doing. After all, there are no museums of "Style and Technique." People don't go to museums to see Van Gogh's *techniques*. People go to museums to see how Van Gogh *thinks*.

I train my kids how to *think like artists,* and I show them how to use their own stories to fuel their creations. I teach them that they don't have to look very far for inspiration beyond their own stories. This usually begins each year with a little game called "If you really knew me you would know..." It goes like this:

If you really knew me you would know . . . "I'm an Artist in Education . . . I won my first art show at the age of five. My Grandma was the first one to put a paintbrush in my hand and I've been doing it ever since. She was a self-taught artist from Lyndhurst, New Jersey. Unfortunately, when the Great Depression hit, she was forced to quit school in the eighth grade to go to work and help support her family, so her dream of a career in art had to be forgotten, only to be realized many decades later the year I was born, winning her first art show at the age of fifty-three. So inspiring! My Grandfather was a boxer who later owned his own milk business. He fought hard through life and died far too young after battling extreme arthritis that had him up to two canes at one point shortly before he passed away."

If you really knew me you would know I once had . . .

"A sister who died during childbirth. An Uncle (my infamous cousin Vinnie) who, before I was born, was part of what is still to this day, two of the longest standing double gangland murder trials in the history of the State of New Jersey.

His trials were made famous because F. Lee Bailey, an attorney you may know from the O.J. Simpson case, was disbarred from practicing in the State of New Jersey—due to his exposing the levels of corruption in law enforcement and in the Passaic's prosecutor's office surrounding cousin Vinnie's trial.

Vinnie was eventually acquitted in both cases, but a year later was sentenced to fifteen years in Trenton State Prison, resulting from a trafficking pinch in stolen goods out of the Alexander Hamilton Hotel in Paterson. He once stayed with my parents while he was on the lam from the Government on his way to Costa Rica where he met his future wife (Dina Molina Lawson), who coincidentally or not, also became a well-known artist."

If you really knew me the last thing I ever expected . . .

"Was to still be *alive*. Was to become a *teacher*, let alone a *national award-winning teacher*. Was to become a *husband*, let alone a *father* to a beautiful Autistic son. The last thing I would have ever expected was to be talking about how to *build relationships* when so many of mine have been the equivalent of tornadoes, leaving a trail of destruction in their wake."

But, everything matters. Even the really bad stuff.

That's the thing that's interesting about life. What shapes us is often the thing we have the least control over—where we come from, and who brings us into the world. Who surrounds us with darkness, or with light . . . All of this becomes what shapes every choice we've ever made.

So, it's not about *what you teach*. It's really *whom you teach* that matters and truly defines *why* you do what you do, is it not? After all, we're supposed to be teaching *people, not curriculum*, right? So, we need to be courageous enough to share our stories with our kids. It completely levels the playing field and makes all the difference in the world. While you may not be able to tell them *everything*, you can certainly give them some of who you are. Then, they will, in turn, give you back exactly who *they are*.

For the rest of my *Building Relationships* workshop, I challenged everyone to also think differently about their content areas. Consider *substance over form*. Reflect on our own time management. You're not alone with how you may feel about all the challenges we were faced with now as teachers. We are all in the midst of what I consider "way too many initiatives at once."

Initiatives stemming from the replacement of the failing *No Child Left Behind* (NCLB) with what I consider an even greater catastrophe in *Race to the Top* (RTT), which, by the way—how *RTT* wasn't the extortion of our states' governors by the President of the United States *is beyond me* . . . to more disasters like *Common Core Standards* and *SLO's* (an accountability method to "measure student growth"). Then there's college and career readiness for our ELL (English as a Second Language Learners), eliminating the "achievement gap" for African Americans, *PARCC* assessments (*Partnership for Assessment of Readiness for College and Careers*) . . .

On and on goes the nationwide over-testing of America's youth. This all led up to the 2015 *Every Student Succeeds Act* (ESSA), which, by the way, was vetoed in Maryland by Governor Hogan, but he was overridden by the General Assembly. So, more disasters are still on the way . . .

What does all this over-testing mean for our kids? Well, in an October 27, 2016 *Time Magazine* article: "Teen Depression and Anxiety: Why the Kids are Not Alright" an alarming 3 million teens, ranging from 12 to 17 were documented having at least one major depressive episode in the past year and over 6 million teens had an anxiety disorder. This, to me, is an epidemic in the making.

In addition to keeping up with a ridiculous amount of new policies, a steady flow of useless acronyms and an overload of content teachers are forced to deliver within nearly impossible time frames, I still challenge everyone this: "How can you possibly teach *curriculum*, or teach *anything* for that matter— without a solid relationship in place?!"

I mean, if your students don't know you, don't trust you, why would they be willing to learn *anything from you?*

Unless they're just being compliant—*which is even worse.*

My kids know exactly what I'm about. And, just like Simon Sinek explores in his famous *TED talk* "Start with Why," remember, kids won't buy into what you do . . . they'll buy into *why you do it.*

So, think about this: "What *can you* be best in your district, in your state, or in the world at?"

This question doesn't beg *what you want to be best at*, it really begs—*what are you good at already*? And how could you become the best at whatever that is, in order to take your strengths and transform those into *your why*?

For example, in art, if you naturally do a lot of contour drawings, you are probably going to be more of a linear painter. That's already embedded in the fabric of your being. You're probably never going to be a thick, painterly type, so I wouldn't pair you up with a Lucien Freud type as a potential mentor since Freud's works are super thick and it wouldn't be natural for you.

In boxing, I'm no featherweight, so it wouldn't do me any good to study featherweight boxers. They're much smaller and faster, which makes their game plan and training regimen totally different from mine. That wouldn't help me in the cruiserweight division. So, naturally, I'll look to cruiserweights and light heavyweights to try and emulate and learn from *style-wise*. For instance, I have a great left hook and a strong overhand right. So, naturally, I'd look to Mike Tyson, Evander Holyfield, and Saúl "Canelo" Álvarez—guys that are great at throwing punches and combinations like me. *These are guys I can learn from.*

So, "What are you best at *already*?"

Use your imagination and figure that out.

"What's your story?" The answer is in there someplace.

In art, based on my lifelong interest in drawing and writing in my sketchbooks, I knew I could be best in the world at *Visual Journaling*, and could use this as a means to take students from point A to point Z. It was something I did naturally already, so I studied it further, to understand it on a deeper level and to be best in the district/state or in the world at. It later turned into my Master's Thesis while a grad student at Towson, and it proved to become a means to forge many great friendships with other like-minded artists who also saw the value of visual journaling as a serious process to understand and inform our final products.

Next question: "What are you *most passionate* about?"

This speaks to *your why.* Why do you do what you do? Why do you teach the way you teach? Why do certain units of study resonate with you on a deeper level than others? Remember, at the end of the day, your kids don't care about what they're doing as much as they care about why they're doing it!

Last one: "What drives your economic engine? Specifically, how do you *fund* your vision?"

This one is for anyone out there that feels money, or lack thereof is in your way of achieving something you want to in your classroom or beyond because it's not. It's your job to go out and get it! Now that we covered *the what* and *the why*, we can get into *the how.*

Now, I've never had to ask my Art Coordinator for a dime. But, when I started ArtQuest, which has turned into one of the largest student art exhibitions anywhere in America, every idea I had was initially shot down. *Mostly due to money.*

I heard things like, "We can't give out prize money. There's no money in the budget for that. We can't give scholarships away. We can't afford signage or backdrops. We can't afford to make a fancy program!"

Guess what—*you can*. If you're willing to put in the hard work it takes to go out and get it. I started out by building community partnerships with local garden centers to do face-painting on the weekends with my students. You know what, beyond making the kind of money I needed to create and sustain the show, we all bonded on those days basking in the sun among hay bales as the crowds flocked to our booth.

We were also getting the word out that, "We're out here from Southern High face-painting to raise funds for ArtQuest." And the community not only got the message, they came out to the show in record numbers!

So, while I'm not a big fan of acronyms and buzzwords, **"IMAGINATION—DEDICATION—HARD WORK"** became three things that defined what we're about. And, *my kids* came up with the acronym. They wanted wristbands with the words inscribed on them and they prompted the painting of these words on my studio walls. This wasn't something I pushed on them. This is what *'shared vision'* really looks like.

Now, when one kid sees another kid in the hallway or out in the community or in the tunnel at graduation with one of our wristbands on they know "they're one of us". *How inspiring . . .*

That's your job, after all—*to inspire*. To make kids feel like they're a part of something bigger than themselves. And if there is a kid not learning something in your class, guess what, the hard truth is—it's not their fault. It's yours.

You need to find a way in. Get them to trust you. Find a way to help them learn and be successful. And every student is different. If you can't find a way in—*it's nobody's fault but yours*.

THESE DAYS there are all these buzzwords floating around. Things like D.I. (Differentiated Instruction), *STEAM* instead of *STEM* (encouraging Art + Design into K-20 Education). On and on the Ed-speak train goes . . . What it really comes down to is *caring*.

Caring enough to do whatever it takes.

In 2012 the New York Times profiled the life of science teacher Jeffrey Wright in a short documentary film, *Wright's Law*. Aside from all the excitement he stirs up for his kids, which I'd liken to some of the great ones—*the Jaime Escalante's, Louanne Johnson's, Erin Gruwell's and John Keating's of the world*. Mr. Wright also has a unique personal story as a parent of a child with Joubert syndrome, which is a rare genetic disorder that only 450 people in the world have. It leaves his son gasping for breath at a rate of 180 times a minute, three times a second. There's not one day that goes by when Mr. Wright doesn't ask, "Why me?" His story is also one, like mine, he shares each year with a new crop of kids.

In the short film, he explains, "When you look at physics, it's all about laws and how the world works, but if you don't tie those laws into a much bigger purpose, the purpose in your heart, then you are going to sit there and ask the question—*who cares*?"

Like me, Jeffrey Wright also believes kids want a greater purpose. For him, he hopes that one day one of his kids will be the one to come up with the cure to help his son. So, *what's your why*?

Sometimes your kids will be the ones to ask you this question.

Early in my teaching career I still remember meeting L.B. for the first time. He was sixteen years old and was living with Mike Fox, another student of mine at the time. This one morning he stopped by during my planning period and began studying a painting I was working on he asked me that very question—*why*?

It was for a *Voices of Violence* series I was creating for ex-Mob wheel woman, now domestic violence survivor and best-selling author, Georgia Durante. The paintings somehow gave him a doorway to walk through. As L.B. started asking me questions about the paintings, I asked him to describe what he saw in them.

With that, he began to tell me how he could relate to the violence. How, when he was nine years old, his sixteen-year-old sister, Kathy, was murdered right in front of him at his birthday party and how his father's been in jail ever since he can remember and his mother's been on drugs so bad he decided to take a chance and go out on his own and live with this other kid —*stay in school.*

So, for all you teachers out there, if you have a kid that's acting out in your class, before sending them right out to the office, it's so important to find out what that kids' story is and what's really going on in their lives.

When L.B. was a senior, *finally graduating,* I was there for his graduation and Lora Johnston, one of our administrators that I became good friends with, came up to me and said, "You know L.B. came running over to me after he walked across the stage and I thought he was going to show me *his diploma*—that he finally graduated—but what he actually wanted to show me was *the card* that you handed to him in the tunnel right before graduation. That was the one thing that was so important to him. You really made a difference in his life, I hope you know that."

It meant so much to me that Lora shared that with me. It was then that I truly realized if you take an active interest in these kids' lives you never know what they can accomplish if you do.

STUDENTS I'VE KNOWN simply function more effectively when they feel respected and valued and function poorly when they feel disrespected or marginalized. When students have a secure relationship with their teachers and a strong attachment to their school they are more comfortable taking risks that enhance learning, tackling challenging tasks, persisting when they run into difficulty, and asking questions when they are confused. Let's face it, building relationships is about making *emotional connections.*

Our children are constantly trying to manage assaults on their self-esteem daily. Some have wounds you couldn't even imagine. And now, living in the age of Social Media where most kids have a cell phone, they're not even safe when they're tucked away at night sound asleep in bed. Their phone could bleep, and just like that, their whole world could change and you wouldn't even know it. It happens in class while you're teaching too.

So, while building relationships with kids, you need to be:

Disciplined. Push them, then push them some more, and expect them to push back. Conserve your time and energy. Avoid all things that break your momentum.

Brutally Honest. But have compassion—try four statements of praise for every one criticism.

A Team Player. Don't think you can do it alone. Everyone needs a mentor.

Available. While building our program I was the first one in and last to leave.

Lastly, be *flexible.* As long as it always works out in your favor. *I'm only half-kidding, of course.*

This is all about developing *your unique vision.* And with vision comes "power," which I believe, is the ability to define reality, and inspire others to respond to your definition as if it were their own. And don't leave out the rest of the staff as potential keys to surround kids with the best support we can. Here are a few more key players that you should really take the time and get to know if you haven't already:

The Custodians and the Cafeteria Staff. The Secretaries and Guidance Department. And don't forget the Business Manager.

This is something I learned from my father and it was the best advice he ever gave me going into my first day of teaching—to take care of people, *especially the custodians.* When he was coaching football he used to buy the custodians their favorite brand of whiskey every Christmas. It became a tradition I'd also carry on.

So, learn the custodian's names, their likes, and dislikes and don't forget about them over the holidays. These are the people that actually make your building run! Every Christmas, I take care of the custodians and business managers, and every Valentine's Day its roses for the Secretaries and Guidance Department.

So where can you fit in? In your building? With your kids? Or with your administration?

What can you bring to your Department's table that's a unique way to fill their needs?

I figured out right away what our needs were when I came to Southern High as a part-time art teacher. *We had no art show.*

There was no reason for a student to take art beyond "liking art," or "liking their art teachers." There were no external rewards for taking the courses beyond that.

So, *I filled a need.*

Our numbers skyrocketed after I created ArtQuest, and here I am today, with one of the largest professionally juried, nationally sponsored student art exhibitions in America.

So, you find the need, replace it with something positive. And, whether you realize it or not, here's your kids' sea of basic needs: *Affiliation—Achievement—Validation—"Power."*

This was something I'd learn from being inside the Los Angeles Good Shepherd Domestic Violence Shelter. Don't ask a victim of domestic violence "Why don't they just leave?" Ask them "Why they *stay*." Replace that need, and they will leave.

This is actually the same model a gang uses to recruit future gang members. So, are you smarter than a gangster?

I've helped make the Arts at Southern High the "involvement canvas" that connects the school to the community at large. We begin with *affiliation*, through our art clubs and National Art Honor Society organizations. We give them *achievement* through entering them in tons of shows and competitions, and *achievement* within our school and community. This brings them *validation* to their role as being "part of something bigger than them." And it leads to our program's *power*, while *empowering them* in the process. So, what will you do that's legendary? What will you create that can live on long after you're retired?

Why did you even become a teacher? My answer has always been simple, "I want to catch kids before they fall."

I want to catch them before they form patterns that lead to one of two places—*dead or in jail.* Not my kids.

Not on my watch.

JACKI BROWN
SPECIAL EDUCATION TEACHER

"I first met Michael Bell at his 'Building Relationships' workshop in 2015. Although I wasn't signed up for his course, I was immediately drawn to his charisma and the visual journals he had displayed about the room. Naturally, I had no choice but to crash his session and participate. Being a first-year teacher in the public school system, and working in a self-contained classroom with students coded as Emotionally Disabled I knew that I would benefit from Michael's experience and advice.

He opened his session in the typical fashion: introductions, ice breaker, etc., then he told us about himself. Growing up learning to paint from his Grandmother, and the violence he encountered. Any other individual may be jaded, but not Michael. He used his experience to help students that others had turned their back on. He taught them to express themselves, their emotions, their experiences, through art. He then turned the focus back to us, his now eager students, and asked us about any personal experiences we would like to share. Some were hesitant, others (such as myself) were eager to share. He commended us for our candor and provided both appreciation and wisdom.

Turning back to his 'lesson', Michael showed us portions of clips from movies like *Freedom Writers* and *Dangerous Minds*. Working with Emotionally Disabled students, I immediately identified my students in the faces of those on screen. He periodically paused the clips to discuss what each teacher had done to engage and cultivate relationships with those students who were more accustomed to people turning their backs on them most of their lives. During the pausing of one of the clips, he said something along the lines of 'Here, she identified the leader of the group. She knows that if she can gain the trust of them, and build a relationship, that she will be able to cultivate relationships with all of them.' Once more, a flash of insight. I knew exactly who the leader of my students was, and that I had to cultivate that relationship with her. I had to gain her trust, gain her respect.

Once the clips were finished, all the pauses and comments wafting through the air for our minds to contemplate, Michael began to share more stories of his students' lives, what they had overcome simply by putting pens to paper, pencil to a sketchbook, and paintbrush to canvas. He showed us their art, their most personal expressions. For a moment, I could feel their pain, feel the tears as they streamed down their faces, and feel the hope. Michael showed us the awards they had won, letters they had written him, and where they are now. It was awe inspiring. Each and every one of them who woke up each morning and strived to do better, simply because one man, their Art Teacher, believed in them.

From here, Michael talked to us about students with disabilities, and once more my ears perked. I have worked with children with Autism and other disabilities for a number of years and was eager to hear what he had to say. He showed us a clip of a father, also a teacher, who had a severely disabled son. The level of dedication, love, and support that this father offered was comparable to what Michael offers his students: unconditional support.

Once more, questions were asked, stories shared, and then attention was drawn to the visual journals that had taken up residency on the desks we sat at. These journals held the very essence of each of his students. Almost as if a piece of their soul was permanently affixed to the piece of art we were greedily thumbing through. He then showed us one of his own visual journals. A deeply personal item that held more pain than I could have imagined. Appearing a little macabre on the outside—a red rocking chair sitting atop a small chest with drawer, a jewelry box perhaps—this visual journal held so much more than I could have imagined. A life of pain, love, struggle, and unmitigated devotion.

I left the two-hour session with a strong desire to change the lives of the kids I was working with. While I had that desire prior to attending Michael's workshop, it was afterward that I also had the tools. I am grateful to know Michael, and to have learned so much from him in such a short period of time."

ELEVEN

CRAZY LITTLE THING CALLED LOVE

A wise man once told me, "We judge a criminal by his lowest moments and a creator by his highest. That we both work from some indescribable force rooted in some deep seeded frustration, and when we explode, there's no turning back."

For me, it became like this *with art and with life*.

Growing up, to anyone on the outside, I imagine we appeared to be a happy family. I know my parents tried their best to give me a happy childhood. And, up until around 2nd grade—*it was*.

But when tragedy comes violently bursting through your door, it comes hard and fast like a tornado. For my family, it was the perfect storm of circumstances and events that shook us to our core and caused such destruction I never quite knew when or where we were going to land.

I spent close to seventeen years of my life as an only child. My mother, Alma went to college to become an elementary school teacher, and my father, Alex, to become a Phys. Ed. teacher. My mother was from Lyndhurst, New Jersey, which is a predominantly tight-knit Italian neighborhood just outside of New York City near the Meadowlands and my father originally came over from Northern Ireland as an only child when he was just ten years old. His family settled in Syracuse, New York. My parents would later meet in college.

Now, the first time I saw my father beat somebody within an inch of their life was at a local *American Legion Social Club*. I was really young back then, but I used to spend many a night at the Legion with my Dad, especially after he and Mom lost my sister while giving birth. It became a tough time for everyone.

My mother was a different woman before tragedy struck home. She used to have all the neighborhood kids over all the time. She used to cook for everyone, make home-made jellies and jams in the summertime from grapevines she grew along our backyard fence. We'd vacation in Clearwater, Florida, Myrtle Beach, Rehoboth and the Jersey Shore. She was this tall, thin, dark-haired woman with an electric smile and this charisma about her I always loved as a child. She looked like a model right out of *Italian Vogue.* I absolutely adored her. I arrived into the world three and a half weeks late, but I still managed to make a grand entrance, arriving on her birthday, of all days. So, for a time things were really good. But when that storm came, *it changed us all.*

It hit the night my mother was due to give birth to my sister. At this point, my parents didn't know the sex of the baby. They were waiting until birth to find out. I had fallen asleep and was dropped off at the neighbors on their way to the hospital. This was my Mom's third pregnancy since I was born. Each of them ended with three or more days in the hospital and multiple procedures. The other two pregnancies were terminated due to internal complications. Hospital records state: two live births, one stillborn and two abortions.

I'm not sure how you get over the loss of a child, let alone multiple children. I know what I went through with Louie, Brenda, and their daughter Angelina. There are no words. My Mom certainly never talked about it. There was a time when she never really spoke at all. You could walk up to her and shake her nightgown and . . . *nothing*. She'd just sit in her rocking chair and just rock.

This went on for about a year and a half or so, the way I remember it all. When talking with my father about it many years later, the thing that stuck with him the most was when the doctor told them she was a girl, and how blue she was in color.

"She was like this bright neon blue baby," he explained to me, still struggling to keep his composure about it to this very day.

He also told me how angry he was with the doctors. How Security had to restrain him after he nearly put his fist through the large plate glass window at the hospital. How they were just in the hospital the week before my mother's scheduled due date and the doctors told them how everything looked fine, but how my Mother still sensed something was horribly wrong. She said she couldn't feel the baby anymore.

I still remember praying, as a young child, when I overheard something about my mother suffering complications during the delivery and how she lost a lot of blood . . . how the doctors were giving my Mom had a 50/50 shot of making it through the childbirth.

I remember praying hard to God, something I still feel guilty about to this day—that if it was between my mother losing another baby or me losing my mother—that I wanted my mother to live. *And she did.*

But she came home a different woman. Not the one I knew. My sister, they named her Amanda, didn't make it. They donated her eyes to save someone from blindness. My sister's memory still haunts me to this day.

Decades later, while taking Master's classes at Towson University, I tried to create a conversation with my mother about all this through a work of art. It turned into this "Red Box" I would call my *Relics of Childhood*.

I found this wooden box, which was essentially an old jewelry box, at a consignment store. I also found a small, wooden rocking chair that I mounted to the top of the box to represent my mother. I painted everything red. Then I drove all the way back to the playground I used to play on as a kid to take photographs of the exact swing set that I used to swing on as a kid.

I printed the photographs on the rough side of photo paper so the imagery would purposefully bleed and mounted them on cardstock with vellum paper in between each photo, to create the feeling that they were *all about memories*.

I hooked chains to either corner of the stack of photographs and bolted the chains into the inside of the second drawer of the box. This way, if you pulled the photos out and let them hang below the Red Box, they would swing just like a swing set. Inside the top drawer I placed baby clothes, never worn, with the tags still on them. I also scattered sealed birthday cards with my sister's name, Amanda, on the outside of each one of them. This was a ritual I imagined my mother underwent each year around the time of my sister's birthday.

I've heard depression described as *rage turned inward*. Also, that it's common after such trauma. My father was resigned to trying to have another child at that point. "That's it . . . no more," he said after losing my sister. This was when the weight of all this began to put a strain on their marriage.

All of this would change most people. For me, I steadily transformed from this happy-go-lucky kid into whatever you see before you today. That picture looks different to different people, depending on who you ask.

My transformation began around the same time our next door neighbor's young child also swallowed a tack and was rendered a paraplegic. We used to go to their house every Christmas and all the parents would party until the morning hours up until that happened. I used to love going over there. I'd fall asleep underneath their coffee table.

It was also around the time Danny Johns and I nearly died of an overdose of children's vitamins that landed us back-to-back in the hospital to have our stomachs pumped. Danny was a childhood friend who was also born on my birthday in the same hospital as me. It's how we all met.

It was also around the same time I nearly lost my right eye, which left a distinct scar. And, a year or so later, my mother lost her father—*her everything*. He died in her arms in his bed in

Lyndhurst. This was a time period that I'd label as the perfect storm of irreversible tragedies . . . all at once.

My Dad later told me my mother thought there was some kind of '*black cloud*' over our neighborhood. He said that 'we had to move.' *And we did.*

But before we moved, I'd spend the better part of a few years watching my Dad coach his way from two back-to-back state high school football championships to building a program from the ground up, much the same as the art programs I've built up. This gift I attribute directly to him. I also got to hang at *the Legion* with his pals on a regular basis. I loved hanging out there with my Dad back then. It must be what it's like for my son hanging out with me and the guys at the boxing gym.

My Dad had this ferocious temper back then, but he'd also do anything for anybody. He'd give you the shirt off his back, and prided himself in breeding champions on and off the field. Now, when I say his temper was ferocious that doesn't really do it justice. *It was truly explosive.* He'd throw down with anyone at the drop of a hat! And he could go from 0 to 100 in a heartbeat. It was this hair-trigger temper, and he'd clock you over the head with whatever was nearby, whether it was a football helmet—which I personally saw him beat someone over the head with, or his belt, which was his favorite disciple tool for me. He just had this penchant for grabbing anything within reach and going to work on you with it if he felt you had it coming. It was how his Dad was with him growing up. *It's all he knew.*

To his defense, I was also the kind of kid that deserved a few beatings from time to time, *trust me*. But when it came to his actual work ethic—well, that was also something that would stick with me as being second to none, especially when it came to football and lifting weights. He lived, ate and slept it back then. And he did just as much good for the guys on his team as I've done for the kids I've helped in art under my tutelage.

I loved helping him draw up new plays as a kid on our dining room table at night. I'd hang in the locker room with the guys before and after the games, and went to a lot of practices.

During games, I'd either hang out on the sidelines as a ball boy, or I'd in the press box. His players used to weigh me down with their gold chains before each game, making me wear them so nobody would "steal their bling" from the locker room.

One summer, one of the guys from his team—a kid my Dad absolutely loved—Brian Sharpeta, tried to bring me along with him to Ocean City with him and his little brother, who was around my age. But when my Dad took a look at the back of Sharpeta's van at case after case of beer stock-piled up to the top he just shook his head laughing, "Hell no, Sharpeta! He's *never* going to Ocean City with you!" Those were good times.

My Dad and Sharpeta were inseparable back then. He was this big fat lineman with a magnetic personality. He was also a typical "meathead" who used to show up late for school, and by late I mean a couple hours late! My Dad would always write him a pass and get him out of trouble. In turn, my Dad made Sharpeta stay late after practice every night to whip him into shape. He would make him run hills until it was dark.

He even took him down to the soccer field to run laps by telling Sharpeta, "The soccer field is flatter and easier to run on." Sharpeta never realized it was twenty yards longer than a football field. And with each lap, anyone within half-a-mile could hear my father barking out, "You call that a lap? Why's your helmet off? It doesn't count with your helmet off. Go again! You've got exactly ten laps and so far I'm counting *none*! Come on Sharpeta!!!"

Sharpeta didn't have a great home life, so I think part of my Dad staying late with him every night was also his way of saving Sharpeta from going home to his old man, who was rumored to be a pretty nasty drunk.

Some nights, as practice was ending, Sharpeta would let out a sigh of relief when the sky would go black over the practice field, only to have all his relief drained from his face as my Dad would go up into the press box and put the stadium lights on. *It was pretty demoralizing*. It's how I'd equate when my college basketball coach used to line the corners of the gym with trash cans before practice started. You knew you were gonna run until you puked.

Finally, all the time and energy my Dad poured into Sharpeta paid off the night he recovered a tipped pass and ran it all the way back fifty yards for a game winning touchdown! When he got to the sidelines, the stadium going wild and cheering after his first career touchdown and he ran right over to my Dad for a huge *attaboy*, only my Dad just broke his balls some more.

"*Sharpeta!*" my Dad barked, "You know you nearly collapsed at the 20-yard line?! I thought you were in shape! You know what an embarrassment it would've been if you ran that ball all the way back, only to collapse at the twenty?! Thank God you made it. Maybe those hills weren't enough. After this game, we're gonna go back to the soccer fields. Now go get some water. You're sucking wind!"

My Dad would smile to himself after an outburst like that. To Tom Marron, Head Coach and partner in crime, they'd have a good laugh. To the players, they thought he was for real. That was typical of my Dad, though. He was a hard ass. He and his former players would have a good laugh about it all many years later but back then, for my Dad, he always knew what buttons to push with which kids. Which ones needed praise, which ones needed more tough love. This was also how it was back then too. Athletes were a different breed of kids. They didn't go running to *Mommy or Daddy* if they didn't get enough playing time. They actually had to earn it. There was a pecking order too. And they didn't go running to the principal's office when they got a bad grade or wanted out of a class because they couldn't handle doing the work. Everything was handled more "old school—in house". That was the number one locker room rule. *Everything stays here.*

With all this newfound discipline my Dad was handing down to Sharpeta, the kid actually got his life together, graduated high school and signed up to join the military. A lot of this I credit to the relationship he had with my Dad. He spent so much time with my father, I felt as though he was probably more of a father figure to him than his actual Dad was. This big fat lineman became a lean, mean fighting machine. But Sharpeta's dreams would sadly become short-lived. It would break my Dad's heart.

He was killed tragically in a motorcycle accident just when things were beginning to go right for him.

My Dad was devastated.

So, as things were getting worse and worse with all these tragedies swirling around our family on the home front, I was spending endless days at football practice with my Dad and late nights with him at *the Legion* where he was trying to drink it all away. Knocking back beers and shots of *V.O.* with his pal Bernie.

ONE FATEFUL NIGHT, everything finally came to a head. My Dad's pals were at the bar feeding me quarters to keep me busy playing *Shuffleboard* while they watched football and drank beers. *Crazy Little Thing Called Love* was playing on the jukebox.

And just like that, a fight breaks out. This one guy at the bar had started jawing back and forth with my Dad about the game that was on TV. Apparently, the guy was a big Washington Redskins fan. My Dad—*not so much.*

"One more word out of you," my Dad said, "and I'm gonna take you by that stupid fucking tie of yours and split your chin wide open on this fucking bar!"

"Oh yeah, go ahead and try it!" And with that—and one sweeping motion of his fist, my Dad took hold of the guy's necktie, and SLAM!!! Straight down. On the bar. Splitting his chin wide open—*as promised!*

The bartender started yelling "Not in the bar Al, take it outside! Take it outside!" So, my Dad dragged him off the bar, still beating the living shit out of him, then he picked him up and slammed him through the first set of double swinging saloon-style doors to the entrance *head-first,* as a melee of screaming and yelling and fighting started breaking out everywhere!

Someone must have bumped into the jukebox during the scuffle because *Crazy Little Thing Called Love* started skipping, which is why I remember everything so vividly.

"*Crazy little thing called love . . . Crazy little thing called love . . . Crazy little thing called love . . .*" over and over again.

I later painted out a more imaginative version of this scene from my childhood. Initially, I titled the painting *Crazy Little Thing Called Love*, but then later changed it, much like the many revisions the painting itself underwent over time. I ended up re-titling it, *House of the Rising Son*, which was a play on words off the 1964 hit song by *the Animals*. It's another song that reminds me of my father—*and my son*.

I used my son as a reference for the younger version of me in the painting, at the jukebox. I put former students in the painting, including Katie Emmitt, Erika Ellis, and Kate Gleeson off to the right near the jukebox, Tyler Mills next to longtime friend and colleague Marlene Kramer at the bar near actress friend Kathrine Narducci, Dominic Capone, and his girlfriend Staci.

I even painted myself into the painting as a present day "stand-in" to represent my father, only in my painting I decided I'd recreate my own real life beating of a kid from so many years ago that landed me in a myriad of trouble as a teen. The work became part of my *Carnevale* series, which was a narrative series of eight 48" X 96" oil paintings on canvases I completed in 2015. Each painting was a "cinematic scene" linked to the other paintings as part of a much larger story, like film stills in a movie. I merged stories from my own life, and stories from my wife Lisa's trials and tribulations, like the time she was robbed at knife-point as a child at her father's Carnival booth in Hoboken. I even placed my father-in-law Bill in the ticket booth as Dominic Capone looks on in painting one, *Boulevard of Broken Queens*. This became my second set of heroic-scale, narrative paintings I ever created up until this point. These became known as prequel paintings to my *Ticket to Ride* series.

Sometimes I'll hear that song, *Crazy Little Thing Called Love* come on out of nowhere, and it immediately reminds me of that crazy night out with my Dad.

While I was scared that night, seeing my father in action like that, he seemed to really know what he was doing. I looked up to my father. Always have. *I wanted to be just like him.*

TWELVE

COLLEGE—THE EARLY YEARS

I moved into the basement of my maternal Grandmother, Violet's quaint little two-bedroom home in Lyndhurst, New Jersey just before making my move into Manhattan to try and make it as an artist back in the early nineties. Even after moving into Manhattan I'd still spend a lot of time commuting back and forth just to have dinner with my Grandma and play cards with her or stay up late sipping scotch, talking about life.

You see, my Grandma was the one who put the first paintbrush in my hand. She taught me how to draw from the time I could barely hold a pencil, so it's that kind of a bond we had.

While it was my mother who carted me around to shows and got me into Creative Arts classes, it was my Grandma Violet that instilled in me "the eye for things" I still have to this day.

She was a true self-taught artist, and I wanted to become one too. Every time we got together she'd have me drawing. Every trip we took into New York City together as a child she'd have me looking at the architecture in the City. She'd show me how to draw the buildings to make them look three-dimensional. She used to take me to *Tavern on the Green* every Thanksgiving, even though she didn't have much money. Just for the experience of it.

After that, we'd hit the *Plaza Hotel* and visit Elouise's portrait. Once back in Lyndhurst we'd order *Paisano's Pizza* and play *Scrabble* and *500 Rummy*. These were our rituals together and were some of my fondest memories growing up.

I was always drawing.

I think my mother could have also been a successful artist if she wanted to be. She could always draw really well too. I guess it just wasn't something she wanted to actively pursue. She, too, can write. She's a very talented woman in her own right.

But the time I spent in Lyndhurst with my Grandma and those memories we shared left an indelible impression on me. These impressions would resurface in my paintings.

I absolutely loved Lyndhurst growing up, which was in stark contrast to my mother and her sister, who couldn't wait to get the hell out of New Jersey as fast as they could once they graduated high school. For me, even though I didn't always live there, I'd still consider myself a Jersey Boy, despite the fact I've spent a great deal of my life in Maryland. It's where I spent what I consider some of "the best times" of my life making my fondest memories. Although, I will say this, when I lived in Manhattan, I also felt that same bond, like a true New Yorker must feel, despite the fact that anyone from Jersey commuting in and out of the City hitting up Manhattan nightclubs on weekends are referred to as "the Bridge and Tunnel crowd." Not me, though. When I lived there, the City became just as much a part of me as Lyndhurst did. So, while my mother and her sister didn't share those same warm childhood memories that I had there, I couldn't wait to get back to Lyndhurst any chance I got.

It's where I'd meet my future wife.

Now, "the Hook," as locals call it, was a small, predominantly Italian section of a neighborhood in Lyndhurst, which is situated in the Township of Bergen County. If you grew up there, you know what it was all about. Everyone knew one another there too. The houses lined the streets and avenues one after the next, some two-family style homes sharing one driveway, not unlike most Italian sections of Brooklyn, Queens, and Staten Island.

The main businesses in Lyndhurst were all along Valley Brook Avenue, Ridge Road, and Stuyvesant Avenue, where my future father-in-law owned *Sorrento's Hair Fashions*. There was also *the Lyndhurst Diner* and *Riverside Park*, which were seated along the Passaic River.

I used to walk across that truss bridge that connected Lyndhurst to Nutley at Kingsland Avenue and play pickup basketball games at the local courts in Nutley in the summertime when I was in high school visiting my Grandma.

When my Grandpa was still alive, he used to take me to the park a lot as a kid. It was just a block down from Page Avenue where they lived. Some evenings my Grandma would even take me with her up to her local artist guild near *Sorrento's* off Stuyvesant Avenue and let me chime in on the painting critiques.

On Sundays, we'd get pastries from *Mazur's Bakery*. And later, during my college years, it would be *Mr. Bruno's* for pizza and the *Lyndhurst Pastry Shop* for, who in my opinion, still makes the best *sfogliatelle* this side of the Hudson River. If you don't know what it is or how to say it, look it up, because you're missing out!

And, as a young girl, my Grandma used to draw lots of pictures of actors and actresses, interestingly enough, much like my own career began, portraying their faces with differing shades of charcoal.

I ARRIVED INTO THE WORLD on April 10, 1971, on my mother's birthday. My Grandma was fifty-three years old at this point. That same magical year, at Christmas, my mother got my Grandma the gift of a new sketch pad.

It inspired her to take up her craft again, which led to her participation in Lyndhurst's historic first Outdoor Juried Art Show in the Town Hall Park.

Eighty local artists entered their work and 1st place in the category of watercolor and other media went to none other than *Violet Vallery—my Grandma*.

This led to her being invited to exhibit at the Town Library that June. In 1973, she took 2ⁿᵈ place in the category of oils in the third annual outdoor art show in Town Hall Park and later that fall, the Art Association of Rutherford awarded her honorable mention for a show in Lincoln Park. In 1974 my Grandma's works were on exhibit at the West Hudson Hospital and then at the First National Bank in Kearny, NJ.

Then, in 1976, the same year I would win 1ˢᵗ place in the first juried art exhibition I was ever entered into at the age of five, my Grandma would also win 1ˢᵗ place in the Rutherford Museum Bicentennial Art Show. The media began to take notice too, and she received features in *the Bergen Record*, *The Leader*, *the Bergenite* and *the Herald News* as stories spread about her special interest in historical villages and buildings.

When asked about her work she explained, "An artist should try to capture happenings, expressions, and sentiments in their own individual way."

The Herald News had this to say about her work:

"The predominance among her paintings of nature or turn-of-the-century scenes of everyday life is a sense of calm, sensitivity and order. With pen and ink, Violet's favorite medium, she creates a world where barefoot boys walk to school along stony paths. She avoids painting people and urban scenes. Instead, she paints out-of-the-way scenes, with people as the background. Her work is now also in private collections throughout the Eastern United States."

When interviewed further about her art, my Grandma explained, "I felt that I was never going to fulfill the dream I had. I stopped drawing and got married, had kids. I always appreciated art. I suppose I was never really far from it as far as my mind was concerned. I see things. Nature's work is always there, but most people just don't look."

MY GRANDMA'S ART CAREER would be short-lived, though. Due to financial hardships and my Grandfather losing his milk business, she had to go back to work at the age of fifty-six.

What my Grandma taught me most during her short-lived career as an artist became one of the most important things an artist can do, which is to "draw a line from your life to your art that is straight and clear."

I learned this lesson and so much more from her, including the lesson of perseverance. While playing her at *Scrabble* or *Rummy*—her all-time favorite card game, she would never let me win. She always said, "nobody is going to just let you win in life, so you better know what losing feels like and get used to coming back from it, even if it takes you a few tries."

Now *I hate losing*. I'd throw a tantrum and want to quit. But she never let me. She'd just hand me the cards and tell me to shuffle another hand . . . not let my emotions get the best of me. Maybe that's where I get some of my relentlessness from.

Now, my competitive streak was definitely born into me from being my father's son. He was tough as nails. Still, to this day, probably the toughest man I've ever known. While his family didn't have a pot to piss in when he came to America, it wouldn't stop him from earning a scholarship to Syracuse University, only to fracture his leg in a couple places playing baseball and have his scholarship yanked out from under him.

What did he do then? Well, since his Dad was working hard at the docks, his mother in the factories—my Dad went out and got two jobs, one working for the telephone company during the day, another bouncing at a local upstate New York watering hole at night.

In four years he saved enough money to put himself back through college, and he found his new home at small school in Tennessee called Tusculum College where he met my mother. They first met when she was visiting the school with my Grandma. It's a cute story actually. He and some buddies lost control of a beer keg they were rolling down a hill on campus and it nearly ran my Grandma over! That's how they met.

My Grandfather passed away in 1981, just five years after my Grandma had to go back to work. This was another difficult time for our family. In particular, *for my mother*, because she was closest with my Grandfather.

Two years later, however, and after many long talks, my Dad agreed to let my Mom get checked out to see if she could carry a pregnancy to full term again. Three years later and many doctor visits, tests, bed rest until her ninth month and a C-Section before her due date at my mother's request, my brother was born. I was sixteen and a half at the time. My parents named him Will, after my Grandfather. *He was a Godsend.*

THE YEAR BEFORE GRADUATING from Lycoming College in Williamsport, Pennsylvania I had spent the better part of the prior two years commuting back and forth on the weekends from Williamsport to my Grandma's in Lyndhurst. I lived down in Vi's basement the previous summer, before finally taking the plunge and moving into Manhattan, splitting rent with a few guys I knew from Williamsport that graduated already. This was one of the best years of my life.

I absolutely loved living in New York City. Frank Sinatra once said, "If you can make it there, you can make it anywhere," and while my time living in the City wouldn't prove to become my permanent residence, it was definitely an experience that stayed with me, and has proven to be a place I'd return to for art business again and again over the course of my career as a painter.

Manhattan is a place everybody should live at least once. And not just for the culture, *but for the hustle*. I mean, you really gotta hustle if you're gonna make it in Manhattan! Everything is so expensive, and if you want to have any kind of nightlife you've gotta find a way to make money.

This is the thing a whole new breed of kids growing up in the new "entitlement generation" is lacking—*the ability to hustle.*

When I first I moved into New York City, my sole intention was to try and make it with my art.

And I did sell a couple of paintings.

My very first big sale came from none other than Matt Harvey, one of my roommates. Harv, as everyone called him, loved this painting I did in college entitled *Lascivia,* which I initially hung in our apartment on West 85th Street and Broadway.

Harv was a great guy and a *hustler's hustler.* He was a star quarterback when he went to Lycoming, and even made the cover of Sports Illustrated his senior year in college.

The year he graduated, he didn't have much cash so he ended up ducking out on his college tuition bill and moved to Manhattan with his college roommate Mike.

Since then, the College put what's now known as "the Harvey Clause" into place. When you walk across the stage you don't receive your actual diploma anymore. You get a piece of paper. Once your bills are paid they mail you out your diploma.

That was just classic Harv.

He liked getting over on anyone. He was the kind of guy who would take all his buddies out to dinner for a huge meal, tell everyone to order anything they want, his treat, and before the end of the meal he'd get up to go to the bathroom and suddenly disappear.

You'd find him laughing his ass off around the corner afterwards watching his buddies sprinting one-after-the-next out of that restaurant after finally figuring out that he cut out on the check and left everyone hanging.

He even pulled a similar move in Manhattan, but with the hospital. The guys were out playing football in Central Park one summer afternoon, which you're not supposed to do, by the way, and here's why—Harv went out for a long pass and was running full speed just as this guy stood up on his blanket. Harv collided with him, smashing in the side of his own face, breaking his cheekbone and shattering his jaw.

Harv had to be rushed to the hospital and somehow made it through reconstructive surgery before slipping out on the bill after giving the hospital a phony name and address. This was just Harv, and only he seemed to be able to get away with it all.

When I first moved in, Harv and Mike gave me two weeks to make rent. They said they'd help me get a job interview at the *Houlihan's* restaurant they worked at on 59th and 5th Avenue across from *the Plaza Hotel*, where I spent so many Thanksgivings visiting with my parents and Grandma gazing up at Elouise's portrait.

So, I was stoked at the opportunity to work there, but it was up to me to close the deal. And if I didn't, and if I couldn't make rent, I was out on my ass. So, I studied a menu they brought home for me and proceeded to interview later that week with the GM, who was this tall, lanky curly red-haired guy named Gary. It went like this:

"Why do you want to work at *Houlihan's?*" asked Gary, staring at me with deadpan eyes, studying my every movement.

"I've always wanted to live in Manhattan, always loved going to the Plaza every Thanksgiving as a kid. It'd be my dream come true to work in midtown right across the street from it," I explained.

Gary didn't give a shit about my story. He just fired back angrily with, "Are you here to take money out of the mouths of my wife and my kids? Are you here to steal from me?! That's what I really want to know!" he shouted back.

"Steal?! NO! Of course not," wondering if I did something wrong, or this was just how he was.

"You ever waited tables before?" he asked, settling down a bit, seemingly satisfied with the sincerity of my response.

"Of course I've waited tables before," I lied. "I'm a great people-person too, good at multi-tasking. I'd be able to handle it," I said confidently—not really knowing what I was getting myself into. Just knowing I had to nail the interview to pay my rent.

"We do $10,000 dollar days here. You know what that looks like? And the patio is packed in the summertime," Gary explained further.

"I can handle it. Believe me," I convinced him.

With that, he smiled, stood up, shook my hand and hired me on the spot and I went home to memorize the menu and computer codes.

Within a couple of weeks, I had the place *clocked*. I was making around $700 a week, working just a few days a week. Plenty of time to go back and forth to visit Vi, and plenty of time to enjoy the City and try and sell my art. I was living the real life version of *the Pope of Greenwich Village.*

Harv introduced me to the cooks in the kitchen and to all the food runners before he left for an assignment bartending at another Houlihan's on 56th and Lex. He gave me the lay of the land. Told me who I could hustle with if I wanted to hustle, and who I couldn't hustle with. Who would rat, who wouldn't and who would want a piece of the action and who wouldn't. Harv told me how it all worked. How they'd order food for entire tables without ringing in the order into the computer, how they'd get the food out of the kitchen once it was up, and how they'd get rid of handwritten checks for those tables. He had a whole system in place. He'd even tell me how they'd change table numbers on checks on the computer so it wouldn't look like a table didn't get sat for two hours or so, in the event that you did succeed in pocketing a table or two in cash.

Sebastian, this funny little Brazilian guy who worked there forever as one of the food runners used to always bitch at all the waiters, "Where's this fucking food go?! Table 303 is table 301, table 305 is table 307. Where's this shit go already?!?" It was pretty comical actually.

They even had this code on the computer that started out as a way for Managers to mess with the cooks and the Manager running "the Wheel" in the kitchen (the one calling out orders and putting checks with food as it comes up.) The deal was, if you punched this certain string of numbers into the computer it rang up with the word "ASSHOLE" across the top of the check. Waiters that were scamming used it to let the cooks know if a check they rang in was for food they already made, as a way to let them know NOT to make the food on that particular check again, and conveniently rip up the order on the Wheel when the Manager wasn't looking. The only reason this needed to be done was if a table paid with a credit card instead of cash.

There was no way of getting around a credit card, plus that was a federal crime and not something that anyone wanted to mess around with. You definitely didn't want a Manager to catch you with any hand-written checks on you either. They'd actually do impromptu searches on us from time to time. The first place they'd search you would be in the bathrooms, so Harv said if you scam, never toss handwritten checks in the trash or try to flush them because sometimes Managers would even follow you into the bathroom waiting for something like that to happen. Harv said to put the handwritten checks in the coffee grinds of an old coffee filter near the beverage stations.

"If they're gonna search through coffee grinds to bust you, you deserved to get pinched!" he'd laugh.

Apparently, this is just how much waiters would be hustling in Manhattan. It was an on-going battle between restaurant owners and employees to see just how far anyone could push things, how much "leakage" they could live with as owners or managers. This was what I figured it was like to hustle like a true New Yorker!

I even started to learn the subways, which I would take to and from work every day, from the 86th street station, taking the 1 and 9 trains to 42nd street where I'd transfer and pick up the N and the R to Columbus Circle and walk the rest of the way along Central Park and past the Plaza Hotel.

Our apartment was a really cool place, and the Upper West Side was a great area to live. It was nothing fancy, and it definitely wasn't a Brownstone or anything, although our apartment building was surrounded by them, and it was really small—but it had a unique layout. When you walked in, the kitchen and the bathroom were to the right. Above it was a small loft overlooking the main living area where Mike slept. Harv usually crashed on the fold-out couch in the living room area just below the loft, unless he had girls over, and yes, I mean girls—*plural*, in which case he'd usually toss Mike's mattress down from the loft and lock us all out of the apartment with an "OCCUPIED" post-it tacked to the door until his party was over.

I'll never forget this one night I came home and as I fiddled with the lock, ignoring his "occupied" sign, I was soon greeted with the secondary lock from the "security chain". I caught a quick glimpse of the two chicks lying down naked next to one another in the middle of the floor as Harv came running to the door as fast as he could.

"C'mon man, it's taken me like two hours to get to this point. Don't mess my night up! Go next door to Kenny's place to crash. Here's the keys!" *That was Harv for ya'* . . .

My room was in the basement—just a short flight down a spiral staircase past the main living area. I liked it there because it was private. I had my own bathroom too. It was tiny, though. I mean, the bathroom door literally hit the back wall when you opened it and you had to squeeze yourself past it and then shut the door to use it, but I didn't mind. I was living in Manhattan, *the City that never sleeps.*

LASCIVIA, was still, to this day, probably my favorite painting I've ever done. It's a 38" X 44" oil painting on canvas of two faces juxtaposed together in profile, face to face, the one on left painted in rich, cadmium reds with a black blindfold over their eyes, screaming at the figure to the right. The face to the right, also blindfolded, with a woman's lips and nose, was done in icy whitish-bluish-purplish tones—her head tilted back, lips partially open, catching drips of water on them.

I purposely left things unclear as to whether it was passion or violence being portrayed. Some felt these two figures were making love, caught in the heat of the moment, while others think they are about to kiss. I leave it up to the viewer's interpretation.

It definitely has elements of rage, passion, uninhibited love-making—*two personalities colliding.* One dominant—at left, in red. The other, submissive—on right, in blues. I parted with the painting for just $400, a far cry from paintings I'm selling today, which range anywhere from ten to twenty grand a pop for that size, but back then it might as well have been a million bucks!

At the time, it was my biggest sale to date, and it gave me some cash to go out with. I was also glad Harv had bought it. And besides, back then, I didn't realize the significance of the piece. I've even tried to re-create the painting several times, but that has proven impossible. I just can't re-capture that certain magic that I painted into the original with such unbridled passion.

When I created the original, I was fortunate enough to also make a small, exclusive limited edition of six Intaglio prints of the painting. These prints were perfect black and white companion pieces to the actual original full color painting. They became a conversation continued, if you will, on a particular subject that was of deep interest to me at the time. I'd expand further on the series after graduation, my first true thematic series which I entitled *the Love Series.*

These were my first *serial works* to date, and each painting was inspired by an original poem I had written. That's where I found the inspiration for all my early pieces—*from my writing.* I'd write these dark, dangerous, seductive love poems and then, based on the things I'd picture in my head as I was writing them, I'd sketch these visions out as ideas for paintings.

My process of painting back then involved finding willing models in my college dorm that would pose for photographs that I would develop in the darkroom as 8" X 10" black and whites that I'd use for reference photos. Then I'd rip, tear, cut up and re-assemble them together as collages for final compositions for my paintings. These days, I can just take digital photographs and use Photoshop. But back then—*this was my process.*

My paintings and prints have always all had a similar feel. Very *9 ½ weeks-ish,* which was one of my favorite Mickey Rourke movies back then. I idolized Mickey Rourke as a kid. Loved him in that film, and in *Angel Heart,* starring opposite Robert DeNiro and Lisa Bonet. I also loved his role opposite Carré Otis in the twisted romance, *Wild Orchid,* and as the rogue CIA agent in *White Sands.* I always felt this strange parallel to Rourke's life and my own. Even though I never met the guy at this point in my life, I could always relate to him and the roles he chose.

The characters he portrayed in his films were just like me. Charismatic, but tragically flawed heroes, mixed with just enough rage to make him dangerous, yet still vulnerable enough to keep him likable. He also began boxing later in life, just like me. He, too, had a strange connection to the Mob.

I also had other early influences on my work. My favorite college professor at Lycoming, Roger Shipley (or Rog, as everybody called him) told me my paintings were very *Edvard Munch-ish* in style. I always found Munch to be one of my favorite artists, and my *Love Series* carried on a similar conversation you'd find in Munch's famous *Frieze of Life* series. Paintings that explore issues surrounding love, life, and pain.

My Intaglio prints also came out amazing. I still have the entire edition, with the exception of one of the prints, which I later gave to Rog, along with another original drawing, *Abjection, Scene 2* from my *31 Nights* series. These were given to Rog in exchange for two of his famous prints, *Alone* and *Fishing*.

Rog played a big influence on my painting career. He was really the only one at that time, besides my family, that encouraged me to continue working at my craft. He knew the type of guys I hung out with, knew I wasn't fitting the typical "artist mold" but he saw something in me. I could feel it. I imagined back then that's what great teachers did. They made someone feel like they mattered.

And, because Roger was also a respected, working artist who pushed the envelope with his own subject matter—lots of nudes, stuff I could really relate to at that point in time—*I listened to him.* He would even call me and wake me up for class if he knew our critique day fell the night after the college's designated partying night. That's just the kind of guy Rog was. The kind I'd end up sitting on a bar stool with one day talking shop, talking art with.

I'll never forget my first memorable critique with Rog. I brought in this *semi-shock art* piece. It was a 14" X 20" gouache painting on watercolor paper entitled *Jealousy*. It was a silhouette a girl on all fours behind a sheet being made love to from behind. There's a candle in the foreground dripping wax, the flame recently extinguished as smoke filters your eye throughout the rest of the painting. Your eye wanders past an old rotary dial telephone on a nightstand with its receiver laying off the hook, to a man's face pressed against the window outside the room screaming in horror as he watches this girl (probably his girlfriend or wife, however you interpret it) having sex with someone else.

Everyone stared at my painting as I pinned it up and they continued to just stare. No conversations were sparked. Just glares. I figured I went too far. Figured Rog would probably tear it apart for one reason or another. That was probably just my own insecurities whispering in my ear at the time, but as it turned out he didn't. He actually went on and on about how much he liked it. How he loved the fact I was taking risks with my work.

He'd go on about how he was "so damn tired of seeing one flowery landscape painting after the next," or something to that effect and that "finally, someone's actually making some work that has some personal meaning to it."

From that day on, the class saw a lot more figurative paintings, a lot more nudes, and a lot more narrative works. Even from people that you wouldn't expect them from, like this one girl Kate, whom I used as a model for many of my early college works that turned into my *Love Series*.

Kate was as straight-laced as they come, but had no problem modeling for me, getting blindfolded, tied to a bed, or getting semi-nude behind a sheet with my roommate Tony to pose for my reference photos. She even worked some nights in the Photo Lab with me, helping me roll film for my photography professor, Lynn Estomin. She would come by to check on me from time to time, just to see if I was actually doing my homework. I liked Kate because she always helped me and never judged me. She knew I was one of the "bad boys", definitely not someone she'd typically hang out with, but she'd become a stable voice that could calm my demons, and would never be someone I'd ever objectify or ever even try to date. Rog liked her too. Her paintings were more illustration-like but mid-way through the year she was making these amazing Georgia O'Keefe-esque watercolors.

Our painting critiques also began to push boundaries, and my work soared. I finally felt comfortable in my own skin going into Rog's class. It felt like home. Nothing I painted was perceived as "too strange, too violent or too pornographic" — it was all just perceived as different degrees of who I was, what I'd seen, or what I wanted to say.

Rog got it. He never judged me, and I appreciated that about him. That's how my Grandma was with me. She never judged. Never saw me as good or bad. *Just loved me for me.*

THE FIRST MAJOR CRITIQUE we had from a well-known visiting artist came in the form of Philip Pearlstein, who was described to us as an "influential American painter best known for Modern Realism nudes".

I thought he was a *pompous ass* right out of the gate.

It wasn't just how he talked *at us* . . . it was the one repetitive slide after the next that he tortured us with prior to him critiquing our work.

It seemed to me like they were all the same painting. The same plastic-like, lifeless nude draped over some couch, or sitting on a floor, not doing anything — *just there*, with no presence. No soul. The paintings weren't saying anything. They struck me as "studies" or some slick, flattened-out Lucian Freud rip-offs. Now, I know Philip Pearlstein had an impressive resume of shows, galleries, patrons, etc. But to me, he was still *a nobody*.

I wanted to be inspired. I wanted to know how to "make it". I felt as though if this was "making it" *I'd pass*. It was time, I figured, to carve out my own path. Definitely not gonna kiss this guy's ass to try and get somewhere. So, while I tried to keep an open mind, it was all going south for me. And I wasn't alone.

One of the sculpting professors introduced him to the class as also being Andy Warhol's roommate in New York, I guess to impress us, but I wasn't a Andy Warhol fan either. Now I just figured out "how" this guy probably "made it" in the Art World — hanging on the coattails of Warhol, *or worse* . . .

So, about an hour passed. His talk was finally over. It was now time for the big group critique. We all laid our work out against this wall in the studio where he chose some at random to talk about. I got the impression he wasn't planning on sticking around long enough to go through everyone's work but stood to wait like everyone else. What happened next, I never saw coming. Nor did the professors.

While we were gearing up for what we thought would be a positive, semi-intimate experience with "one of the great ones" everything went terribly wrong.

He was brutal!

You could hear the proverbial "pin drop" as he tore apart one kid's work after the next, for this reason, or that. Some of which I could understand, but only to a point. I just kept thinking to myself, "C'mon, give the kid a break . . ."

I wasn't the only one either. One of our professor's wives, who was this young, vivacious "art mom" to all of us kids at the college, she was getting agitated too. But no-one seemed to be willing to slam on the brakes and halt this critique that seemed to de-rail before everyone's very eyes. I kept glancing over at her, catching her occasional winces as Pearlstein continued his barrage of hyper-critical rants about this work and that work. There was definitely a moment brewing. The kind of moment that would become one that would resurface again and again throughout my adult life—the moment to step in when no-one else would.

And so I did.

The moment couldn't have come sooner either. A girl he was criticizing had just burst into tears as she was trying to justify why she did what she did in her work, how her work wasn't finished yet, but she would try harder to fix it. I couldn't take it anymore and finally jumped in with, "Why don't you critique mine?"

The room seemed to freeze. Our "Art Mom" (sculpture professor, Jon Bogle's wife) gave me this look, like "Yesssssss!!!" All the other professors seemed to put their heads in their hands like, "Noooooooo!!!!"

Me, I was like, *"It's on now!"*

And with that, I continued, "You might be able to make that girl cry, if that's what gets your rocks off, makes you feel more of a man, but why not try me on for size? *I guarantee you I'm not gonna cry.*"

I stepped forward, chest out, chin up, anger boiling in my eyes, ready to snap him in half if I felt I had to.

Then, *nothing.*

He gave me one of the biggest softball critiques of my life. It was almost apologetic, as he backtracked and he suddenly tried to reel everyone back in.

"Pathetic," I thought to myself. "What a fucking pussy."

I don't know what Rog felt about everything, but I also knew Rog was a lot like me, so I figured he didn't mind how I disarmed Pearlstein the way that I did.

Me, *I felt good*. I didn't give a rat's ass about his critique at this point anyway. For me, it wasn't about the work anymore, it was about standing up for every other kid in there that he put down.

The Other Side of the Mirror was the work that Pearlstein critiqued. It became the second piece I sold in New York while living in the City that summer. I sold it to this girl named Veronica, another waitress at *Houlihan's*, originally from Virginia Beach.

It was a 16" X 20" gouache on watercolor paper of a girl lying in bed alone, her lips parted in the heat of passion, sheets disheveled. Beside her, is a large mirror on the wall portraying her reflection as she's being ravaged by a devil-like figure in the mirror, strangling her as he makes love to her while a young child holding a candle watches on in horror in the shadows near the doorway of her bedroom. She's not someone actually intended to be "present" in the room, but she does serve to represent the "childhood-self" of the girl being ravaged, watching on as her "adult-self" on, what I refer to as, *the Other Side of the Mirror*.

This painting was also created using lots of cadmium reds and cool cerulean blues. It became another painting in my *Love Series* done in a similar palette to *Jealousy* and *Lascivia*. I felt I was on to something with these narrative works, so I kept going.

All in all, the Pearlstein experience taught me one major lesson. Never let anyone intimidate you along your journey. And, no matter what anyone says about your work, the right person can still come along and buy it.

I suddenly had a new taste in my mouth when it came to the Art World, though. I certainly wasn't star struck anymore, that's for sure. It kind of just affirmed what I thought already. It's not about what you know or how good you were, it's about *who you know*.

I wasn't interested in becoming another Pearlstein though, riding on anyone's coattails. I just wanted to be appreciated for being me and I wanted my work to be purchased for being what it was. That's the only way I saw it from that point on.

That critique with one of the "major players" in the Art World really put things into perspective for me.

Two decades later, in October of 2013, I was invited back to Lycoming to be honored alongside Barbara Lovenduski Sylk, a 1973 Lycoming graduate, and trustee at the Pennsylvania Academy of Fine Arts to receive the Dr. James E. Douthat Outstanding Achievement Award, given in recognition of alumni who have achieved significant accomplishments that reflect positively on the college. 2013 would become the year I would be honored with a trifecta of three other national teaching awards.

The new President of Lycoming College, Kent Trachte, was this exciting guy who decided to have a solo exhibition of my *Ticket to Ride* paintings at his President's mansion on "the Hill" in Williamsport for what would become the first in a series of exhibitions the Trachte's would host at their home annually.

My opening reception came later in the weekend, which began with a chauffeured ride through the city in the back of a slick black 1929 Packard, as part of the Homecoming parade. Me, my wife and son (then, just six years old), were driven onto the 50-yard line of the Lycoming Warrior's football field as my award was announced over the loudspeaker, at which point Carmen leaned out of the car and waved to the roaring cheers from the crowd. It was a proud moment for us all.

From there, we were celebrated guests of President Trachte for the Homecoming Football game in his skybox, and my son got his picture taken with all the Lycoming Cheerleaders in the end zone. Brooke Long, an art student at Lyco', arranged this for us.

Later in the weekend, I stood in Pearlstein's former shoes, giving an artist talk to aspiring undergrad artists in Professor Seth Goodman's painting classes, critiquing their work one-on-one shortly afterwards, just like Pearlstein did when I was a student at Lycoming. Only, I didn't give a boring slideshow of *one lifeless nude after the next lifeless nude* like Pearlstein did followed up by the attempted destruction of everyone's hopes and dreams. I shared *my story* with them, which allowed them a secret window into the soul of my work and why I painted the types of violent, narrative scenes I painted. I, in turn, encouraged them to share *their stories* with me. I assured them I was only there for them, to give them encouragement and advice. Afterwards, Seth's classes attended the opening of my solo exhibition of my *Ticket to Ride* paintings at President Trachte's mansion, which opened up to the public that evening.

I enjoyed spending time with Seth's students, providing them with meaningful feedback in a non-threatening way. The interesting thing about the connection between Seth and I was that Seth got his MFA from Towson, studying under Nora Sturges. I got my Master's from Towson the same exact time as Seth was there, and I also studied under Nora, so we both came from a similar school of thought and painters. We just never happened to cross paths until I returned for a show at Lycoming, where Seth was now teaching.

Later, I shared my story with Seth about my nightmare of an experience as a college kid that I had with Pearlstein. He started cracking up laughing because he had a similar run-in with him when Pearlstein juried a show that Seth was in years earlier. He shared the same sentiments—the guy was *strangely brutal* when talking about other people's work. It made me feel better knowing I wasn't alone.

ROGER SHIPLEY
LYCOMING COLLEGE PROFESSOR OF ART

"I came to Lycoming College in 1967 to teach various studio disciplines in the art program. Michael Bell was one of my early students. I taught Michael drawing, painting, 2D design, color theory, and printmaking. The art program at Lycoming emphasizes a one-on-one approach with its teaching method so I soon found that getting to know my students on a personal level was quite easy.

Michael came to Lycoming not knowing what to expect having to acclimate himself to college, the social aspects of dorm life and the individual freedom college life provides. It was clear to me from my first encounter with Michael that he was having trouble as a freshman with college life and what was expected of him, but also that he had considerable artistic talent and had little difficulty expressing himself in the various disciplines I was teaching him. His artistic images were uniquely personal and aggressive in their execution.

As was the custom in our program, I got to know Michael quite closely. In the first semesters, he was having difficulty settling down and was getting into trouble in his dorm life. There were times when his campus life was interfering with his commitment to class and I had to make numerous personal contacts with him to get him to attend class. There was an incident that put Michael's college career in jeopardy and I was called on as his professor to support his appeal to be allowed to stay at Lycoming.

I saw a very strong student in Michael with all sorts of artistic talent and did not want to see him leave Lycoming. I wanted him to be given a second chance and fortunately, I was able to convince the Dean of Students to allow him to stay.

As the years passed, Michael and I became close and the teacher/student relationship we developed allowed his artistic talent to grow and mature. I saw exceptional work being done in all his classes. Michael came to Lycoming as an aggressive street smart kid whose temperament had gotten him into trouble in his early campus life, but it was becoming a very strong influence in his art and we worked with this throughout his four years.

His artistic images were uniquely personal and aggressive in the use of color and subject matter that were oftentimes disturbing to the viewer. To this day his personal encounters and his approach to life greatly influence his art. Michael has become a very successful Artist and a committed Art Teacher. It has been a joy watching him grow and achieve success in all that he has accomplished in life being honored by his school district, state, and by Lycoming College for his artistic achievements, including the Dr. James E. Douthat Outstanding Achievement Award, given to him in 2013 in recognition of alumni who have achieved significant accomplishments that reflect positively on the college. I still remain a dedicated friend."

THIRTEEN

CROSSROADS

In the summer of 1994, I graduated from Lycoming College. Now I either I head back to the streets of New York, or try to secure gainful employment in the field of education. At this point, my mother pretty much begged me to try and get a "real job." I reluctantly agreed.

I found my calling during my junior year while at Lycoming and knew teaching was what I should probably be doing. Otherwise, there was a great chance I'd end up dead or in jail.

While the lure of the streets is always going to be the wild beast inside me I have to keep tamed, it was visiting a high school that turned me on to teaching. Specifically, during an education class, I took with Professor Rachel Hungerford. I spent the day at Loyalsock High School, where I'd eventually complete my student teaching under Paul Barrett. But it was my first visit there that proved to be the most eye-opening experience. Now, I absolutely hated high school growing up. There was nothing inspiring about being a teenager for me, and teaching certainly wasn't a profession I ever considered going into until I was out in the field and "saw myself" in the many faces sitting in those classes on that day. I wanted to help them. *Anyway I could.*

I wanted to do for them what nobody did for me.

I connected with a few of the kids immediately as I'd circulated the art room, asking them what they were working on and why they chose whatever subject matter they chose. I'd ask them stuff that Rog would ask me about my own work. Not questions for the sake of making small talk. Questions that would help me gain some insight into their lives, as a means to help me unlock the door to the place from which all they were creating was coming from, find out *their why.*

There was also another reason I cared so deeply. As a teenager, I got into a lot of trouble. The kind of trouble most people don't walk away from. The kind your parents have to put up their house for, in order to secure your bail.

The kind of trouble that put me face to face with twenty years to life.

Now some people, when they feel pressure, *they fold.* When I'm squeezed, *I focus.* Everything goes silent. It's like the sounds of a locomotive train growing louder and louder in my head, churning faster and faster as I'm nearing the brink until I see red and any sounds around me immediately turn to silence. My quiet turns inward and explodes back out as *pure rage.*

It's like that when I'm in a fight. I never remember much afterward. Everything goes dark. It's almost like I black out and go to another place in my mind. It's quiet there actually, amidst any chaos or violence. Minutes or hours could pass and I couldn't tell you the difference. I'd only see the aftermath of what's been done once the dust settles.

I'd liken it to when you're driving someplace far in your car and when you get there, you can't remember even getting in the car, let alone how you got there. The only difference being this is how I am amidst total chaos, not the quiet solitude of your car as you get lost in a song or two.

When everyone seems to panic just when all hell breaks loose that is when I'm at my calmest. For me, that's when everything seems to slow waaaaay down, as if I'm watching it all with my third eye, my artist's eye, from a distance in slow motion. Sometimes I just snap. After all, *I am my father's son.*

Now I still, to this day, believe there deserves to be a special kind of hell for the douchebag that almost cost me twenty years of my life. Anyone who beats up on girls, rapes or abuses them—I believe they deserve the kind of punishment I was happy to deliver unto him at that point in my life. But I was just a kid back then. What I didn't think about were the consequences of playing judge, jury, and executioner—or what it could potentially cost my family, how long a trial might drag on for, and what it could mean to my future. I was just a kid, like so many other future teenage students of mine who made one very bad decision.

My mother had given birth to my brother Will at the age of forty-two. Giving birth to him seemed to silence her demons, while mine were just beginning to grow. I wasn't a good kid anymore. I was hanging with a really bad crowd, and Will was my parents' main focus now. But, being there for my little baby brother Will was probably the one thing that kept me from turning "really bad" in the end because I loved being big brother to him. He was my "everything" back when I was young.

As he grew, I'd roughhouse with him to toughen him up. I played lots of football with him from as early as he could walk, me on my knees, him trying to get past me from a narrow stretch of carpet between my father's pool table and the steps down in our basement. I figured, he'll never face anybody in his life that's tougher than me, so if he can put up a good fight against me he'd be good to go against anyone else. It used to break my heart whenever I was away from him, especially when I later went off to college. I'd hide my tears every time I'd watch him wave goodbye from his rear car seat as they pulled away after a nice long weekend visit.

Knowing my reckless nature, I guess I never knew which time might be our last together, even from the moment he was born, so I always cherished every moment. And, as he grew older, I made it a point to never miss one of his football games, from his Pop Warner little league games all the way through high school. He was a good kid leading a totally different life than the one I led growing up, and he was even being raised totally differently.

My parents were older by the time they had Will. They slowed down a lot, probably due to the fact I exhausted them. My brother should thank me for that! My Dad's temper had waned. My Mom seemed at peace with her sadness, and I simply wanted Will to have a better life than I carved out for myself at the time.

As normal as things probably appeared to most people on the outside, looking back on it all, I can see how fucked up I really was as a kid. How self-destructive I was, doing things like shutting the car headlights off while driving down the windiest of roads just to see how far I'd make it without crashing. I'd end up totaling two of my parent's cars and wrecking a third before graduating. I liked playing chicken.

I also had a high tolerance for pain. As a kid, I used to test it by doing the craziest things, like when you'd get a mosquito bite on your forearm, for instance, I'd try and see how long I could hold the part of my forearm with the mosquito bump on it down on the car's sizzling hot dashboard on a summer afternoon before it left a mark. It was actually soothing to me, reminded me I was still alive inside at that time, as bizarre as that may sound.

This would become a familiar pattern that would resurface later in my life in the form of numerous tattoos I'd get inked into my skin to serve as a visual map documenting all the battles I've fought and the triumphs of all I've overcome.

FOURTEEN

INKED

My first half-sleeve, *St. Michael, the Archangel*, began in the summer of 2012 after a tumultuous year spent trying to save the life of one of my Scholastic Art Regional award-winning photographers, Tommy Taylor. This tattoo, inked by national award-winning tattoo artist Ty Pallotta, would become my first of many large-scale tattoos done by Ty, and getting inked by him down the Jersey Shore each summer thereafter would become our ritual.

Getting inked became a celebration of the closing of one chapter, and the opening of another—a tribute to "new beginnings". For me, like boxing proved to later be, getting inked was better than therapy.

Tommy Taylor's chapter began with me breaking the news about his troubles to my Advanced Placement (AP) Photography class. I first assembled them all into a small semi-circle in the back of my studio. I always treat my kids like family, much the same as I remembered how my Dad was with his players back in the locker room. A family doesn't keep secrets from one another, so I had to tell them. You could hear the proverbial "pin drop" as I began to explain the severity of Tommy's situation.

Now, Tommy was a kid who was always in trouble. This was nothing new. As a child, he grew up in Paterson, New Jersey, which was another reason I probably bonded with him so quickly. He also seemed attracted to all things dangerous, just like me as a kid. And, he, too was fascinated with who my painting clientele was. We hit it off immediately. He loved gangsters, and we seemed to live very parallel lives.

I urged him to "draw his line from his life to his art" over the course of his junior and senior years, and this took the form of a haunting series of photographs he took while trespassing inside a condemned mental institution. This was an annual tradition of many AP Photography students that began with Leigh Rogers, who left her AP visual journal behind for future generations of photography students in my classes to read, and, of course, she left detailed maps with instructions on how to gain access into the many abandoned buildings she'd take photographs in. One of Tommy's award-winning photographs became a shot of a lone tricycle left abandoned amidst the rubble and graffiti.

This award-winning image proved to become very prophetic.

"Tommy won't be coming back to school today," I explained to the class. "He might not be coming back the rest of the year, or maybe longer. I wanted you to hear it from me first before all the rumors start flying around. I know some of them have probably started already. I want each of you to know this is a *kid I love*. So I'd appreciate it if you didn't feed into any of those nasty rumors. If anything, help me squash them. *Out of respect.* Does anyone have any questions? Ask me now, because we won't be having this conversation again . . ."

"Is he, okay? I heard there was a gun involved?" one girl asked. Some of the other kids started to break down and cry as they began to grasp the magnitude of the situation. Rock stars like Paige Shryock, Sarah Bailey, Amanda Kenney and Tyler Mills. They knew it was serious by my tone, and by the fact that I, myself, was fighting hard to hold back tears.

"He's going to be okay," I tried to reassure them. "I'm working on getting him bailed out."

I also assured them I didn't know anything about *any gun*. I told them not to spread a rumor like that around either.

"All I know is he's in a lot of trouble and he needs our prayers and support," I explained. "I have a friend that's a lawyer and he's agreed to help Tommy and take his case. Tommy's a good kid that just made a very bad decision. That's about all I can tell you." *A good kid that made a very bad decision.* A familiar echo from my past. A scenario I knew all too well.

WHILE I CAN'T GO INTO DETAILS about exactly what I'd done some twenty years prior to Tommy's situation, the consequences I faced as a teen were just as grave, probably even worse. In my situation, the scumbag I served up some justice to for trying to rape a girl I was close with also had a family member on the police force and inside the court system's offices. So, as soon as I was arrested for what I had done to this kid, I was stripped naked and thrown in what prisoners call "the hole." No phone call. No nothing. I still remember the asshole that tossed me in there telling me "We're taking your clothes so you don't hang yourself."

"Hang myself?! I'd never give them the satisfaction, the crooked fucks," I thought to myself.

I may have been a punk kid back then, but even if I was scared, I wouldn't let them see it. I figured it wouldn't change anything anyways. I might as well stay tough—outwardly at least. Inside I was dying and suddenly terrified for what my future might hold. Would I ever get to see my little brother again?

It was November, so it was deathly cold in the hole. There was no heat, just the cold cinderblock walls and the concrete floor. No lights. You couldn't tell whether it was day or night, what time it was, how long you'd been in there. After a while, your eyes adjusted to the blackness in some strange way. Maybe it was just my imagination though, because in the complete blackness you have no physical bearings other than feeling the walls, but you could still dream. I imagined I was someplace else—*someplace warmer*. But that didn't help.

Over the course of my time in the hole, I lost close to twenty pounds just from shivering day and night. When the cops figured they couldn't rattle me, they decided to finally officially book me and when they finally took me to arraignment, I was placed in shackles, like I was some mass murderer or something. Over what, I still couldn't figure out? While I did tune the kid up pretty good, I still couldn't understand the severity of the charges, or what I'd later learn was *really going on.* As they paraded me through the courthouse one of my mother's friends just happened to be walking past. *Not my proudest moment.*

"Michael??!! Is that you?!" she exclaimed.

"Call my mother!" I yelled to her.

My parents surely didn't know where I was, because, at that time in my life, it wasn't uncommon for me to stay away from home for a few nights at a time here and there. They knew how I was, and remember, this was also back before cell phones and *constant contact.* And, the kind of kid I was back then, it was good news *not* to get a call from me.

It was either sheer luck or by some guardian angel's doing that my mother's friend happened to spot me that day, because up until that point I wasn't even afforded the customary phone call. All protocol when it came to me or my buddy went out the window. I didn't even know where they took my friend. I hadn't even seen him since they picked us up. And he was just in the car with me that night. Why were they punishing him too? Even after I asked for a lawyer countless times they just kept interrogating me for hours on end before tossing me back into the hole.

This would all work in my favor while presenting my defense later on. I'd have to literally sign my life away so that I wouldn't sue the state in exchange for my freedom, all because of the crooked, deplorable things they did to me when I was in their custody. Regardless of what I did, I figured the scumbag I tuned up did ten times worse. I guess at the end of the day I just wanted to be tough like my father. Most boys probably do growing up, but now I just figured, "leave it in the lawyer's hands. That's what they're getting paid to do. It was somebody else's problem now."

Years later, when reading about my own family's infamous cousin Vinnie and his four-year murder trial, as described by Dorothy Matzner in her 1973 memoir "Victims of Justice," we, strangely enough, seemed to share a similar disposition.

VICTIMS OF JUSTICE, 1973
By Dorothy Matzner

"Vinnie, perhaps because he was more accustomed to suspicion than the rest of us, took the attitude that the whole thing was his lawyer's problem. He had total confidence in Bruno Leopizzi. If Bruno had told him to jump off the George Washington Bridge, Vinnie would have asked, 'Which side?'

Vinnie is a quiet man with tastes and style that don't fit the clichés of the world he lived in. I think he was self-conscious about his background when he was around us and went out of his way to be especially polite. I never once lighted my own cigarette in Vinnie's presence. He was always ready with a match, even when he was wearing handcuffs."

THESE WERE ALL THE THINGS racing through my head as I headed out to visit my student, Tommy, in the detention center where he was being remanded until his bail was set. He was so glad I came. All these thoughts surrounding my own secret past were swirling around in my head as we talked in the visitation booth by telephone.

It broke my heart to see him on the other side of the plate glass wall between us. Before I hung up, I told him I loved him and that I'd help him and to stay strong. I raised my hand and pressed it flush against the glass partition. He did the same, his hand against mine, and then the guard came to take him back to his cell. I watched him the whole way as they took him back.

Reflecting back on all this, it's interesting how life works. Had I not gone through what I went through at his age, I wouldn't have had the first clue how to help Tommy Taylor. I wouldn't have any real advice for him at all.

What I did know is that Tommy was scheduled to go into *Gen-Pop* (General Population, lumped in with all the other prisoners) the following week. This was something I knew I had to prevent. I had to get him out of there! A one hundred thirty-five pound kid tossed in with career criminals and grown men twice his size and age was a recipe for disaster. This much I knew. So, I called his Mom and begged her to get him out soon as bail was finally set. *She agreed.*

Just before his transfer, we were luckily able to bring him home where he'd be safe until his trial date. He would have to wear an ankle bracelet and needed to stay out of any trouble whatsoever. I reminded him to be extremely careful, and that it would be best for him not to even talk to anybody about what happened until his trial is over, so there'd be no surprises.

MY PARENTS HAD TO PUT UP THEIR HOUSE for my bail, and once they did, my father couldn't believe how much weight I lost. Me, I was just happy to see my little brother again. But just as soon things calmed down, those crooked cops returned to indict me on even more heavier charges—*on Christmas Eve, of all nights.*

I'll never forget seeing my little brother's sweet little face screaming as the red and blue lights were flashing outside our home, "Mommy, Mommy, the police are here to take Michael away! Don't let them take him away again!" *It broke my heart.*

To make matters worse, you're not gonna believe what happened to my buddy who was with me that fateful night. Let me preface this with the fact that he did *absolutely nothing* besides go along for the ride. If anything, he probably saved that scumbag's life by racing out of the car when things got out of control to drag me off the kid. What happened next I wasn't expecting. He also got hit with a slew of bogus charges too, by *those same crooked cops*—just so he couldn't testify on my behalf.

"Pretty smart of them," I thought to myself. *We were both officially screwed.* To this day, I can't listen to Bing Crosby's "I'll be Home for Christmas" without getting depressed.

FIFTEEN

ST. MICHAEL THE ARCHANGEL

Back when I got into trouble, my trial date was set for nearly a year later. I imagined this would still be the case for Tommy. My lawyer at the time was this great, charismatic guy who looked strangely enough exactly like former President Bill Clinton.

He petitioned for my release immediately after my parents retained him and put up their house for my bail. He felt, despite the fact that my grades up until this point were less than sub-par, if I did make a miraculous improvement grade-wise and stayed out of trouble over the course of the rest of this year, it would give a Judge and Jury a reason not to flush my life down the proverbial toilet. He said it would show there was still "hope" for me as a potentially productive member of society. I figured it was worth a shot. My parents fought for me to make that happen.

This would become the same strategy I suggested to Tommy Taylor's lawyer, Joseph Laumann, who was a friend of mine that I first met when he was a substitute teacher at Southern High working on his law degree. He agreed to help me out by taking Tommy's case for lowball fees in exchange some artwork he wanted to be done by me.

The only thing with Tommy's situation was, our Administration wasn't being as receptive to Tommy returning to school. They felt he was better off being home-schooled, to prevent any further incidents from happening. I understood what was really happening, though. He was going to be a major disruption. Plus, I imagine they were probably pretty fed up with him at that point and didn't want to deal with him anymore.

I also knew how kids would react to Tommy's potential return to school since it's something I, myself, had also already gone through.

I felt the whispers. Saw the uncomfortable glances. I actually watched kids walk out of their way just so they didn't have to walk directly past me and make eye contact with me. It was pretty disheartening. It saddened me. I felt like an outcast.

Up until this point in my life, I prided myself in pushing my shoulders back, chin up, glaring at anyone I could in order to make my presence felt, daring anyone to knock the chip off my shoulder. I liked it when people were afraid of me. Now, it just felt too real, I guess. There was a genuine reason for people to fear me now, but I didn't like the feeling anymore and didn't want people looking at me like they were. I became withdrawn, sullen, and generally started just staying in my bedroom to catch up on my studies, which I needed to do anyway, now that my life depended on it. My lawyer was counting on me to do my part, as were my parents, so I did my best. While I was praying for a miracle, I couldn't believe it when one actually came my way, and like I said, I had to literally sign my life away for it to happen.

FAST FORWARD TO MY COLLEGE YEARS—I got myself into more trouble and nearly got kicked out of college, all over a similar scenario—*coming to the aid of another damsel in distress*. Only this time I had the kind of friendships with professors like Rog, with my roommates Tommy Navarro and Tony Luci, and with my new best friend from town, Louie Miele, to help me through it all. I wish I had a supporting cast like these guys as a kid.

Navarro would blast anyone he felt someone was looking at me differently wherever we went on campus. He would bark out things like, "Whadda you lookin' at? You gotta problem with him or something? I didn't think so!"

Nobody messed with Navarro. I appreciated that about him, but at the same time, I didn't want any more trouble. I put my family through too much as a teen, and now, I just wanted to find a way to stay on campus and mind my business so nothing else bad would happen. Keep my grades up and wait everything out, like you would any category five storm. Stay in the bunker until it was safe to come out again.

But with friends like these guys, they wouldn't let that happen. They'd say, "You're not stayin' in again tonight. No way! You're goin' out, and don't worry, nobody's gonna even look at you twice. They do it'll be the last thing they do!"

Navarro was reckless. Brazen. But he also had an eye for surveilling the scene. I think he could see things happen too before they actually did, the way I could. I liked being around him. He kept me feeling alive the rest of that year.

We even had a few laughs during winter nights at *the Old Corner*, which was this local joint Navarro's friend Frankie bartended at. Frankie's family owned the place, so it was a safe place to go. *Nothing* would happen to me at *the Old Corner*.

So, as the snow began to fall and pile up that winter, once my studies were done for the night, they'd drag me out and we'd pile on a few drinks there and have some laughs. At this point, I wasn't sure how many more free nights like these I would have, so I obliged every time they dragged me out.

One night we headed out so late that when we pulled up the only parking space Navarro could find was one right under this fire escape across the street. This would also prove to be a night that Navarro would have one too many *Calderone's*, as he called them. This was the name of a guy he smashed over the head one night with a bottle of beer, like something you'd see right out of a scene from the movie *Goodfellas*. From that moment on, a round of *Miller Lite's* were ordered as "a round of *Calderone's* over here!"

Later that night, as Navarro got a little *ubriaco,* as he would say, we prepared to head home. He was pretty blasted, but we weren't worried because his Dad knew everybody in town, and *the Old Corner* was just a couple blocks away from campus anyways. *What could happen?*

I mean, the cops wouldn't bother Navarro for the most part, no matter what he seemed to ever do. I figured that was probably why he always carried himself like he owned the town. He was completely fearless. All 5'4", nearly 190 pounds of him. He was a bull. So, end of the night, we headed back for his car, which stuck out like a sore thumb no matter where we went. It was a white, mid 80s Caprice Classic four-door Sedan with blackout limo tint windows. It looked like a pimp mobile.

As we pulled out, Navarro looked over his shoulder to back up but cut the corner too close to the fire escape. Somehow it hitched itself to the corner of his front bumper and he was dragging it, cursing as he jerked the car back and forth to shake it loose. It was pretty hilarious, actually. I glanced around to see if anyone saw us. I was still worried about cops, even if he wasn't. I'd always feel this way, for the rest of my life—always looking over my shoulder, even if there wasn't a reason for me to. Well, that night no-one was around to notice, nobody except Frankie, watching from the doorway of the bar—*laughing his ass off.*

We finally made it home, and the next morning Navarro's Dad somehow hadn't spotted the damage to his bumper, which Navarro was able to push back into place for the most part.

FAST-FORWARD TO ROUND TWO, the next night at *the Old Corner.* Navarro's cousin wanted to come out with us so we headed over the bridge to South Williamsport to pick her up and have dinner at Mikey Palermo's joint.

After we ate, Mikey's daughter joined the three of us and we headed back *to the Old Corner.* It was still snowing pretty hard, and by some stroke of chance, the only parking spot left was beneath that same fire escape. *"Here we go again,"* I thought.

The girls in the back seat were both clueless as to why we were arguing about whether to park there or not.

"What are the odds? C'mon, nothin's gonna happen. Thank God it's here. Least we've got a spot," Navarro argued with me.

"Ok, if you say so," I shook my head as he parked.

At the end of the night, Navarro was pretty hammered again. We all were. Only it wasn't as late as the night before, and there were still people milling around outside *the Old Corner*.

This time he made sure he carefully turned the wheel near the fire escape, backed up ever so slooooowwwly. His arm was over my headrest as he peered beyond the girls in the backseat to study his maneuvering, and to make sure he didn't hit any cars parked directly behind us as he inched his way out of harm's way.

"You see, I told ya' . . . Nothin' to worry about! We're home free." He smiled at me. As he did, he looked straight ahead, hit the gas—*only we were still in reverse!*

Slaaaaammmmm!!! We hit this brand new Cadillac Eldorado parked directly behind us, flush into their driver's side door.

"I think I saw somethin' jump when we hit!" I exclaimed.

"Whadda ya' mean—*jump*?" Navarro asked.

"I mean . . . I think there's a guy inside," I said. "We better go check and see."

"Alright. You stay here. I'll go check it out."

Sure enough, there was a guy inside. *Also hammered.* Way worse than we were, though. I was cracking up at how Navarro approached the car. With his wingtips and double breasted overcoat, collar up, newsboy cap on, the brim shielding his eyes from the wind as it whipped cold air and snow across the parking lot. As he arrived at the guy's driver's side window, he rapped against it with his ring finger to get the guy's attention.

"Excuse me . . . Ummm, sir? You awake in there, pal?"

The guy hit the button on the inside of his driver's side window and it started to roll down. "Yeah? Whadda you want kid?" the guy groaned.

"I think we may have ummmm, tapped your door a little bit. *Just a little damage*. Thought you might want to take a look at it."

Now, this was no small tap. The whole side of the guy's door was caved in. His Caddy was *fucked*. But Navarro could talk his way out of a Turkish prison, and this guy was pretty wasted.

"Look, kid, you don't want the cops here. And neither do I. So get the hell outta here, will ya!" he barked.

And with that, Navarro quickly jumped back in, tossed it in gear—in DRIVE this time—and we were off. I can only imagine the look on that guys' face the next morning when he saw the damage to his Caddy. *Ouch*, I imagined.

That next morning we went to church in town. I remember his sister shaking her head as Luci, Navarro and I walked in making the sign of the cross.

"Will you get a load of these guys? It's a wonder the walls don't fall down," she said.

Father Andy did the service. He was affiliated with the college too. He was a young priest, as far as priest's go, probably in his early forties, and we used to talk to him a lot whenever we'd pass by his campus residence since he was always outside smoking cigarettes. He'd smoke and curse, just like any one of us. It wasn't a put on either, to be like one of the guys or anything, that's just how he was. I think he also drank a little too much wine from the vestibule, but who was I to judge. Navarro told him a little of my situation, and he said he'd pray for me. He also told me about this new Campus Parish Priest at Lycoming. His name was Father John Ludway.

FATHER LUDWAY was new to Williamsport, even younger than Father Andy, and brand new to the campus. He was gauntly thin with red hair, glasses and a red beard in kind of a goatee.

I introduced myself to him, and he explained how he was trying to bring more students into the Sunday services so they could increase the size of his new Parish.

I told him I would try and come by. He then mentioned that Father Andy told him I was in some trouble . . . and he asked if I wanted to talk about it . . .

Now, I wasn't looking to re-hash everything with some guy I just met, let alone some new Priest, but Father Ludway had this way about him. He just seemed genuine. *An honest man.*

In my world, those were few and far between. So I went out on a limb and told him my situation. Told him about my volatile past and how I always wound up in these crazy situations. I figured since I was tough enough to help someone, and had developed a certain skillset that most kids didn't at my young age, I should do what's right. Even though that often meant doing something wrong to defend what I felt was right. I explained to him how whenever I saw something going down, I'd step in and get involved, and more often than not, I'd take the heat for it.

As I waited for him to pass judgment and toss me right out of there, or perhaps be generally dismissive, *or worse*—be like my Mom's pastor back home. He basically told my Mom right in front of me, "He's not a good boy anymore. Let him go."

I mean, *who says that*? I'd never step foot in that church again. But Father Ludway surprised me. He didn't judge me. Nor was he dismissive. He was kind. Genuinely concerned. So what did he do with this new information from a kid like me?

He gave me keys to the chapel.

You believe that? He literally *handed me the keys.*

He also gave me two *St. Michael Prayer Cards*, which would prove to be something that meant more to me than anyone would ever know. He told me to keep one in my dorm room and take another home with me, just in case I ever lost one. He said St. Michael would help protect me. He went on to explain that St. Michael is one of the greatest of all Catholic Saints.

"He's the patron of protection, for those who have fallen, for soldiers, and artists," Father Ludway explained. "He was the leader of God's army and knows what it means to face evil and imminent danger."

He said St. Michael's prayer with me. It would become one I would soon memorize in that empty chapel over the course of many lonely nights sitting in the dark by myself, reciting it over and over:

"Saint Michael, the Archangel, defend us in battle.
Be our protection against the wickedness and snares of the devil.
May God rebuke him, we humbly pray. And do thou, O Prince of the
Heavenly host, by the power of God, thrust into hell Satan and all
evil spirits who wander the world for the ruin of our souls.
Amen."

ONE BEAUTIFUL WINTER NIGHT, one that I'll never forget, I prayed there in the chapel for hours, while sitting all alone in the darkness. I never turned the lights on when I was in there, partly due to my own paranoia. I knew Father Ludway gave me permission to go in whenever I felt I needed to, but I didn't trust that Campus Security would see it the same way.

I also didn't feel at this time that I deserved such an honor, to even be granted access to such a place. I didn't feel I was worthy, so sitting in the dark, like being in a self-imposed "hole" was just fine with me. This way, it was just me, my thoughts—*and God.*

The snow began to fall again as I finally emerged out of the chapel. It was probably well after midnight and the entire campus had fallen silent. Not a soul was out. It was as if the whole world had suddenly gone still. It was so still I could actually hear the snowflakes falling gently as they began to quietly blanket the night's sky. I could hear my breath as I walked, and I listened to the snowflakes softly land on my face and my jacket, the snow crunching beneath my shoes. It was a magical night. I felt like I was being cleansed by the purity of the white snow.

It literally made me want to cry as I walked. I don't know what it was. Maybe just the flashbacks from my youth, when I was once afraid I'd ever get to see such beauty in nature ever again, at least not for a long, long time.

It was all coming back to me . . .

But, as I stared up at the sky and marveled at the freshly falling snow as if this were the first time I had ever seen it, something compelled me to keep walking past my dorm, all the way to Father Ludway's residence on campus.

When I arrived at his doorstep I knocked eagerly. He opened the door to me after a few minutes, wiping the sleep from his eyes, I said to him, "Father, I know how I can help your Parish. I know what I can do. I'm going to fill it like you've never seen it filled before. You'll see. I'll do this week's reading for you. And I'm going to fill the chapel. You won't lose the Parish, Father. That much I promise you."

He simply smiled, with no hesitation, just a calm, steady tone and said, "I know you will, Michael, I know you will. Get some sleep. I'll see you at Mass on Sunday."

I felt exhilarated. For the first time in a long while. I asked Luci and Navarro to help me get the football team, some of the fraternities Luci's older brother Ben knew, another future roommate of ours Michael Susi, and a lot of the girls from the sororities to come out to the service on campus that Sunday. And they all came out. The place was packed. *Standing room only.*

There weren't even enough chairs for everyone. I proceeded to do my reading. Father Ludway did the rest. Everyone was moved by the whole thing. It helped to have the "Who's Who" of the campus there to reinforce this notion that it was "cool" to go to church. This trend continued weekly. And his Parish grew. It wasn't just a temporary thing. Father Ludway's higher-ups were more than impressed. They couldn't believe the work he had done in such a short time. It was unheard of. Definitely not the size of the services the other ministries on campus had.

We made an impact.

At the year's end, I hugged Father Ludway, Rog, and the rest of my friends from college goodbye, not knowing whether I'd be back to campus or not, given the new trouble I was facing again, but I had done my part. I even finished the semester with straight A's. *Straight A's*, can you believe it?

I left the rest to our lawyer to do his job, entrusting my future with his ability to do his best by me. I had done my part and stayed out of trouble. I also kept Father Ludway's *St. Michael Prayer Cards* with me at all times, in my pocket. He said they would protect me. *And they did.*

ON THE MORNING OF TOMMY'S TRIAL I prayed to St. Michael to fight alongside us, and I prayed to God to save Tommy, much like I was saved over two decades ago while sitting in his shoes.

As I slipped into a suit and tie, I stared into the mirror, preparing myself to sit by my student's side as he faced his judgment in court. It took me back to when I prepared for my own battle in court as a kid.

I remember it being a beautiful sunny day, just like the day my Grandfather passed away. I went outside with my little brother and rolled around a few times in the grass with him, hugging him tightly and holding him up in the air above me as I stared up at the trees.

I soaked up the moment, not knowing whether it would be my last one seeing my little brother for a long, long time or not. Not knowing if I'd see the trees again either, or smell the grass, listen to the sweet sounds of nature, all the things most people on any given day take totally for granted.

These are all things I didn't take for granted anymore, especially now, like just listening to the beautiful sound of the rain, the purity of year's first falling snow, the coolness of the wind whipping through my hair, or the tranquility of the moonlight on the quiet winter nights I'd walk to and from the Lycoming College campus chapel that had become my own personal sanctuary when troubles befell me in college again.

These were all things that heightened my sensitivities as an artist later on, and while in some ways they hardened me, they also made me even more empathetic. These became the memories that I reflected on as I got dressed for Tommy's day in court.

Way back when, on my own day of judgment, I recalled my parents telling me all the things I shouldn't be doing . . .

"Don't do your hair like that! Don't slick it back, *comb it to the side*. Don't wear *that* shirt and tie, wear *this one*, it looks more conservative. You want to look like some innocent kid—*not like, well . . .*" they paused . . .

Like a criminal . . . I imagined is where they were headed, even though they never finished their sentence. I know they were only trying to help.

This whole ordeal drained them completely, emotionally and financially, but I was still stubborn and wasn't having any of it. I made my peace with God. I felt like I already lost the most valuable thing most people take for granted in life—*time*. And back then, I was potentially facing plenty more of it.

But even so, I truly felt that if I was going to be judged, I should be judged for exactly who I was, not someone else standing before the court trying to fool someone. So, I got dressed as "me" and let the chips fall where they may. At least they couldn't take that away from me. But let me tell you, there's no more humbling an experience than standing before a Judge as you hear the fateful words, "All rise" as you wait for some perfect stranger to deliver your fate, whatever that may be.

REFLECTING ON ALL THIS as I got ready for Tommy Taylor's day in court, I knew he'd be feeling much of the same emotions. God had mercy on me and blessed me with vindication, on more than one occasion. I was hoping Tommy would experience the same good fortune as I had been blessed to receive.

As I got dressed, my subconscious must have been working overtime to calm my nerves, because I all of the sudden remembered something funny that happened after one of my own ordeals. It was something I hadn't recalled in many years, but it made me laugh and lightened my mood . . .

The summer after I signed my life away so I wouldn't sue the state in exchange for my freedom, I ended up having to do some community service. Once I got a good look at the attractive thirty-something community service caseworker I had this bright idea that if I flirted with her, maybe—*just maybe* she'd have mercy on me and hook me up with a "cushy" air-conditioned office job.

Well, I did—only it was with her, in her office, and she turned out to be a *total psycho*.

I'll never forget my father shaking his head at me as the phone rang, again and again, late one night as we were watching a ballgame on TV.

"You better get it," he says. "Don't want her violating the terms of your agreement, do you?"

I took the call and then asked my father to borrow his car so I could go meet her.

"Well, guess you gotta go, don't you?" he says to me, half laughing at me, half pissed off at me. "Thought you were preeeeetty fuckin' smart, didn't ya'?"

Once summer was over, I broke it off *extremely carefully* with that caseworker and I prepared to go off to college with a clean slate. In hindsight, it was just like Father Ludway would later say to me . . . "St. Michael, the Archangel, he's always in your corner."

I imagined a lot of other people have always been in my corner too, like my Grandfather, the boxer, who probably fought alongside me in spirit, or maybe his father, Arcangelo dalla Valeria, who bore the name of the Archangel himself. And it was always just when I started to feel like my life was like a page out of the Book of Job, I always suddenly felt alive again. There must have been a reason I had to keep going through such ordeals.

I'd later learn it would be to help the kids that I teach.

Finally, many years later, in my fifth year of college to be exact, I completed my student teaching, which I felt was now my calling and I earned my Bachelor's degree in Fine Arts.

I kept those St. Michael prayer cards given to me by Father Ludway in my pocket for the next twenty years.

They were like magic.

The day Tommy Taylor was finally released on bail, I gave them to him.

"A beautiful, honest man—*this Priest*, gave these to me once. He said they'd protect me, and they did. I believe they will help protect you too," I told Tommy, hugging him tightly.

And they did.

It took until the end of what felt like an excruciatingly long year, but my lawyer pal ended up getting Tommy a plea that allowed him to go free with "time served" for good behavior. I sat with him in court, *in his corner*, as the Judge rendered his verdict.

And, while Tommy wasn't able to return to school and finish out his senior year, he was thankfully free to live outside the walls of jail again. I was also able to submit his AP Photography portfolio for him while he was incarcerated, and he passed. He also did enough to graduate and was permitted to walk across the stage to receive his diploma with the rest of his classmates.

That summer, I breathed a deep sigh of relief after the outcome of everything working out in Tommy's favor. I reflected on all of it as I drove back to New Jersey to get my first major tattoo—a half-sleeve of *St. Michael the Archangel*.

This was a really special piece for me because I no longer had the St. Michael prayer cards with me anymore. To this day, whenever I talk with Tommy, and we still keep in touch, he texts me a picture of the prayer cards.

"They're a little beat up," he'll say to me, "but they're always with me."

SIXTEEN

SORRENTO'S

My Grandma always got her hair done at *Sorrento's Hair Fashions* on the corner of Page and Stuyvesant Avenue. I knew Bill, the owner, from visiting there a bunch of times as a kid, but it had been years since I'd been up there. My Grandma was always trying to set me up with Lisa, Bill's daughter, but, as I'm sure you can probably imagine, anybody your Grandma is trying to set you up with immediately conjures up imagery of some librarian-type. So, I always stayed away from that one.

But, on the weekend of my twenty-fourth birthday, I drove back to Jersey from campus with one of my college buddies, Brian Farber, who also happened to live just down the road from my Grandma's in Palisades Park, which is situated off Route 17 past Teterboro Airport.

We were gonna make a weekend out of it. Stay local with his buddy they called "Stitch" in Palisades on Friday night, and then meet up with my old pal Gus on Saturday night in the City. Gus used to work as a Manager at the *Houlihan's* on 5th Avenue I used to work at, and we stayed in touch. Gus was a great guy. Now he was managing the Empire State Building location and he invited me down for birthday drinks on the house Saturday night. Who was I to refuse?

Farber dropped me off at my Grandma's on our way back into town and headed home to catch a nap, before picking up Stitch and me to go back out. I figured I'd do the same, and visit with my Grandma for a while, try my hand against her in a game or two of Rummy. Only, she wasn't home. And she was *always home*. Then I saw the Post-it note on her side door. It read, "Up at *Sorrento's* getting my hair done. Back home soon."

Now, Farber had already pulled away, and Vi didn't leave me a key. So, I figured what the hell, I'll take a stroll. *Sorrento's* was just at the top of the hill, so I went up to surprise her at the Beauty Parlor.

And, just as I walk in, there she was — *Lisa, Bill's daughter*. It was like the scene out of *the Godfather* when Michael met this beautiful Italian girl from "the other side" and immediately felt lovestruck, as if by a thunderbolt of lightning. And let me tell you, Lisa was definitely *no librarian-type*. She reminded me of Marisa Tomei from the film *My Cousin Vinny*, only prettier.

Jet black curly hair, all teased up high, wide bright blue eyes that sparkled just like a young Liz Taylor, and this tiny little figure with an incredible set of legs. She couldn't have been more than 5' tall, maybe a little over 110 pounds soaking wet. She looked simply stunning and had this bubbly personality that made me feel as though I knew her almost instantly my entire life. She had that effect on everybody, though. That, to this day, is one of her strongest assets — *her incredible personality*.

I guess from growing up in her parent's beauty parlor she learned great people skills early on. She could sell sand to the Arabs. Lisa is still the biggest seller of my paintings to date. She also had this innocence about her, which was something that I certainly never had been around before. At least not with the kind of girls I was going out with. It was disarming to a guy like me. She was street smart as hell, *but innocent*. She was also from the neighborhood, which I loved, along with her thick Jersey accent, and the fact that she came from a really tight-knit Italian family.

Her father Bill was also just like his daughter. Back in the day, they used to call him "the Boss" since he looked a lot like Bruce Springsteen when he was younger. Bill and Lisa were two peas in a pod. It was probably where she got her "gift of gab." He knew everybody and was definitely the king of the castle at *Sorrento's*. The salon was his stage, and everybody would hang on his every word. The things that came out of it were hilarious! He had this thick Neapolitan accent and everybody loved him. Especially my Grandma, who had been coming to him to get her hair done for over thirty years, and my Grandfather before her, who used to go up to *Sorrento's* to bullshit with Bill and hang out with the "street guys" on the corner by the Candy Store.

Bill came over to America at the age of twenty-one as Pellegrino Molinaro, from Ponte, in the Province of Benevento, the Campania Region of Italy. His family owned a two-hundred and fifty-acre farm. He was the oldest boy in the family, one of eight (three other brothers and four sisters). His father sent him over to America to carve a path for his family, and start a new life for himself. His second oldest brother would be the only one to ever join him in America, also ending up working as a hairdresser, first with Bill, and then later he went off on his own after he and Bill had a major falling out. They are still estranged to this day.

Bill's third brother Carmine died around age thirteen. He was born with a hole in his heart and passed away due to complications surrounding that. His youngest brother Amore stayed in Italy and ended up running their family's farm with his children. His sisters Giuseppina, Vittoria, and Candida all stayed in Italy too, with the exception of his fourth sister Carmela, who moved to Australia, where she still lives today.

When Bill came over to America he met Olga, who also had an interesting story, emigrating from Trapani, Sicily around the age of twelve. She was adopted in Sicily, and had to wait in a foster home for a year for her new family to finally send for her in America. When she finally met Bill many years later, she was living in Nutley, New Jersey, also as a hairdresser, and the two ended up getting married on the day of America's first *Superbowl*.

They eventually bought the whole building on the corner of Stuyvesant and Page Avenue, ran *Sorrento's* together, lived in one of the upstairs apartments for a time and rented out the other two stores, which were Embroidery Store, Athletics Apparel Shop, and the corner Candy Store. Olga had a terrible time having children, just like Lisa would later experience. She would also survive a life-threatening brain tumor that sidelined her for over a year and would cost everyone their share of emotional and financial hardships. Their tragedies hit just after Bill built their family a new home out in West Milford, complete with an in-law suite for Olga's mom, Josephine. Only, Josephine fell in the shower while still at her apartment in Newark, hit her head and developed a blood clot in her brain. She had to have surgery at the same time Olga needed brain surgery. It was too much for Lisa to take care of her brothers and father for a year *plus her Grandmother*, so Josephine ended up moving into a nursing home after her surgery as Olga thankfully recovered. To this day, it's one of the reasons why they're all so close. They, too, went through the fire together.

So, as I walked into *Sorrento's*, I found my Grandma in Lisa's chair as Bill was in the middle of telling some wild story.

"So he says to his wife—you want *steak* tonight? You need money to go *shopping*? Listen to me sweetheart, you see this twenty dollar bill? *This one* belongs to me. You see the one in the mirror? *That one* belongs to you!"

Everyone was laughing, hanging on his every word, for the punchline. Back then you could smoke freely, so you could also cut the cigarette smoke in there with a knife. Between the smoke from the old betties in curlers and all the hair spray it's a miracle the place never exploded beyond just laughter!

Bill would go on, "Aspete, aspeta—so the husband comes home late one night, opens the Frigidaire and there's all this meat! Sausiche, brachiole, capicola, *you name it*! So he drags his wife out of bed to the Frigidaire and yells—*what the hell is all this*!?"

Everyone's cracking up at this point. Me, I was just listening, smiling to myself while trying to make eye contact with Lisa as she finished my Grandma's hair.

"So he says to his wife, what'd you do, *rob me*? I told you, *no buyin' nothin'*! Where'd you get the money for all this?"

Bill lifts up his smock to the mirror at his hair station, like he's the wife in the joke *flashing us* with her nightgown and says, "You see *that*, between my legs? Yeah, *that one*, in the mirror? *That one* belongs to you. You see *this one*?"

Bill points to his smock now as he delivers the punchline . . .

"*This one* belongs to *the butcher*!" The whole place burst out laughing hysterically!

You could tell going into *Sorrento's* for one minute just how much everyone loved Bill, and that Lisa was his pride and joy. So, I smiled at my Grandma, and she made light of the fact that she locked me out of her house by saying "I have no idea what you're talking about" as she smiled at me, watching me trying to make the moves on Lisa.

I asked Lisa if she wanted to get together that weekend. That it was my birthday coming up, and how could she refuse a guy on his birthday weekend? But, she still shot me down cold. Told me she had to work the next morning, that Saturday was going to be a busy one and she already had plans.

So, I smiled confidently and told her I'd be back tomorrow to change her mind. I paid for my Grandma's hair before Vi could get to the register and then headed home with her to shower up and meet up with the guys.

I told them all about her. They even started a pool that weekend to see how many times she'd shoot me down. And they all placed bets on the fact she'd definitely never go out with me. They actually were taking BETS! *Those bastards*.

But I still kept going back. Still to solid "no's" but I kept going. She never gave me her phone number, so I couldn't try calling her, only at the salon. I didn't even know her last name. I tried to look it up under the last name *Sorrento*, like the salon, but couldn't find anything. Turns out it wasn't her last name. So, when I stopped by one last time, I gave her Farber's house number so she could reach me there if she wanted to.

Still, no phone call.

So, we finally went out celebrating Saturday night with Gus in the City and then planned to head back to campus late Sunday night. My birthday wasn't officially until Monday but this was when we were celebrating it.

So, there I was, sitting at the bar at the *Houlihan's* on 34th and 5th, at the Empire State Building location. We began doing shots just as another guy down the end of the bar yelled down that his birthday was also April 10th. So, we started sending rounds of drinks back and forth . . . *all night long.*

Finally, I turned to Farber, "What the hell's wrong with me? Why do you think she won't go out with me? C'mon. Be straight with me. With this one, I can't get anywhere."

"I'd go out with ya'," was his sarcastic response, as he laughed, "Ahhhh, whaddaya mad for, because you lost money?"

I thought to myself, "Well, technically the weekend's not officially over, *maybe there's still hope . . .*"

Sunday afternoon finally rolled in, and I was still racked out in Farber's basement on the couch after our night of partying and making late-night vodka sauce over pasta that we devoured at four o'clock in the morning. Farber was already up and out and wasn't due back for a couple of hours. I think he was playing softball with a bunch of guys or something. He was a fitness freak that way. He reminded me of Rocky, as in Rocky Balboa. You could never stop him from working out. That's just how he was. Even after a weekend of solid partying.

And then the phone rang.

It was Lisa. "She finally caved," I thought to myself. We ended up talking for hours. Right up through when he got home. I smiled at him when he looked at me and mouthed the words, "Who you talkin' to?"

He couldn't believe it. *She actually called me.*

I'd spent the better part of the next few weeks visiting Lisa whenever I could, driving back and forth to Lyndhurst from Williamsport with Farber every weekend.

Six months later I proposed.

SEVENTEEN

THE RAINBOW ROOM

I had the proposal all planned out a few months in advance. And while this wasn't a "shotgun wedding" it certainly would go off with a bang! *First things first, I had to ask for her hand.* It's the right thing to do and being who her father was, it was the only thing to do.

The only problem was Bill's virtually impossible to get alone, especially at *Sorrento's*. So, when Lisa invited me to spend that Thanksgiving with her family in the fall of 1995, I felt that was a great opportunity. I had never been to their house before. They had moved out of the apartment above *Sorrento's* many years before Bill finally could afford to build this large home in West Milford, which is a very rural area of New Jersey approximately an hour West of New York City. It's surrounded by lots of rolling hills, tons of trees, and it was home to Greenwood Lake, one of the largest lakes in the State and was nothing like Lyndhurst.

Bill loved to hunt and fish and growing up on a farm in Italy, so this was probably as close as you could get to that unless you lived in Pennsylvania or Upstate New York. The first time she drove me out there to her house I thought we were in another time zone. It was way out there. I couldn't believe Bill commuted that far every day. Now I understood why Lisa said she and her Dad started driving separate to and from work after a while. I had never even been West of Route 23 before, aside from going to college in PA. I only knew Jersey as Lyndhurst, Nutley, Belleville, Paterson, the Palisades, Hoboken, those types of places.

Thanksgiving with their family was great. They had tons of food and Lisa's family entertained all night, with a steady flow of Lisa's friends and their families stopping by. By now, I had already asked Lisa's mother Olga and I laid out my intentions to ask Bill. But, even at his home, it was still proving to be impossible to get the guy alone!

So, around midnight, as everyone started heading out after taking their last sips of wine for the evening, in the blink of an eye Bill rose from his spot, placed both hands down firmly at the head of the table and said, "Well, goodnight everyone. I'm going to bed. Ci vediamo domani."

And just like that, he was outta there!

Headed upstairs to bed.

I couldn't believe it. I looked at Olga as if to say, "What do I do now?!" She shot me a look back nodding me towards the stairs to go after him. So, I took a deep breath and headed where I imagined no man ever would venture—*to Bill's bedroom.*

Now I had no idea what his bedroom looked like. It was that one place in their house that no-one ever went. It was "off limits." Bill's domain. Who knows what the hell went on in there?! There were all kinds of crazy thoughts racing through my head as I walked up this expansive, never-ending curved staircase leading to his upstairs bedroom. His was the only door to the left. As I slowly approached the door I could hear the muffled sounds of a *New York Rangers* hockey game on the television.

Bill loved falling asleep watching sports. Never one for a movie. Occasionally the news. But always sports. He also had these da Vinci-like sleep patterns, passing out in the blink of an eye. Partially due to the fact that he was such an early riser, always up around 4:30 in the morning, come rain or come shine. This was how he was brought up as a kid on the farm in Italy.

So, after the first knock, I knocked again. He finally grumbled, "Olga, that you?"

I opened the door a crack to find him lying half asleep already. I probably just woke him up.

"Michael? What is it? Come on in . . ."

Here we go . . .

I walked in, sat down beside him on his bed and dove right into my schpeale.

"Bill, I wanted to come to you and ask you in person," I said, "to ask you if I could have the honor, *and for your blessing*, for your daughter's hand in marriage."

He sat right up in bed, smiled at me wide, reached over to give me a hug and we kissed on both cheeks. "Of course, Michael. Thank you for asking me. You have my blessing."

I was on top of the world—*until the next morning.*

Bill came downstairs and hit me with, "Michael, I was pretty drunk last night. You didn't come by my room and ask me anything, did you?"

All I could think of was, "You've gotta be kidding me. I have to do this all over again?!"

My nerves immediately shot through me, and I think he could see it written all over my face.

"I'm only kidding." He smacked my cheek and smiled. "Took a lot of balls comin' in my room like that, though. Gotta give you that."

We both shared a private little laugh. Me, I shit the bed. Lisa kept staring at me, trying to figure out what the hell we were joking around about. I could tell she knew something was up. She's intuitive that way. Always has been. And Bill has always been a ball-breaker like that. I mean, the first meal Lisa ever cooked for me in front of the whole family Bill said, "It's good Lisa. Shrimps are a little tough, but overall, it's pretty good."

Like I said—*he's a ball-breaker.*

But he was also a phenomenal cook. He was probably in the kitchen more than Olga. They both were good cooks, but anything Bill made was "the best". Just ask him, he'll tell ya'!

It was pretty comical. He didn't do it to throw digs or make you feel bad. He just liked what he liked, and that would consist of *anything he made*. And everything was fresh. He'd make eight bushels of Roma tomatoes every September, jarring enough for the whole entire family for the year with his restaurant-quality tomato press and strainer he had shipped over from Italy. And occasionally, he would also do thirty gallons or so of homemade wine in early October. Before purchasing motorized press, he used to do it all the old fashioned way, cranking it by hand. He's a maniac that way. His forearms are stronger than most twenty-year olds are. I still, to this day, sometimes need to bang the tomato jars open with a knife because he's got them turned so damned tight.

AFTER THANKSGIVING, I began working on a portrait of Lisa in gouache on paper. I wanted to present it to her as a gift on her birthday, matted and framed behind glass, the night I also planned to propose to her. I loved giving her the gift of my art because that's a "forever kind of thing".

Art, as I still look at it, is something timeless. Unlike a photograph, which is a captured moment, it's an accumulation of an experience, an "arrived-at-moment" through hours in the studio, layers of drawing and painting. That's what makes all the difference to me when it comes to my own work—the layers and layers of meaning. And a painting can also, if done right, capture the emotions poured into the piece. I wanted to give Lisa my love, and I figured, as an artist—this was the very best way.

The painting itself was nothing as provocative as many other pieces I'd later do, nor as narrative. Just Lisa dressed up, holding a single Rose in her hand. I did place a diamond ring on Lisa's finger in the painting, though. Something I'd do again many years later in a painting for Dominic Capone of him and his girlfriend, Staci. He planned to propose to her on camera at my gallery opening in Chicago for his reality television show *the Capones*, telling Staci—"Look at Michael's painting of us. You notice anything? On your finger?" *With that, he got down on one knee.*

Looking back on Lisa's engagement portrait, it wasn't particularly great from a technical standpoint because I was still honing my skills as a painter at that time. Back then, hands, in particular, always gave me trouble. I'd always seem to make them smaller than they should be for some reason. But, back then, especially at an engagement party, it wouldn't be something anybody would be honing in on. That was just me being critical of my own work, but over the years I've gotten really, really great at capturing people—and not just their likenesses either, but who they are *on the inside*.

That, to me, is the ultimate goal of a portrait. Capturing a likeness *is easy*. Anybody can capture someone's likeness from looking off of a photograph or by using a projector, which is the industry standard for most art school grads anymore. The "grid method" days are over due to the advances in technology, but even so, something technology will never be able to help with is *capturing one's soul.* That's a whole other ballgame.

That's a whole other level of artist that can capture that in a painting, and one very few out there are truly capable of. That's the difference between college and the pros.

It's why celebrities have sought me out to paint them. It's why the likes of America's most infamous seek me out to do what no-one else is capable of doing—capturing "their soul." Their essence. Who they really are. *Inside.*

I liken it to that feeling you get when you meet someone for the first time, but as you get to really know them their face actually changes. They look different than they did when you first met them. Some for the better, some look worse. That's their personality surfacing. That's capturing "their essence." That's why working from a single photograph of someone whom I've never met never really does it for me.

It's because everybody looks so different in every photograph. Why we're not reducible to one single image that says "that's us!" At least not in photography. That's what's so difficult about capturing someone's soul. But it's what I do best, better than any artist out there.

I think I've been able to get so good at capturing my subjects' soul because I get to know them on such a deep level. Deeper than most. I look at it as a commitment to my craft. I pay my paintings respect in that way.

And while I spend a lot of time on the surface, *it's the inside of my subjects* that I'm always really after.

But, for this particular portrait of my future wife, on this particular night, it was just something that I wanted to create for her to always take her back to this special night in her mind whenever she'd look at it. It was, for me, just one gift of many I planned to give her that evening, only this one was too big to carry around with me all night, so I left it back at her house, where her mother was throwing Lisa a surprise party, relying on the fact she'd say yes—*talk about pressure!*

Her Mom invited all her friends and family, their relatives, my family and my Grandma. It would be a party of about thirty people or so scheduled to be at her house later that night when we got back from our evening in the City.

NOW I HAD TO SET MY PLAN into place. I first had to make a reservation at a fancy joint, because if you're going to do something, you've gotta do it right. My plan was to propose at the place where my Grandma always took me every year around Thanksgiving time as a child—*Tavern on the Green.*

That was "our thing". Even though my Grandma didn't have any money and all we could order was a huge plate of french fries, I didn't care, because it wasn't about anything but the experience of it all. Making that memory. Being able to say we ate there. If you've never been there, *Tavern on the Green* is located in Central Park near the Upper West Side. It had a huge glassed-in atrium and tons of stained glass throughout the restaurant. It's a historic landmark in the Park, and one I wanted to take Lisa to after first taking her on a handsome cab ride (horse and carriage) through Central Park just before proposing.

So, I made the reservation.

TWO MONTHS PASS . . . and it was nearly Lisa's birthday. I've got the ring. The painting is done, matted and framed. I picked up some other things to put some gifts inside other boxes of gifts, one box smaller than the next, so she'd keep opening down to more and more until finally arriving at the box with the ring inside last.

I decide on a whim to just "triple-check" my reservation. Not that I needed to, but, I figured why the hell not, one more time can't hurt, since this was the very week I was headed into the City with her for her big night.

So I call and guess what—*they don't have my reservation!*

"You've got to be kidding me!?" I yelled. "Check it again!" After all, I was just triple-checking! I had already called a month prior and two weeks again after that. Everything was all set.

"Sorry pal, restaurant's been booked for a private party. They wiped all the reservations off the book" was this guy's response.

Now, what was I going to do?

I mean, this is New York City. Any place you call that's worth proposing at usually has a three to six-month wait-list. So, I started calling around.

Sure enough, every place I called pretty much laughed me off the phone with the customary, "Umm, you really have to book this place a couple months in advance, we're sorry."

Now what? I mean, I can't propose to her at a *TGI Fridays*! Just not my style. I needed someplace intimate, someplace epic even, but every place I called was booked solid. All the top restaurants were. So, I decided to make *one last phone call.*

This call would be to a man I couldn't even invite to my wedding due to some very complicated reasons, and while I vowed to stay away from trouble, which included not being indebted to friends of mine in "the life" —*this was a last resort.*

So I made the call. It went down something like this . . .

"Sure Michael. Sure, sure. Something nice. I got it. No problem. I'll call you back in five . . ."

A few minutes later, my phone rings.

"You're all set, kid. *The Rainbow Room*. It's really nice there. Perfect place to propose. It has a slow moving, revolving dance floor and everything. I even got a dozen long stemmed roses being delivered to your table half way through dinner from a florist I know nearby around the corner. That's on me. My gift to you. Bring a lot of money with you, though. There's no prices on the menu at that joint."

"No . . . prices?"

"I'd bring a couple grand."

"A couple . . . *grand*?!" I laughed, not positive whether he was kidding or not. "I'll make it work. I can't thank you enough. You know, if I could invite you—*to my wedding and all* . . ."

"Say no more. Fuhgeddaboudit, kid. I understand. Listen, this is my gift to you. Say no more. Buona fortuna. Be well."

With that, he hung up. As for me, just to double check, I immediately called *the Rainbow Room* back and got the same guy on the phone I spoke to a little while ago when I was calling all over the City trying this place and that. He recognized my voice right away as I asked if he had my reservation.

"Yes, you're all set."

"But, I called you like twenty minutes ago and you said you were booked solid and you had to book there at least six months in advance. You did say that, no?"

His response, which I probably figured I had comin' to me by now, "That was also before, well . . . Listen, you still want the reservation, or not?"

"Of course."

"Alright, we'll see you Friday night then."

And just like that, we were headed to *the Rainbow Room*.

Now, this is definitely "the place" to make memories, as both John and Peter Gotti would say to me over the years as being one of the only important things in life besides family.

"Make memories," they'd both say. "Make as many as you can." This was advice passed down to them from their iconic father, John Gotti, Sr. *And I was about to.*

ON MARCH 1st WE HEADED INTO THE CITY. Lisa was wearing this beautiful white outfit. I was in my best double-breasted dark teal-colored suit with a matching tie and kerchief. I drove in over the Upper Level of the GWB so we could see the big city lights over the Hudson. I did my customary loop around the 79th Street basin, just like I would back when I lived in the City, turned left onto Broadway and found parking on the Upper West Side, somewhere between Broadway and West End. From there we caught a cab to midtown Manhattan to grab a quick drink at *Houlihan's*, where my old roommate Mike was still bartending. He was in on it but almost let it slip after pouring us a drink and yelling "Congratulations!"

"On what?" Lisa asked as I mouthed the words behind her "Shhh . . . it's her birthday" as carefully as I could.

"On your birthday," Mike quickly recovered with, "Congratulations on your birthday night out in New York City!"

From there, we walked across the street and through the Plaza Hotel. I snapped a photograph of Lisa in front of Elouise's portrait and then I took her for that handsome cab ride around Central Park. It was the first one I was ever on. I guess it's one of those things where if you live in the City you never do the touristy stuff, like visiting the Statue of Liberty, or going to the top of the Empire State Building. It was nice, though. Brisk out, but nice. Then we were dropped off at *the Rainbow Room*. The whole time, I was carrying this big shopping back with "birthday gifts" wrapped up inside it that she kept asking me about. I told her not to worry. I would let her open one of them at dinner.

"Where are we going for dinner?"

"You'll see."

I never liked telling anyone my plans. Letting anyone know what I'm thinking. That's always how I was. You ask me a question and I'll just smile. So, when we arrived at NBC Studios she was curious. Were we there to see a show? Where was dinner taking place? Once inside, we took the elevator to the 65th floor, and there we were.

The Rainbow Room.

The place was elegant. I felt totally out of place, I mean, we were two kids just twenty-five years old at that time, so we definitely were the youngest ones there. As I entered, I tipped the maître de a $20 spot, got seated. To this day, neither of us could tell you what we ordered, what we ate, if we danced or how much it cost. I do know it was a lot. But I brought enough. The night was a total blur. But in a good way.

About half way through service came the roses. And, shortly after, I started handing her presents to open right there at the table, one after the next, eventually leading to the final one nestled carefully in the smallest box of all.

The crowded room began to gaze over anxiously as Lisa finally unwrapped the last box.

Moments later, the place burst into a loud roar of applause after I took her hand *and got down on one knee . . .*

"Will you marry me?"

EIGHTEEN

RAGS TO RICHES

Bill and Olga spared no expense when it came to their only daughter's wedding, and six months later, on August 10th we exchanged vows. But, the narrative of our life would prove to be just as complicated and filled with as many unexpected twists and turns as the narratives embedded within my art.

Lisa's oldest brother, Peter, got sick the night before our wedding at the rehearsal dinner and had to be hospitalized. I remember him sitting in the car before he was taken away saying, "I'm really sorry Michael." He ended up okay a day or so later, but missed the entire wedding. My mother and father-in-law were devastated. I always loved Pete though. We had a connection from day one. Pete lived in Brooklyn for a while, so we'd always swap stories about the City. He and I remain close to this day.

Tommy Navarro, my old college roommate was also in the wind and would prove to be a "no-show" for the wedding.

He said he was "jammed up" in Florida, whatever that meant, so my younger brother, Will, went from being an eight-year-old junior usher to being in the wedding party, walking with my wife's girlfriend Christine.

Since it's a tradition for the groom not to see the bride the day before the wedding the guys stayed the night at the hotel where the reception was to be held the next day, and I spent the night drinking martinis with her father Bill and my best man, Louie at the hotel bar 'til around 4 A.M. I woke up in bed next to Bill early the next morning with a huge hangover. He was already up getting dressed, about to head back to the house to greet the photographer for pictures when he arrived.

"Don't be late, Michael" he yelled to me as he headed out.

Lisa made sure that little detail wasn't left to chance, though. She sent the limo for the guys first. Me sleeping with her father the night before the wedding also became one of the running jokes among my pals throughout the reception.

"So, heard you slept with the father before you slept with the bride. How was he?!" my pals would joke.

We were all introduced and came out to a crowd of around two hundred and fifty friends and relatives from all sides in tandem. Lisa and I came out to a round of applause as Tony Bennett's classic *Rags to Riches* played as our theme song.

Once the reception was underway, a huge circle gathered around Bill as he danced to *the Tarantella* as everyone clapped along. This is a song that no Italian wedding would be complete without. I can still picture Bill dancing around with one of the old betties from *Sorrento's* with a napkin on his head!

Lisa also got in on the action with her Dad and Godfather Victor, twisting and twirling around to *Run Around Sue*. And lastly, we got "our dance" to Tony Bennett's classic Italian love song, *Because of You*. He would graciously autograph our wedding photo as a gift to us, writing *"Because of You . . . Tony Bennett."*

But, the good times would later prove to be too few and far between for us that night. Lisa started breaking out in these hives half-way through the wedding, and before the evening was over she was so swollen we had to rush her to the hospital. So, there we were, while everyone was back at the hotel partying, at St. Joseph's hospital in Wayne, with me and my mother, as Lisa got a shot in her ass while still in her wedding dress.

If we were in the era of Social Media back then a photo of that posted to *Facebook, Instagram* or *Twitter* definitely would have gone viral! The next morning we were scheduled to fly to the Caymans for our honeymoon. Seemingly better that next morning, we hopped in our Limo, headed to Newark Airport and flew out, but while on the plane the hives resurfaced. By the time we got to the hotel she had a fever. I went to a local pharmacy and got some medicine, stopped by the liquor store for a bottle of *Johnny Black*, anticipating a long night ahead, and made it back to the room.

We had this beautiful view overlooking the Caribbean. I never saw waters so clear and crystal blue. You could see right to the bottom of the beautiful colorful coral reefs. I immediately shut the shades, poured myself a drink and didn't open the curtains for the next four days.

I TENDED TO LISA DAY AND NIGHT, but her condition steadily worsened. I didn't know what to do. By day four she was so swollen and her body was bright red like a lobster I thought she was dying. So I took her to what was the equivalent of an emergency room on the island.

It was lucky for me I'm a cash kind of guy because we just got married and insurance wouldn't kick in until November. I was just hired full-time as an art teacher at Southern High, so I had to pay for the hospital visits all out-of-pocket.

The running tab was now up to two grand!

I still remember the doctor, black as night, with these big wide white eyes. All medicine was labeled by hand. It was a scary scene. The receptionist told me as we arrived, "You should have come an hour earlier it would have been cheaper."

How was I supposed to know they were running happy hour specials at the local hospital down there?

So, she got yet another shot, of God knows what, since it seemed like a bunch of voodoo doctors down there and nobody seemed to know what was wrong with her. At first, I thought it was a reaction to shellfish, but it couldn't be that because she hadn't eaten anything much in days, and nobody else got sick from anything at the wedding. I was baffled.

I called my mother when we got back to the room and explained the situation to her and that we needed a flight home. But there was nothing available.

"No flights out", my Mom said. "I've been trying."

She suggested telling Lisa *a little white lie*. That we got a flight booked back for the next day, just in case just knowing she had a way home might help from a psychological standpoint. Even if my mother couldn't get us a flight out until the following day, maybe just her knowing we'd be going home would help.

So, after telling Lisa we were going home the next morning, that night, I decided to take her outside to get some fresh air. We had been in the room nearly a week with no sunlight.

So, I carried her out to the shore.

We sat and watched the stars as the calm of the waves softly lapped at our feet. I held her there all night until we both finally passed out in each other's arms right there on the beach. We woke up the next morning to the Caribbean Sea washing up over us, soaking us wet with morning waves of the warm, salty, crystal blue ocean like something out of a movie. The sun was just starting to come up as we lay there, the water washing over us.

And then, the strangest thing happened—*she looked better!*

I don't know if it was the Caribbean night air, the idea that we were headed home, whether the medicine finally kicked in, or God intervened with my favorite angel, Archangel, Saint Michael, but her swelling finally went down. She didn't feel warm anymore either. She looked like herself again.

"It's so sad that we have to go back today. I feel like I'm okay. I wish we had another day to enjoy all this. It's so beautiful here."

Then I broke the news to her . . .

"Well, here's the thing," I confessed, "We really don't have a flight back. At least not until day after tomorrow."

She just shook her head and smiled. So, we crammed as much as we could of the Caymans into a day and a half. We snorkeled, swam with the stingrays at *Stingray City*, and had dinner at the fanciest restaurant there, which was filled with these exotic birds throughout the place. We definitely made the most of every minute left there before flying back, and we never found out what it was that made her so ill.

Whatever it was that she had returned again when we got back home to our new apartment. Her fever got so high I ran and got ice, lined the bottom of the tub with it, filled the rest with ice cold water and lowered her into it to try and shock her fever down before rushing her back to the hospital. It was literally that close of a call. I couldn't understand why I kept nearly losing her.

I remember hearing our wedding vows in my head and saying to myself, "God, you're really putting me through this in sickness and in health thing really fucking fast." But what are you gonna do? She was my responsibility now. I owed it to her father to make sure I took care of her. I wouldn't let her die on me.

So that's how our marriage began. These would be the first days of our new life together. It was a strange series of incredible highs and lows that would prove to be the ebb and flow of our life together. Always dramatic. Never uneventful, that's for sure.

Eventually things calmed down, and I began trying to figure out how I was going to also "make it" as an artist, especially in Maryland—which is definitely not the hotbed for artists who painted anything besides what I'd call "boat paintings," you know, pretty scenes of the Chesapeake Bay, stuff like that. I've also heard them once referred to as "couch paintings," which always struck me as pretty funny. Couch paintings—meaning, if they look good over your mother's couch, *don't do them!*

I'd later state it more profoundly in a *TED talk* in New Jersey two decades later in 2016 before a packed house at Bergen Community College, "The most important job of any artist is to draw a line from your life to your art that is straight and clear."

At this point, I hadn't stopped painting completely, but I also hadn't lined up any shows. I was still figuring out "who I was" as an artist. "What would be the thing that I'd be known for," I wondered? *So, I began drawing that line . . .*

Below (from left): Scholastic Art National Medalist art by Carley Meredith, Shanna Dunlap, Meghan Segreti, Kat Milbradt, and Hannah Larney.

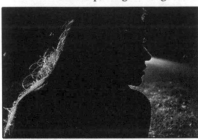

In New York City celebrating with my first five Scholastic Art National Medalists
Hannah Larney, Kat Milbradt, Shanna Dunlap, Meghan Segreti and Carley Meredith.

At the nation's first NAEA Creative Industry Studio workshops
in Washington D.C. with NAHS Officers Mikayla Hennessey,
Hannah Larney, Shanna Dunlap and Sienna Broglie.

In Washington D.C. being honored with my two back-to-back National Award Winners Louis Fratino and Katie Emmitt at the U.S. Department of Education.

Out on the town celebrating with Peter J. Gotti after being honored with my wife Lisa and my 2015 National Scholastic Gold Medalist Sienna Broglie at Carnegie Hall in New York City.

Enjoying a Gurkha Louis XIII with the Teflon Son, John Gotti, Jr. on the High Line.

At the 2016 NAEA National Convention with my 7th back-to-back National Rising Star winner Sienna Broglie in Chicago. I promised her Mom, "*No Gangsters!*" Does a late night dinner in Chinatown with Al Capone's great-nephew Dominic Capone count?

Our son, Lil' C "the Butcher" choppin' it up in his first year at the boxing gym with his trainer, Coach Wolf, at the ripe young age of just 7 years old.

Tony "Ace" Acevedo, Me, Lil' C and Autumn Wolf in training, year one. We told C to pretend like he was hitting Wolf for the photo and he clocked him! Tony laughed, "That's the best punch ever thrown in the gym!"

Lil' C was hooked on boxing since being ringside at gym favorite Sean "Rocky Lightsout" Cormier 's first fight. We'd roll with him to the Golden Gloves with Arthur Neal, Tony, Me, Lil' C, Sean's son and Clint Pratt.

Lil' C's first flight across the country to watch boxing future Hall of Famer "Sugar" Shane Mosley ringside give the fans the KO they were looking for at the Forum in L.A. In the VIP area we met the great "Showtime" Shawn Porter.

MOSLEY MAYORGA II

AT THE FORUM BROUGHT TO YOU BY CHASE

WATCH LIVE ON PPV 7PM PACIFIC
SATURDAY AUG, 29TH

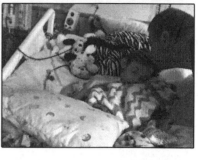

Louie with his beautiful daughter Angelina (above).
Top right: Big Nick "the Hulk" (whose son Vhito
fought Cancer alongside Angelina), me, Louie and
his eldest son Louis, Jr. at Children's Hospital in
Philadelphia one week in, fighting for a miracle.

Opposite page: Me as best man at Louie's first wedding with his crew of
Scott Phillips, Steve Malizia, Tommy Savel and Marc Sortman. Below is me,
my Dad and Tommy Navarro at the wedding. (center) With Lycoming College
mentor Roger Shipley, Seth Goodman, my Goddaughter Alex, Louie and his
Mom Marie at my Ticket to Ride opening in Williamsport. (below) Lil' C with
the Lyco Cheerleaders, and waving to the crowd in a chauffered 1929 Packard.

Outside the church at Louie's second wedding.

Carmen rescuing his new puppy Nero the week I began writing this memoir.
Middle: With my boxing trainer Arthur Neal, working on being better men.
Carmen's fascination with trains led to inspiration for works in my *31 Nights* series.

Back in my Studio working on my famous portrait commission for John A. Gotti for the cover
of his memoir, *Shadow of My Father* that made the cover of the *New York Daily News*.

My Grandma Violet picked up her paintbrushes and began winning art shows in Lyndhurst the year I was born. I followed in her footsteps winning the first art show my parents ever entered me in. I'll always be grateful to my family for sitting through all those shows with me.

Michael Bell Wins First Prize in Art Show

My Grandpa Bill was a boxer. That's him from his early days (center). Every Thanksgiving we'd all go into New York City as a family. Below is the crowd watching me draw. On right, I'm being interviewed by the press for winning 1st prize in the first art show I ever entered at age 5!

VINCENT KEARNEY, JR. 29. Numbers runner for friend Gabriel DeFranco. Accused of helping to kill both DeFranco and Judy Kavanaugh.

Bailey Ousted in Murder Trial

Paterson, N. J. –UPI– F. Lee Bailey was removed Friday as a defense attorney in a double murder trial for what the judge termed "gross unethical conduct."

F. Lee Bailey

MURDER NEW JERSEY STYLE

Top: My infamous cousin Vinnie, acquitted in the longest double murder trial in the history of the State of New Jersey. Below are my Godparents Jeannie and Billy, Lisa at *Sorrento's* with her Aunt Mary, and me with my Mom at one of my Godparents' summer pool parties.

Down the spiral staircase was my realm in our New York City Apartment
on W. 85th & Broadway. Top left is longtime Bel Air pal Mike Z. from HS.
Top right is me and Gus, Manager at *Houlihan's* on 59th & 5th Avenue,
circa '93. Top center are my NYC roommates Matt Harvey and Mike
Neyhart, and (right) out and about with Mike in Manhattan.

Above is me and my little brother Will, (right) with Lycoming College Art
Professors Roger Shipley and Jon Bogle at my Senior Show. Bottom (left)
with roomate Tony Luci and art classmate Kate, and (center) is my 38" X 44"
Lascivia oil painting that my former NYC roommate Matt Harvey owns.
Bottom (far right) me after getting my first tattoo while living in Manhattan.

At my Grandma's just hours before proposing to Lisa at *the Rainbow Room* in Manhattan. Afterwards, at Lisa's surprise engagement party with my future father-in law, Bill Molinaro, as Lisa opens her portrait.

Lisa in front of Elouise's portrait in *the Plaza Hotel* March 1, 1995. Grammy Award-Winning singer Tony Bennett autographed our wedding photo, dedicating it to us with "Because of You" . . . our wedding song.

Top: With my best man Louie and one of Lisa's bridesmaids, Christine. Then, a dance with my Mom and Lisa doing *the Tarantella* with her Dad hours before flying off to our roller coaster of a honeymoon in the Caymans. Above right, kissing Aunt Helen, mother to my infamous cousin Vinnie.

My Father and Mother, my Grandma Violet, my brother Will, and next to Lisa is her Father and Mother with Kevin (Lisa's Godfather, Victor's son).

NINETEEN

MY ROOKIE YEAR

When I began my application process for teaching, I literally applied everywhere. New York, New Jersey, Pennsylvania, Maryland, you name it. My first bite was in Maryland. Harford County wanted to interview me, so I went. The interview went great and I was promised a job verbally, so I rented an apartment early that summer and was gearing up for my first year teaching. Only, Harford County stopped returning my calls as the summer drew closer to the end, and I suddenly found myself with a year's lease on an apartment and no job. *Thanks, Harford County.*

So, I took a job waiting tables at a local *Ruby Tuesday* restaurant in Bel Air to make ends meet and I kept re-applying for jobs in education wherever I could. I was still painting, but Maryland wasn't the venue for my current body of work, which was edgy and figurative, with many of the paintings filled with sex and violence. So, for now, my dream of making it as an artist would have to wait. It was then I began drawing a line from my *parent's life* and focused finding a career in education.

Finally, one afternoon, I got a call from Southern High School, which is located in Harwood, Maryland, about sixty-three miles south of where I was living. I interviewed with them and they hired me as a part-time art teacher. What that meant was, I'd essentially be in the car more than in the classroom. Classes back then were only fifty-five minutes long, and being part-time I'd have to share a room with two other art teachers, Roxanne Weidele and Jean Teitelman, and teach in their rooms during each of their planning periods 1st and 2nd periods every day, before returning home to catch a quick cat nap and head to the restaurant at noon to work a double shift.

The principal at that time, Don Buchanan, was one of the last members of what'd I'd label as "the good ole' boys club." Having served as principal of Southern High for the last seventeen years of his career, he promised me if I did a good job, he'd hire me back full-time the following year. *He made good on his promise.*

ONE YEAR LATER, here we were, living in Maryland. I had a full-time career in its infancy, and my wife took a job at a local hair salon so we could make ends meet.

George Trotter was Principal Buchanan's right-hand-man. He was a tough, but fair assistant principal who also looked out for me, being I was new. Instead of doing what Administration now calls "walk-throughs" where they come into your room with clipboards in hand, checking off the generic *Administrivia-style* checklists before quickly exiting, leaving feedback in your mailbox in very impersonal ways, George would just pop in. And he'd stay. He'd make it a point to be in my room daily to simply make sure kids knew that *he knew* what was going on. None of his "walk-throughs" had anything to do with checklists. He preferred to just be out and about, not hiding in his office. If ever there was a "Street Boss" as I would say in my "other life" George would have fit the bill in the education world. He knew the pulse of the school and seemed to have this uncanny gift to know what was going to happen before it would happen. He made it a point to know personal things about you too, and he'd ask you about your family. He did that with every teacher. *That's just how he was.*

I guess it's the "un-teachable" qualities like George possessed that most administrators today are really lacking and need to be "re-taught". George always put you on the offensive in front of the kids, making sure your entire class knew that they should be paying attention to you because you had something to offer them. And it was *always* the students' fault with George, not *the teachers'*. That was just George though, always preaching ethics to the kids and always 100% positive with the faculty and staff. He was like Buchanan, old school in that way. I wish they made more guys just like him. Every word out of his mouth was geared towards something "great" you were doing, to pump you up. Stuff like that. This was a guy you *wanted* to work for. You *wanted* to produce for. He actually knew who all the kids were, where they lived and who was raising them.

He and Buchanan made the place feel like one big family, not some data-driven numbers crunching building that cripples their administrative staff and teachers with an exorbitant amount of endless meetings filled with minutia.

Since Don Buchanan's eighteen-year reign at Southern High, I've seen eleven different principals. Buchanan was truly one of the last of the "great ones" and I miss him.

He was a man of great character, and I learned a lot from him and from his administrative team in the one short year that I spent under his leadership.

But times were changing in Administration, and this would forever become the trend.

TWENTY

THE ADMINISTRATION

An administration at any school can really make or break the culture of a building. Over the course of my twenty-plus years I've seen them come and go due to retirements, promotions, some to demotions, deaths, you name it—on and on I could go. I will tell you this—the building I've worked in always ran its best in the Buchanan era, prior to this "new Administration era" more focused on data than on getting to know the students, teachers and the real climate of a school. Our building has actually run best when no-one has been at the helm, and I don't mean that to be sarcastic. It's just true.

More often than not, over the years and constant changes, with new groups of administration coming and going, they've always proven to just get in the way, busy working on this new initiative or that one, many which would undermine the previous leaderships', and all of which, for the most part, were putting stuff into place not based on the true needs of the kids in the school but more on what's going to make them or their superiors look good, or help satisfy their ability to "move up the corporate ladder". It's politics. Anybody who doesn't think education is economically and politically driven is living in a world with blinders on.

Typically, your staff, if they're good—and most are, deep down—will get the job done if you just stay out of their way and let them actually teach. Most teachers get into teaching because they generally want to make a difference in children's lives for the better. Now, my experience in schools as a kid would directly contradict this statement, but I'm still an optimist. I have seen my staff pull together and bond under the duress of extreme circumstances—in the form of bomb threats, racial tensions boiling over, murders and suicides. You name it—*I've seen it.*

On the other hand, those teachers who move into administration, many do it for the money, since it's the only opportunity for financial advancement in this profession, or worse—*because they couldn't hack it in the classroom.*

That's just the reality of it. Education is this weird system where there's actually no other way to become promoted from a monetary standpoint unless you go into an administrative position. I believe the structure of the overall system needs to change. And I don't mean performance-based pay. That *definitely* doesn't work. Look at what the city of Chicago churned out when moving to that model. That should have given the Government all the data they needed to know this was a bad idea, but *there's money in over-testing kids*, and where there's money to be made, kids' best interests fall to the wayside. There really needs to be a system in place that rewards growth without penalizing for lack of "student performance". Just reward great teaching—*beyond National Board Certification*, which I earned back in 2010.

And there needs to be *fewer meetings! For everyone.* Principals included. Everyone in the new "data-driven" culture has created a monster in the form of an exorbitant amount of meetings that inundate the faculty and administration with so much "extra busy work" it's virtually impossible to have any extra time to create the culture of a "family" or get to know anybody at all.

Looking to go into administration? I hope you like meetings, administrative duties and responsibilities. Here's just a few:

Athletics, Sports Boosters, Assemblies, Homecoming, Spirit Weeks, Pep Rallies, Administrative Event Coverage, Internships,

Discipline, Advocates, Behavior Interventions, Student Parking, Student Obligations, Transportation, Field Trips, Clubs and Contracts, Facility Usage, Building Repairs, Technology Liaisons, Schedulers, Parent Teacher Organizations, Teacher Duty Rosters, Work Release Liaisons, School Websites and Social Media, Pupil Personnel Liaisons, Testing, Professional Development, School Improvement Plans and Teams, Advanced Placement Programs and Teams, National Honor Societies, Attendance, Yearbook and School Publications, Faculty Council Liaison, Substitutes, Principal's Designees, 504/IEP Plan Liaisons, Equity Teams. *Oh, and did I mention testing . . . on and on it goes . . .*

Now, Southern High, I soon learned, was either someone in administration's first stop or it was their last. In our county principals get paid based on the size of the school.

Southern High, while being in the second largest county in the State of Maryland, was the smallest school in the entire county, typically capping out at only 1,100 students. South River, a school just five minutes down the road has more than double that with nearly 2,300 students.

If you were a new principal just starting out, Southern High would probably be your first assignment, and if you did well, you'd be promoted from Southern to a larger, higher paying, and more challenging school. But just because it's the smallest school doesn't mean it goes without its share of problems. It's just easier to contain them because the problems are typically coming from a smaller population than any other school in county.

So, that also meant that if you were Principal, or any administrator for that matter, and you were *sent to Southern High* from any other school in county—*it was a demotion*—make no mistake about it.

You were either being penalized for something, being placed there because it's where you could foreseeably do the least amount of damage, or you were being "forced out".

I've seen all three of these scenarios over the course of a couple decades during my tenure. At the end of the day, sadly, it's always money that dictates the job description, which person goes where in any profession for that matter, and that's how it went for our administration. So, when Don Buchanan retired in 1995, Southern became a revolving door and training ground for new principals.

I taught my very first full-time year as a newly married, second-year teacher under the leadership of our new principal, Cliff Prince. Cliff was a former middle school art teacher, turned guidance counselor, and now first-year principal. Cliff was a good guy, but, in my opinion, it was a bad move to send him to Southern for his first tour of duty.

At that time, Southern High was still very "Southern", for lack of a better word. Not much diversity, if you know what I mean. And for Southern to have their first African American principal, well, to say he wasn't met with his share of adversity would be an understatement. I personally felt like Cliff was being set up for failure. It probably didn't help that Cliff dressed impeccably sharp and owned both a Porsche and a BMW, both of which he drove to work and showed off to all the kids. I knew why he was doing it, to show them all, "Look what you can achieve", but I'm not sure everybody saw it that way.

Back then, South County was a unique place to live with a lot of proud, hard-working, blue-collar residents. It still had its *Mom and Pop* stores. There was an eclectic mix of boaters and farmers since there was an abundance of water shoring up against most areas where our kids lived in the form of the Chesapeake Bay, and there were still plenty of expansive pockets of farmland to grow crops or breed horses.

No-one that grew up in South County wanted big corporate businesses coming into town, and the locals fought hard alongside the South County Chamber of Commerce to protect the "historical" aspects of the area. A few places back then even still had tobacco farms, and since Southern High was only within twenty minutes of the Washington D.C. corridor, anybody could be sitting on prime real estate, so there was also a lot of new money beginning to be mixed with old money. Then there were several trailer parks and some families with no running water.

Now, the old money came in form of land owners that were sitting on property worth millions that were passed down through generations. But you'd never know it if you were judging them by what they looked like or what they drove. They were hard working, blue collar for the most part, and weren't planning on capitalizing on their property or ever selling it. The new money had the McMansions built in newly built neighborhoods and these kids drove to school in Daddy's Mercedes.

If you're reading this and that was you, don't get offended. *I'm not judging*. Just telling it how it is. Painting the picture of South County much the way it is even today. There were huge trailer parks right up the road from million dollar estates. You could also be a millionaire living in a newly built place right next to a shack with no running water and thirteen cars all piled up on the front lawn, twelve of them not running or up on cinderblocks. *This is just the way it is.*

And this is all due to the zoning, and how there are no neighborhood associations that people have to pay fees into that put some "quality control" into making sure people take care of their properties and maintain them. This is pandemic across most of Anne Arundel County, not just South County.

AS A TEACHER—you only get one chance at a good first impression—with your kids, your staff and your administration.

So, at our first "Back to School night" everyone eagerly awaited to "meet the new principal", especially since there hadn't been a new one at Southern High in eighteen years. I planned on making a great first impression with my new boss too. I dressed the part, wearing one of my best suits, tie, and matching kerchief—*my signature dress style.*

Funny thing was when I saw Cliff, his suit and tie ensemble was like a mirror image of mine. We hit it off immediately. He told me he was impressed with how I dressed. Said he "liked my style." That we'd have to get together, sit down and talk sometime. And we would over the next three years, quite often.

Now, this was my first year with my own room. The previous year I was just part time and shared space in Roxanne and Jean's rooms, which, for any new teacher, can be a nerve-racking experience. If you care about what you do, you also want the teachers whose room you're teaching in to see you doing a great job—and you wanted to leave their room in the condition it was before your hour of instruction began. So I did my best to "put in my time"; paying attention to every detail, and because of my work ethic, I was rewarded with a full-time job, despite my extremely small class sizes. I think Principal Buchanan just did what he said he'd do because he was a man of his word and because no-one would question his decisions. I mean, after all, the guy was an icon there.

Buchanan knew all the *muckety-mucks* (as my new head football coach buddy, Russ Meyers, used to refer to them as—you know, the big shots at the Board of Education with the fat cat salaries that you have no idea what they even do all day). He knew them all and Southern was definitely "Buchanan's school". I mean, this guy was a guy who used to stand on a step-stool in the middle of the hallways with a megaphone yelling at kids to get to class—*and they listened*. He was a former Physical Education teacher and most of the kids and their parents either respected him or feared him.

This was new territory for Cliff, though, and this being his first principalship, he was also under a microscope. At that time, I didn't understand the way "numbers worked" or how class sizes were allocated, how to recruit, how to build a program—nor did I feel it was my place to know. I mean, these decisions were up to Roxanne, the Art Department Chair back then. She had been there as Southern High's very first art teacher when the building initially opened back in 1968 and she did her entire tenure there, working for over thirty years at Southern. Who was I to question anything? She was also a well-respected, local artist in the community and was very well-liked among the kids. She was originally from Brooklyn, so we also immediately hit it off. Roxanne and Jean made me feel right at home.

They looked out for me like I was their prodigal son. But they also felt I didn't know too much and had a lot to learn, which I would agree with—but I was great with the kids. Because I was young, close in age to the kids at that time and street smart, even the roughest of kids seemed to listen to me, relate to me and gravitate towards me.

Cliff's first year we had a record high number of bomb threats. So, *times were definitely a-changin'* as the saying goes. These bomb threats were, of course, to make him look bad, all by the hand of our student body at the time, and all in retaliation for a lot of things that began taking a turn for the worse morale-wise in the building.

Cliff wanted to bring about change, bring South County into the dawn of a new era. I'd liken it to Obama's first year stepping into office as President of the United States. But, *change* wasn't what South County wanted. The white kids felt as though Cliff favored the black kids, which really wasn't the case, and the black kids thought Cliff wasn't "one of them" and was this flashy guy with a *Beamer* and a *Porsche* not in touch with his people. This was also not the case, but in education—"perception is reality".

I was also becoming too loose with discipline in my own classroom, as were other teachers in the building. Finding that balance as a new teacher is difficult. You want to be the cool teacher, but at the same time, you want to maintain law and order. Back then, everybody smoked in school and fighting that battle was becoming a major problem since we were just moving into the age of "smoking is bad for you". When I went to school even the gym teacher would smoke from his office in the gymnasium during class. This definitely was not the case these days. They were trying to stop kids from smoking in the bathrooms, and teachers were trying to stop kids from leaving class to smoke.

My new room in my second year teaching was located at the very end of G Hall, in an old auto body shop (back when they used to teach auto body at the schools) so it had its own garage, back door, and a bathroom within the room. I mean, the place was huge, and hard to manage due to its size.

I was trying my best to keep kids in class and not have them roaming the halls on my watch, so I let them use the bathroom in my room. Well, that backfired on me.

One day a kid went in there to smoke, decided not to flush his cigarette but put it out in a trash can, and set the trash can on fire, which triggered the fire alarm. Not only did the whole school have to evacuate, the sprinklers went off in my room and put the entire place under about six inches of water. The local fire department came. It was a new teacher's nightmare! Cliff even had the head custodian padlock my bathroom door shut in my room. How embarrassing is that?!

But, life went on, and so did my second year teaching—which still felt like my first, since it was my first year with my own room, and I was literally all the way across the entire school from the other two teachers in the Art Department. Roxanne and Jean were still upstairs in their rooms all the way across the other side of the building, so whenever I needed anything, I'd have to go see them on my planning period or after school because it took so long to walk from my room downstairs to theirs. But, one of the cool things was I was in the hallway with all the custodians and got to know them really well.

I always chose to eat lunch with our custodians over eating with the teachers in the faculty lounge. Who wanted to listen to negative shit in the faculty lounge on your lunch break anyways? Plus, the custodians were cool to me, and I'll tell you this—if you want to know what's really going on in your building be nice to the custodians, the secretaries, and the cafeteria staff. They know what's gonna happen in the building before it happens. And, they also know the kids—in a different light than most do, since some of the kids are, in fact, their nieces, nephews, or children even.

One of the greatest things I think I've ever been told by anyone in my school, besides from one of my kids, was a custodian. Many years after I had won "Teacher of the Year" and all that, one of them pulled me aside one morning.

"Mr. Bell—You're cool—You're cool because you never changed. You're the same man that walked in here when you first started. You always think of us (custodians), always ask me about my family. You're a good man."

What isn't cool is the opposite of that—*not knowing your kids or your staff.* Not knowing, for instance, as an administrator, when it's one of your teachers' birthdays. Especially when you decide it's time to head down to their room and tell them their position is being cut for the following year, that they are going to be effectively "excessed"—which means, *you're out of a job next year.*

This is exactly what happened to me, and it's a moment I'll never forget. I'll also never forget the administrator that did that to me. He'd later get promoted to become a principal at another school—*go figure.* He was a total jackass. I mean, *who does that?*

On my birthday of all days!

When he got my reaction, he immediately backpedaled with "I'm so sorry. I had no idea it was your birthday today."

"It's YOUR JOB to know it's my birthday!" I yelled back. "Especially if it's the day you are deciding to tell me I'm gonna be out of a job!"

What a fucking asshole. Some old ways die hard, I guess. Not the smartest thing to do—yell at your administrator. Definitely not something I'd recommend anyone else doing. But I figured I was history anyways. I was young and hot-headed. And, if he didn't give a shit about me, why not burn that bridge to the fucking ground! *It felt pretty good too.*

What was the point in holding back now anyways, after he shattered my world on my birthday, of all days?! For me, it was worse than that, though. My wife left her whole family and everybody she knew behind—*all for me*—all because I had a steady career with healthcare benefits and could provide a good life for her. An honest living, at that. Now, what did I have?

Nothing.

I was totally devastated. How was this gonna fly? What would I tell her father?

What was I going to do now?!

TWENTY-ONE

IT'S A WONDERFUL LIFE

A funny thing happened in my second year, the year that I got excessed. When I was at my lowest, a few guys came to my aid, much like Clarence did for George Bailey in *It's a Wonderful Life*.

And, much like that timeless Christmas classic, these guys would not only help save my ass, but if they didn't, a whole lot of other lives would have been changed forever, and in many cases, might never have been saved either. I love these men for what they did for me, most of all because I know it's something they didn't have to do but did anyway.

This kind of selflessness from someone I would least expect it from would prove to also become a familiar pattern in my life. *One I've also paid forward.*

If you're a new teacher, or new to whatever job you're starting at, this chapter is a testament to why it's always best to be nice to everybody and get to know everyone you can.

People skills. That's what matters most. *Trust me.*

One of the first guys I met and struck up a friendship with was Russ Meyers. Russ was also new to Southern; hired the year before I came aboard to teach Physics and take over as Head

Football Coach. Russ was from upstate New York and we were both huge Syracuse fans, and while we'd be an odd combination to peg to become close friends just by our contrasting appearances alone, fate intervened one night and he became a very dear friend to me over many years. He'd introduce me to the guys that would soon work to save my job. He'd later dole out an annual "Coaches Choice Award" at ArtQuest that has also become a fan favorite.

My friendship with Russ began under the strangest of circumstances. I was working a shift one Thursday night at *Ruby Tuesday*—still living in Bel Air, still commuting over an hour one way through my second year teaching (which I continued to do for the next ten years), *when in walked Russ . . . with some girl.*

Now Russ is someone you'd recognize right away in a crowd. He looks and sounds like a head football coach should. Kind of a cross between Andy Reid, former NFL Football Coach of the Philadelphia Eagles—and Dennis Franz, the actor famous for his role as Andy Sipowicz on the once popular TV show, *NYPD Blue.* Russ was short, heavyset, red hair, mustache, abrupt—to the point, and he didn't seem like one to turn many beers down. So, when he happened to wander into my gin-joint one Thursday night, I immediately spotted him from across the bar, watched where the hostess sat him, and quickly took him over the biggest twenty-three-ounce beer on tap.

He was totally startled—*like he just saw a ghost.*

"Funny you'd be all the way up here, some sixty miles away, no?" I said. "We work at Southern together. I've seen you around. You're the football coach, right? Least I could do was set you up with a beer. It's on me. And there's more where that came from! Whatever you want, I'll take care of you. Just let me know when you're ready for another . . ." I assured him.

I kept his beers flowing the rest of the night, and the next morning as I pulled into my parking spot behind the building where the custodians parked, near the receiving docks—*there here he was.* Standing in my spot as I pulled up—*just waiting for me.*

He immediately pulled me aside, "So listen, here's the thing. I appreciate you taking care of me last night. But, that girl you saw me with—*that wasn't my girlfriend*. Now, I'm not the kind of guy to do something like that, believe me, but my relationship has been kind of on the rocks, and I got set up on this blind date . . ."

Now I'm cracking up.

"I figured—*Bel Air*—now that's totally out of the way," he continues, "Nobody's gonna see me there! I mean, there's what, a hundred restaurants in a two-mile radius? Something like that?"

"Sounds about right," I said, listening to him rationalize.

"So, that didn't happen," he declared. "Me being at your restaurant last night—*that didn't happen, alright?*"

"I didn't see a thing," I assured him.

"I did appreciate the beers, though," he chuckled, "despite the fact that just before you dropped the first one in front of me I just got through telling my blind date how I didn't really drink much, that kind of shit. She was a nice church going girl, you know what I mean?"

"Hey, I get it. Say no more. It never happened," I reassured him.

"What was I gonna do, though, not drink them?" he laughed.

"Well, you might find me working at the bar more often than not, pretty soon. I just got cut, didn't you hear?" I told him, as we started heading into the building to start the school day.

"Really? Man, I'm sorry to hear that. Let me ask around, see what I can do for you," he said.

With that, Russ got to talking with Ray Ciupek, Science Department Chair at that time, who was also an old-timer who had been in the building quite a while. Ray also happened to be friends with John Aylor, head of the Tech-Ed Department at Southern. I think they all played golf together or something.

Aylor's room was located on the corner of G and A hall. He had two adjoining rooms. His main room was in A100, where he taught Architectural Drawing, and it was situated on the corner of the main hallway of the school. It was the first room you saw as you entered the building from the teacher's parking lot. He had a connecting room in A100 to G101, which opened out into G hall that he used as a Production Studio for one of his Tech classes.

Both rooms had hardwood floors because they both used to be part of an old gymnasium in the school. G101 even had metal chain link fencing over all the windows because it was once used as a small gym for a local elementary school that was being housed in G hall the year I was hired. I substituted for that elementary school my first year while teaching part-time and even played kickball in that room, which would later become my permanent home and future art studio for the rest of my career.

Now, Aylor and I got along great. I'd always make conversation with him whenever we passed each other in G hall over the course of my second year teaching nearby his room. He also took pride in knowing all the custodians by name and is someone I'd definitely consider a man's man—*a teachers' teacher.* John was a strong guy, intimidatingly tall with a graying goat-tee and had twenty-five years in the game. The kids all respected him. Especially the troubled ones. He gave them structure. He was tough. Firm. But likable. And he knew his shit. Especially when it came to Architectural Drawing classes.

"Heard you got excessed," he said to me in passing one day. "I think I can help." *Word traveled fast, apparently.*

"I was talking with Don Richter, Social Studies Department Chair," he explained, "He has a .4 position available, and so do I. That would mean, if you'd be interested in teaching out of area for a year, you'd have to teach two Social Studies classes—two lowest level World Civilizations classes for Don, and two Architectural Drawing classes for me. What do you think?"

"John, if it saves my job and keeps me at full-time for next year, I'd teach anything. It's either that or I tell my wife I lost my job to kick off our marriage. I'm definitely down for teaching anything that's gonna keep me full-time!"

So, Don and John went in with me to see Cliff and he went for it. Cliff liked me and wanted to keep me in the building. Our Art numbers were just so weak it didn't justify keeping me, even if he leveled out all the art classes in the Department with lower numbers. So, this is what year three would look like: Staying one Chapter ahead of my kids in *World Civ*, and doing my best to figure out what the hell I was doing in Architecture, where I wasn't just teaching a Level 1 class, it was a combined class of Levels 1—4—all in the same room, all doing different projects.

Today, they'd call that "differentiated instruction." For me, it was called flying by the seat of my fucking pants teaching seven preps. But I was good at doing that. Working in the restaurant business helped me to learn to do that. Being street smart and living in New York City helped me learn how to do that too.

Talk about learning how to multi-task! That's what it was all about in that Architectural Drawing class. It felt more like I was bartending than teaching. Everybody needed something different and I had to figure out ways to do it seamlessly and appear in charge, even though I clearly didn't feel that I was.

"There are many of you here in this room," I explained to them one day, "that quite frankly, know a lot more about Architectural Drawing than me. I'm going to learn it though, and I'm going to do my best to help you go above and beyond with Mr. Aylor's help, but I'm also going to need some of you to help me out in here. You upper-level kids—I'm gonna need your help teaching some of the Level 1 kids. And if you help me, I'll be able to help you faster," I asked of everyone.

And they all bought in. We got along. We made it work. They respected my being straight up with them from the beginning and they all helped me out. It was a great group of kids that I'd continue forming strong bonds with, some that would last a lifetime. Kids like Shean Prunier, who went on to graduate and later did three tours of duty as a sharp-shooter in Iraq.

He called me on New Year's Eve from across the globe and wrote me letters while he was away just to let me know he was still alive and thinking of me. On Shean's birthday in 2016, I sent him a picture of one of his letters I kept. His reply:

> "Thanks to you talking to me like a man and treating me like one [in high school] it made me make a man's decision and do something with my life instead of wasting it. We'll meet up again my friend. Thank you. – *Shean*"

Then there was Nick Finnamore, who came from a big Italian family in South County. He was a kid I was always getting out of trouble with our administration. His mother would call me before she'd even call the office after a while. His family would later do my Professional Artist business cards for me, and I'd later teach his younger nieces, nephews, and cousins and be invited to his family cookouts.

And then there was Chuck Grower, who at that time I taught first in my Architectural Drawing class, but later in my Art classes, and I still also remain friends with him to this day, just like the others. Chuck was originally from upstate New York, near Buffalo, and we also hit it off immediately because of our New York connection.

And, naturally, every time I'd pass that lovely administrator that I tore a new one after excessing me on my birthday, I'd simply smile a little "all-knowing smile," the kind that says, "Thought you were getting rid of me, didn't you." He'd shake his head at me.

He probably couldn't believe I was still there after all that. I know he wasn't out and out trying to get me when he did what he did, it was just the incompetence of it all that left a bad taste in my mouth. Can you blame me?

So, advice to any bosses out there reading this, if you're going to fire someone, check and make sure it's not their birthday. Because that's a lousy thing to do.

After all those strings that those guys took the time to pull for me—*look at my career now.*

Look at where I've come from and what I've built.

Imagine what never would have happened, had guys like these not come to my aid and gone above and beyond what they had to do in order to "create an opportunity" for me? It's rare these days for anyone to go out of their way for someone else, let alone a young kid fresh out of college who hadn't even proven himself yet in the education arena. This would prove to be one of my greatest opportunities, and one I would seize, and never take for granted.

Imagine all the lives I would never have been able to help. Some years, I can honestly say, *it's a wonderful life.* Now it was totally up to me to capitalize on this opportunity.

There was a reason I went from a .4 part-time position to a full-time position right back to part-time in art. But numbers were numbers. It was just business. So, now I'm looking at the big picture. I asked myself "what are we missing?" What would be a "game-changer?" It soon became obvious. There was no art show at Southern.

Now I know a lot of schools have "Art nights" where they collaborate with different departments, some schools even put on a show. But we had nothing at Southern.

This could be the game-changer.

This could be my contribution to our department.

My future legacy.

JOHN AYLOR
TECH ED DEPARTMENT CHAIR (1980—2011)

"Teaching in an electives area in a public school system as a young teacher is precarious at best. This type of position requires an instructor who is competent, enthusiastic and most of all flexible. This flexibility can require an instructor to teach out of area in order to keep a full position. This becomes one of the principal's most difficult parts of their job description—determining next year's staff.

Back in the late 1990's, the Art Department took its first cut, shortly after Michael Bell joined his new department. Being the head of Southern's Technology Education department, I requested to have Michael teach Architectural Drawing in order to keep his full-time job. Our principal, Don Buchanan said to me, 'We have to keep our good new teachers here!' We were all on board.

It is easy to determine who is a 'born teacher' and Michael fits that bill. Michael even told me once how he and his family finished off his own basement in his new home. So, he has a practical domain that welds well with his artistic nature (a great formula for teaching Architecture, I thought).

The class went seamlessly. I'd go into the class and see the students were on task and enjoying their work. I loved teaching Architecture for several decades and I knew when I got these students at the next level after Michael taught them, they were ready.

I consider Michael a very good friend and have enjoyed watching his vision for the Art Department grow."

TWENTY-TWO

ARTQUEST

In 1998, in just my third year teaching, all the while teaching only part-time in art—I created *ArtQuest*, Southern High's first annual student art exhibition. This would also prove to be an important part of my legacy.

I first pitched the idea to Roxanne and Jean and they were excited about it. I then pitched it to our principal, Cliff, and since he was an Art guy, he also loved the concept. Said he'd even donate $100 towards food, refreshments, some grapes, cheese platters, and stuff like that. He even brought a boom box and a bunch of Jazz CDs to play at our first opening (this was before *YouTube, Pandora* and live streaming). More importantly, I pitched it to the kids and they were incredibly excited!

I felt as though if we created an art show that was unlike any other, it would create a spark, and also become "a reason" for kids to take art beyond whether they liked a particular art teacher or not, and beyond what classes they liked or didn't like. This would become a place for them to showcase their talents, and do something big for the community to also see.

With that said, these things take a lot of behind the scenes work, and they take money if you want to do it right. So, for the first year, I agreed to do the show in the Media Center, since the art teachers who taught the biggest populations in the building (Roxanne and Jean) were both upstairs. This was definitely not my first choice, but as long as everyone agreed to get their kids involved, who was I to complain? *Baby steps, right?*

And, in 1998, Southern was due to get another school housed within a wing of our building the following year. Just the eighth graders from Southern Middle School this time, which I'll tell you in advance, was a disaster of monumental proportions. Whoever decided *that was a good idea*—to put eighth graders in the same building *as seniors*—they must have sat a little too long in their Supervisor's cubicle.

I mean, not just for the immaturity factor, but for *the dating factor alone*, this was a very bad idea. It got gross too, *really fast*. But, let's not get sidetracked here . . .

With the new knowledge that eighth graders would be coming to Southern next year, I decided the best time to launch our first ArtQuest was on an incoming eighth grade Parent Information Night. At least we were guaranteed some attendance, right? I also invited the Music Department to play some string instruments during the evening, and we lined the place with easels and a few display panels we built. It became just one big group show. No major prizes being given away, just ribbons for the first, second, third and honorable mention. The night was a success.

This did for our Art Department exactly what I thought it would do—it sparked renewed interest in kids taking Art throughout the building and as a result, I was promoted back to full-time again the following year, this time just in art. *Our numbers really grew.*

The next year Roxanne announced she was retiring. Cliff called me into his office.

"Roxanne came in to see me today," Cliff explained. "She says she wants me to put Jean in as Department Chair next year."

"Sounds good to me, Cliff," I responded. "I appreciate you taking the time to let me know."

Jean and I got along great. So now, all I wanted to do was to help make ArtQuest continue to grow, do a great job taking over the painting and drawing classes for Roxanne and support Jean and our Department as best I could. But I also knew there was only one way for the show to grow. *We had to change the location.*

So here's where having a strong vision comes in. Be sure and always listen to yours. *Never doubt it.*

When I first came up with the concept for ArtQuest, I envisioned the entire community showing up. I envisioned having numerous categories with lots of prize money. I envisioned it being a place to showcase the best artists in the school, not just make it an "everybody gets a gold star" type of environment. Something more competitive, but also equitable and accessible to all kids.

I also wanted to market the show. Make it bigger than anyone ever imagined it could be. The quiet, serene environment associated with the Media Center wasn't the place for it, but while Roxanne was still here, I played along and kept it there for one more year. But, once she announced retirement, I'd be taking over the painting and drawing classes. I had to make some major moves. The first one being—*my art room location.*

Aylor offered up G101 to me, which was that room with the adjoining door to his, the one with the palladium style floor to ceiling windows with north lighting and hardwood floors. I knew instantly this would be my new home.

Roxanne petitioned to move me upstairs into her old room next to Jean, but I wanted my move to be into G101 next to John. It was a "guy's hallway". No drama. Just men. I loved being in that hall. And the room was an Art studio just waiting to happen. It was also in an area of the building no administration ever came because there were no problems. We handled our own, and they left us alone down there (excluding the time that kid almost set the room on fire down in G104 my second year teaching).

But, I had learned from my mistakes, and kids were starting to know and respect me in my third year. I figured we could hire someone new and have them go upstairs in Roxanne's old room.

Cliff agreed that the decision on where I was to go when Roxanne retired wasn't anybody's but mine and despite the fact that I was being met with some resistance on what I wanted to do. Ultimately I knew deep down what was in my best interests, and I stuck with my gut and stayed downstairs in G101 to grow our program from there. This was better, due to the room's proximity to everything in the building, so I proceeded to *sell the sizzle!*

HOW DO YOU SELL THE SIZZLE? Step one—*sell the dream.* Share with everyone what ArtQuest could mean for our school and community to the public at large, and then change the location of the show to a larger venue, which, in my case became the cafeteria. I planned on transforming it completely and filling it with the kids' artwork for an epic one-night show. The cafeteria is literally is right outside my door off of my G Hall corridor, and it was on the first floor, not too far from the main entrance to the school, which would also help with attendance. I mean, nobody was realistically going to try and *find ArtQuest* by trekking through the school all the way upstairs to the Media Center.

Step two—*fundraise!* We needed money, so the following year I planned to start finding ways to purchase stuff to make the show even bigger. While we may not have had money in the budget to pay for mats to frame up the artwork really nice, or for prize money (which I thought would be the thing that would really sell the show to the kids) we certainly could go out and get it!

And not by selling candy or *Joe Corbi's Pizzas* either.

I wanted to make some *real cash.* So, I called around, eventually met with the Director at Homestead Gardens, which was one of the largest local garden centers in the area, and asked if they wanted face painters for their upcoming Fall Festival the following school year. They said "Absolutely!" So, I asked if we could charge $1 or 1 ticket per design and keep 100% of the proceeds for the school's art department as a fundraiser for ArtQuest. They felt it was a win-win. So, my partnership with Homestead Gardens was born.

That next fall we raised around $2,000 face painting over the course of four weekends. Plenty of cash to set up numerous awards categories for the kids. Also, plenty to start ordering large quantities of canvas, stretcher strips, and oil painting supplies. I wanted to get these kids painting on large 4' X 4' canvases in oils like I was with my own art. Finally, we could do more. During the weekends I spent out there in the field with my kid's face painting I was able to form bonds with them.

This ultimately became an annual tradition and one that allowed me to get to know my kids on a deeper level, outside of the classroom. They'd help me spread the message about ArtQuest. They'd help rally around my vision for where our program was headed.

Since then, I've added a summer fundraiser, working the Annapolis Irish Festival and I secured a second face painting location, *Greenstreet Gardens*, which helps our Department earn around $5,000 in face painting annually. You'll never hear our Department complaining about the lack of funds, low budgets to work with, or not having any materials. We simply go out and get it! We fend for ourselves and our kids have it all! They go without nothing! In addition, we began selling ArtQuest t-shirts to support the show and selling program ads to local sponsors.

Step three—*make a quality hire*. And, in the spring of 1999, Jean and I made one in Marlene Kramer. She's taught alongside me ever since and did an amazing job breathing some enthusiasm into that third position, as well as some new energy into the ninth graders in our entry level Foundations of Art classes. She had this amazing energy about her!

As a result, I could just focus on developing our Drawing and Painting program, which truly is the crux of *any* great program. Hiring Marlene made the ultimate trifecta! She moved into Roxanne's old room, where she and Jean hit it off great and we rock-and-rolled like this for another seven years until Jean finally retired and Marlene moved next door into Jean's old room.

Let this be your motivation to you to do what you envision. *Dream it. Create it. Become it.*

Because I'll tell you this, every single idea I initially had for ArtQuest—every idea that was totally shot down for reasons like "We don't have money for this or that, it's wasteful . . . we can't give away prize money for awards—it's just money going out the window . . . the show will create an environment where there are winners and losers. It's too competitive. We can't do the show in the cafeteria. It's too big of a space and too much work for a one night show . . ."

Well, despite all these initial concerns from lots of different people, it all worked. *Everything*.

So, never let anyone deter you from your dreams, if you believe it in your heart and imagine it in your mind. It's what I've done, and ArtQuest has since become one of the largest and most community inclusive student art exhibitions in the country.

Now we not only showcase students and give out awards totaling $2,000 in one night in over sixty—yes, SIXTY different categories! We also get local businesses to donate prizes towards our cause, like Art Things, Inc. in Annapolis, Homestead Gardens, and Greenstreet Gardens.

These great businesses became major sponsors annually.

THE NEW MILLENNIUM YEAR OF 2000 became the pivotal year we moved to the cafeteria and was the first year we announced a "Best of Show" category; one that would have that student's name engraved on a large plaque I bought for each subsequent winner thereafter.

Our first official "Best of Show" winner was Zoe FitzSimmonds. She also became the first student I was able to get into a college—my alma mater—Lycoming College.

She'd go on to study under my former mentor, Roger Shipley. She and I have kept in touch over the years and I even got to attend her Senior Show of amazing large figurative paintings. She was really special to me.

I only taught Zoe for one year while at Southern, but to take her from where she was into painting a series of huge 4' X 4' canvases for ArtQuest to getting her into college was a huge accomplishment for me.

What started out small—*grew*—*exponentially!*

We grew so large we've expanded the show into the main lobby, into the cafeteria lines, and into the alcoves of the Auditorium just across from the cafeteria. We even have a stage with a huge backdrop of sponsors and our very own Red Carpet for kids to take selfies on before the show starts. We created a "Community People's Choice Award" with a suggested donation of $2 per vote, all proceeds going to the student artist with the most votes.

I even got the Faculty in on it, getting them to throw in for a "Faculty People's Choice" Award. The administration wasn't left out either, as they contribute $100 towards an "Administrator's Choice Award". Why get all these different groups to contribute? Because I wanted the entire faculty and administration to have a reason to come out and see the show, see these kids in a totally different light, many of them in a light they've never seen before. If they contributed funds towards something, they would have a vested interest in seeing the return on their investment—which would literally show its face on the smiles of the kids chosen for their selected winning category.

Nearly a thousand people in the community poured out. And we've continued to grow, while still keeping ArtQuest 100% free to the public. It's better attended than most football games.

We've also grown to exhibit not only Southern High's talented student artists but we also now showcase the Southern Middle School artists and Elementary feeder schools. We've even been able to give our National Art Honor Society students a showcase to highlight their scholarships; announcing them to the packed house on the stage.

Along the way, we also found a way to differentiate the Advanced Placement rock stars from the pack of other kids participating in the show too, in order to give them some street cred, if you will. They now get their own exhibit space, which they have to invent or build.

When the show first started, we simply had everybody lumped together in one large group show. Now, we lump the intro level students together, which includes Foundations of Art, Studio 1 & 2 students (2D and 3D), with Photography 1 & 2 students also exhibiting work on panels together. Level 1 & 2 photo students are allowed to print 5" X 7" and 8" X 10", while our year-long honors Level 3 students can print 11" X 14", and AP students have no size restrictions.

This was all purposeful; intended to make kids want to move up in level in order to show their work in a larger capacity and eventually earn the "AP challenge", which is to create their own "solo exhibition" somewhere within the cafeteria. And let me tell you, they bring it! These are some of the most conceptually as well as technically exceptional works and displays you'd ever want to see, from Drawing to Painting to Photography to 3D. One photography student last year, Nate Huber, actually built a huge barnwood backdrop with a metal awning. He even brought in hay bales to exhibit his AP Photography Concentration on, since it fit with his theme of nature, hunting, and fishing. Bob Costa, then member of the House of Delegates, bought Nate's entire display.

In 2011 Seth Millman created his own newsstand, which made sense conceptually, with his work being on cardboard and newsprint, and he even created flyers that read: "Seth's Newsstand." He passed them out to the public as they entered ArtQuest in order to get people to come see his work.

In 2012 Paige Shryock was the first one to venture into the cafeteria lines. She had this vision to put up panels with white sheets behind her photos. Her work contained a lot of imagery with sheets in them since her theme was about "the Dreamworld".

So, I asked Terry Rigsbee, head of the cafeteria, if that was okay and she said sure! That's how quickly things can happen and change the course of everything. Students have been showing in the cafeteria lines every year since. Paige went on to do a collaboration with me for her BFA Thesis Exhibition at *Ole Miss*.

We grew so much over the following years so we began creating an online presence. I started my own website around

1998 or so, and in turn, I started promoting our students' work online. As the show grew, especially after our first tremendous show in the cafeteria in 2000, a funny thing happened—the world beyond the walls of Southern High and the immediate community started to take notice. This led to a phone call that came in one day that went kind of like this . . .

"Hello, is this Michael Bell?" this woman asks.

"Yes, this is Michael."

"Hi Michael, I'm Kathy Kahre. President of ArtQuest, Incorporated, based out of St. Louis. Are you the one that's promoting something about *ArtQuest*?"

I wasn't sure exactly where this was headed. "Ummm, yes, that would be me," I said, hesitantly.

"Did you realize when you started this show that you're infringing on a Registered Trademark? I'm the owner ArtQuest, and we've gone to great lengths over the years to protect our name . . ."

"Ms. Kahre," I quickly interrupted, "Please let me explain. It's a kid's show. It's not a business or anything . . . a high school student art show that I started up a couple years ago."

"A kid's show?" she hesitated for a momentary thought. "Ok, tell me more about it . . ."

"I would love to!" . . . and so I went on to tell her all about it, how I didn't know anything about the name *ArtQuest*, it was just something I made up for the kids here, locally.

I was hoping we weren't going to have to change it since it was just finally starting to stick with the kids and with the community, but I also understood it was her right to shut us down. I actually appreciated the fact that she called me and didn't simply send a "Cease and desist" letter, which would have been her prerogative, and would be the case in most instances today.

What she did next blew me away.

"Michael, it sounds like you're doing a wonderful thing down there for those kids. How would you like to be *the only one* who has permission to use the name *ArtQuest*, for your kids' show?"

I was elated!!!

To top that, she also cut us a check for $500 to put towards prize money on her behalf. I've put her picture in our program and give the audience some of her "words of wisdom" every year since. And each year since she's also sent us a check, as a donation to help support the prize money we dole out to kids at the show. How amazing of a woman is this! Talk about turning a negative into a positive! It's things like that, when they happen, that restore your faith in humanity and make the job worth doing.

So the year 2000 was a pivotal year, and a wonderful one, with ArtQuest being such a huge success.

But also one marred in tragedy . . .

TWENTY-THREE

ST. PATRICK'S DAY

O n March 17th, it's a "given" in the United States that everyone pretty much celebrates St. Patrick's Day, whether you're Irish or not. Me, being half Irish, I'd also get into the spirit of things, if for no other reason—for my father, who hailed from Belfast. Our student population was no different. Give teenagers an excuse to drink, and they'll party. And, there were always quite a few South County kids that typically partied pretty hard.

Keith Rogers was a rock star art student of mine, and he was definitely going places, much like his classmate Zoe who went on to win ArtQuest that year. Both had a tremendous amount of natural ability. Both painted epic floor-ceiling murals in my room.

Keith was a graffiti artist initially but I turned him into a painter. I imagined him going off to college, much like Zoe, for art. He loved working large and I was just the man to help him hone his skills since I also loved creating large scale murals.

The first one I ever did was back in '98, the same year I created ArtQuest. I truly felt at that point in my artistic career, the most important thing you could do was to get your work seen, get it out in the public eye. I thought that if I could just get my work on some huge building for the world to see, it would lead me to super stardom, and I was pushing this concept with my kids while also trying to lead by example.

My wife, Lisa, was working at a small hair salon on the outskirts of Baltimore at that time. This guy Jerry just happened to sit in her chair one day and explained to her how he recently bought a large nightclub on Route 40 called *Attitudes 3000*. It was along a busy corridor for people commuting in and out of Baltimore City. She told him about me and my art, and he said he wanted to do something to the outside of the place to spice it up.

So, we held a meeting, I sealed the deal and I painted what is still, to this day, the largest mural I've ever done all by myself—all with brushes, no spray cans.

It's over ten feet in height and stretches close to a football field's size in length. The mural was a tropical theme, with Tiki torches by the entrance doors, cascading waterfalls, grottos, palm trees lining back into the distance to create depth, things like that. It turned out great. It was my largest commission to date at that time. This also led to more mural jobs.

I ended up doing two large murals in the children's bedrooms of a doctor's home. Then, a *Roman Baths* theme against the backdrop of a spa-tub styled bath in another woman's home. I even did a huge *Ancient Ruins of Rome* mural in our townhouse which traveled from an overhang beam over into a large slanted sunroom wall. I'd show my kids my work, and in turn, it would inspire them to want to do the same.

So, when Keith, Zoe, and a couple other kids (Nancy Pullman and Rachel Thompson) wanted to create murals like mine, I figured what better place to start than in my room. My studio was huge, and with my hardwood floors and north lighting, it was ideal for some murals to add some ambience to the space.

Since I was still in the building stages of our program, and since this was my first year in my new studio space, I figured it would be the perfect time to supervise these kids as they painted some murals. I could even pitch in when they needed help. After all, since finishing the huge mural on a very challenging textured wall at Attitudes 3000, I trained myself on what works and what doesn't, and how to make a textured wall work in your favor, especially using cinderblocks to your advantage, which is what most high school walls are built with. There are lots of dimples, so instead of working against it, I learned to work *with the dimples* by painting the first coat a slightly darker color and then by brushing over it delicately with a lighter color it created the effect of blending. This became an easier way of working for me. So I also taught this trick to my four students painting their first murals.

Nancy and Rachel created one on two walls in the back corner of my studio of a castle, a sky, rocks, water, and things like that. Zoe tackled the very back alcove of the room of the Golden Gate Bridge in fiery reddish-yellow colors lighting up the sky, and then she went below the bridge with the lower half of the mural, creating an underwater scene in contrasting bluish greens. Keith tackled the wall adjacent to Zoe's mural. He began one of his huge rocky landscape scenes.

On St. Patrick's Day, Keith went out and partied with some friends a little too hard. He made it home safe but then went back out late that night after receiving a phone call from a friend of his. By this point in the night he was well beyond the legal limit, definitely shouldn't have gone back out driving anywhere, but he did, and he lost control of his car and died tragically that night.

This was my first experience losing one of my students.

Unfortunately, the word "first" is the operative word here. There have been more since Keith, too many in my opinion. But, when it came to Keith, it was especially hard being we were really close, and I knew his family.

I was asked to speak at his funeral.

That, too, was a first. *It was heartbreaking.*

I'll never forget my principal, Cliff, coming down to my room, telling me to leave early—go over and represent Southern at the funeral.

"They don't want me there," Cliff explained. "You're who needs to be there. Go. Don't leave me any plans. Just go. Do your thing. I'll watch your classes myself."

And he did. I told him he should pick up a paintbrush again while in my room. Instead, he wrote me this long letter explaining how sad what happened was, how he wished he was back in the art room again inspiring kids like I was, not disciplining them as he was at his current position. I still have his letter to this day.

MARCH 22, 2000
Cliff Prince

"Mike, I didn't mind at all sitting in for you today. I know that when 'the boss' is nice and does the same thing as his staff, it is difficult for people to accept (without thinking, 'What is he up to?') Actually, I am a nice person who is willing to do what's necessary to get the job done. You actually did me a favor today because you could much more appropriately represent the school during this time of bereavement—You have a special bond. I appreciate all that you do for the kids. You remind me of me when I taught— fewer problems than most teachers, great relationship with the kids and community . . . You will find that once you are in my position, and this is just a matter of time, you will know about that which I speak. By the way, the class went well. Again, thanks, *Cliff*

P.S. – I really wasn't in the mood to be creative today. I had an alcohol bust yesterday and a drug bust today (*marijuana*). It was too blatant to ignore. I keep catching them as they do their thing."

WHILE CLIFF WAS BUSY WATCHING MY CLASSES as he wrote me this letter, here I walked into the funeral—greeted by tons of paintings done by Keith spread out throughout the reception area.

I met with his parents first, giving them a hug and kiss. I remember all these eyes on me as I walked through the packed house to greet his parents and view his body.

All my art kids were there, and some I didn't know, watching what I was doing, looking for cues as to what *they should be doing—following my lead.*

I also remember seeing the kid who urged Keith to head back out again that fateful night to meet up with him, despite the fact Keith was way too drunk to be driving anywhere. It infuriated me just to see him here at the funeral.

"What was this asshole doing now?!" I thought to myself, as I watched him, amidst all the tears and condolences being spread around. He was busy running around asking people for hair gel that he said he needed to fix Keith's hair.

This kid was just an asshole through and through right to the end. It was also something that sparked a memory from my own Grandfather's funeral. How everyone was trying to fix my own Grandfather's hair.

My Grandfather had this wild, wavy full head of hair right up until his death, and everyone felt the funeral parlor combed his hair "too perfect." It was "too slicked back and straight." They wanted to mess it up a little and bring back its natural waviness. It was the strangest thing to remember from my Grandfather's funeral, but it's actually one of the only things I really remember about it.

These thoughts also took me back to my Godfather's funeral. He died young from emphysema and stuff brought on from years of smoking and drinking. I remember seeing all these people, some relatives, some friends of our family, all standing outside the day of his funeral smoking their brains out. I thought, "How disrespectful."

My Godfather just died of smoking, and here everybody is, *outside smoking*. I remember thinking, as only a kid probably does at that time, "Why can't they wait? Have some respect for my Aunt Jeannie who is burying her husband. Can't they hold out one hour without a cigarette to go smoke on their own time, and not do it at my Godfather's funeral?"

But, like Chazz Palminteri said in his famous film, *A Bronx Tale—nobody cares.*

So, as I watched the "hair gel" situation play out, it literally took every ounce of my being not to just toss this asshole the fuck out of there, right then and there. Believe me, I wanted to. *Badly*.

But what would that have done for the student body, for Keith's family, for my reputation for that matter? So, I just bit my tongue, figured karma will take care of this douchebag one day, like many of the others that have crossed my path. I just took a deep breath and focused on what I was going to say about Keith when it was my turn at the podium.

Later that spring, I spent the better part of an evening painting over Keith's half-finished mural with multiple coats of lead white wall paint. I'd organize a showing of his work at ArtQuest, and do a nice spread for the newspaper on him, but his mural couldn't stay. It was something that was becoming an unspoken issue in class every single day. I'd notice kids just getting lost in, *staring at it*. A piece never to be finished. A constant reminder of *wasted talent*. It was killing my kids to look at it. It was making them sad, and me sad. So, I painted over it. I cried to myself as I did. The first brush stroke being the hardest.

If you X-Rayed my wall I imagine you'd still see it there, beneath layers upon layers of white exterior wall paint. For me, I still see it. It's always there, even to this day, as is Keith—in my heart and in my thoughts. And, like a lot of kids, I still, to this day, don't party on St. Patrick's Day because of it. It's amateur hour out there anyways. *Definitely not my scene*.

I'll always think of Keith on St. Patrick's Day, though.

CHUCK GROWER
CLASS OF 2000

"We're all products of place. Products of our environment. Shaping our experiences and framing up how much bleakness or how much hope surrounds us.

These are words from a man that means much more to me than one page can express. I first met Michael Bell in 1997 as my 9th-grade Architectural Drawing teacher. I had an instant connection to him. Since he wasn't much older than me, and a fellow New Yorker, when he spoke I definitely connected and listened.

Flash forward to 2000, my senior year of high school. During the same year, I lost a friend of mine and a fellow student in Keith Rogers. I had never lost anyone I knew in my life at that point and didn't know how to deal with my feelings at the time. It was the very next Monday after the passing and one of my teachers wanted to have a discussion about the passing with our class.

During the discussion, a fellow classmate shared an opinion on the passing I did not quite agree with. After hearing his opinion I completely lost it and had to be removed from the classroom. Shortly after being removed I met with Mr. Bell outside of his classroom. Instead of reprimanding me for losing it in one of my classes he hugged me and calmed me down.

He said to me, 'Every person has to deal with their choices. Your friend made that choice, sadly. He was headed down a dangerous path.'

He then said that he would have been heartbroken to hear if that would have been me. These words have been with me ever since. Fifteen years later, Mr. Bell is still very much a huge inspiration in my life and I will always be honored to call him family!"

TWENTY-FOUR

THE HAMMER

Some of what Cliff eluded to in his letter to me the day he covered my class so I could attend Keith Roger's funeral—the part where he says, "You will find that once you are in my position, and this is just a matter of time, you will know about that which I speak," well, that was Cliff referencing him grooming me for administration, to follow in his footsteps.

He saw something special in me early on, and so I began taking coursework in Administration and Supervision at Loyola College. He even had me substituting for various Administrators when they needed to be out of the building for meetings and such numerous times throughout the year to get some experience behind the wheel, so to speak. I even substituted for him as principal of Southern High for an entire week when he was out of town. And, I did a good job.

The faculty loved when I was at the helm. They could actually teach when I was in power. Mostly because of the fact that not only did I have a great relationship with all the kids in the school, they also knew when I had my walkie-talkie with me I wasn't just playing the role. If they messed up, I was there to dole out punishment. I wasn't there as their friend, or as someone that would sit them down for a therapy session. All the stuff that made me great as a teacher wouldn't work in administration. Up there I was known as "the Hammer". And I brought it down. *On anyone.*

I bounced so many kids out on suspension my first day at the helm that the rest of the week I was literally bored to tears, combing the hallways, popping into classrooms just looking for something to do. I figured this must have been how my former administrator George Trotter had all that free time to visit my classes when I first came to Southern. He handled things the same way. And, since I didn't have to answer to any of Cliff's "higher-ups" for suspending too many kids from school, what's the worst thing that could happen to me? Send me back to the classroom? Please, do me the favor! In hindsight, I was probably daring them to. Truth is, I never really wanted to follow in those footsteps.

Then came along this one kid, let's call him *Benny.* A pretty tough kid, according to the other teachers and kids, but also a typical bully, which to me meant—*probably not so tough.* He was also giving every teacher he had *major problems.* He already made at least two trips to the office before 9 A.M. every single day, either for threatening a kid in his 1ˢᵗ period class, another for his 4ᵗʰ lateness to his 2ⁿᵈ period teacher's class, stuff like that. So, I tried to "scare him straight" into following the rules.

"I'm not playing around with you! You get another tardy, you're suspended!" I told him. Our policy back then stated that on tardy number five you're automatically suspended—the fourth was an after school detention, which I knew he wouldn't show up to serve. Prior to that—on your third it was detention with the teacher, which of course, he'd never show up for either.

So I continued, "You threaten another kid, you're gonna have to deal with me!" I made it crystal clear for him not to show up in my office again the rest of the week, let alone the rest of the day.

He didn't say much at all in response to this, didn't even look me in the eye, kind of shrugging the whole meeting with me off. Shortly afterwards, I had him escorted back to class.

Now, looking at this kid's file, it was a train wreck. Funny thing was, he had a girlfriend who was the sweetest kid ever, and she came from a really nice family who supported our annual ArtQuest, and even she couldn't help him.

He was spiraling wildly out of control. Even I could see it. As a kid, I had been there too. And, looking at the size of his file I knew I'd probably see him again, so I prepared for him. This one particular day, he finally did wind up back down the office after being physically pulled off a kid in his 3rd period class for another bullying altercation (which was becoming a daily occurrence). Apparently, he was flicking stuff at some kid who finally confronted him verbally for messing with him and so he retaliated, jumping up, tossing his desk over and getting in the kid's face. The teacher had separated them in time, but this was it for him. He obviously didn't take me at my word.

This was the last straw.

After I was radioed down to the classroom to get him, I immediately did what I felt would be the opposite of what he'd be waiting for. While he was probably waiting for me to lay into him, I didn't say a thing—the entire uncomfortable walk back to the main office—*not one word.*

As we arrived back at my office, I asked the Administrative Secretary who was stationed just outside my door to take a break. "Go grab lunch, whatever you want," I said, "but don't come back for an hour." She looked at me, and at the kid, kind of puzzled by the request, but obliged and left.

This made him curious. *And a little nervous.*

Next, as we entered the office I asked him to have a seat. I quickly yelled over, "Can you hear us over there?" to the Business Manager at the time who shared an adjoining wall with mine.

"Yes I can, Mr. Bell, what do you need?" she replied.

"Can you take a lunch break for me? We could use some privacy. Maybe an hour?"

"Sure thing, let me just get my things and lock up."

Once she was gone, he was starting to get fidgety in his chair.

I proceeded to walk over and grab a sheet of black construction paper and a roll of masking tape that was laying in front of him on my desk that I had grabbed from my art room prior to his returning to the office. He turned, curious now as to what the hell I was up to, and watched me proceed to cover the clear glass partition window that allowed someone the ability to look inside the office with the black construction paper.

Then, I took my keys out, proceeded to make a big show of my locking the door from the outside so no-one could get in, trying the lock several times to make sure it was secure.

Now he was starting to sweat.

I then made my way back to my desk, still not saying one word to him, and I began taking off my jacket, then my watch, then I unbuttoned my sleeves, rolled them up, then loosened up my tie . . .

"What's goin' on here?! What's this all about?" he barked.

"You're such a tough guy. Pickin' on all these kids that are smaller than you that won't fight back . . ."

"What're you talkin' about? I'm not gonna fight YOU!" he exclaimed.

"What happened to the tough guy tellin' all those kids to go fuck themselves? That you're gonna kick their fucking asses in front of the whole class. Where's that tough guy?!"

Now, I had no intentions to ever lay a hand on Benny, nor would I have even if he did decide to take a swing at me. That's territory *I'm trained* in handling, from my youth. But I wanted to see what he was really all about.

And up until now, Benny had built up such a wall that even those closest to him couldn't scale. It was a familiar wall I had once built around myself at his age. It's how I recognized it so easily. But what happened next shocked even me—he slumped down in his seat and broke into tears. Not out of fear, but a legitimate breakdown of probably everything he had been going through in his life up until right then.

"You don't understand!" he screamed out to me. "You just don't understand what I gotta go back home to! Suspend me, do what you gotta do. I don't care. Just, don't hit me," he cried.

Then it was me, shedding tears for this kid who shared a piece of himself with me I knew nobody else got to have.

His guard was completely down, the mask was gone. And so was mine. Now we were just two people left alone to figure this thing out. I wasn't his principal anymore. I wasn't his teacher. I was now more to him than any adult in that building, perhaps even in his life was, simply because I cared. I cared enough to go to the furthest extremes just to get him to open up to me.

"Just so you know, Benny, I wouldn't have hit you even if you had taken a swing at me," I told him as we hugged. "What happened to your parents anyway? *Tell me what happened . . .*"

He proceeded to tell me *his story*. I quickly figured out where all his anger came from. I understood it well. Now I just wanted to help him. And I could tell he knew I wouldn't bullshit him either. He spent three years of his career at Southern racking up this tremendous discipline file, but no-one knew his story—*no-one until me*. And look at what it took to get it out of him.

"You're just a kid. It's not your fault. None of this is your fault," I assured him. And, from that moment on, *he believed me*. I also got more involved in his life, and stayed in it, long after that day.

I sat down with every one of his teachers over the next week to shed a new light on him and his story, in hopes they'd give him a second chance.

They respected me enough as one of their own, so they agreed to work with him for me. I promised them he wouldn't behave the way he'd been behaving for them up until this crucial turning point in his life. Administration helped too, coming to me first whenever he slipped up a little bit, even long after I returned to the classroom once I gave up substituting for our principal and administrative team.

Over time, Benny's mask of anger finally subsided. He was actually a really nice kid, once he let the anger go. Once he realized that there was another way out for him. He finally graduated and gave me a big hug at his graduation. I got an even bigger hug from his girlfriend for the transformation he underwent the rest of that year that ultimately led to his being able to walk across that stage.

THIS TURNED OUT TO BE Cliff Prince's last year at Southern High School. *I walked him out on his last day.*

Leaving with Cliff that day felt like one of those poignant, cinematic moments that happened every so often throughout my life. I remember it vividly.

We left together through a back exit through the receiving docks, which was located around the back of the building where the custodians all park. I escorted Cliff through the dark tunnel of the receiving docks out to the bright, warm sunlight beaming off of his shiny black Porsche that awaited him for one last drive home from Southern on this warm June afternoon.

I hugged him, told him I'd miss him, which I did, and still do. He's probably still, to this day, right up there with Buchanan as one of my all-time favorite principals. Why? It wasn't because of any record-setting data, that's for sure. It was because he took the time to care. About the kids. About me. About my career and about the future of the school. Above and beyond the call of duty. Even if the kids didn't see it that way at the time. He took it all to heart, and I love Cliff for that.

He, in turn, hugged me back and wished me well. He assured me my career was just getting started, and whatever I did to stay true to who I was. That the kids needed more people like me in this profession.

And then he drove away.

Cliff was a good man. Misunderstood by many of the kids back then, but instrumental in helping me develop as an emerging leader in our building. I learned a great deal from that man. He was a great mentor and being his "hammer" was a remarkable learning experience.

TWENTY-FIVE

A MENTOR INFLUENCES OUR BEHAVIOR

Despite losing Cliff, I was still feeling ambitious and inspired. ArtQuest was on the map! Another summer was coming to a close and the 2000—2001 school year is about to kick off.

Our Department, while still small with just three of us, was young and ambitious again. Jean was renewed with excitement as our Department Chair and was heading up our 3D programs of study. I was heading the painting and drawing classes and began introducing more and more kids to painting larger-than-life on canvas in oils as early as sophomores, which is an experience most kids wouldn't get until they reached college.

There was also a new Coordinator of Art, Mark Coates, who was hired the previous year to replace Elizabeth Grimaldis, who had been at the helm for more than a decade. Mark was ready to bring change to the county's art programs and in a BIG WAY! Mark would also prove to be one of those few great individuals that came along in my professional life, like the great prize fighters, one every ten years or so, like Roger Shipley at Lycoming, and later—Dr. Jane Bates, Nora Sturges, and Michael Weiss while doing my graduate coursework.

Mark came from a neighboring county where he was a rock star art teacher in his own right, easily the best in his county. Taking over as a new Coordinator, he definitely came with a clear-cut vision for what a successful program needed to look like.

He was in the trenches for twenty-one years as an educator with Howard County Public Schools where he was Department Chair at River Hill High School. While there, he became one of Maryland's very first teachers to earn National Board Certification. He was also awarded the National Art Education Association's National Teacher of the Year, co-taught the Gifted and Talented Program for Howard county, served as a Maryland Art Education Association Secondary Division Director, later serving as a National Art Education Association Officer, all the while still teaching high school seminar programs at the National Gallery of Art in Washington D.C. and still carving out time to head to Maine once a year to do *Plein air* paintings in oils from direct observation, maintaining his dedication to his craft as not just an educator, but as an artist.

I think this is so important. *Never stop being an artist.*

How can you teach kids how to be one if you're not one? After all, you didn't get into the education arena in order to STOP being an artist, so why would you let this happen to yourself? I've seen too many art teachers over the years that aren't making any real art! How can you possibly lead by example, help kids get real world gallery experience, teach kids how to gain commissioned portraits, do public mural projects, things like that, if you, yourself, haven't done it? So, Mark was also a teacher's teacher. And, among Mark and his circle of colleagues they'd tell you— we're not teachers. We're "Artists in Education". *Big difference.*

So, as an artist in education, Mark wanted to bring our county to another level, and he had the high expectations and the expertise to get things done. He also liked what he saw over the past year visiting my classroom. He saw that I, too, was a working artist that had a gift of relating well to the kids, and he wanted me to take my gift to the next level. I think, maybe, he saw a little of himself in me. He also wanted me to instill the kind of enthusiasm into some new programs he wanted to bring into the county with the same high stakes competitiveness and maniacal drive that he had once taught these programs with. Programs like the Gifted and Talented Visual Arts Enrichment Program, which he formed in 2000, serving the "best of the best" students in grades 6—12 based on a portfolio audition process.

I would first co-teach the program as the high school educator along with Jo-Ann Howard, a teacher at George Fox Middle School at the time. I'd later bring Marlene Kramer, our new hire in 2000 from Southern, on board to teach the program with me when Jo-Ann left teaching for administration in 2008.

Mark also wanted to bring computers into the county's Visual Arts Programs, so, who better to pilot the program and write curriculum with him than *yours truly*. Over the course of the following year we wrote curriculum for a new Photography and Digital Processes course, Mark secured a tremendous grant, and we built a computer lab in the alcove of my studio, complete with twenty-four computers, internet access, and Adobe Photoshop.

The defining moment for me with Mark came the day he asked me to take off school for the day so he could take me around and show me some of the top art programs around the state of Maryland.

He said it was important to show me these programs in action, not because what I was doing was wrong or anything, but to show me just how far I could take what I was starting to build if I was willing to put in the work—*which I was*.

The experience was eye-opening, to say the least. We traveled by car late that spring all over the state, visiting schools Mark previously taught at, and ones he felt were equally as acclaimed. He introduced me to some of the best teachers in the state, whom I've gotten to know very well over the years.

We visited programs like River Hill in Howard County where I first met Gino Molfino, Mark's future successor as Coordinator.

Then we hit Towson High School in Baltimore County to visit Duane Sabiston and Linda Popp (Baltimore County's future Coordinator of Art for a short time).

I'll never forget Duane saying to me, "You've got a great mentor here in Mark. You'll go far with him, kid."

Ten minutes with Duane and he could teach you how to see color like you've never seen it before! He had this innovative approach I still use to this day of using white porcelain cups and white saucers as a still-life against a bright white foam board backdrop, and a solitary studio light equipped with a pink *Chromalux* light bulb (now you can use *GE Reveal* bulbs as a more economical option) and a clear plastic viewfinder with blue cellophane covering the viewfinder. *Blue cellophane is the trick.* You simply hold the blue cellophane viewfinder over the pinkish light while staring at the white on white setup. Once your eyes adjust and see everything as bluish in tint, you quickly whip the viewfinder away from over the studio light with the swiftness any magician or matador pulling away his red cape would and—*Voila!* You see fiery reddish, pinkish tones on a white on white setup.

I also learned from Duane how shadows radically change shapes by using these cylindrical objects as a still-life. Duane prefers to call them "micro-labs". *Micro-labs, Ellipses, and Eclipses* using a solitary studio light as though it were the sun rising slowly over a neighborhood of tea cups as stand-ins for houses.

When I show this to kids I ask them questions like, "Do you think now is a good time to paint? Early morning—Yes! Lots of shadows! How about now? Twelve noon? Absolutely not, no shadows, just direct light. How about twilight? At that magical "golden hour" just before the sun is about to go beyond the horizon? YES!!! YES!!! YES!!!!!"

So, I learned a lot from spending the day traveling the State to the "best of the best" programs around. I think this was the single most important learning experience for me early on in my career as both an artist and educator, even more, important than my student teaching experience—spending the day with rock stars making huge waves in our field.

I was able to see and feel what a quality arts education actually looks like "in action" from more than one teacher, seeing multiple approaches and styles.

And, after spending an afternoon around Duane with his incredible tireless energy, you just wanted to race right home and paint. So I did! I created large self-portrait while looking into a mirror in one long late afternoon sitting on my back patio in oils on paper. The painting began in the dead heat of the melting hot sun, and I finished it as the sun was setting, wearing sunglasses and my partially unbuttoned dress shirt. As I painted it, I kept hearing the references Duane would use to help "describe colors" not as just concrete colors, but as things associated with other things. Things like "cotton candy clouds" or his references to Steinbeck, "the sunset *bled* into the valley . . ." Having Duane in your ear was like having John Keating from *Dead Poet's Society* in your ear describing, "Don't just consider what the author thinks. *Consider what you think!*"

In addition to learning how "a mentor influences our behavior" Duane also made me feel as though painting is "action-oriented." Not some quiet, solitary practice. In order to capture how you felt at a certain time or if you are making a painting that was about a memorable moment in your life—you need to paint it that way.

Like a method actor, I began getting into character, forming the expressions and gestures for my own paintings as if they were my own. I began communicating through color and brush strokes all the things my paintings were meant to scream out to the viewer. I've been working that way ever since.

While "out on location" I also took in the fact that all these classrooms I visited didn't look like classrooms at all. They looked like working art studios. They had no desks. In place of desks were these wooden benches called "drawing horses", which essentially were wood benches built with plywood and 2′ X 4′s that had a vertical piece of plywood on the front of the bench, so you could straddle them, prop a drawing board up against the end and do figure drawings or work on still-life drawings and be able to see both your subject and your drawing at the same time. These also served as podiums, if you flipped them up on their base, so you could place a still-life on top of them.

The studio spaces also all had these white Homasote panels lining the cinderblock walls, which served as an easier method of displaying work because you could simply pin work all over the Homasote panels instead of just along one thin line of cork strips, giving the room a much greater "gallery feel", while enabling you to be able to display a lot more of the student's artwork. So, what did I do? I went right out to *Home Depot* and began building drawing horses and panels with some of my kids.

WITH ALL THIS NEW AMMUNITION in my wheelhouse, I made a to-do list that summer in my visual journal to kick off the 2000 - 2001 school year with a bang! This was my list:

1. Throw out desks
2. Prepare Studio like a working studio
3. Give a successful presentation of the new GT Program
4. Prep wood for building drawing horses
5. Set up new Photo lab.

Once we got back, Mark asked me to present our success with the GT Program to the rest of the art educators in our county, to encourage them to submit portfolio entries, with our emphasis on observational drawing and visual journaling—*my specialty*.

It went well and the teachers seemed receptive—as receptive as teachers are at the beginning of a new school year. Everybody really just wants to get back in their rooms and set up, not sit through boring meetings, but once the meetings were all done, the year was off to a blazing start. Mark made me feel like a "somebody" and I took the bait and ran with it!

He even bought me this very "fitting" apron for my studio and had the words "**ART GODFATHER**" printed in bold letters across the top of a *Mondrian* print. I hung it in my studio. Mark was so awesome! In turn, I made my kids feel like "they were somebody." Mark agreed to be my featured juror at ArtQuest in the spring of 2001. I saved a note he wrote to me afterwards.

APRIL 26, 2001
Mark Coates

"I really appreciate what you're doing for these kids. I also liked the fact that all your kids showed up for you to receive their awards. That speaks volumes about how much they respect you and the program you're building. Consider finding ways to highlight your seniors in years to come as the show grows to give them some more clout too. Great job overall. Congratulations on the tremendous turnout from the community."

I FINALLY BEGAN TO FEEL like I actually knew what I was doing from this point on. Chrissy Biederman just became our second ArtQuest "Best of Show" winner, and it was a close race, followed up by Seton Hurson, a girl who I helped get into Parsons that year. She was my first art school kid! I was so happy when I heard the news she got into Parsons. It always starts with one. This gives you a roadmap for others to know what it takes to get there. I never went to Art School so I had no idea up until then.

You always need that first one, and Seton was mine.

The next fall she'd be headed off to New York City, and I'd be continuing pursuing my dreams of building my art career and building this art program. Giving both my equal attention, multitasking like crazy, *leading my dual lives.*

In the classroom one minute, off to meet a painting client the next, flying by the seat of my pants trying to figure it all out. Your first few years teaching truly are all about flying by the seat of your pants! But I wouldn't have it any other way. I was at my best under pressure. I'd later come to learn, the great ones usually are.

I also loved the fact that Mark practiced what he preached, which was to continue being "an artist in education".

He didn't want teachers to stop being working artists in order to teach, as though it was going to interfere in some way with the work that was to be done in the education arena. He felt, well, like I did, "How can we lead if we're not leading by example?"

So, I got busy lining up some portrait commissions here and there through my new online web presence at MBELLART.com.

Lisa helped me line up other commissions through patrons of hers at the hair salon, plus I was still waiting tables at on the weekends in Bel Air, so I'd get the occasional painting client through that venue, even though the bar scene really isn't the best place to find painting clientele. But things were happening, nevertheless.

Then, one night I had a dream that I wrote down in my sketchbook the next morning. In my dream, Rog, my former college professor from Lyco told me in it to "sign up for my Master's classes over break."

I felt like the dream was a sign. *A prophecy, maybe.*

So, I followed it and applied to Towson University. Marlene Kramer, the new teacher we recently hired in 2000 agreed to also apply with me. We thought it'd be worth a shot to try and do our Master's Degrees together, to keep each other motivated.

Seventeen days later I received a phone call from a woman at the University verifying my application. I was accepted into Towson's Graduate Program to get my M.Ed. in Art Education. I met with Dr. Jane Bates shortly afterwards. She'd prove to be another great mentor in the upcoming chapters of my life and someone who would help me to develop my Master's Thesis on *Visual Journaling*.

This was all the beginning of something really big.

I could feel it.

TWENTY-SIX

9/11

The experience of 9/11 was life changing on so many levels. I also believe it did exactly what the terrorists had intended for it to do—change America—*perhaps, forever.* Anyone born after 9/11 might not understand what the world was like up until then. And, whether you're an artist or not, you might not realize the impact this day had on the art world.

The drastic changes in the real estate market in the aftermath of 9/11 still influence the investment landscape of today, and since the art world and the real estate market typically go hand in hand, artists took a major hit. And no-one was prepared to step up and tackle the role of expressing what words could not possibly describe, as art has historically done so well over the ages.

Art precedes language. It's the reason that over time, no matter what the crisis, no matter what the situation the world always looks to artists as the innovators. We are the visionaries who not only express what society is feeling but are the creative minds who help figure out what to do next. But, given the nature and the complexity of what happened on 9/11, no one was adequately prepared to respond to it. I was one of them. The day before 9/11 I wrote this in my visual journal:

Monday, September 10th

"Last night I got invited to go to Joe Gannascoli's restaurant, *Soup as Art* in Brooklyn, NY. Joe plays Vito Spatafore on HBO's *the Sopranos*. I'll be doing paintings for him and putting other work of mine in his restaurant. He's going on Howard Stern to promote it. We're doing autographs and signing prints. It's going to launch my career into stardom even more!"

Tuesday, September 11th

"I received a call from my wife Lisa at 9:10 A.M. She told me a plane hit one of the World Trade Centers. It sounded like an accident until she called me back and told me of a second plane hitting the second tower. Then my heart sunk. I announced what happened to my 2nd period class. I'm worried about my friends and family . . ."

MY DRIVE HOME THAT DAY was the eeriest drive I've ever taken in my entire life. There was literally no-one on the highway. And I mean *no-one.*

As I traveled from Anne Arundel County through the Harbor Tunnel through Baltimore City I was the only car in sight.

There weren't even any cops.

It was like the world stood still for a moment and everyone had decided to batten down their hatches and stay inside, afraid for what was next. It felt like Armageddon.

As I was driving home I got a call from Joey G. He sounded panicked and upset beyond words.

"Mikey—we lost half our neighborhood brother. Half the fuckin' neighborhood! Guys I knew my whole life. Literally. Everybody's . . . GONE! I don't know what's gonna happen now, but obviously, the restaurant signing is off. I wanted you to know. I also wanted to ask you a favor . . ."

"Anything Joe," I responded with, equally as devastated. "What can I do?"

"Can you do a painting of someone for me? *Robert Cordice.* He was in Squad 1. A young kid everybody loved," he explained.

"Yeah, I can do that. My wife's childhood priest was Father Mychal (9/11's first known casualty), so say no more . . ."

"These guys were first responders," Joe went on to further explain, "I'm sure you can imagine . . ."

"I can brother, absolutely . . ."

Then Joe hit me with . . . "the guys are organizing a benefit at the East Shore Inn, South Beach on Staten Island. I'd need it like within 48 hours, though. That even possible?"

Now, a lot of artists I know would never be able to pull off something like this, at least not with any degree of quality. Most wouldn't have even agreed to attempt it. But this would become my hallmark.

I'd do one of these "stay up all night, paint 'til you drop marathons" again and again over the course of my career. For Joe, for Dominic Capone, and for John Gotti Junior.

I always do whatever it takes. I always "go". I always get the job done. So, I agreed immediately. I am a firm believer that everything happens for a reason. There's a reason It was me that had been hooked up with Joe. And there was a reason he asked me to do Rob's portrait.

As it turned out, there were more coincidences surrounding this other than Father Mychal being 9/11's first known casualty. Rob's mother, Caroline Calicchio Cordice, just happened to work in the same office building downtown as my wife's childhood friend Christine, who happened to thankfully be out of the office the day of 9/11. So, this became another connection I had to Rob, and to 9/11. Not to mention I still had tons of friends in the City.

And then there was *Seton.*

She was the girl I sent to New York City to go to art school at Parsons. My first "art school kid". My stomach dropped. I immediately thought about her, where she was, and if she was okay. I tried to call her but all the lines were down.

So, I poured my energy into an all-night black and white acrylic painting of Rob that took me into the next morning, where

I returned to school to put the finishing touches on it. Once dry, I rolled it up like a scroll, packed it and overnighted it to Joe for the guys at the fundraiser in Staten Island. Christine ended up going to the fundraiser and said my portrait looked fabulous hanging like a huge banner above all the memorials, in honor of all those fallen heroes from *Park Slope's elite Squad 1.*

One month later, on October 14th, we would finally do that print signing with Joe at his restaurant, *Soup as Art,* which was located on the corner of 84th and 3rd Avenue in the Bay Ridge section of Brooklyn.

I brought Lisa, her father, Bill and her mother Olga, and Lisa's friend from her hair salon along with me for the experience. I loved having them there with us. For Bill, he was right at home.

I also brought along with me a huge portrait of Joe from a famous scene he commissioned me to paint depicting him "whacking Jackie, Jr.," along with a large acrylic painting of the New York City skyline with the twin towers in it—a painting I had done prior to 9/11.

Christine and her husband Kurt showed up too. Kurt ended up helping with the 9/11 relief efforts. He worked in the city as an underwater welder prior to helping organize crews to help clean up the city and search for survivors. He loved the painting so much I ended up giving it to them. After all, he'd done to help so many countless others, and with the strange connection we had to Rob I felt they should have it.

This would mark the year of my very first celebrity print signing, one of many I'd end up doing with Joe and others over the years, and let me tell you, it was an experience! You know the expression, fake it 'til you make it? Well, that's how I was rolling.

I had never been around any celebrities before, up until this point in my life. But, I had been around my share of gangsters, and I grew up idolizing the likes of John Gotti, and guys like him.

I started painting pictures of him back in when I was in college, and I'd later do some drawings for his eldest daughter, Angel, who insisted on purchasing them from me, even though I told her I'd be honored just for her to have my art as a gift.

I GREW UP LOVING MOB MOVIES. *Scarface, The Godfather, Goodfellas,* and *the Sopranos*—the show Joe was now starring in. And, since much of *the Sopranos* took place in the same neighborhoods that were so familiar to me—*Lyndhurst, Nutley, Belleville* . . . being around Joe just felt so natural.

So, the day I drove up to Brooklyn to pitch in and do 9/11 relief efforts with Joe, we smoked cigars all afternoon with my father-in-law Bill, while signing autographs and prints for charity at a few tables we had set up outside his restaurant on 3rd Avenue. It was like a huge block party, lots of tents set up selling Italian sausage and peppers, lots of memorabilia, and something I'd liken to *the Feast of San Gennaro* that was held every year in Little Italy. Joe's Dad also stopped by. He wasn't a huge fan of the Mob movies. But he was a huge fan of his son, Joe, and he was an old timer so he and my father-in-law hit it off, talking to one another in Italian over the course of the afternoon.

While I didn't sell a hell of a lot of prints, we all had a blast. About half way through the day Joe started drinking pretty heavily. He had a cooler inside the restaurant and had one of his waitresses refilling our cups for the better part of the afternoon. We took lots of pictures. Especially with guys from the *FDNY*. We donated any money we made to help the families of the fallen firefighters from Joe's neighborhood, and Joe treated me great. He also loved his painting and became one of the earliest champions for my painting career that was just now getting underway. Later that night we all went out for dinner before heading back home. The whole experience became what locals labeled as the "3rd Avenue Festival of Hope" and was a great way for New Yorkers to come together and do our part, in any way we could.

Throughout the rest of the year there were a lot of artists who tried to figure out ways to respond to 9/11, but there really wasn't anyone dealing with the human form, until I saw Eric Fischl's sculpture *Tumbling Woman*. Now, Eric wasn't even an artist who was on my radar at the time. But, as I began taking classes at

Towson with Nora Sturges while completing my Master's degree, I would learn of Eric's work. She thought he might be a good fit for me as a potential contemporary artist mentor since he dealt with controversial subject matter and literally brought narrative figurative painting back from the dead—all things my art was also about.

Eric would turn out to become one of my heroes in the art world. Someone I'd grow to admire, befriend and appreciate on many levels. He was also someone who would end up helping me launch my now worldwide *31 Nights* movement many years later at the 2012 NAEA National Convention in New York City. I was there doing my part to also help him promote his *America: Now and Here* movement, which was a traveling multi-disciplinary art exhibition featuring artists, playwrights, and poets.

In the wake of 9/11, Eric would explain that he was "better at understanding victims . . . responding to vulnerability." This is also something I can relate to, being a champion of many different causes over the years, ranging from domestic violence and anti-bullying to Autism. Eric believed the lessons of death are really about how one survives it. He wanted the public to be able to have a conversation about it. *At least be open to one.*

But a writer at *the New York Post* described his sculpture in such violent terms that readers thought it depicted a moment of impact. This created an adverse reaction on the public's opinion of the work. Eric responded with, "The writer was projecting her sense of violence onto the piece and blaming me for it. And this created a kind of hysteria around the sculpture. Certainly, that wasn't the response I wanted. My piece came out of grief and was meant to be shared. I wanted to sit with those who had suffered directly, to sit with my society, my country, in a shared way."

And while Fischl's sculpture was only supposed to be on view for a two-week period, it was sadly withdrawn after eight days. He didn't object, stating, "The sculpture wasn't site-specific, it wasn't a commission. And it was never my wish to make a sculpture that seemed to make people miserable." He saw *Tumbling Woman* as "a healing tool".

He misjudged the potential reaction to his belief that "one of the ways to heal is to make visible the things that hurt us, so they can be dealt with." He sincerely thought America would be ready for that—that his sculpture would *help people heal*. In 2016 this sculpture did finally get its perfect forum. It was selected for exhibition at the 9/11 museum's show "Rendering the Unthinkable: Artists Respond to 9/11". I'm so glad it found its home there.

As an artist, I've also been very empathic, sometimes to a fault, like I imagine Eric also seems to be. I tend to take on the pain of others in my work, and while re-creating tragedy sometimes it becomes ingrained into the very fabric of my being. So much so that whatever I'm working on has its way of picking up a trail of energy, much like a tornado would, and it becomes totally consuming. Literally, whatever I'm working on shows its face in what's on television, songs on the radio and in the face of people that mysteriously and not-so-coincidentally emerge or re-emerge in my life during the period of time surrounding whatever I'm working on.

You know the expression, "Words are powerful . . . words are events . . . words can change things?" Well, so are paintings. Paintings are events . . . bundled up energy, packaged up on canvases for the world to unpack . . . Paintings can also change things. You, as artists, often become what you create. So, a word of advice to all you artists out there, "Careful what you say, careful what you write, and careful paint or draw. It finds a way of coming true, or coming to life in other different forms."

It certainly has for me over the course of my life.

SETON HURSON ROSSINI
CLASS OF 2001

"During the four-hour drive from Annapolis to New York City, I didn't say much to my parents. I was too busy lost in thought, worrying if I would be good enough to cut it at *Parsons*, wondering if my roommates would be nice and (as cliché as it sounds) if I'd make any friends. The 'Foundation Year' at *Parsons School of Design* is notorious for quickly weeding out those who aren't fit for the program. And although I felt as prepared as possible—I had purchased every required art supply from erasers to X-Acto knives—I couldn't seem to shake the anxiety in beginning a new chapter. It was a feeling I knew all too well.

Over three years prior, I nervously walked into my first class at a new high school—Studio Art: Level 1, instructed by Michael Bell. I recall the first drawing I ever did in that class. It was a charcoal drawing of two hands cupped together, aimed towards the sky–as if they were pleading to the gods, 'Please, let me make it through my first week at school, through this awkward *new girl* moment!'

You see, I had joined Southern High School halfway through my freshman year. I was a transplant from Texas, dropped into a small rural Maryland school. It was light years away from my norm, and I was a newbie in a school of seasoned locals.

In high school, as most teenagers do, I wanted so badly to find my niche. I'd always loved art, but the community that existed in Mr. Bell's classroom was so much more than an art class. He fostered an environment that was inclusive, challenging, creative and collaborative. It was the perfect place for me. Truth is, I'm not the best painter but that didn't matter. Mr. Bell doesn't care if you're painting the next Mona Lisa or finger painting like a toddler. All that matters is that you're creating. At some point along the journey, you'll discover your talent.

There were never any judgments, just encouragement, and that ever-so-helpful technical instruction. 'If you hold your brush at this angle, the waves will look more realistic,' and 'your colors will pop more if your highlights are a true, bright white.' It took a couple years, but in that classroom, I grew from a beginning art student to a confident high school graduate, headed to art school in New York City.

Technical skills aside, the artistic confidence and independence that I gained in Mr. Bell's classroom helped me survive an incredibly difficult freshman year in college. It was early September of 2001, and although I wasn't prepared to begin my adult life at the same time as the events on 9/11, what helped me get through that first year of college was my passion for art and the ability to channel my emotions into my work—something I first learned in Michael Bell's classroom.

Fifteen years later (really!?), I am an award-winning designer and a cookbook author (*Sweet Envy: Deceptively Easy Desserts, Designed to Steal the Show*). Although I didn't pursue a career in the fine arts, I use those skills as a designer on a daily basis. Creativity has its ebbs and flows, we all have our versions of 'writer's block.' But what is (and always was) inspiring is the fact that Michael Bell is not just a teacher of the arts—He is a working artist, striving to create something compelling and beautiful every day.

That doesn't go unnoticed by his current and former students alike. And as I continue to move forward in both the culinary and design world, there isn't a moment that I look back and don't see the path coming straight from Mr. Bell's classroom."

TWENTY-SEVEN

LIFE IMITATES ART

Does life imitate art? I believe it definitely can. I also know art can be downright prophetic, in various forms. I've seen it in my own work, and if you examine history you'll see it there too—in words, songs, videos, photographs, paintings, you name it. Think about rappers like Biggie Smalls (Notorious B.I.G.) coming out with his first LP titled *Ready to Die*, and his second entitled *Life After Death*, portraying himself as a hearse driver on the cover.

And then there's Tupac Shakur, coming out with *Death around the Corner, How Long Will They Mourn Me, Is There a Heaven for a G*. In a music video Tupac even went as far as to portray himself as an angel in heaven rapping about how he was shot after leaving a theater with a friend, which is eerily similar to the way he was shot in real life, only he was leaving a Mike Tyson fight, not a theater, but *he was with a friend*—Suge Knight, and died two days later on September 13, 1996.

How about the famous photograph captured by Annie Leibovitz of John Lennon and Yoko Ono on December 8, 1980, just hours before Lennon was murdered outside the Dakota building on the Upper West Side of Manhattan? That photograph literally catapulted Leibovitz into super stardom status. It was the very last photograph ever taken of Lennon alive, and the photograph itself is chillingly prophetic. It depicts Yoko Ono completely clothed, dressed in black, staring off into the distance, beyond him, somewhat detached from the scene as John, in stark contrast, is completely nude, kissing Ono's cheek as he's curled up against her in a fetal position, as if he's a baby going back into the womb.

Coincidental or prophetic?

Going back even further in art history, there is the famous painting *Portraits d'Enfants*, exhibited in 1883 by John Singer Sargent. Its composition was criticized for its "four corners and a void" and how the children seemingly do not have any relationship to each other. What's interesting about the psychology of the piece is what happened to the four children in the painting, which is something Sargent couldn't possibly have known while painting them.

None of the girls ever married. Florence and Jane, the two rear daughters off in the shadows of the painting, were said to have become mentally or emotionally disturbed later in life, much the way the painting portrays them to be. Mary Louisa and Julia, the two girls depicted in the front of the canvas remained close as they grew older, just like in the painting; and Julia, the youngest — the only one actually doing anything in the painting (playing with a doll on the floor), became an accomplished watercolor painter. Did Sargent sense all this and pour it into the painting, prophetically acting out their future roles on canvas? There's no way to know for certain, but there is something to be said about the role of an artist as a prophet.

I think it's about being completely in tune to not only what you're seeing in front of you as an artist, but what you're "feeling" and "experiencing". I've often said that while painting a portrait capturing someone's likeness is the easy part. Capturing someone's soul, that's a whole other ballgame. And that's always what I'm after — what's beneath the surface, *behind the mask.*

REFLECTING BACK ON MY EXPERIENCES creating art and on 9/11, I always return to an early John Gotti painting I did in 1998 entitled *Gotti, America*. I depicted Gotti's face in profile on the left side of a 36" X 48" horizontal canvas staring out into what's filling the rest of the picture frame at right, which includes: Lady Liberty holding her tablet marking the Declaration of Independence; the American flag waving along the top center of the canvas, gradually fading into the Italian Flag in the top right corner; and red subway lines beginning along the side of his face, leading to other subway lines that lead your eye throughout the rest of the canvas. At the bottom left corner of the canvas is a dark area with an angled aerial view of lower Manhattan, in particular, of the Twin Towers. It's one of my favorite paintings from early on in my career and was reflective of that particular time period.

Angel, John Gotti's eldest daughter, doesn't like the subway lines in the painting, though. She's told me it looks like her father is bleeding, which wasn't my intention. But, I've had other people give me a different interpretation, that the subway lines represent "the Gotti bloodline". I prefer that interpretation. It might even hold more weight with her brother John, Jr. because the year I completed the painting was also the year he was indicted and went through the first of his four trials, following in his father's infamous footsteps.

Everything that's built into that work makes up what the painting "is of". What "it's about" sometimes becomes a different thing altogether. At the time I was lashing out about "our land of the free" and how I felt about the Government spending millions of taxpayer dollars on surveillance and manpower to put away the likes of a man like John Gotti because of what he stood for; meanwhile, terrorists, who were out there plotting and scheming to do far worse than anything John Gotti ever did, were in close proximity to neighboring boroughs right across the Hudson River in nearby Jersey City. There literally have been dozens of documented counterterrorism failures on the road to 9/11 as agents in New York offices remained so obsessed with bringing down "The Dapper Don". *And this is not just my opinion.*

In Peter Lance's book *Triple Cross*, Lance documented through evidence obtained in *302's*, that if the Feds devoted as much energy to surveillance of *Sphinx Trading* in nearby Jersey City as they did on John Gotti and to *the Ravenite Social Club*, they might have been able to pick up on two of the hijackers who obtained their fake I.D.'s illegally just prior to hijacking the airplanes they crashed into the World Trade Center and Pentagon.

So, *Gotti, America* was initially my visual response to the Government's relentless pursuit to put John Gotti behind bars at all costs, which led to his eventual incarceration, death, and then the relentless pursuit to try and put his first born son away. This painting was my creative take on how I felt about our Government's abuses of power and our "liberties and freedoms."

And, like Fischl did with his imagery, I also discovered a way to construct meaning in my work by telling stories that were based on things I actually knew about. My narratives were also rooted in collaging imagery together to form a story, much like I was doing back in my college years while creating my *Love Series* paintings. Collage, for me, simply became my process for mimicking how the mind works, by breaking the world of images down into fragments of memories torn from their original context, placing them into a new context—*my point of view*. And, our point of view comes from *our experiences*.

My experiences enabled my narratives to become embedded into the fabric of each painting I'd create, and my work became more authentic because they were based on things I, too, had experienced on some level.

John Gotti, America became a jumping off point for the more recent painting I did for John Gotti's eldest son, John Junior in 2015 that would become the famous cover art for his best-selling memoir, *Shadow of my Father*, depicting him and his father, John Gotti, Sr., as colossuses over Manhattan. I also brought back the subway lines into this painting, and the Twin Towers, re-visiting the notion that those towers might still be standing and all those lives might not have been lost had the Government not been so obsessed with "getting Gotti".

Was my original 1998 *Gotti, America* painting prophetic? Who knows? It certainly became the topic of a conversation between me and his son, John Junior as I was working on the narrative painting for the cover of his book.

This also raises the question: "Do we know, as artists, what we're actually doing when we're *in the moment*?" Are we painting out our future? Or a self-fulfilling prophecy? Are we making things happen by what we say and do? Is life imitating art or the other way around? Or is it just all coincidence?

How about Vincent Van Gogh's famous painting, *Wheatfield with Crows*, painted in July of 1890? The painting shows several paths through the wheat fields, essentially leading to nowhere, as black crows circle the dark skies above, perhaps foretelling Van Gogh's own tragic end. Did Van Gogh know this would be one of his very last paintings? Is that why he painted it the way he did?

We will probably never know, for certain.

I do know I felt the hairs on my body stand on end for some strange reason as I was painting *Severed Ties*, which is a large 48" X 96" narrative painting—one of eight in a series entitled *Carnevale Italiano*, which essentially is a prequel series to my *Ticket to Ride* paintings. They illustrate events that happened involving my wife at a Carnival in Long Branch back in the early 1970s, using vignettes from my wife's childhood, mixed with events from my own childhood, re-configured to tell a much larger tale— all of which leads up to my *Ticket to Ride* paintings.

To describe the scene in *Severed Ties*, I portrayed myself in the center of Mulberry Street during *the Feast of San Gennaro*, smiling up proudly at a Ferris wheel. Standing to my right is my father-in-law, Bill, and to my left is Dominic Capone, with a smoking gun in his hand. Behind him is a Cotton Candy Stand, which references *Sweet Screams*, the painting just before this one, which depicts a few severed heads stuffed into cotton candy bags hanging in what looks like a meat locker.

There are other shadowy, roughly sketched out figures in *Severed Ties*, one carrying what appears to be a body bag, the other figure—a ghostly likeness to Dominic's great-uncle, Al Capone.

The reason my hair began standing on end though was because as I was painting it, for some reason, I decided to chop off the necktie I was wearing in the painting. The floral red-on-white bamboo pattern on my tie was an homage to the same bamboo floral print on the chairs in Eric Fischl's *The Bed, the Chair* series. But, the decision to sever the tie also led to the title of the painting, which I began in 2012 and finished early in 2013, prior to my Grandmother's passing and the subsequent ties that would become severed for a few years between me and my family, just as my painting seemed to foretell. So, did I suddenly recognize the metaphor I was painting as I was painting it? *Maybe I did.* There must have been a reason I subconsciously did what I did. Maybe I felt it coming.

As artists, we all have a language that reflects techniques we use in our paintings, but nothing that accurately articulates the language our paintings actually speak. Painting is just indescribable that way. That gets back to why I feel it is so important for artists to "draw a line from your life to your art that is straight and clear". Patterns repeat themselves like life, and as history often does. It's like we're swept up into a riptide of our creations.

Edvard Munch, a Norwegian painter and another one of my heroes in the art world, someone you may know best from his iconic 1893 painting, *The Scream*, also had similar "prophetic" experiences with his art. In a diary entry, *Nice 22 January 1892*, Munch described his inspiration for his painting:

"One evening I was walking along a path, the city was on one side and the fjord below. I stopped and looked out over the fjord—the sun was setting, and the clouds turning blood red. I sensed a scream passing through nature; it seemed to me that I heard the scream. I painted this picture, painted the clouds as actual blood. The color shrieked. This became *The Scream*."

While we all remember *The Scream* for its iconic image, you should know that over the course of his lifetime Munch created 1,008 paintings, 15,391 prints, 4,443 drawings and watercolors and 6 sculptures.

So, you never know what you're going to be "known for" or which painting will eventually "make you" well-known, so you keep pressing forward. You simply keep working on your craft. One work after the next. Munch had the courage to expose his own traumatic life situations through his art. That's what seemed to matter the most. You have to keep going, not for the external rewards, but for the internal ones. The external ones will follow.

In Munch's *Frieze of Life* series he dealt with a lot of pain and destructive relationships that he encountered in his life. He worked out his inner sufferings in constructive, as opposed to destructive ways—*through his paintings*. I admire that. He puts it all out there.

He's been quoted as saying, "No longer shall I paint interiors with men reading and women knitting. I will paint living people who breathe and feel and suffer and love." This is what it was all about for Munch.

And, for me, much like a method actor, I need to "live out" whatever I'm painting to make your experience (as the viewer) more authentic. So, I also inject my own life in a lot of the subject matter that I paint, for good or for bad. If it's personal to me, I'll spend more time with it, re-creating the experience in order to re-frame it and understand it with more clarity. This also allows the world a glimpse into my personal thoughts and it informs you what it's like to be me. I'd explore these personal narratives even further through many drawings and paintings from a body of self-portraits entitled, *Images of the Self*.

So, is art prophetic?

I'll leave that up to you to decide. Either way, art keeps finding ways to challenge not only the viewer but the maker. Fischl once said, "Listen to your paintings. It's a search for meaning. Finish the painting by discovering its true meaning."

I just keep asking myself as I'm working, "What am I *really* trying to say?"

And then, I proceed onward.

TWENTY-EIGHT

DREAM IT. CREATE IT. BECOME IT.

Most people don't understand just how much we all operate in two worlds and live *dual lives*. We wear our public masks and keep our private one tucked away in a drawer. We have our work persona and our play persona. Our family life and the life we project into Social Media for strangers that often feel as though they know us better than they really do.

We give the people what they want. We all become travelers and witnesses. And everybody's story begins someplace. It's up to us whether our journey is defined by where we come from or by our maniacal drive to fight our way out of that place.

What does our journey truly map? Does it reveal its secrets to us like hidden truths we awaken from after a lucid dream? Do our most poignant memories return to us and re-appear in random details around us like the pattern of our Grandmother's wallpaper? Or is it the pattern of a cycle that keeps repeating . . .

Our visual journals can help us remember these moments in life. They can also help us get through some of our worst. They can map where we've been, document familiar patterns forming in our lives, and help us to predict where we're heading.

Mine have become many things over time. They've been a place for me to deposit anger; a place to make a "Wheel of Fortune" where I'd write out my dreams and desires; a place to draw out floor plans for a dream home, as I often did alongside my kids while teaching Architectural Drawing class; a place to document "actual dreams" and then try and interpret them, or revisit later to see if they actually came true. They've also been a place for me to document actual places I've been through maps, photographs, collaging them with spontaneous thoughts, poems, and self-reflections. It's a place to not only think something up but a place to *get something down*.

One thing I've also learned about living a creative life is that *you are* what you give your attention to—*artistically*.

You dream it. You create it. You become it.

And, while I was *dreaming it*—"It" being, ways to "make it" as an artist, and ways to become better for my kids at my career in art education—I was also *creating it*. There's a narrative in our lives, just like there's a narrative in our careers. And I was steadily becoming everything I was surrounding myself with.

AFTER MY FIRST PRINT SIGNING in Brooklyn during the wake of 9/11 with Joe from *the Sopranos*, my name began to get out there among those circles. I'd liken it to a cartoonist developing a following at Comic-con, only for me, it was Gangster Art and Mafia enthusiasts. It wasn't something I purposely set out to do, but it was something I did plan on getting some considerable mileage out of after the fact. After all, I had just done work that a lot of artists out there couldn't say they had done, and, since *the Sopranos* were just beginning to be a huge deal, my name was circulating amongst fans of the show all over the country.

I made it my mission to do my best and to always maximize whatever opportunities came my way. No matter how big or how small. The reason being, sometimes it's not who or what you set out to meet or do that becomes the thing that turns out to be the most important. It could be someone you meet on the plane. It could even become someone else who comes from out of nowhere just because of what you've done or who you're now perceived to be associated with. So, I kept the train rolling.

In early summer of 2002, I got another mural job through Lisa, this one for her boss at that time, Michele Brunner, owner of *the Salon at May's Chapel* in Timonium, Maryland. They had a really large home and wanted to do something unique with their kids' bedroom, so I transformed it into a scene that went from Oriole's Park into the Baltimore Ravens Stadium. Even though we're *Giants* and *Yankees* fans in my household, I made it awesome for them, with lots of unique perspectives to open up the wall space in ways that made you feel like you could walk right into the mural. That, to me, is the cornerstone of any successful mural. It doesn't close in a space but opens it up. Makes you look at it just a little bit longer, finding new things hidden in it every time you look at it.

Then, on the last day I was finishing their mural I received a phone call out of the blue from a woman named Georgia Durante.

That's how quickly anything happens. How quickly pages turn and new chapters are written.

Georgia said she found me through "friends of friends" of *the Sopranos*. She also said she knew guys in "the life" and heard about the artwork I did of John Gotti. She went on to tell me how her life was "like the real life *Sopranos*" and how at one time she was also "the Kodak Girl," labeled one of the most photographed girls in the country. She went on about how she grew up in Rochester and became a "wheel woman" for the Mob, how she once met Carlo Gambino, Boss of all bosses during her heyday prior to moving far away to California to get away from "the life" after her husband committed suicide while under Federal indictment with her gun. She shared with me how her experience behind the wheel pulling E-Brakes, coupled with her move to *LaLa Land* ultimately fueled her desire to start up her own stunt driving business, which she still owns to this day, *Performance Two, Inc.* Now she wanted to fill her colorful life with some art and wanted to commission me to paint her portrait.

I thought it all sounded interesting enough. All this was long before shows like *Mob Wives* and *the Real Housewives of New Jersey* came out. It turned out that she also wrote a best-selling novel about her life, which she mailed out to me immediately, so I could familiarize myself with her story while I began painting the first of what would turn into numerous narrative portraits of her. The first work referenced her book cover. It was done in oils on paper in black and white featuring her holding a smoking gun, wearing a gangster's fedora and a polka dot blouse, staring at you, the viewer—as if she's just shot you. I had fun with the piece, especially trying to capture an essence of beauty and darkness all at the same time. She talked a lot in her book about the two different sides of her—*Georgia White* and *Georgia Black*.

Georgia White was the domestic violence survivor. She was the demure, childlike girl with big dreams and wide eyes.

Georgia Black was the gangster. The survivor. The killer that lurked deep inside of her.

I didn't realize how different these two women were or how prominent of a position they took up in her physical makeup until I finally met Georgia in person and spent a considerable amount of time getting to know both Georgia White and Georgia Black; an interesting concept I could relate to, living in two very different worlds myself.

After completing her first painting, Georgia said she had an opportunity for me to get my work out there among Hollywood's *Who's Who* if I'd be willing to donate a painting for the *Hugh O'Brian Youth Leadership Foundation (HOBY)*. This way, she said we could finally meet face to face, do an unveiling at her Hollywood home and talk about future works, while also helping me gain increased exposure for my artwork out in L.A.

JUNE 12TH WAS THE DATE of the event, and Georgia said she could get one of my pieces featured as a major auction item, so I decided to go for it. I could also feel this surge of "something big" starting to happen for me with my art career. *Finally, I thought!*

So, with this being my first trip out to Los Angeles, I planned on making it a memorable one. I'd do my first live auction, make a big success of that, potentially get some big money clientele out of it, and get to know Georgia better. In addition, Lisa and I could make a little vacation out of it. While planning our trip, Georgia said she wanted to introduce me to Denise Brown while I was out there. Denise is the famous sister of Nicole Brown Simpson, O.J. Simpson's slain ex-wife. Georgia had become a domestic violence activist after going through a brutal relationship with her deceased husband and was good friends with Denise. She figured we should also meet, in the event I wanted to become involved in donating any work to help benefit "The Nicole Brown Foundation". So, we were gearing up for an exciting, busy week.

On Georgia's recommendation, we booked a room at *the Sportsmen's Lodge*, which was in close proximity to her home. We also rented a car—and all the final arrangements were put in place. The Sportsmen's Lodge was also running a hotel package, coincidentally or not, to "Book a room for $209 plus room tax to get VIP Tickets" to take a free shuttle to/from *MOCA* to view the Warhol Retrospective that was on exhibit from May 25—August 18, 2002. "Warholmania" they called it, anticipating a sold out event. This was not for me, being that I'm no fan of Warhol, but I felt it might be something of a good omen—the fact that they were promoting an artist and art at the time *yours truly* was making his first trip to L.A. to have his first live painting auction.

First order of business was to ship out a large 45" X 58" painting from my "Love Series" entitled, *Another Side of the Mirror*, valued at $5,000, which was based on what my selling point was at that particular time in my young art career. Initially, I had a hard time parting ways with the piece because I really liked it. It was hanging in the hallway of our new townhouse and I grew fond of it over time.

The painting was inspired by photos I had taken a few years prior—it was a montage of a model I blindfolded and tied to a chair as I dripped water from an ice cube over her lips and face for the painting. In the dark background of the painting I also included a montage of a silver mixing bowl, lit candles, some silk ribbon, a mask—all combined together as double and triple exposures through the process of darkroom manipulation using multiple photo negatives. These photos were taken back in my college years at Lycoming but were still fueling my paintings at this point, and a continuous conversation I was having in the form of my on-going *Love Series*. Nowadays, the opening bid for a painting that size would fetch triple what they opened with. But this was my very first live auction, my "introduction" if you will to Hollywood, so I was happy to donate it for a good cause, an educational cause at that, in order to get my name out there.

So, *Another Side of the Mirror* was to be officially auctioned in front of a large, affluent crowd at a $500 per plate dinner for "the 2002 Albert Schweitzer Leadership Awards" at the Regent Beverly Wilshire Hotel in Beverly Hills. The event would be hosted by Hugh O'Brian, founder of the HOBY Organization and former actor, who was also apparently known for his starring roles in the 1955-1961 ABC western television series, *The Life and Legend of Wyatt Earp*. He was an old timer. I never saw the show. It was way before my time, so I had no idea who he was. But I did recognize some of the other old Hollywood types there that night as I was introduced to upon arrival, including Art Linkletter, William F. Austin, Pat Boone and Lou Ferrigno (*the Incredible Hulk*). They were all there to be recognized for their contributions through philanthropic endeavors and business leadership. There was even a local reporter covering my newfound success in a June article in the South County section of *The Capital* newspaper in Annapolis, and in turn, my students and their families would be able to follow my journey to Los Angeles in the news, since school was out for summer. It was all a really exciting time!

But, before all this, Lisa and I planned to spend an entire week in sunny California taking in the sights, and enjoying some downtime by the pool while getting to know Georgia. I would do the first of what would become many painting unveilings at Georgia's beautiful Hansel-and-Gretel-style North Hollywood home that she since calls "the Enchanted Manor".

But things took a quick turn to the land of the weird, and when I say weird, I mean, well—the bizarre, the haunting, and the frantic—you name it, like something right out of a movie.

First, on Monday, June 10, 2002, just one day prior to our heading out to Los Angeles I received a call to my cell from an Unknown Caller: "I just wanted you to know . . . a certain someone who's been in the media a lot that you painted quite often passed away today. Out of respect, before the news was everywhere, I thought you should know. Be well, my friend." And with that, they hung up.

A few hours later *there it was*, all over the news: "Mob Boss John Gotti Dies at the age of 61."

Gotti, Sr. had been convicted back in 1992 of racketeering conspiracy—including six alleged murders—and was sent to the country's toughest and only Level 6 Supermax Federal Prison at that time, *the U.S. Penitentiary in Marion, Illinois*—with no possibility of parole. He died there of brain and throat cancer.

The day after he passed away, on June 11th, we flew out to L.A. When we arrived at *the Sportsmen's Lodge* we called Georgia, who welcomed us to Hollywood over the phone. We told her we were going to take a swim, rest up, get unpacked and then come over later that afternoon to do the unveiling of her painting.

Only, most of the afternoon I kept getting interrupted by these strange calls to my cell phone from various "Unknown Callers" asking if I had any John Gotti prints available for sale. Back then I had my cell phone on my website as being "my studio number" in the contact area, so my phone number wasn't a big secret. I assumed the calls were due to Mr. Gotti's untimely death, and personally thought it was in real poor taste to be calling me about memorabilia one day after his passing. Definitely not something I was interested in entertaining or profiting from in any way. I'd just say "no, I'm sorry," and I would hang up.

While I drew and painted a bunch of pictures of Mr. Gotti, I wasn't selling them. Unless someone really had some special request for a particular commission, I preferred to keep it "in family". Gotti's oldest daughter Angel appreciated my artwork early on. She even purchased the first drawing I did of her famous father coming out of court.

Under the circumstances, I didn't find it totally unusual to get art requests by phone, but what was unusual was the number of calls about "Gotti" and the way the calls were going. They seemed like people were trying to "keep me on the phone" if you know what I mean, for whatever reason.

And as I'm fielding this call and that call, my wife, Lisa spotted this guy . . . let's just call him Mr. Smith, because he looked like *a Smith*—he kept glancing up at her, but not in a flirting way, just in a creepy "watching you" type of way.

He was older, probably late 40's or early 50's, had sunglasses on, dark hair parted neatly to the side, and everywhere she went she said that she felt his eyes on her.

It all began with occasional peeks over his newspaper from across the pool, as he sat in a lounge chair, and then it escalated when she decided to go up to the room for a minute.

If he was spying on us and trying to be inconspicuous, he wasn't doing a great job of it. But Lisa is also pretty good at spotting this kind of thing, growing up the way we did, and as I said, she spotted him almost immediately—as soon as we hit the pool. *Like alarm bells going off in her head.*

I dove under water as if going to do a lap, as she headed upstairs to our room. I watched her as she left. When I came up from under water I noticed the guy also rose and quickly proceeded to follow her past the gift shop and up the stairs.

Now, I raced out of the pool!

My cell phone started ringing just as I got out. This time it was Lisa. It kept cutting out due to bad reception though, so much so I couldn't understand a word she was saying.

I screamed, "Call me back! I can't hear you!" And I grabbed a towel and started running past the lobby to the elevator, trying to get her back on the phone.

Still no signal.

Then my cell phone finally rang . . .

"Unknown Caller"—*again.*

I canceled the call, and then it rang once more. Only this time, it was my buddy Louie just calling to say hi. I rushed him off the phone, impatiently pacing back and forth in the elevator, waiting for it to re-open to our floor, and then—*Ding!* The elevator doors finally opened.

I raced out of the elevator, ran around the corner. Still dialing her back. *Still no service.*

Finally, I spotted her, standing outside our door trembling.

"What's the matter? What happened?!" I asked her, huffing and puffing from my frantic race back up to our room. "He followed you, didn't he? The guy with the newspaper?"

She nodded yes, and then explained to me in a fast but low whisper outside our door, all the while, her hands still shaking . . .

"I went up the steps and saw him following me from seeing his reflection in the gift shop window so I did a loop. Nobody goes in a complete circle, but he was still behind me, trying not to be obvious. When I finally turned to yell at him . . . '*What the fuck do you want*?!' he disappeared."

"So what happened when you went in?" I asked, my eyes motioning toward our door, which was cracked partially open . . .

I figured she had been inside already.

Lisa immediately put her finger up to her lips, "Shhhhhh . . ." she whispered.

"What?! What is it?" I whispered.

"It was *like this* when I got up here. I didn't get the chance to go in yet," she said.

"*You mean . . . ?*"

"Yes. I'm *not* the one who opened it. And I know we locked it before we went downstairs."

"You think anybody's still in there?" I began inching closer to the door, trying to carefully peek inside.

"I don't know. What should we do?" she asked.

"Call for Security. I'll go in and check it out," I said as I reached for the door lever.

"I'm not leaving you!" she exclaimed.

"Ok, well just stay here in the hallway and keep a look out for me while you call the front desk and ask for security. If anything goes down you run! Okay? And I mean if you hear *anything*. I'll be right back. Stay here," I tried reassuring her.

And then I headed inside, carefully inching the door open ever so slowly, as to not make a sound, listening for any movement inside. But I didn't hear anything. The room looked empty.

So I slowly moved toward the bathroom door, stepped inside, staring at the shower curtain. I took a deep breath and then flung the shower curtain back! *Nothing*.

From there, I checked the closets, under the bed, checked outside on our balcony—*still nothing*. It didn't even look like anything was taken or touched. It was strange. But it felt like someone had been there—as if their energy was still lingering about in the room. Like we arrived just a moment too late to catch them there.

But why us? Who would want to be in our room? Were they planting bugs? Was it because Gotti passed? Was it because we were going to see Georgia?

These were the kind of things that raced through my mind as I started checking our bags for anything that might have been stolen, tampered with, or planted. If anything was planted on us, any tracking or listening devices we certainly couldn't find them. And believe me—*we looked hard*.

When a security guard finally arrived, they asked us if there was anything missing, and they took a look around the room, which seemed fine. The only problem was when they shut the door to check our lock, our key all the sudden wouldn't work anymore. The security guard even admitted, "Hmmmm, this is strange. Let's try it again."

Nothing.

Then he tried his master key. *Again—still nothing*.

"Now this is really strange," he said, fumbling with his tools to try and get into the lock.

He ended up having to disassemble the door and replace the whole locking mechanism.

Two things immediately crossed my mind:

1) "Who has the kind of equipment to override a hotel's lock system, totally disarm it, disable it, and render it useless?" and . . .

2) "Why us?"

It took the guy over an hour to take the whole lock apart on the inside of the door frame to replace it. By this time, it didn't matter, the hotel accommodated us by giving us another room. But for Lisa and me it didn't matter. New room or not, she didn't feel comfortable, or safe, and neither did I. So, I decided to call Georgia and ask her if we could come over a little earlier than we anticipated.

"I'll explain it when we get there," I said to her. Being who she was and the company she kept, she understood what that meant—*not on the phone.*

AFTER WE ARRIVED BACK AT GEORGIA'S, bags already packed and in the trunk of our rental car, she said she would put us up in her guest house for the rest of the week.

Upon meeting her for the first time, she immediately struck me with her charm. She had this infectious laugh, these penetrating eyes that I could tell had probably seen a lot over the course of her lifetime; a lot she was probably also hiding behind them and that beaming smile of hers.

She was wearing this matching yellow Pant-suit outfit and looked the part of a gangster's girl. I could tell she'd been around "the life" and was the real deal. We all hit it off immediately.

Her house itself was filled with lots of knotty pine lining the interior walls. There were large wooden beams extending throughout the ceilings, a huge green carpet in the main living area just beyond her rustic kitchen that had lots of hanging copper pots and pans, and a few fireplaces throughout the entire place. As we made our way through her living room, there were tons of 8" X 10" photos hanging gallery-style covering an entire wall of Georgia with different Hollywood celebrities she's doubled or worked with in the stunt driving industry; stars like Farrah

Fawcett, Cindy Crawford; some Wiseguy-types like Big Frank D'Amico and Pat Reale; and ones with the "old timers," guys like Hugh O'Brian, Dom Deluise; feminist lawyer Gloria Allred, Lori and Morton Downey, Jr., and the likes of whom I was about to all meet in person for my first painting auction.

As she walked us through her home to the guest house, our suitcases in tow, through her living room to another great room that also had a cobblestone fireplace, a huge gleaming parquet floor and knotty-pine walls with a full floor-to-ceiling bookshelf that also doubled as a secret passageway to a hideout, we finally landed at the guest house entrance. She told us the most fascinating stories along the walk, about how she spent the better part of two weeks when she first moved to L.A. hiding from the Feds *and the Mob* in that secret room. The Mob wanted to know if she told the Feds about her husband. The Feds—they wanted to know much of the same. She just wanted to escape with her daughter and start life anew. Not pledging allegiance to either side, although, keeping her mouth shut about anything in regards to the Mob.

The corridor that led from that great room into the guest house also had its own foyer with an entrance-way out of the house and a doorway into the guesthouse, so she could keep it open when she wasn't renting it out. Before entering, I swear I saw a shadow of a face screaming in the wrought iron bars of the exterior doorway in the foyer.

It stopped me in my tracks and I had to look, twice. I immediately felt like the place was haunted.

Once inside, her guesthouse was quaint, with couches, our own fireplace and Murphy's bed that pulled out from the wall. Just beyond this living area was another room with a kitchenette and sunroom with exterior doors to her backyard, where she had a pool and a treehouse with a swing. It was like a little oasis smack in a Cul-de-sac in Hollywood.

So, we dropped off our bags and headed out to the pool to take some photos together for future publicity. Georgia couldn't wait to see the painting, so I unveiled it in the main foyer of her home. Generally, when I do an unveiling of any type I make a big deal of it, complete with a red silk sheet to drape over the work until the moment of the actual "reveal". I want to capture someone's initial reaction and make it a special moment for them, one they'll never forget. So, I did the same with Georgia and she loved it. She hung the painting, once we took some photographs on either side of it for her scrapbook, on a wall near the knotty-pine bookshelves in her main foyer.

After finishing with the photo op from her unveiling, we all headed out through her office to her pool to drink some wine and all get to know one another, swapping stories like that. We all knew familiar names that swam in similar circles, and Georgia made Lisa and I feel right at home.

While enjoying some wine, Georgia pondered the possibility that the FBI might have been the ones that broke into our hotel room. First was the Gotti angle, as a possibility, but again—why?

The only thing I could think of was that the day before, one call I did return was from Helen Lucaitis, then a reporter for *Court TV's Hollywood at Large*, who wanted to ask me for a quote about Mr. Gotti in the wake of his passing, and why I chose to paint pictures of *the Dapper Don*. I figured maybe her article went live and the Feds were wondering why I was even someone to be contacted for a quote in the first place. Maybe I wasn't a blip on their radar until then? My paranoia was probably just taking over, but who knows.

Then there was my relationship with Joe and his *Sopranos pals*. Let's just say there wasn't a ton of "acting" going on in the show. Some of the actors were guys who grew up around people in "the life". This could be another possibility.

Maybe someone in our circle wasn't who we thought they were. Given the nature of the company Georgia kept, which incidentally was the title of her book, we figured maybe she was the reason? This was another possibility. But it had been years since her problems with the Feds. Georgia then mentioned there might be another possibility was that the Feds might be trying to track down the whereabouts of her former tenant . . .

She said the woman that rented her guest house always paid her in cash, was on a month-to-month basis and one day, when Georgia went inside the guesthouse looking for her she noticed a bunch of fake I.D.s' the woman had obtained, hidden in a dresser drawer. She appeared to have a lot of aliases.

A couple days before our trip to Los Angeles this woman apparently packed up and vanished. Georgia felt she was probably "on the run" for whatever reason and so that became another possibility for our run-in at *the Sportsmen's Lodge*. I thought this reason was probably most likely what was really going on. But, to this day, none of us know. Nothing ever resurfaced about it.

That evening we just ended the night with more questions than answers, but tomorrow was a new day, and it was also the night of *the Albert Schweitzer Leadership Awards*.

My very first live auction. My night to shine.

My night to "Dream it. Create it. Become it!"

I couldn't wait!

TWENTY-NINE

THE HOBY AWARDS

I t was June 12th, the morning of the Albert Schweitzer Leadership Awards, which was essentially a night for the *HOBY foundation*, and I couldn't sleep a wink. Neither could Lisa. We slept on Georgia's Murphy's bed and all night long I kept feeling like there was someone in there with us, just hovering over our bed for some reason. It was freezing cold too, which didn't make sense, being we were in Los Angeles in June.

All night long we froze in there.

I even tried starting a fire in the fireplace, but it didn't make much of a difference. When I asked Georgia about it, she told me that there definitely were some ghouls following her around—one being her ex-husband Joe, and perhaps in others. She went on to explain how when she first remodeled the guesthouse many years prior, after first moving to LA, the construction crew found hundreds of newspaper clippings about MISSING GIRLS plastered beneath the wallpaper, coating the walls of the bathroom. It doesn't get much creepier than that!

I kept thinking about being surrounded by all those newspaper clippings as I shaved my face in that very bathroom, wondering if the home was once a slaughterhouse of some sort to some serial killer. I definitely felt the presence of something in there. The next morning, sleep deprived but still anticipating a great day, we got dressed. I was donning the only tux I ever owned, one I bought just for this trip out to L.A. Nothing too fancy, but what I could afford at the time.

Lisa looked elegant in a long black dress and a sheer top, her hair slicked back. Georgia spent the day getting beautified; her mid-shoulder length blonde hair feathering out on both sides, wearing a shiny black top and matching pants with long pointed tipped high heels and a pinkish-coral tuxedo jacket.

When we arrived at the Regent Beverly Wilshire Hotel, I couldn't get over the opulence of the place—and it's history. I knew famous stars such as Elvis Presley, Warren Beatty, and Steve McQueen have all lived in the Hotel and had walked the hallways I was about to walk, but it was also pretty cool that a film I saw when it first came out—the Julia Roberts' film Pretty Woman—was shot on location here. Georgia promised to take us for a walk down the Hollywood "Walk of Fame" afterwards to see where all the stars put their handprints in the cement.

We took some photographs together in the main lobby and then Georgia autographed a few of her books for a silent auction. My painting was on prominent display for the live auction and you couldn't miss it as soon as you walked in. It was right next to this large bronze bust of Hugh O'Brian, and a huge landscape painting of the New York City skyline by a local Laguna Beach artist who seemed pretty well known around the area at the time.

I was immediately impressed by her brochures. She had her artwork packaged on pamphlets to pass out, one on every seat for this $500 per plate outing. Apparently, she made a living out of her own local gallery and would take helicopter trips over major golf courses all over the world and take aerial photographs of the major tournaments. Then she'd return home to paint the scenes, on commission, from whatever the venue was.

I thought it was a pretty unique niche she carved out in the world for herself, and I also saw it was great marketing on her part to have all these glossy, heavyweight tri-fold pamphlets with her one-page bio on the inside once you opened it up. Unlike me, she definitely had some major financial backing.

Remember, this was long before companies like *Vista Print* — where you could order your own print-on-demand merchandise at the click of a button for an affordable budget, and I was still new to all this. I was still learning, but taking it all in, and like everyone else, was hoping to snap some photographs with some of Hollywood's icons and hope they appreciated my artwork.

So, the silent auction finally closed. Dinner was now served, and about half-way through dinner, it was time for the live auction.

My larger-than-life sized painting, *Another Side of the Mirror* was brought up on stage first.

One of Hugh O'Brian's old timers started reading my bio, describing me as a "Celebrity Artist to the Stars" and then he went on to describe the "dark, mysterious world" of my *Another Side of the Mirror* painting. I distinctly remember him, immediately after reading off some background behind the painting, saying to the crowd, "Oh, I don't know if I like that," in reference to the "dark, mysterious" description of my painting he was reading.

Now, I don't know if he was trying to be funny, if the write-up on the painting was a little too morbid and he was trying to make light of it, or what? Either way, *what an asshole!* It didn't help start the bidding process, that's for sure. I started to feel this stinging in my cheeks . . . *the sting of embarrassment.*

I looked around, waiting—waiting for what felt like an eternity for the first bidder, but there was nothing but *crickets.*

Not one bidder for my painting.

So, they finally said "take it away," *next item —*

I was humiliated. Lisa could see it all over my face, but I tried to remain brave and shake it off as if it didn't sting my pride as much as it did. The woman with the New York City piece was up next. I definitely felt this woman was going to sell her piece since she was local, and appeared to have a strong clientele base in L.A. But then, a strange thing happened, not one bid for her either! Finally, after a few moments of coaxing, someone local who knew her placed an opening bid, which was around $1,500, far below whatever she typically would sell the work for. I mean, my opening bid was scheduled to start at $5,000, let alone $1,500. She told me at our table just prior to the auction how she could usually get around $10,000 for a painting that size at her gallery.

She started getting just as antsy. After the opening bidder, no-one else came back with anything and now her embarrassment turned to anger. She leaned over to her husband also seated at our table and said, "The frame alone costs more than fifteen-hundred bucks for that piece! No way I'm letting it go for that."

And then I heard her say, "I'll buy it back myself if I have to!" And she did.

With the very next bid, she bought her own painting back. Afterwards, she tore the guy in charge of the auction a new one. She told them they didn't do us any due diligence in the way of marketing the auction. That it was just a bunch of seat fillers and all they cared about was getting their $500 for the tickets but that no-one had any intention of actually buying anything there that night!

She was right. Everyone there just wanted a few photos with celebs, indulge in the open bar and $500 a plate dinner. The guy concurred that she was right. He admitted they dropped the ball on seeking out actual art collectors for our works in advance, and that they made enough on ticket sales that basically, they weren't concerned one way or another whether anything else really sold.

Talk about a fucked up, humiliating first live auction.

The thing I became increasingly concerned with though was what would happen to my painting? After all, if they didn't give a shit about marketing it, would they care even less about mailing it back to me? I mean, my situation wasn't like the other artist's situation—where she actually bought it back because she had one bidder that would have taken it otherwise. Not one bid on mine. What happens next?

I immediately asked Georgia. She said she'd look into it for me. Finally, the coordinator of the event said they would ship it back to me if I agreed to pay for the shipping. Now, this was a big piece. It already cost me a lot to ship it out there, but I was fine with it as long as I could get the painting back.

Well, another lesson learned.

When we finally left Los Angeles to head back to Maryland the head of Hugh O'Brian's foundation stopped returning my calls. To this day, I have no idea who has *Another Side of the Mirror* or what became of my painting.

Thanks, Hugh O'Brian and the *HOBY Foundation*. You're a real class act! But, I kept my mouth shut. I knew Georgia had a longstanding friendship with the guy and I didn't want to be disrespectful, but I also started doing my homework.

Now, the HOBY organization is quoted as being "an organization dedicated to training and nurturing the young leaders of tomorrow. Its mission—to provide lifelong leadership development opportunities that empower youth to achieve their highest potential."

What I'd later come to understand is I should've done my research when it came to donating anything to any charitable organization, *let alone this one*. But, this was my first auction, so I learned a hard life lesson. The lesson being, many "charitable organizations," become places for people in the public eye to unequivocally line their own pockets in order to continue to afford a lavish lifestyle they once led while in the Hollywood spotlight. This isn't "new news" but for a kid in his twenties just starting out in the art world, it was a learning curve. After all, these definitely weren't my type of people.

When I did return home and looked through the past notable recipients of Hugh O'Brian's *Albert Schweitzer Leadership Award*. They included: Former Secretary of State Madeleine Albright, President & Mrs. George H. W. Bush, Lynn and Richard Cheney, Secretary of State and former First Lady Hillary Rodham Clinton, Elizabeth and Robert Dole, President and Mrs. Gerald R. Ford, David Foster, Lynn and Foster Friess, Raisa and Mikhail Gorbachev, Vice President and Mrs. Al Gore, Lydia and Charlton Heston, Dolores and Bob Hope, J. Willard Marriott, General Colin Powell (Ret.), President & Mrs. Ronald Reagan, General Norman

Schwarzkopf, Ted Turner, and former California Governor and Mrs. Pete Wilson. *On and on that list went . . .*

On my particular night, it was *Art Linkletter.*

"Welcome to Hollywood, Michael Bell," I thought to myself. What a sucker I felt like. From that day on I vowed to myself, "Never again."

Never again will I be humiliated by the likes of Hugh O'Brian or any "charitable" organizations that operated in that manner. *Never ever again.*

I did learn a lot on that trip, though. And I would make my way back into the spotlight again and again throughout my career, learning more and more every step of the way. Life lessons I'd share with my kids in my classes and with fellow artist friends.

Joe, my *Sopranos* pal, scheduled me to come back and do another 3rd *Avenue Festival of Hope* in Brooklyn with a few more of the guys. I lined up two more portraits for Tony Sirico (who played Paulie Walnuts on the show), and another for John Fiore that included him, Joe Pantoliano and one for James Gandolfini.

I eventually had one of Georgia's large paintings auctioned off a few years later in Hollywood. Georgia auctioned it off with popular television host Mario Lopez and boxing's first successful woman promoter Jackie Kallen at a charity benefit to help support Trish Steele's *Safe Passage Foundation*, which she founded to equip women and children of Domestic Violence to become productive members of society. This would also become one of many upstanding domestic violence charities I'd help support over the course of my career with Georgia through more successful auction sales of my paintings.

THIRTY

DRAWING ON MEANING

L ife after my first big auction went on, and I finished out the summer of 2002 teaching the GT Program and dedicating my time to a young crop of aspiring artists. This was my second year teaching this program under Mark Coates' leadership and it was really taking off. We had a great group of kids, with an exciting blend of projects that became a unique blend of conceptual and technical approaches. All of which were designed to get these 6—12th graders "thinking like artists" and experimenting with a wide variety of media out on location.

We'd do *Plein air* painting out in the public eye. Some locations included: downtown Annapolis by the City Docks; some days it was all about hiking through Quiet Waters Park; and at least once in the fall or summer, we'd take the kids to the Baltimore Museum of Art, to the Hirshhorn or to the National Gallery of Art in Washington D.C. to do drawings inside the museum and outdoors in the Sculpture Gardens—all are traditions that still carry over into present day.

Marlene and I also started our graduate coursework at Towson with Dr. Jane Bates. I developed ideas for beginning my

Master's Thesis on *Visual Journaling*, while Marlene focused on printmaking. And while Jane was busy pushing my creative thought processes in the realm of research, we also started taking some exciting Graduate level drawing and painting classes with the kind of artists that literally helped me push amazing boundaries from a technical skill and conceptual thought standpoint.

Jane was great for me from a research standpoint, being a published author herself, and proved equally as invaluable to David Modler, who was another art student of hers I'd later befriend and spend many years collaborating with, presenting at national conventions. David would become a professor of Art Education at Shepherd University and together we'd create a pipeline for his student artists at Shepherd who were from Maryland to come intern with me at Southern High. Jane always used to say to me, "You've got to meet David Modler. You guys would hit it off!" One day, she got to see us presenting together at a national art convention and couldn't have been prouder.

My studio professors/artists at Towson also became new mentors and sources of inspiration to me, and they truly changed the way I looked at my own process of painting.

They were Michael Weiss and Nora Sturges.

Michael Weiss taught me during his inspiring class called "Drawing on Meaning", where I learned how to apply emotional context into physical works of art, and how to teach my kids in my own classes how to do the same. While I always did this naturally in my own art, it was the first time I realized this could be a teachable practice that could be meaningful and therapeutic at the same time.

In order to draw on meaning one must create with purpose; drawing from experiences in our own lives as inspiration for the work. Art can be as subjective as it is objective. And while meaning shifts from person to person, it all comes from our point of view, which is based solely on the viewer's prior experiences. Take the topic of religion. Whose God is the "real God"? No two Catholics believe uniformly; nor do two Muslims. Perception is their reality, which is rooted in their experiences with their religion and their point of view is formed based on these experiences, in addition to *what* they've been taught and *how* they've been taught.

These are the kinds of deep philosophical and artistic conversations we'd have in Michael Weiss' "Drawing on Meaning" class. Michael was like an art encyclopedia. He knew everything there was to know about art and about the history of art throughout the ages.

And then there was Nora Sturges. I love Nora. She really taught me how to paint with oils. Up until then, I was essentially "self-taught", but I was eager to learn. And she was easy to learn from. She had this way about her that was very nurturing to me. It felt "safe" being in her studio, which is the kind of atmosphere I've worked to cultivate for my own students over the years.

She introduced me to the Grisaille and Verdaccio methods of oil painting, taught me glazing and scumbling, and introduced me to painting on MDF Board, which I, in turn, also teach my own aspiring art students how to do to this day. Nora also taught me how to have "good palette hygiene" as she put it. She said I worked so heavily and aggressively and that I needed to slow down, take my time, and do more mixing in my palette than on my canvas itself. She also encouraged me. It was easy to want to work hard for Nora. She was so sweet, so reserved, and an absolute perfectionist when it came to knowing her stuff and understanding how to paint. There's no way I could ever put a measure on the impact Nora, Michael, Jane and the other professors that embraced me since my early years prior with Roger at Lycoming. I wish I had people like that around me in high school. These were truly inspiring individuals.

Since those early years, and throughout the course of my adult life, I've read a lot of motivational books written by a wide range of authors, from artists to billionaires. In every book I've ever read, there's always been some personal tragedy that has taken the author beyond "their why" and into "their how and their what." Translation—they all knew *their why*, but they also figured out "how" to create their "what". How they got those "gallery shows". What they learned that directly contributed towards taking them to that next level. Therefore, I'm going to share this with you too. The kind of things that go on in my studio long before the works hit the galleries, long before the awards and accolades were handed out.

In order to give you this knowledge, I have to return to the place where my stories are always first born—*my visual journals.*

I've amassed well over thirty volumes of visual journals over my lifetime, which is right on pace with the amount Picasso amassed during his lifetime. In them lies my secrets. My art-making process. My notetaking. My sketches. Plans. Goals. My dreams. Some realized, some—still awaiting realization.

On the first page of every sketchbook I create, I always draw a ballpoint pen rendition of *Lascivia*, which is that first painting I ever sold in New York City—the one I sold to my roommate at the time, Matt Harvey. I always make the sketch tiny, approximately 3.5" X 3.5" in the bottom right corner of page one. And, with each new volume, I give it a number and a title.

The volume I'm looking at now is entitled, "Personalities . . . in the Spotlight . . . deepen the mystery," which is written in scratchy ballpoint pen. Inside the next page are some inspirational quotes. Some are from Sun Tzu's *The Art of War* and Machiavelli's *The Prince*. Others from Joseph Murphy's book *The Power of your Subconscious Mind* and from a book by Catherine Ponder entitled, *The Dynamic Laws of Prosperity*.

Around the same time I became immersed in visual journaling, Nora turned me on to the work of Eric Fischl, whom I've aforementioned in regards to his 9/11 sculpture and for his *the Bed, the Chair* series. Nora said that while I didn't necessarily paint like Fischl, his content and ways of thinking were right up my alley. *And she was right.*

Eric painted these psycho-sexual suburban dramas on larger-than-life sized canvas. They were essentially figurative scenes about the ironies that took place in suburbia; specifically about life growing up as a child on Long Island, where everyone in the middle class was trying to "keep up with the Joneses" and hiding countless family secrets. Eric would bring these secrets to light through his paintings—secrets juxtaposed against the backdrop of the 1970s and 1980s.

He also explored very personal issues in his work; things like his Mom's alcoholism, his discovering puberty, questions surrounding whether his parents were "swinging" in the era of free love, and his Mom's proclivity towards nudity in the home as being "normal". These were where all departments of Eric's work shined. He carved out a unique niche in this genre of suburbia, which was a genre nobody at the time was tackling, so it became his alone.

"What would become *my genre?*" I thought to myself.

I remember reading a quote from Eric that I wrote down in my sketchbook about how he frames up his experiences: "Art gives us permission to experience and have an experience while framing it in a way that makes it socially acceptable."

I, too, was ready to push boundaries with my work—*just not in the land of suburbia*. For me, my realm was *the Mob*. Stories surrounding power, sex and violence.

People in "the life" was a world I was all too familiar with. After all, these people were friends and family to me, and I was close enough to it all that I could tell these stories in an authentic way unlike any other artist of my time. I wasn't an outsider looking in on this world.

Time to paint.

Time to "rage against the dying of the light."

THIRTY-ONE

LAKE POWELL

Michael Weiss told our class about his upcoming solo exhibition at the Numark Gallery in Washington D.C. on Friday, September 13, 2002. We were all invited to attend.

This would prove to be another one of those instances where "I'd always go", which always led to something huge. *Something life changing*.

At this point in my career, I was extremely curious what went on at art exhibitions. I never had a real gallery exhibition of my own work beyond my senior show at college, which doesn't really count, and this was at a well-known gallery in Washington D.C.

Eric Fischl had exhibited there once early in his career too, so I wanted to see what went on, what a *real exhibition* looked like, what you did at a gallery opening *as an artist*. I considered this an opportunity to "take notes" while preparing for my own future.

After all, gallery shows were not something prevalent in "my world" or among the type of guys I hung out with, so this was all new territory for me, and I wanted to soak it all in . . . learn as much as I possibly could before going out into the world on my own as a potential gallery artist.

So, amidst all this learning and my fascination with changing the way I was thinking and perceiving life and art, and just before Michael Weiss' opening night was scheduled to take place, I received a call from Georgia.

She invited Lisa and me to vacation with her and some friends and family in Lake Powell in order for me to take some photographs of her for a future painting commission or two.

The timing was extremely emotional, as we were coming up on the first anniversary of 9/11, but again, I felt it was important for us to "just go" . . . whenever an opportunity like this presents itself. Therein lies half the battle—the importance of just showing up. Whether it be to an art opening, an invite to participate in something new, or just showing up to put in some work in your studio, or at the gym . . . even when you don't feel like it.

James Gandolfini, the famed actor who played *Tony Soprano* once said, "There's a lesson to be learned in just showing up; showing up every day, honing your skills—even when you don't feel like it. There is a lesson in that."

And, I believe this, wholeheartedly. After all, I was living proof of this. Show up for the process, and create an opportunity for yourself. See what happens from there. Make the most of whatever comes your way.

This was around the same time period that I also began incorporating text into my paintings. I started to ask whoever I was painting to incorporate their own hand-written text directly into the background of my actual works. Whether it be random thoughts they had, a poem they wrote—just something that put "their physical mark" on my pieces. I guess, early on, I always loved collaborations. I loved learning how people think, and why they think what they think.

Instead of my paintings becoming "my own private window into their soul," my work started becoming more of a collaborative effort, and one where I was literally "inviting my subjects to participate in the painting's creation by allowing them to make their mark on my canvases. Sometimes I'd allow their text to show through, sometimes allow it to be completely illegible.

Georgia wrote a poem that I ended up basing her next painting on entitled, *The Arrival*. Now all I needed was a photograph of her for the painting itself, which she insisted had to be taken at Lake Powell.

So, we packed our suitcases, and with the opportunity to travel out West again, we decided to make the most of it. I booked us a flight to Phoenix so we could rent a car and drive five hours through beautiful Sedona and experience the West Coast on our own. We thought it would be fun making little stops along the way at authentic, local Mexican restaurants, places like that.

WHEN WE ARRIVED INTO PHOENIX and rented a car, it couldn't have been a better decision. The drive through the desert, lined with cactuses and breathtaking sunsets was indescribable.

It's just like you'd imagine seeing in the movies, only better. It was romantic. We felt like gypsies traveling from place to place, without a care in the world. And we stopped at the most delicious "hole-in-the-wall" Mexican restaurants along the way, one, in particular, was just outside of Sedona, which I would describe as being like a little oasis in the desert. There literally is also nothing like traveling through the canyons of beautiful red rock into Lake Powell. Words simply can't do it justice.

Lake Powell itself is a reservoir on the Colorado River, straddling the border between Utah and Arizona. It's essentially like being in the middle of the Grand Canyon on water. Georgia had rented a 50' houseboat and among her gang that lived with us on the houseboat for a week was: Aida Bogosian, owner of famed *Michael B. Jewelers* on Ventura Boulevard in Los Angeles and one of her girlfriends; Georgia's parents—Angelina and Pooch; this funny guy named Jim and his son; and Georgia's daughter, Toni.

Georgia's poem, "A Desert Flower," which I kept in my sketchbook and in my mind throughout the course of the trip while searching for that "perfect photo" of her for my painting served as inspiration for me.

Georgia's poem read:

A DESERT FLOWER
By Georgia Durante
"A Desert Flower
Growing from a Barren Rock
Standing Alone
Its beauty is something one wants to possess
but beauty can only be captured by the mind
and held in the heart
It cannot be possessed
Like me, it takes on a lonely quality
Blowing mindlessly in the wind
with no direction
Waiting to be picked
only to wither and die."

Alongside the poem in my sketchbook, I split the poem up down the middle and wrote: "Georgia White" on left, "Georgia Black" on right. I took copious notes and did thumbnail sketches, writing things like, "vulnerable, trusting; a hill; dandelions blowing petals; a sundress; wildflowers in hand; face turning from the light to face the dark; teardrops turning into blood on the sand; red rock, flowers emerging from cracks in the red rock; spirits floating like the haunted house in *Disney World*; lighting a cigarette; ivy growing on rock; spider webs glistening; Georgia White and Georgia Black staring at one another in two paintings."

These would transcend into ideas for future paintings of her.

Then I started thinking about a triptych. "Three sides to every story. Going beneath the surface. His side, her side, the truth somewhere in the middle. Who will the audience identify best with?" I asked myself, as we drove through the red rock canyons into the most beautiful destination I'd ever seen—*Lake Powell*.

We unpacked at the hotel on premises where we'd be staying just for the night and went into town to do some shopping for the week. Food, alcohol, stuff to make campfires, toiletries, things like that. And, after spending the first night in the hotel, the next morning we all pitched in to fuel up the houseboat, boarded and shoved off, leaving the navigating up to this guy Jim's younger son, who had apparently driven huge houseboats the size of this one before.

I had no clue when it came to this stuff, and I didn't think Georgia or anyone else on the boat did for that matter. The views were amazing, no matter which direction you looked. It was like the Grand Canyon on water. We were all seeking out the perfect grotto, something with a romantic waterfall of crystal blue water in a little private alcove of red rock.

It was funny, though, the eclectic mix of people aboard. Georgia could fit in with anybody, as could we, but it was still comical. Aida and her girlfriend were still bejeweled with Beverly Hills' finest diamonds and gold, dressed in designer swimsuits, high heels, and designer sunglasses, dancing around to Greek music on the top deck while drinking Belvedere vodka and smoking cigarettes.

Lisa fit right in with the girls, though. They were so much fun, and Georgia and I talked privately from time to time about the creation of her paintings when the opportunity presented itself. Georgia didn't want to monopolize my time, but I could tell that she also felt a breath of fresh air surrounding these paintings. For her, it was a reason to move forward. After all, I was someone interested in her story. I empathized with it and was interested in making it come to life and immortalizing it through my art.

This was important.

It was my first real venture into storytelling on a much deeper level than ever before, since it was someone else's story I was now telling. I had to understand it completely, in order to get it right and become intimately in tune with her, as my subject, in order to breathe the kind of energy into my brushwork that accurately captured her story.

I never stopped to try and understand "why me" or what this meant for future work, or where it might lead, I just knew this was what I felt I was supposed to be doing at the time. It was a wave I needed to catch and ride out until it was time to get off.

THE FIRST DAY ON LAKE POWELL we got beached and it took half the day to finally get someone to tug us off the land, so there'd be no taking photos on day one. Just some funny ones of me and Jim trying to push this fifty-some foot houseboat off the sandbar we were stuck on, as we pushed and pushed while buried in about three feet of mud. We knew we had to break free soon though, because once it hits night you can't see. You literally have to find a place to make camp at least an hour beforehand or you're totally screwed because it's literally pitch black out on the lake. So, we finally got another boat to stop and help tow us out, and we soon found a place to make camp about twenty miles down the reservoir.

That night we all carried folding chairs and a table out and made a campfire around the setup, roasted marshmallows, and everyone had dinner together. We all took turns cooking stuff throughout the week. Lisa loves to cook, so she pitched in, and Aida was also a fabulous cook, so between those two and Georgia's Mom, we were pretty set! Plenty of drinking went on into the early morning hours and eventually Lisa and I passed out on the rooftop deck of the houseboat watching the stars at night. There was no night air, no bugs. It was just perfect. Not too hot, not too cold. *Just right.* A perfect early September night out in the middle of the darkness on the waters of Lake Powell.

The next day I was determined to get some photographs, and I took them whenever I could. Lisa and I also did some hiking over the red rock. We had never seen anything like Lake Powell before. It was so gorgeous. Georgia pointed out spots where they filmed movies like *Planet of the Apes*, and we explored while taking lots and lots of photographs.

I finally got the shot I was looking for with Georgia late in the afternoon as she leaned back on the boat drinking beer and watching her parents interact lovingly with one another. She had this look of calm come over her face as she watched them. She was also seated next to this chain from the boat that was dangling.

I loved the metaphor—*unchained*—and I snapped the shot. This would become my painting entitled *The Arrival*, a 14" X 18" oil painting on paper done in black and white using the Grisaille method of underpainting I was perfecting back home working with Nora. I liked it in black and white so I never went into the painting in color. At least not until later when I explored the idea as a much larger oil painting on canvas that was close to eight feet in length. Black and White became a theme from early on with how I saw Georgia as these two contrasting selves, Georgia White and Georgia Black, so I left the painting that way.

I'd later work from another photograph I saw in Georgia's home of her staring out a window in what resembled a maid's outfit. That piece would be titled, *The Departure* and would become a companion piece to the painting I did of her on the boat. This painting would be about the moment Georgia decided to leave her small town of Rochester, New York and embark on a new life. I also included the reflection of a train in the window, as a metaphor for her boarding and moving on with a new chapter in her own life at that point. That was *her departure*—the painting on the boat was *her arrival*. Two contrasting elements again. Georgia White and Georgia Black.

Then something strange happened during the week. Her Dad suffered some kind of a stroke, or paralysis shortly after we took off and was bound to a wheelchair for the duration of the trip. I assured Georgia that I felt like he'd be okay. She feared he was dying. That wouldn't prove to be the case. Both her parents would live on for another thirteen years after our trip.

There would prove to be an emotional impact on me when painting works like these. I mean, it's a real commitment. Doing the research, living with my subjects, getting to know their most innermost secrets. I become immersed in their memories and circumstances surrounding their lives as I work. Mix this with my own haunting past, which always seems to creep back in, and it's always a recipe for me to sometimes get lost. Lost in their pain. Lost in my own sadness and loneliness at times. Sometimes it hurts to explore what's below their surface because I'm always somehow digging mine back up again with it all. It can get really dark there at times. I hear their voices. I wish I could have been there to help them earlier—but then, I remind myself that they all experienced what they did in order to lead them to the place they are in today, same as me.

It's literally the road behind us that's gotten us here.

My imagination also plays its role in the interpretation of everything. Some of what I add to a painting comes from what I've experienced while spending the kind of time with my subjects that I do, on a deeper, more personal level than most artists might be comfortable with. Also, on a level that most artist's spouses might not be comfortable with. So, thank God mine knows exactly who she is and what she's about, and for that reason, it's how she understands why it is I'm doing what I'm doing. Anybody else would never understand why I'm doing what I'm doing or my process behind my paintings. In the end, the experience in total creates more of an autobiographical experience than anything else. I'm telling a story—*visually*—based on my ability to bring what's inside them, often deep inside them—*to the surface*. I guess that's a special gift I have. I know it when I've accomplished it.

So, by week's end, we're scheduled to fly back on September 10th, which was the one promise I made to Lisa before leaving. She's not a huge fan of flying in the first place, so I promised her we'd leave on the 10th, not on the first anniversary of September 11th, which was just one day out.

But then a freak storm hit.

So, on the 10th, we literally had to stay anchored due to the severity of the storm. We kept waiting it out, waiting it out, Lisa growing more and more anxious with each passing hour. Finally, we both realized the inevitable. We weren't going to make our flight. Then, by some stroke of luck, I finally was able to get cell phone service, so I re-booked us a flight out of Phoenix the next day without penalty. We spent one more night on Lake Powell and headed back on the fateful first anniversary of September 11th.

THE DRIVE BACK through Phoenix was fine, but the plane flight was a different story altogether. *It was downright eerie.* There was literally *no-one* aboard our flight. Out of fear, I suppose. Totally empty. I mean, you could sprawl out across three seats and sleep if you wanted to. There was next to nobody on the plane—except for this one Muslim passenger of Arab descent in the aisle directly across from us, and he had Lisa totally freaked out.

Now, I'll preface this by saying I'm the least prejudice person you'd ever meet, but when it came to that fateful first anniversary of 9/11, even for me it became a little alarming seeing this Arab guy seated across the aisle from us reading the Koran backwards. I assured Lisa not to worry, he probably wasn't a hijacker or anything, I mean, there was hardly anybody on the plane for Christ's sake! What would be the motive to hijack it?

But regardless, Lisa grew more agitated, especially after he asked the flight attendant for *actual silverware* for his in-flight meal. He said that he couldn't eat with the plastic utensils. Lisa couldn't believe the flight attendant actually gave him a fork and a knife. From that moment on, I was on the defensive.

"Here," Lisa instructed me, "Dig through my purse. Find something—*anything* that you can make a weapon out of—and make it fast, just in case. Keep your eye on him . . . If he does anything—*you finish him.*"

These were my instructions. But all I want to do is sleep. I was exhausted. But now I'm forced to keep one eye open on this shady dude reading the Koran, who is also now armed with a knife and fork for the remainder of our five-hour flight.

So, as I'm drifting off to sleep here and there, Lisa keeps hitting me with "Wake back up!" *It was brutal.* When we finally touched down safe and sound I reflected on just how profoundly 9/11 changed everything, including everybody's perception of even the silliest of things—like asking for silverware on a plane. It's so sad what's happened to totally change the world we live in, all due to those tragic events surrounding 9/11.

It changed the face of war. It changed the economy. *It changed everything.*

Once home safe and sound, I continued my ever-growing conversations with Georgia Durante. We'd talk over the phone on a frequent basis as I was busy painting scenes from her life. I was learning from doing these paintings and enjoyed the connection I had with Georgia.

She was teaching me as much as she could about the entertainment industry as I was helping her cope with her tumultuous past through my artwork. I was also discovering new approaches to connect the dots between what Michael Weiss and Nora Sturges were teaching me. I felt there was a reason Georgia and I was destined to meet, and I was trying to figure it out.

When I learned more about her years of physical abuse suffered at the hand of her late husband who eventually committed suicide with her gun after being faced with either Federal Indictment or his own executioners within the Rochester Mob, I began understanding more and more what this series was supposed to be about.

Years ago, I'd come to someone's aid by meeting their oppressor with violence as judge, jury, and executioner. And, I paid a steep price, one that nearly cost me twenty years of my life. Now I was coming to someone's aid through my art, trying a new approach. One in which the proverbial "pen is mightier than the sword." This approach would become transformative to me, as a person, and as an artist. I never realized I had the power to change someone's life for the better with my art. But it wasn't just "my art" that was empowering for Georgia, as others I'd soon meet would step up to the plate and commission me because of what they saw in the creation of this new series.

In the end, I never made any real money off of any of these works. Georgia has a couple. Many of the originals I still have. But it was the time I spent working on the paintings that mattered the most. The phone calls, the conversations we'd share, my simply taking the time with another human being to truly understand their story, who she really was, what she'd really been through and how I could bring all of this understanding to the surface through a work of art.

That's why I say, "While I spend a lot of time on the surface of my paintings, it's the inside that I'm truly after." I wrote a rough draft about the works while creating an artist's statement in my sketchbook later that September. I'd later change the title of the series from *Wounds to Wisdom* to *Voices of Violence*. It read:

WOUNDS TO WISDOM
Artist's Statement by Michael Bell

"*Wounds to Wisdom* explores and examines the psyche of individuals and the circumstances that surrounded their (devastating) wounds. While studying their stories through a series of narrative portraits, we are invited to experience the results of their outward circumstances artistically while learning that it is possible to rise above patterns and cycles surrounding our past and present decisions to make life a triumphant experience. As viewers, we can appreciate our own vulnerabilities that give us the strength we need to grow, live, love, and 'gain wisdom' about our present circumstances. The point is *Immortalization. The Objects*—I want them to become an essential ingredient in the artwork. Symbolic metaphors, but not so engaging that they narrow the overall viewer experience—the objects should not be locked in a time period."

AROUND THIS SAME TIME PERIOD I struck up a friendship with Sofia Milos, an Italian/Greek actress best known at that time for her recurring role on *the Sopranos* as Camorra Boss Annalisa Zucca. We exchanged frequent e-mails and talked once and awhile on the phone about the portrait I began for her and I shared photographs of it with her as it progressed.

Sofia was also very soulful, like Georgia, and had both a spiritual side as well as a dark side, to some degree. Like Georgia, I sensed she also hid a lot behind her smile. I always knew when she was busy, and when she wasn't because we'd talk more frequently when she was in between roles.

Every conversation we had centered on "positive energy" and she helped me to incorporate her same "spirit" into my painting through our talks.

So, with Sofia's painting started, Georgia's paintings in progress, I got a phone call from Joey G to do a second *3rd Avenue Festival of Hope* in Brooklyn at his Bay Ridge restaurant on October 20th. I also lined up another potential mural client and some smaller drawing commissions online through my "Gangster Art" fans frequenting my website.

Time to make another to-do list in my visual journal.

On top of all this, Georgia invited Lisa and I back out to her Hollywood home to spend Thanksgiving with her and a gang of her old Hollywood friends, along with a couple old school friends of hers from 29th Street in Manhattan. If you know the neighborhood, you know the kind of "friends" I'm referring to.

Thanksgiving in Hollywood this year? Sure, why not!

I figured this would be a great opportunity to try something new. Instead of just snapping photographs of Georgia to work from for future paintings in this ongoing *Voices of Violence* series, I also wanted to start some of the paintings *from life* and not just work from photographs (*which is always best*). In a sense, it was me "living life like an artist should." And by that, I mean REALLY getting to know Georgia as my subject over several hours of drawing her from direct observation.

This was initially something that began as just an idea, one I never really ventured into before other than in college while taking nude figure drawing classes, but it was something I was really interested in trying with her. I was interested in examining the effect working from life might have on my painting process, and on my overall final products.

Georgia was game.

So, I also touched base with Sofia Milos, figuring I'd kill two birds with one stone, and line up a painting unveiling with Sofia while we're back out in L.A.

She, too, agreed and wanted to do her portrait unveiling at *the Four Seasons* in Beverly Hills. Who was I to say no to that?!

It was also around this same time that I met another artist, Michael Sprouse. The relationship I'd forge with him would also prove to be one that would change the course of my work and would prove to be the kind of brotherly bond I'd never had with another artist before him.

And it all happened because I said "yes" to going to Michael Weiss' upcoming show at the Numark Gallery.

Always go. *That's my motto.*

Jean Teitelman, Roxanne Weidele and Principal Cliff Prince with me at Southern High's first ArtQuest in 1998. Below is John Aylor, the Tech Ed teacher that helped save my job, former student Chuck Grower and ArtQuest's first "Best of Show" winner Zoe FitzSimmonds in 2000. This also became a year marred in tragedy with the death of Keith Rogers.

In Brooklyn helping with post 9/11 relief efforts, selling art and autographing prints with longtime *Sopranos* pal Joseph R. Gannascoli (*Vito*). Father Mychal was my wife's childhood priest and was the first recorded casualty of 9/11. My portrait of Robert Cordice was donated to support Brooklyn's Squad 1.

Lisa with her Dad (left); and Joe and I (right) working the crowd at our booth outside Joe's Bay Ridge restaurant at that time aptly named *Soup as Art*.

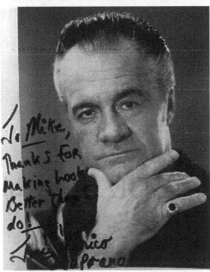

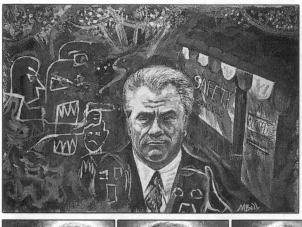

Early John Gotti paintings and charcoal drawings ranging from 1990 - 2002.
Angel Gotti, the Don's eldest daughter, owns most of the drawings.
The center ones are of Gotti and Dellacroce in the Ravenite Social Club.
Below is my prophetic 1998 *John Gotti: America* painting with the Twin Towers.

In 2002 at my first Hollywod portrait unveiling for Georgia Durante, ex-wheel-woman for the Mob. One day later I was at my first $500-a-plate gala with Hugh O'Brien, Art Linkletter, William F. Austin, Pat Boone and Lou Ferrigno. It was the last time I'd ever see my *Another Side of the Mirror* painting.

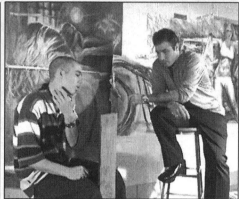

I didn't let my first disasterous brush with the Hollywood Art Auction scene halt my momentum. I flew right back out to Georgia's home and began a new series of paintings entitled *Voices of Violence* that would change my life, L.B.'s life and countless other lives forever.

My art began to take me places. This trip was to Lake Powell on America's first anniversary of 9/11 to take photos of Georgia for more paintings. My next Hollywood auction was a huge success, with this painting going for $12,000.

2003 proved to be an exciting year. I met Michael Sprouse, then gallery owner, artist, future lifetime collaborator and dear friend. I had a solo exhibition at his Zwaanendael Gallery November 1st, spent Thanksgiving in Hollywood, did a portrait unveiling in Beverly Hills for actress Sofia Milos and then two collaboration art shows with Michael.

Sofia autographed a *CSI: Miami* script that Michael and I auctioned off along with our first collaboration art painting, *Never Was*, to help save the Milton Theatre. Then we created more collaboration paintings for an *Ireland* show. I even painted my Dad.

THIRTY-TWO

THE TWO MICHAELS

As I began writing this chapter about my experience meeting Michael Sprouse, now a dear friend of mine of the better part of well over a decade, the interesting thing is that I was actually doing it from his computer (*without him knowing*). It was Saturday night, December 12, 2015, and he had an art opening the next afternoon entitled, "Portraits and Ponderation" at Lula Brazil in Rehoboth Beach, Delaware.

It was a sprinkling of colorful new abstract paintings and some of his signature narrative portraits, which are often paintings based off of vintage photographs of people long departed, some of which Michael gathered from flea markets and antique shops. Michael channels their inner spirit and brings his own intuitive take on their story as he paints them, breathing new life into their souls.

Now, it's been years since Michael has had a solo exhibition, or been active in the gallery scene, but it's how we first met—in Washington D.C. at his Eklektikos Gallery. Since I hadn't seen Michael in over a year, I thought it would be a nice surprise for me to show up the night before his show and celebrate with him, plus it would be great to get together with him before Christmas.

Funny thing was when I showed up at his house and texted him to see where he was he hits me back with this:

"Hey, champ! At dinner holiday cocktail party in D.C."

D.C.?!!! I couldn't believe it. *Son of a bitch!*

Lisa told me I should've called first. I just figured there's no way he'd be anyplace else but home the night before his opening. Worst case scenario—he'd be out on the town and I'd just meet him out someplace for drinks. I had Lisa text him the day before asking for his address under the guise of needing it to send out Christmas cards (and so I could plug his address into my GPS, since I'm horrible with directions). After a few back and forth texts (being that he didn't believe me that I was actually standing on his doorstep—after all, he's known me to be a bit of a prankster) I snapped a selfie in front of his wreath holding a bottle of scotch and a fistful of cigars. His response:

"Holy shit! *You ARE at my house!* Haha! You rock. Stay the night, I'll tell you where the key is. I'll be back in the morning. Party with me tomorrow night. I love you for this man! God! It would have been awesome! Fuck. So wish I was there."

So, there I was. All alone at Michael's home in Lewes, Delaware while he's in Washington D.C., writing this very Chapter from his very own computer. At least I'm being productive, right? After all, everything happens for a reason.

I figured it was a good time to reflect and write while I was there since he's someone who has had a profound effect on my career as an artist and on my way of seeing the world. Michael and I have also talked about writing a book together too on numerous occasions, because we collaborate so well.

Over the course of many years, we've painted paintings together and done shows together, packaging them as "two-man exhibitions". He knows me better than I know myself, probably, and the same goes for me when it comes to him. He's one of those kindred spirits that comes along once in a lifetime and no matter how many years go by when you're with them it's like no time has passed. That's the kind of brotherly bond Michael and I have shared over the years, over the ups and downs of the art world, and over the course of numerous different career paths Michael has undergone. Currently, he's the "On Air Arts & Entertainment Reporter" for *WRDE NBC Coast TV* and he's since founded his own *TwinFin Media, LLC* Production Company. But when we first met he was a *gallery owner*, so, let's start there, where he happens to be right now as I type this—in Washington D.C.

This is where the story of "the two Michaels" begins.

I RETURNED HOME FROM LAKE POWELL on September 11th and got ready to head to the Numark Gallery in Washington D.C. for Michael Weiss' show that was opening just two days later on September 13th. His show would remain on exhibit through October 26th but I really wanted to surprise him and show up at his opening. I had a lot to do this month from the moment our plane landed, preparing to head back for my second appearance in Brooklyn with *the Sopranos* in October, but I decided I should really go to Weiss' show, out of respect for him and all he'd been doing for my own personal growth as an artist.

With that idea in mind, I unpacked, sifted through a ton of e-mails from when we were away and without a computer (remember, this is before the age of the smartphone), and there pops up an e-mail from none other than Michael Sprouse. He wrote me that he was doing an online search for his own website to see how his search engine rankings were doing and my website popped up. He checked it out, and said something to me along the lines of, "As a gallery owner, I'm really not one to reach out to other artists, since they'd soon be looking for a show with me, but I did appreciate your work and wanted to let you know."

He also went on to say that while he didn't know where I was located (being my website doesn't say where I live), but if I was ever in D.C. to drop by his Eklektikos Gallery and say hi.

Of course, the very next thing I did was first check out his website so I could see his work, and check out his gallery to see if I could find a picture of him to see who in fact he was. Right away, after looking at his hauntingly timeless contemporary portraits, I could see we already kind of worked like one another. While our styles weren't exactly the same, they weren't all that different either, and I could see a little of the same techniques I applied to my paintings in his. So, I e-mailed him back almost immediately, telling him—as synchronicity would have it—I was, in fact, traveling to D.C. for Michael Weiss' art opening and if his gallery was nearby, I would gladly also stop by and meet him. Funny thing was when I mentioned that Weiss' show was at *the Numark* on 406 7th Street NW Michael immediately responded back.

"That's my address! Cheryl's space is literally right next door! We share an adjoining wall with the Numark Gallery. We've definitely got to meet!"

So, on Friday the 13th, just two days after returning home, I headed off to the Numark Gallery in D.C. Curious thing also was, as I wrote this Chapter in 2015, it was also the 13th, the thirteenth of December, well over a decade later, and well after midnight.

When I arrived in D.C. for Michael Weiss' show I found parking around the corner and headed in. The Numark and Eklektikos galleries were side-by-side on the third floor of the building. So, up the stairs I went. As I walked up the stairs I passed this really tall guy with a floral printed Hawaiian-type shirt headed downstairs with a couple other gallery patrons. I couldn't tell you who he was with, but there was something about him that caught my attention. Almost like your soul recognizing the soul of another's energy somehow. I actually took a second glance back down at him as he headed outside wondering to myself—*was that Michael Sprouse*? He admitted to me later that he did the same double-take on me as I walked past him on the steps. Upon returning back inside, we passed each other once again. Michael turned and finally asked . . .

"Are you Michael Bell?"

"I sure am. *Michael Sprouse*?" I asked, figuring it was him.

"Great to meet you!" he smiled. "I'm headed back outside for a quick smoke. I'll be back shortly. I'll meet you back inside."

ONCE INSIDE THE NUMARK GALLERY, which was situated to the right of Eklektikos, Michael Weiss greeted me at the door. He was dressed to the nines in a suit and his highly enameled glossy abstract works lined the studio walls. This was the first time I ever saw Michael Weiss' paintings.

He purposely never let us see his own personal work in class, and now I knew why. He was pushing my boundaries with my realism, yet he was working completely abstract with shapes morphing into one another, like a series of ovals, almost plasma-like paintings as if you were looking at something under a microscope. Very organic in nature. Lots of overlapping colors, shapes, some allowing underpainted parts to show through, others more opaque.

"So, what do you think?" Michael Weiss asked me. "Still going to follow my advice now, after seeing my work?" he chuckled.

"Of course!" I responded confidently, still taking it all in.

I made light of the fact that I must have had total surprise written all over my face, not expecting such abstract works based on the manner in which Weiss was teaching me. But I got it. This is what being an artist is about. Finding your own voice. Your own signature style. Creating a series of works that are cohesive.

And, his show definitely was cohesive. It also seemed to generate a lot of interest from the public too. It's one of the reasons I wanted to attend his show. To see how it's done.

I'd never had my own solo exhibition of my paintings—not like this, at a "real gallery". While I had my first Hollywood auction, which was a total flop, and also had my first brushes with celebrities who were now buying my work, the gallery scene was all new to me. While some of my celebrity clientele were starting to catapult some buzz into my career, and I did have lots of commissions lined up in the form of murals and charcoal drawings of gangsters, which seemed to be *my genre*—I hadn't had any real showings of my work at an *actual gallery*. So, I was there to watch and to learn. I liked the energy. I liked watching him work the crowd. I imagined . . . *one day that could be me.*

I had no idea this would be the night that would also begin a life-long friendship and take my own art to a whole other level.

After a while, I shook Michael Weiss' hand, allowed him to get back to his patrons so he could generate some more sales and told him I was going to stop by the gallery next door and meet its owner.

As I entered Eklektikos, I took a quick glance around at the work that was hung—*also a series of abstract paintings*—but definitely not the polished version I saw next door by Michael Weiss, and definitely not the works I saw online by Michael Sprouse. These were works by a local artist who had apparently befriended Michael Sprouse. They were *kitschy* paintings, all consisting of a colorful array of dots on canvases accompanied by a tremendously over-inflated artist's statement that ran over into a second stapled page. The kind of statement that could've been extracted from a medical journal. It was confusing at best, but I tried to look back and forth and make the connection between the artist's statement and the work itself. As I was trying to figure out what I was looking at, I spotted Michael Sprouse watching me study the work from across the room. He began to make his way over to me through the crowded opening.

"Michael Bell! Great to finally meet you again man. Glad you made it into my gallery!" he exclaimed.

Michael also must have caught me glancing back and forth between the statement and the paintings and asked me, "So, what do you think of the work?"

Now, this was my first meeting Michael, so I definitely wasn't going to blurt out what I really thought of the artist's paintings. It's not like me to be insulting anyways. Maybe I just didn't get it? Maybe it was *me* that was missing something, I thought. Michael quickly re-assured me, quietly, so as not to be within an earshot of anyone else. "It's ok," he whispered. "You can tell me."

"At the end of the day, despite what I'm reading, and despite what I'm seeing, these are just . . . *dots* . . . aren't they?" I asked, glancing back and forth at the artist's lengthy statement about the "dot paintings" in front of me.

"Sadly, *they are* just dots," Michael smiled. "Come on, let me take you back around the corner here and show you some of my pieces. So glad you could make it down to D.C."

And, just around the corner, there they were—the haunting, narrative portraits I saw online of all these women's faces. Beautifully painted, soulful even. Realistic, but not, due to the bright palette of splashy colors and drips.

It's like the works came to life when you stared at them long enough in the same way one feels the Mona Lisa is staring at you no matter where you walk, no matter what angle you try and sneak up on her. This was the same effect Michael Sprouse built into the eyes of these contemporary portraits. I loved them.

And, I even bought a $35 print of "Wind" off of him.

We went on to talk downstairs over cigarettes on 7th Avenue. I was really glad that we met. Even hearing Michael in action at his galley talking to patrons and making sales (not of his particular artist's work that he was showing, but *of his own work* during the opening, which cracked me up a little). He also reminded me of myself the way I dealt with potential clients.

He was a people person. He knew what to say, when to say it and he had this charm about him. A certain *charisma* that seemed to be exactly the way I was.

Our stories were similar but extremely different at the same time. His middle name was even the same as mine—*Michael Douglas*. And while we shared similar dark stories surrounding our respective childhoods, we both grew up on very different sides of the tracks and hung in extremely different circles . . .

MICHAEL HAD A ROUGH UPBRINGING, definitely not a privileged kid by any means, and he also took his fair share of abuse in one tragic form or another throughout his childhood. This also certainly shaped the origins behind why he became exactly who he became. The story of Michael "the Artist" began after experiencing the tragedy of losing his mother to cancer at the young age of twenty-three youngster living in Kentucky.

The loss was so profound it haunted him his whole life. A friend of his told me once that when looking at his early paintings his mother seemed to be present in every one of his works. With his mother's passing and his Dad turning their home into a shrine to her, everything began weighing too heavily on Michael and it all became too much for him to bear. So, his father, whether he recognized this himself or not, decided to send Michael off with literally just enough bus fare to take him to Washington D.C. to pursue his dream of becoming an artist. It was there where he met George Thomasson while working as a waiter. George became his life-long partner and co-owner of the Eklektikos Gallery.

This would be the last show I'd see at Eklektikos. Michael explained to me later that night that he and George were thinking about moving to the beach to pursue some other careers. That Lewes, Delaware was an up-and-coming town and a lot of their friends from D.C. had already moved there, due to the escalating violence that was becoming pervasive in the nation's capital.

Michael explained how gallery sales were on a quick yet steady decline ever since 9/11. Cheryl Numark was also going to shut her doors soon, or at the very least, find another location. He said everybody seemed to be jumping ship, and so was he.

I was just glad I got to learn what I needed to learn while visiting D.C. for Michael Weiss' show. That night sparked an ever-growing, amazing kinship as artists and a life-long friendship. This is how it all began for Michael Sprouse, in his own words:

AUGUST 8, 2016
Michael Sprouse

"In the spring of 2015, I hit the big half-century mark on the timescale of existence. It designated fifty times that I had ridden that crazy, speeding, twisting and turning, screeching and purring life locomotive around the sun. I celebrated the day accordingly with family and friends. There was a party with plenty to eat and drink. There were gifts, hugs, toasts, vocal and digital declarations of love and hopes for another fifty more.

It was a perfect celebration.

But I realized throughout the day that a man doesn't reach an age milestone without at least a few moments of contemplation and realization. It's as if the psyche won't allow it. There's no denying them. The thoughts follow you throughout the day. They hide in the shadows wearing a long trench coat where they try to get your attention with a *'Psst—Hey buddy'* whisper rasp and the promise of a new watch on the cheap. Other times, they walk right up to you, grab you by the chin and force you to look them straight in the eye.

Eventually, you listen to them. This isn't a particularly enjoyable experience for me. Over the years, I've become someone who isn't fond of spending much time focused on the past. Sure, I'll recant a funny story every now and then. Or perhaps I'll share some intense experience from my youth with someone over one too many glasses of red wine. But overall, it feels like wasted energy to me. I'd rather focus on what's in front of me or plan what I'd like to see ahead. The past forever vanishes. All that remains are thoughts disguised as memories. They cloud and change like a brewing storm over the horizon. It may be perfectly sunny where you are, but somewhere in the distance, you can see the gathering clouds and a distant flash of lightning and maybe experience occasional claps of thunder.

The flip side of that, however, as I have discussed with Michael many times, is that you can't really be who you are now without the experiences that are behind you. I may not like to spend much time looking in that direction, but that doesn't change the fact that each and every second spent traveling on that long stretch of life highway is still present in every 'now' moment of your experience. It is with that perspective in pocket that I am sharing some of my stories here, at least part of it now because it brings me to the present moment where my invaluable and irreplaceable relationship with one of my most cherished friends, Michael Bell, shines like a beacon in the fog.

In the spring of 1990, my life was very different than what it is now. I was twenty-four, living in my hometown of Bowling Green, Kentucky. My mother died about six months' prior at the age of fifty-two after a long battle with cancer. I moved back into my parent's home several months before her death to help with the very stressful and sad situation as well as to help raise my younger brother who was around nine at the time.

My father, with whom I had a rocky relationship, to say the least, was a blue-collar worker struggling with undiagnosed depression and a barely controllable alcohol addiction. Understandably, my mother's death only exasperated the situation and his demons. I was a young, talented artist with zero focus or direction, floating in and out of crappy jobs and haunted by the darkness of having just lost my mother. We had very little money, very little joy and life was dark, heavy and obscured with the aftermath of a parent's early death. It was quite honestly one of the worst periods of my existence.

I spent the majority of the time between my mother's passing and that spring focused on escapism. It was a time of intense drug use, binge drinking, and casual sex. I floated in between feeling completely numb or trying to feel as alive as possible. That meant great risk-taking. How I made it through that time physically unscathed, not incarcerated, healthy and alive is still, to this day, a mystery to me.

And then one day, my father did an amazing and completely uncharacteristic thing. Somehow, through the dreadful darkness of what must have been his new yet completely shattered existence (one that I was too young to comprehend at the time), he found a moment of clarity and he did something for me that changed my life forever.

He bought me a bus ticket.

It sounds like a little gesture, but it was perhaps the most important thing, in retrospect, that he had ever done for me. My sister, who is a little over a year younger than myself, had found her own way out of the gloom by marrying her boyfriend at the time and moving with him to Washington, D.C. a few months prior to my mother's death. This wasn't a selfish act on her part whatsoever. It was not an easy decision for her and she only married and moved away with my mother's complete blessing.

It was a wise and brave decision. Without my knowing, my father had contacted my sister and informed her that he was going to purchase a bus ticket for me to D.C. He wanted to know if I could live with her and her husband for a short amount of time until I found work and a place of my own. *She agreed.*

In short, one afternoon my father announced to me his plan. He told me that he realized I was wasting my life in Kentucky and that I had to go out on my own into the world. He told me that he had purchased a one-way bus ticket to Washington, D.C. and that I could live for a little bit with my sister until I got on my feet. He could spare $75 dollars and a small suitcase that he had picked up at a thrift store so that I could pack some clothes.

I took him up on his offer.

Two years after arriving in Washington D.C., I met my amazing life partner George. One year later, we opened a small art gallery in Georgetown which, through tremendous hard work, eventually become known as one of Washington, D.C.'s top ten contemporary art galleries.

Some nine years later, I met my incredible life-long friend Michael Bell at an art opening after an uncanny string of, what we now believe to be, universe driven synchronicities. That was a life changing experience as well and one that will find its way into more chapters of future stories undoubtedly.

I'm not sure where this ride is going. I can only look at what I like to think is a map that I created and do the best that I can to guide the train along the tracks that form in the present moment. But I do understand, now more so than ever before, that sometimes, when you least expect it fate steps in.

It doesn't scream from across the room or try to lure you from the shadows. It whispers in your ear, sweetly and wisely like a lover. It will ask for just a micro-moment of your attention. It doesn't demand, it offers a choice. If you listen to that whisper, that timeless source of wisdom available to everyone, then your life may very well possibly change into something amazing.

I know mine did." – *Michael Sprouse*

THIRTY-THREE

THE BIRTH OF COLLABORATION ART

I t's rare when artists work together. It's very rare when artists work together on a particular piece. To find someone who is compatible with you stylistically, also someone who has that same artistic vision that you have is rare. – *Michael Sprouse, November 29, 2003, at the opening for the Milton Theatre Project.*

Michael has been reading tarot cards ever since he was a kid. He knows them like the back of his hand. We'd talk about his experiences conjuring up the dead over scotch and cigars in his studio in the spring of 2003, often well into the night, sometimes even pulling all-nighters while drinking and reading tarot cards. This led to some readings he'd do for Lisa and me in the garage studio of his new home in Lewes, Delaware, where we'd engage in deep, intense conversations about art and life.

I imagine our magical friendship could be likened to that of Matisse and Picasso, or between Edvard Munch and Stanislaw Przybszewsky, or perhaps between my contemporaries, Eric Fischl and David Salle. It also led to our first collaboration painting that would be auctioned off to benefit the restoration of the Milton Theatre nearly a year later. And it all happened so naturally.

We even filmed it, not recognizing the importance of it at the time, just documenting what seemed like just a really fun night. Aida, one of Georgia's close friends, who was on the Lake Powell trip, had this really great Sony Camcorder. She showed it to me when we were on the lake. It was so small and took such great quality footage I just had to get one for myself as soon as we returned home.

And, as it so happened, I brought it with us to Michael Sprouse's house the first time Lisa and I were invited up to stay over and hang out with them for the weekend. Lisa started filming us doing our tarot card readings so we could remember what was said. I, too, would be documenting everything with notes and thumbnail sketches in my sketchbook. Michael also kept a visual journal and had these great little ballpoint pen drawings tacked up to the walls of his studio. It was a great little space. He put up this large black curtain across the back of the garage to separate the space and had a couple large *La-Z-Boy* recliners, a table filled with buckets of water, acrylic paint tubes, a scattered assortment of paintbrushes and boxes of vintage photos he'd use for references. Candles were also everywhere. As were the sounds of Billie Holiday, along with other 1920's jazz and swing crooners playing in the background. And, of course, several of his haunting narrative "face paintings" were either hung about the studio or were leaning up against one another against the studio walls. It was a good place to get messy and artsy while drinking and doing tarot card readings.

I'm not sure exactly what sparked the idea to create a painting "together" but we were so charged up that night that we decided to paint. The process began with us sifting through a bunch of Michael's old vintage photographs. We talked about who the people might have been, and why someone might have discarded their photographs. We discussed the story behind this one photo album Michael found in an antique shop, which was filled with love letters between this man and this woman. There were photos of them taken at different places together. They looked so happy, and then—on the last page—was a wedding announcement card. But it was a wedding invitation for the man—*and another woman*. We tried to imagine what might have happened between them. How might she have lost him?

From this conversation, we decided to find a photograph that appealed to each of us to paint together. Michael searched to find one from his vintage stack—someone that was dead and gone, and since I really only fancied myself as painting "the living" I thought it would be more intriguing to juxtapose a narrative between someone dead versus someone that was still alive.

So, I combed through some more magazines Michael had lying around for a model who was older but still living that "spoke to me" for whatever reason and grabbed my attention to use for my piece to this collaborative puzzle. I stumbled upon someone that reminded me of Grace Jones from those old James Bond movies. This model was probably in her forties or fifties. Michael found a very young silent screen star. From there we tried to determine "the why". Why did we choose who we chose? Not just for the aesthetic value of the photograph or the way the woman we invariably chose looked, but why them? Why were they supposed to now be paired together in a narrative? What's the relationship between the two random people? What could we create a story around? Then I headed over to the canvas with an idea I explained to Michael:

"We could make it a piece that would push and pull against each other. Essentially, once we get each of our images started, I'll work on yours some, then you work on mine some and back and forth we go together until it comes together into one complete style and it won't look like two different paintings on one canvas. Does that make sense?" I asked Michael.

"Cool. Very cool!" he exclaimed. *And off we went!*

We initially divided the canvas nearly in half with charcoal. It was a decent sized 30" X 40" canvas. Mine was a close-up of a woman's face on the right side of the divider. Her mouth partially open, teeth and full red lips meeting halfway down the center of her face at the divider, only her left eye fitting into the frame. And then, on the left side of the canvas, Michael began sketching out a full face of his woman—someone from back in the silent screen era of film. As we sketched ours individually, we began contemplating the relationship between the two works. Once sketched out as a rough charcoal drawing, we began painting. And Michael began channeling his thoughts out loud as we'd take turns painting through the night, working on sheer energy and excitement as the painting began to come together as one narrative piece. Me in my guinea tee and short sleeved patterned *Tony Soprano-esque* shirt, black dress pants and dress shoes (which I always wore—you'll never find me in a pair of jeans, I don't even own a pair), and Michael in his white Gold's Gym t-shirt splattered with paint and a pair of old painter's blue jeans.

"I think that artists, people that are creative, are born that way," Michael began explaining as he started our painting. "They're born into this world this way. There are leaders, there are teachers, there are people that just follow, but there are groups of people that are just meant to be artists. Regardless of what type of art they are creating, they have no choice in the matter. Regardless of what they do in life, they are gonna *create something* and if they can't they go insane." Michael talks now to Lisa as she's filming all this, now shifting his brushwork over to "my side" of the canvas.

"Really?" Lisa asks . . .

"Yeah," Michael continued, "and what type of world do we live in if we didn't have artists? Think about time. Think about life and the way it's documented—*it's through the arts*. If you didn't have them, or if they didn't do it or if they *couldn't do it* what a bleak, bleak world we'd live in. People don't understand—every time they see a commercial or every time they go to the store and pick up, say a pair of pants, or something there that they like— there's *an artist* behind that. In this society, it's almost lately like we're trying to ignore it or try not to even think about that. Or when society does recognize it, they think it's some elitist thing that's out of their reach or something they've been trained against appreciating because they can't do it themselves. Therefore, it's only for the 'special' chosen few. *And that's sad.*"

Michael then began adding touches to the eye of my woman on the right side of the canvas. Drips began cascading down the canvas with each brushstroke. A signature move for both of us, coincidentally, or not.

"You're right, I know what you mean," Lisa agreed.

Michael Sprouse continued, "I'm only just thankful that somehow Michael and I and everyone else in that group rose above that mindset. Because where would we be without it? I can't even imagine. Ever since I was a little bitty kid, you know when they ask you 'What do you want to be when you grow up?' A fireman—a hairdresser—whatever—I was like . . . *I want to be an artist*. I remember kids in my class laughing. *Laughing at me*, you know. And well, here I am, at thirty-eight, and look what I'm doing!" Michael laughed as he continued to paint.

When I look back and rewind the video footage of this memory, I can hear the sounds of crickets chirping from outside in the summer night. It was really late into the night, and the studio had grown dim, with the exception of the candles that are lit and studio lights illuminating the canvas we were painting.

Lisa caught my intense stare as I was contemplating my next move on the canvas. My face was lit with that Rembrandt-like lighting from a nearby studio light bulb shining upon my face— the rest of it immersed in shadows and darkness.

"I love the sound of crickets," Michael said, as I approached the canvas and he took a step back.

I loaded up a palette and continued where he left off.

"Is that Pthalo Blue?" Michael asked me.

"Yeah, I use Pthalo Blue a lot in my oil paintings as a glazing process," I explained.

"I don't usually use it so purely like this, like we're using it right now, but I like it . . . it's such a great, great color." Michael negotiated as we began attacking the canvas at the same time.

"When you look at these two [faces] on the canvas now," I asked Michael, "what do you feel the connection is between them, if any, on any type of level? What do you think?"

"Well, I mean, my initial reaction, and I only say this because

I also understand what it is that we're doing here, is in terms of her looking into her future . . ." Michael pointed from the vintage photograph of the young woman on left to the contemporary model I chose to paint to her right.

"This is really about the show," I interjected.

"Absolutely it's about the show . . . absolutely!" Michael exclaimed! "Because these are both, I mean, we're making them sort of ambiguous, but they're both people involved in performing and being out there. That's what's so magical about what we're doing, in my opinion. We're painting a portrait that is inspired by artisans. We're artisans ourselves. And we're melding these two. This is an image of an actress who is very, very young, just starting out. And this other image is of someone forty or fifty years later. That could be her . . . *who she turned into.* Time passes yet they both have these similarities. That's what's so amazing about this process of collaborating. We've taken people that are forgotten and gone, and we put them on a canvas together and suddenly *they're alive again*! That's what's so empowering about it. It's like you're creating a new life for these people," Michael proudly explained.

"Absolutely!" I completely agreed.

"Who would ever think, if you were these people, that when their photo was being taken on that day—*sixty, seventy or eighty years later*—that two guys who have this great connection . . . *two artists* would get together and decide to paint their portrait? When you think about it, *it's uncanny*, it really is. But that's the beauty of making art like this. You never know what's gonna go on. Are we bringing them alive again? And then, is their energy out there somewhere—alive?" Michael continued to ask me these rhetorical questions as he mixed up some more colors in his palette.

"I think so. It's immortalizing them in a way," I said. "It's letting them know they were important and they should not be forgotten. And for whatever reason, *they've been chosen.*"

"Yeah, that's what's so weird about it," Michael explained, "I mean, who are we to say that it's not there? That it's not this weird symbiotic relationship? I mean, we've talked about earlier about how cool it was how we met and everything. How do we know that those same laws don't apply to the people that become subjects that we choose to paint? We don't. When you think about it, we absolutely don't."

We pressed on and continued painting until sun-up. My familiar pattern of pulling all-night painting sessions was also a familiar pattern for Michael.

Lisa eventually crashed and fell asleep in her chair. We didn't stop until the painting was complete. When we finished it we knew we had done something special, we just didn't understand the magnitude of what this would do for our friendship and our artistic talents. It's an interesting bond that takes place when you're painting with someone. Not just alongside someone, but actually "with" someone, as a total collaboration.

Most people that would see the painting afterwards would invariably ask the same questions, "So, who painted what side, or who painted what parts?" But this wasn't the case at all.

We got completely comfortable throughout the process of creation with painting it totally together as if it were done by one artist.

This level of trust between artists is rare. It's one you just have to be completely comfortable with as you realize the changes the other artist might make to your own marks are just part of the process and you just have to embrace that fact and never get too attached to any of your marks, until you both step back and can live with them. It's part of the evolution of the piece itself, and there must be a "reason" your counterpart made the changes they made, and then you, in turn, build off of them and also make changes to their work—*as if the marks were your own*. Simply put, you *embrace change*. You understand that there are no such things as mistakes, just "negotiations".

These negotiations between Michael and I became intuitive very quickly. Not something we even talked about. We never once said over the course of our all-night marathon painting session, "Are you okay with me painting over this area over here . . . or are you okay with me adding this or that?" *We just did it.*

Just like we wouldn't ask such questions of ourselves when we painted our own paintings, we just did what we felt deep inside, and eventually arrived at a moment where we became the viewer. The moment of completion. When there's nothing else that needs to be said within the work. When there's nothing formally distracting or missing. When you just step back and say, "Ahhhhhhhh, yessss—I believe it's finished!"

This would be the first in a series of collaboration paintings Michael and I would create together, as we worked towards putting together several shows over the next couple of years.

So, while I headed home to prepare for my October print signing with my *Sopranos* pals in Brooklyn, and then another trip back to Hollywood in November to spend Thanksgiving with Georgia and do a painting unveiling for actress Sofia Milos, I also kept in touch with Michael along the way.

We plotted and schemed and made plans for future exhibition opportunities together every time we talked. And Michael, being the ever moving entrepreneur that he was . . . he also decided to open up his own new gallery in Lewes, called the Zwaanendael Gallery of Art, aptly named after the Zwaanendael Inn, on the corner of 2nd Street, which was the hotel directly connected to his new storefront gallery space.

This would be the place Michael would introduce me to his own clientele with my first solo exhibition on November 1st of 2003 entitled, *Michael Bell: Recent Works*. This would also be the site of a follow-up show, *the Milton Theatre Project*, our first two-man exhibition of works on November 29th of 2003 to help raise money through an auction of our first collaboration painting *Never Was*, along with prints, autographed photos from my *Sopranos* pals, Sofia Milos, Georgia Durante and others.

It would also be the site of our second two-man show, "The Ireland Show" that we'd launch on St. Patrick's Day, March 17th of 2003. It was another back-to-back busy year for me in the art world, paving my own way as only I knew how. *On my own.*

Doing it my way . . .

THIRTY-FOUR

THE 3RD AVENUE FESTIVAL OF HOPE II

Prior to all these shows with Michael Sprouse, I was still committed to finishing Sofia Milos' painting, and spending time with Georgia over Thanksgiving to continue the narratives in that series. I was also finishing up some paintings to take with me to Brooklyn for round two of the *3rd Avenue Festival of Hope*, so I was charged up and was painting up frenzy!

I prepared lots of prints to take with me to Brooklyn, in addition to the new paintings I was to unveil for Joe Gannascoli, John Fiore, and Tony Sirico. The day of the festa was to be held on October 20, 2002, just a little over one month after returning from Lake Powell with Georgia and meeting Michael Sprouse for the first time in Washington D.C.

My world was opening up to new friends, new colleagues, new techniques, and also the opportunity to travel. This was what being an artist was really about, I told myself. Not those endless hours in solitude spent in the studio with yourself, your thoughts and your canvases. For me, it was about forging new relationships, which could extend outward onto my canvases. And, while 2001 and 2002 were both huge years for me on that front—meeting Joey G and my new *Sopranos* pals while helping out with 9/11 relief efforts, I was also doing pretty good in the education arena—being named Southern High's first ever "Teacher of the Year" in 2001 in a small ceremony that took place in our school's media center. Then, in 2002 I was named the *Maryland Art Education Association's (MAEA)* "Most Outstanding New Art Teacher of the Year." While these were nice honors, my career in the art world was also finally starting to take off!

So, I continued to focus on building up my professional painting career. I'd dedicate myself to my craft, and continue making the most out of every opportunity that came my way, always still "going" whenever there was an opportunity, all the while, beginning my coursework towards my Master's Degree with Dr. Jane Bates, Nora Sturges, and Michael Weiss.

I kind of knew what to expect when traveling back to Brooklyn for my second 3rd Ave Festival. I knew what to take, what not to take, stuff like that. Joe invited actor John Fiore (who played Gigi Cestone on *the Sopranos*) to join us for this round. These two had become friendly on the set of *the Sopranos* and became very close friends back then. Joe also got me another portrait commission a couple months earlier for Tony Sirico (who played Paulie Walnuts on the show) and so I got that painting framed for him to bring with me, along with a painting I did of Joe, Joey Pants (Pantoliano) and Fiore playing craps, which would later go to actor John Fiore. And, since Joe and I were becoming better friends over the course of the past year, he invited Lisa and me to make more than just a day of it in Brooklyn, which sounded like a blast, so we agreed.

Once there, typical block-party-like festivities were underway and we were all set up at our booth, which was lined with Fiore's DVD's and photos to autograph, my fine art giclée prints and Joe's t-shirts. We jokingly used to call Joe *the T-shirt king*, but he's since become *the BottleSkinz King*, creating a mini-empire in 2015 with a line of water-cooler covers emblazoned with the logos of NFL teams on them. He joined more than one hundred and fifty NFL licensees who pay royalties to line up with the league.

This guy simply knows how to *step in shit*. It's just how he is, though. Personable, brazen, bold and ultra-confident. To me, in hindsight, this was just Joe finding his own way to "draw a line from his life to his own art" as I say, since he's an avid sports fan. Yankees and Giants, just like me, all the way!

We began taking photos with fans of the show. I started selling prints I made for Joe, plus we took some publicity photos of us all together for the unveiling of my two new paintings I mentioned earlier, which Tony Sirico would graciously sign over a nice autographed photo of his own to me that read:

"To Mike, Thanks for making me look better than I do. – *Pals, Tony Sirico.*" This is the kind of guys these were. Down to earth, street tough, fun loving wise guys that became like long-lost big brothers to me.

The sunny October day was definitely fun-filled. We couldn't have asked for better weather. Sausage and pepper stands in full force. Huge crowds of patrons lined 3rd Avenue in Bay Ridge, Brooklyn. The iconic Verrazano Bridge served as a picturesque backdrop for photos to be taken with *Sopranos* fans. Lots of FDNY firefighters and NYPD officers came over to also pay their respects and take photographs with us too, although for Joe it was more of an honor for him than the other way around. He loves these guys and supports all they do whole-heartedly.

John Fiore and I got along great too. He's a piece of work. A "ham-and-egger" as Joe would call him. Basically, a total bullshit artist, but he also reminded me of slightly younger, slightly more street-tough Dean Martin with a Boston accent. All these are fine qualities of great actors, right? John was also more of a comedian than anything else too, I mean, between him and Joe, you're laughing your ass off most of the day with the shit they'd say to their fans. Lisa and I were dying laughing!

But, as the day rolled on, and as Joe's waitresses from his "Soup as Art" restaurant kept refilling our cups with scotch or beer, or in Joe's case *both*, Joe became increasingly belligerent, which was funny because everybody in the crowd just thought he was playing the role. He wasn't though. *This was Joe just being Joe.*

All three-hundred-plus pounds of him, playing the part. At one point John leaned into me and said, "If Joe gets one more scotch in him we're not gonna sell a fuckin' thing. Just look at this guy over here . . ."

At this point, Joe grabbed one of his 8" X 10" glossy photos he was autographing, held it up over his face, and tossed a couple over to us to follow suit, just before this old lady could snap a photograph of all of us.

"Hey, what'd you do that for?!" the old woman asked.

"Whadda we look like lady? *Animals at the zoo*?! You want a picture? Buy a t-shirt, buy a print from Mikey over here, or one of Johnny's DVDs. Then, you can take all the pictures you want. Until then, *hit the bricks!*" he yelled out.

"See what I mean?" John laughed, shaking his head as he fired up another cigarette.

"Yeah, I get it, pretty funny, though, no?"

"Listen, I need to make some dough over here. He's killin' me this guy! We gotta cut him off pretty soon, no?" John pleaded.

By the day's end, Lisa's friend Christine and her husband Kurt joined us again for year two in Brooklyn. I counted up our sales, which weren't spectacular by any means, but it was enough to head out to a really nice Italian restaurant for dinner while Joe went home, got changed and took a power nap before meeting us out later on for drinks—*round two, Brooklyn style.*

WHEN JOE FINALLY ARRIVED to meet us back out a couple hours later he pulled up curbside at this local watering hole in a shiny, new Cadillac Eldorado. This was a big step up from his old beat up 1980s model Mercedes two-door he had the previous year. He joked that "Jimmy [Gandolfini] bought it for me."

I wouldn't be surprised if he actually had.

From everything, Joe's told me about him, may he rest in peace, he was one of the most generous guys on the planet. He even helped Joe get his restaurant some major foot traffic after doing an appearance there one night. Sick as a dog, and hating any media coverage of any kind—he still showed up for Joe. That's the kind of guy he was. He sat for hours with a line around the block and signed autographs inside, took photos with every single fan while Joe kept the media at bay outside his restaurant. I'd later do a pastel piece of him and Jamie-Lynn Sigler, who played his daughter Meadow on the show.

Day one of the festival was over, and so we all piled into Joe's new Eldorado—me in the front, Lisa, Christine and Kurt squeezing into the back, and we were off to paint the town red. Every place we stopped for a quick drink Joe would leave the car running. He'd flip through a Rolodex of windshield hang-tags, "*FDNY, NYPD, Handicapped . . .* " and depending on where we were, some stops he'd double-park in front of whatever joint we were about to hit, toss one of these hang-tags in his dash, leave the car running and off we'd go—*into the bar.*

Joe must've caught me glancing back at the car.

"Don't worry about the car, Mikey. Nobody's gonna take the car. It'll be fine," he smiled and winked at me.

And so, we'd go in, and the bartenders all knew him.

Everyone did.

We'd do a quick shot or drink of some sort, and then Joe would say, "Okay, let's bounce!" Then we'd pile back into his ride, and off to the next joint. This was our "warm-up" for a night of partying with "Vito," Joseph R. Gannascoli.

As the night rounded 10 P.M. or so, Joe says, "Want to go to a night club opening?"

"Absolutely!" we all exclaimed.

So, off we went to Staten Island. When we got there John Fiore was already there. He was wearing a black suit and had a cast on his hand. He said he was in the City getting new headshots and hurt his hand somehow. He hugged and kissed me hello, and was cracking me up with his assessments of Joe's new found fame.

This was in reaction to the crowd going wild the minute Joe walked in, greeting everyone with open arms, making sure everyone in the joint knew he had arrived.

"Will you look at this guy?!" said John. "I'm a freakin' Capo! I'm in Tony's crew for Christ's sake. Everybody knows my name one day . . . and then they whack me on a toilet and it's like they don't know me. Then this guy moves in, and will ya' get a load of him already?" John motioned to Joe, standing up on a chair with both arms open wide greeting his public at the bar like any rock star would. "Nobody even knows *Gigi* anymore!"

I assured John that I liked his acting. I told him I appreciated when he gunned down Patsy Parisi in the car, how he held his hand over his ear when he blasted the first point-blank shot into his head in the scene. Told him it made the scene more authentic.

"Thanks, Michael. Not a lot of people would catch a move like that. I *wanted* to make it more authentic. Bring something to the scene that *wasn't* in the script," John explained.

"It was a great move," I said. "I look at everything like it's a painting," I told him. And what John did, I'd go on to tell him, was pretty amazing, because he found a way to capture the element of "sound" and its effect on what happened, even if the TV was on mute, for instance. It could still sustain the suspense of the scene, even without sound effects, just like a painting can. I mean, how hard is it as a painter to capture sound or even temperature in a work of art? It's pretty damned difficult. So, I appreciated what he had done in that particular scene. And, he, in turn, appreciated the fact that I recognized it and acknowledged it. He'd go on to tell me how many directors would watch their films in complete silence before watching them with sound. If the scenes held their interest *visually*, and if they could interpret what the scenes were about *without sound*, then the dialogue and background effects would serve to enhance what was already acted out. If not, the scene would probably be re-shot.

We partied late into the night at that club opening. They served us hors d'oeuvres and cocktails over the course of the evening that were all, as Joe put it, "on the arm," which means "on the house", for all you *non Mob-speak* readers out there.

At the night's end, we left the nightclub and Joe said, "I gotta make a quick stop."

We all looked at one another. Where were we gonna go at this hour? But, he was our ride.

So, he drove to an apartment complex where he got out and disappeared into the night for what began to drag on like an eternity. Finally, about forty-five minutes later Joe emerged from over the top of this hill with a few cardboard boxes in hand.

Huffing and puffing over to the driver's side, out of breath from the walk he said, "Sorry it took so long. Here—for you—for waiting," he explained, handing me the boxes.

I didn't open them until we got home. They were filled with cologne samples. Hugo Boss, stuff like that. There was enough for a whole department store to pass out. But, that was just Joe.

Unpredictable. Hilarious. Generous. *All of the above.*

Before we left Brooklyn Joe also cut me a check for my artwork, and he talked to me about setting up some more gigs together, more print signings. We bounced around an idea to do a whole "Dinner with the Sopranos" night at a few different venues. Me, him and John. Everybody would try and set something up in their respective cities and we'd go from there. Me, shooting for something in Baltimore's Little Italy, and John in Boston.

WHEN I RETURNED BACK HOME I lined something up through yet another hair client of Lisa's. Joe started promoting it. He had started doing "call-ins" across the country on different radio stations for his "Sopranos predictions" on up-and-coming episodes. Now David Chase, the producer of the show, never let anyone near any scripts other than the lines they had to read for their specific scenes, and according to Joe and some other cast members I've been friendly with over the years, David was insanely strict about letting any potential spoilers out of the bag early—so Joe's talks were specific just to Joe and he never gave anybody anything of value. It was more just promotional for Joe and for the show in general. After all, Joe didn't want David to whack his character out in some bizarrely embarrassing fashion, as he'd become somewhat famous for.

His genius behind the creation of the show was simply something everyone appreciated and respected to the utmost. I mean, this was a show everybody who was Italian in the Tri-State area wanted to be on if they could, and it was one everybody watched religiously for the realism of the characters everybody could identify with and for the neighborhoods they shot the show at on location in North Jersey.

Joe started promoting our "Dinner with the Sopranos" idea on Baltimore's *98 Rock's Morning Show*, hosted then by a trio of Kirk, Mark, and Lopez. This was an exciting thing for any restaurant to buy into. I mean, for any of *the Sopranos* to come to Baltimore was a big deal, let alone a restaurant in Little Italy. These actors typically wouldn't travel for *anybody*. James Gandolfini, for example, hated doing media-related stuff whatsoever, so to line up something like this with these guys was exciting and new for the City of Baltimore.

We said we needed $3,000 up front. 1K per man. That was it. With that, fans could share food and fun with us, take photos, receive free personalized autographs and fine art prints, and they could also buy additional merchandise Joe and John planned to bring, in addition to me bringing my own set of prints to sell and sign. What would something like this cost a restaurant? Not much. Churn up some pasta, put out some light anti-pasta and you're set. It would be all profit. We'd just leave it up to the restaurant owner to promote it and sell tickets to make back his three grand, which, like I said, *is peanuts* in terms of an "appearance fee", especially since we'd be bringing something exciting and new to Baltimore.

A strange thing happened though. Shortly after Joe started promoting us on *98 Rock* to those morning show guys, all the sudden the restaurant owner in Little Italy started giving us excuses for not wanting to come up with our appearance fee up front. *He kept stalling*.

Turns out, one of the guys from that morning show apparently told the restaurant owner we weren't "big enough names" to be asking three grand for our appearance fee, which is crazy in itself. The even funnier thing was that the restaurant owner started tossing around the last name "Gambino" like it was supposed to intimidate us into lowering our appearance fees.

Big mistake.

I first called my old college roommate, Tommy Navarro, who lived in Little Italy for a short stint and even worked as a waiter at this particular restaurant for a short time after we went our separate ways; me moving into Manhattan and Tommy heading to Baltimore, then Virginia, and eventually making his way to Clearwater Beach, Florida where he'd find permanent residency.

While in Baltimore for a short stint, Navarro lived at 908 Fawn Street in Little Italy. When I asked him about the whole "Gambino" thing he burst out laughing hysterically. Said that's the whole reason he left Baltimore. He went there looking for some "action" in Little Italy but found nobody was mobbed up. "Just a bunch of old-timers," he put it to me, "running Grandma or Grandpa's restaurants. Definitely nobody in 'the life' living there. No *tough guys*, that's for sure."

So, I asked around some more. I called in some favors from some old friends in New York and asked the bold question:

"Is this guy *a Gambino*?" I asked. "Is he *with* anybody?"

And it was just as I thought—*no relation*. Not *with anybody* either. On top of that, my New York connection said, "You tell this punk if he's goin' around sayin' he's connected or somethin' because of that name he needs to shut his fuckin' hole before somebody pays him a visit he'll *never forget!*"

I decided to pass on delivering that message, especially if this guy was a "civilian," but I did pull the plug on the whole *Dinner with the Sopranos* venue taking place in Baltimore. It was a shame too. Somebody's bullshit ego got in the way of a good time making some good money and some great memories.

Joe asked me to wait, though . . .

Apparently, he had something more diabolical in mind. If you don't know Joe, he's a bit of a *wiseguy*, and can also be a nasty fuck if you rub him the wrong way.

Case and point:

"Make sure and listen to the *98 Rock Morning Show* tomorrow," he urged me.

This was when he was due to call in for his weekly *Sopranos predictions,* or whatever the hell he was calling it at the time. You know, free publicity is all it really was.

And so here I was, back at Southern, teaching a painting and drawing class that next morning just waiting for Joe to come on the radio, and then, there he goes! The broadcast went something like this:

Radio Guy: "So, we're here this morning again with Joseph R. Gannascoli, *Vito Spatafore* from *the Sopranos* with our scoop on what's in store for the next episode Sunday night of *the Sopranos.* Joe, what can you tell us?"

Joe: "Well, first I'd like to say thank you to you guys for promoting the event we talked about recently. Our whole 'Dinner with the Sopranos' thing with my artist pal Michael Bell in Little Italy in Baltimore . . ."

Radio Guy: "Certainly. How're things coming along with that?"

Joe: "Funny you should ask, because, after *further inspection* we quite honestly would never eat, dine, or do an appearance of any sort at a *rat joint like that* even if they paid us *three MILLION dollars!* I mean, us not being *'big names and all'*—isn't that what youse said?!" Joe yelled out over the air.

I burst out laughing! I couldn't even put it into words exactly how perfectly Joe put that douchebag restaurant owner on blast before the radio station just as quickly cut Joe off and went to commercial once they figured out where he was going with everything. It was too funny! That was Joe though, God love him.

So, no appearance in Little Italy in Baltimore. That turned out to be a total bust. But it did afford us a few laughs. It also affirmed the fact that the three of us really got along so well that we should probably line up some more appearances together.

A couple weeks later I got a phone call from Harry Lawrence inviting me to participate in the world's first "Golden Age of Gangsters Convention" in Chicago.

Harry was beginning to organize this event for the upcoming year and I told him I was down. I immediately called Joe and John to see if they'd want to do it with me. They agreed.

Harry had already reached out to Georgia, coincidentally, who was also going.

So, we worked out the details. Harry would fly us all out and put us up at the hotel where the convention would be held, all expenses paid, and we'd have a booth where we could keep the entire proceeds in lieu of an additional "appearance fee".

Everyone was happy with that.

So, we booked that appearance, and I began preparing for our Thanksgiving with Georgia and to do my painting unveiling for Sofia in Beverly Hills.

It was a busy, busy month again . . .

THIRTY-FIVE

THANKSGIVING IN HOLLYWOOD

I'm not sure what a Hollywood Thanksgiving looks like. I didn't even know what to expect. Lisa and I were used to cooking up a storm, from huge trays of anti-pasta, making stuffed red bell peppers, stuffed hot cherry peppers, cracked olives, trays of fresh mozzarella, prosciutto and provolone with some baked ziti or lasagna in the mix (or, as we'd say—*fresh muzzadell', braajh-oot and baked ziti with rigott'*).

But when we got to Georgia's on Sunday before Thanksgiving she had already made arrangements to pick up most of the feast later in the week, which she had catered. Turkey, stuffing, condiments, stuff like that, were all coming from a restaurant owner she was friendly with.

Lisa still ended up doing some cooking (you can't keep her out of a kitchen, plus she's like her father, never one to sit around and watch anyone else work). She made some olives and gutted some red peppers to roast, along with stuffing some of those peppers with her family's amazing signature recipe of putting hand-pulled fresh Italian bread (or at least the best we could find in L.A.), eggs, fresh grated Parmigiano-Reggiano, chopped olives, fresh parsley, garlic and olive oil . . . *simply delicious . . .*

It was a nice change of pace to see how the other half of the world lived—out in "La La Land"—but I did miss the huge spread at my father-in-law's table, although it could put ten pounds on you just looking at it! And I missed Vi, and our annual trip to New York City, despite the fact that I never went back to *Tavern on the Green* after they fucked me on Lisa's proposal.

So, in Thanksgiving prep mode, we continued to help Georgia move the couches in her living room, which was an open space next to the kitchen where we pieced together some folding tables, creating one super long table, which we draped tablecloths over and seated a bunch of folding chairs beneath for all the guests she was anticipating (around twenty chairs or so).

Prior to venturing back out to the West Coast, I had been working on Georgia's portrait from the photos I took of her in Lake Powell and planned to surprise her with an unveiling of this, and another work I had completed, entitled *The Departure*, which was inspired by that old photograph of her staring out the window in what looked like maid's attire. The train I added into the piece reflected in the window dramatized her wanting to leave her small, Rochester town and hop a train to New York City and make it big. I was pleased with how both paintings turned out.

I also finalized Sofia Milos' painting before leaving with it. I wrote her before we traveled back out to the West Coast about how my process of painting was becoming much more important to me than the actual finished product, although I understand how that final product was the thing valued most by those who commissioned me, and we talked about how I felt my paintings were becoming *prophetic*, in ways beyond my comprehension.

Could I, in fact, create my own destiny, one way or another, through my paintings? Or was I simply re-framing situations and circumstances in my art? These were questions I was beginning to ask of myself, and in turn, were questions I asked Sofia . . . if the experience of being painted by me was real or therapeutic for her in any way it seemed to be for Georgia?

This is how Sofia expressed her thoughts on this, via e-mail:

OCTOBER, 2002
Sofia Milos

"The reality of what occurs with chain images, of where people might be stuck in after a painful occurrence and how that works, but also how the awareness today of that can restore responsibility in re-creating/replacing these images with the present time (not past) images based on our new and constructive choices. Responsibility also will put one back into control as that is what responsibility is in big part.

Understanding has 3 components: Communication about it, have a reality or agreement of what's real. And have an affinity for what is *now*. You have to understand something first before you can be responsible for it and regain your desired control over it. 'It' being *your environment*. Thus, it's your images you create your present and future with. So I agree with you. I also have an understanding of that process and I am still learning. That's what I meant." – *Sofia*

I'M REPLAYING ALL OF THESE CONVERSATIONS in my head as we finished setting up for Thanksgiving at Georgia's. Once everything was done, we all hung out, laughed the rest of the day away and talked arts and entertainment stuff, drank wine, and I shared ideas I had for future paintings. I also showed Georgia my plan for the week of Thanksgiving and what I wanted to do with all the materials I brought with me, which consisted of heavy-duty cold-pressed watercolor papers, charcoals, and watercolors.

I explained how I wanted to begin each work, in what locations around her house I wanted to work in and the symbolism behind everything I had in store for her. I showed her some of the ideas I rough-sketched in my visual journal.

On a page in my sketchbook, I showed her a black ballpoint pen sketch I did that depicted Georgia sitting on her bed holding the back of her neck as she stretched, staring at her own reflection in her mirrored closet doors. I wrote below it:

TAKE PHOTOS:
Promo: Georgia and Michael with her gun, books, paintings.
3 by the Treehouse—Georgia writing, Michael drawing.
3 in the Bedroom: triangular composition. See Georgia's back, her face in the mirror, a close-up and one of her bare back.

Later that night we ventured back to her guest house for another unsettling night's sleep. You do remember our last stay there, right? Well, we did our best to fend the haunted evil spirit of her late husband off, because the next day we would be headed off to do painting unveiling number two at *the Four Seasons* in Beverly Hills with Sofia Milos.

The next morning we toured Beverly Hills before meeting Sofia at the famous hotel restaurant for lunch. It was cool how, as we traveled down Sunset Boulevard, once you officially enter Beverly Hills, all the street signs turn white. That's something I recall very vividly about it. The houses all turned into mansions. Gorgeous mansions too. Some on flat streets, others in the hills. Definitely a much different way of living from the East Coast in North Jersey and New York City, but very cool. I also loved how the huge palm trees lined the streets of Sunset Boulevard.

Once we arrived at *the Four Seasons* early that afternoon I valet it and we headed inside. We got there first. The place was opulent. We headed to the outdoor restaurant and got a table for four, not knowing whether Sofia was flying solo or bringing her publicist, which ended up being the case shortly after she arrived.

I spotted her valeting her silver BMW. She's easy to spot, looking the part much like most movie stars I imagined would, walking in like she owned the place, large sunglasses, big hoop earrings, long dark curly hair flowing with each confident stride she took, pretending not to notice everyone whispering and pointing as she entered the room.

She was wearing this sheer, brownish-orange patterned bell-sleeved top that was see-through across her mid-drift, with matching plum colored pants and high heels. She immediately hugged and kissed us both on both cheeks as she greeted us, hailed the waiter and asked them to bring over some Italian sparkling water for the table. Her publicist arrived shortly thereafter and also joined us for lunch.

Sofia sat beside me, Lisa on my other side next to her publicist and we ordered a light lunch. Over lunch, she showed me some surgical scars, which I hadn't noticed, but that seemed to be bothering her, probably just in the event I did notice, from a terrible car crash she was in with a friend of hers recently somewhere in Brazil. She was worried it would affect her career either in acting or modeling, and definitely was going to limit her physical activities for a while.

I just pointed her to mine along the right side of my eye and said, "Our scars are like a roadmap that leads us back to where they originated, and how strong we are for overcoming them. You look beautiful, don't worry about it."

And, with that, after some more light conversation, we headed out by a terrace near some trees for privacy, away from paparazzi and also to serve as a nice backdrop for her painting unveiling, which we'd take photographs of with us together with her portrait.

I quickly did *the reveal*, in front of a busy lunch crowd of on-lookers who immediately recognized Sofia, and seemed fascinated with what was going down. She absolutely loved the painting and in particular, how I painted her. It was done in oils on paper, which would prove to become my favorite combination for doing commissioned portraits. It's become a great combination for me over the years for capturing realism, which is what Sofia wanted for this piece. It's the same "oils on watercolor paper" formula that would work for me years later for John Gotti Junior's painting of him and his iconic father for his *Shadow of my Father* book cover.

Sofia's painting was 13" X 20" and I had a custom frame made for her. She wanted it stained light for her home in order to match its décor at her Miami apartment, so I obliged. I worked off of a photograph she sent me from a series of headshots she had done prior to being on *the Sopranos* and *CSI: Miami*.

She thought I made her look flawless and captured a certain magic gleam in her eyes that she loved. I also agreed, and after now finally meeting her face to face for the first time, I also thought she looked much younger and even more attractive in person than she appeared on camera.

As we were leaving, I took one last glance back at Sofia getting in her car after the valet arrived with it. I smiled, as Lisa pointed out the stuffed animals lining the entire back window of her Beamer. Too funny, I thought. *Another unveiling complete!*

One thing I noticed right away about L.A., more specifically, about the people I met in L.A., was how important "image" was. I noticed a few things right away in a short couple of days. One, anybody who was anybody or who wanted to appear to be anybody drove an "expensive name brand car" meaning—*BMW, Mercedes*, those types of vehicles . . . but they weren't always new. They were mostly older models. The name was important, but the year—*not so much.*

The second thing I noticed was *the attire*. The labels on clothes mattered. The bling mattered. When spending some time around people with "real money" I realized how quickly they actually know what kind of suit you're wearing without even asking.

It was that kind of world.

I once had a conversation many years later with a wealthy art collector, Leonard Sylk, who told me he was once walking along Rodeo Drive in Beverly Hills and a salesperson literally came out of this "appointment only" store to greet him as he was walking past in order to invite him in. The reason? He spotted his *Brioni suit* as he was walking past the storefront window. Can you believe that? *That's L.A. for you.*

The process of getting ready for any big event also seemed to be something that was also made a real big deal of. Georgia hired someone to come to her house, get her outfit ready and do her hair and makeup before any event. She didn't "put her face on" by herself—at least not for a big $500-a-plate gala.

The third thing, the *food didn't matter*—unless you were going out in public, then it had to be at a place where you'd "be seen".

Now, this one would be a deal breaker for me falling in love with L.A. I love my food. I couldn't live with some model that kept the fridge barren while their freezer was stocked with booze. Just not my thing, sorry. I'd rather have the opposite.

But in L.A., it seemed like it was *fend for yourself, order in,* or get someone to *cater dinner.* Not a lot of cooking going on. Not a lot of money being spent on things in the house that wouldn't necessarily "be seen" by the public, if that makes sense.

It didn't seem to matter if someone's home wasn't updated with new furnishings, or if the fridge even had any food in it. It would only matter what people (the public) would see. Or what the location was. *The zip code.*

That seemed to matter.

Back in New York City, my only experience with that was what area code you had. If you met someone with a 212 area code you knew they were Manhattan. If it was 718 you knew Queens. In North Jersey, it was 201. But, for us, Lisa and I, life was different now. We cared about what our bathroom fixtures looked like, and we loved a packed fridge sparing no expense on food, both of us loving to cook, which wasn't the case in L.A. But this was Hollywood, and you had to adapt to the culture and climate of your surroundings.

It seemed like in Hollywood there was this mask everyone had to don in order to "keep up with the Kardashians," so to speak, even though up until this point—*the Kardashians* weren't even a blip on the Hollywood radar.

Aside from their father's infamy due to his longtime friendship with O.J. Simpson, Kim Kardashian's star wasn't even born yet. She was still just fourteen years old back when O.J. contemplated suicide in her bedroom just prior to his famous police car chase in Al Cowling's white Bronco along the 405 Interstate.

Our drive back to Georgia's Hollywood home resurfaced many visions for me from O.J's car chase along the 405, partially because while touring Beverly Hills we actually went on the 405 before heading back over to the 101 to go back to Georgia's.

It's only about a 30-minute drive. That, and Georgia wanted to introduce me to Denise Brown sometime later that week. I didn't get the chance to meet her during our first trip out to L.A., but the domestic violence charities were definitely something I was still interested in contributing towards so I was looking forward to the possibility of meeting Denise. We talked on the phone already and seemed to hit it off, like I did with most clients.

WHEN WE RETURNED FROM MY UNVEILING in Beverly Hills Georgia seemed tired, so we put off beginning her paintings from life until Tuesday, November 26th. Later that evening we all went over to Georgia's friend Aida's, who we first partied with on the houseboat in Lake Powell.

We had dinner with her, and we met two of her sons, Michael and Arthur, while we were there. Her place was like a little palace in Studio City, with beautiful marble floors, a resort-style pool with cabanas out back. Aida's husband, Michael Bogosian, apparently had this house in addition to another place in Beverly Hills. They owned *Matthews*, the jewelry store carrying their brand name, *Michael B. jewelry*.

This proved to be a dangerous liaison, as Aida invited Lisa to join her the next day out at the jewelry store while Georgia and I began some of her paintings—in order to give us some space so we could get comfortable and get down to work. Of course, she found some jewels she wanted, while I was busy working.

I proceeded to work at a feverish pace to try and accomplish everything I bulleted in my sketchbook that next morning. I also wasn't sure how long Georgia would be down for "sitting" as a live model, so once Lisa took off for Aida's jewelry store to hang out I got right down to business.

We started in Georgia's bedroom. I figured, let's break the ice and get the most intimate works out of the way early. This would help Georgia to become more comfortable later on as each work progressed. So she disrobed, climbed into bed and then I asked her to re-enact what it felt like each morning as she woke up.

She proceeded to sit up in bed and rub the back of her neck. She had been in physical therapy for it at one point. Her ex-husband used to beat her and abuse her daughter on a regular basis, and one time he hit her so hard that her spine was nearly severed in two places near her neck. So, I came up with the idea of doing this first piece as a diptych, which essentially consists of two panels that are positioned together as one. I took two sheets of the large, heavy-duty cold-pressed watercolor paper that I pre-gessoed before flying out and laid them out, one on top of the other and then I offset them, so they wouldn't line up just perfectly, placing one sheet slightly to the left of the other. Just by a few inches—*symbolic of her neck trauma.*

And then I began the drawing. The separation between the papers naturally was placed at the base of her neckline as I took various photographs of her to work from, and feverishly sketched her from life in charcoal while sitting on the floor of her bedroom.

And then we did another; one of her lying down in the bed simply staring back at me. I asked her to imagine something that completely contrasts the pain she'd undergone and imagine the most beautiful, positive things that she could. Once the rough sketches were at a place I felt comfortable leaving them at, I asked her to get dressed and meet me in the foyer. I didn't tell her what to wear. From there we proceeded out back near her tree house. Lisa just arrived back and shot some photographs of us working. Both of us sat opposite one another in reclining pool chairs, me straddling mine with my drawing board facing Georgia as she sat with a legal pad writing out what it felt like to be drawn by me:

NOVEMBER 27, 2002
Georgia Durante
"To be at one with another mind. Two separate thoughts coming together in a creative process. No words spoken. The eyes speak to each other in quiet thought. Powerful. Peaceful. Does he know? *Maybe so.* On a deeper level than I may even know. He sees deeper than I dare to go. But his truth will open the doors to my hidden fears and the fears will come to the surface and be set free.

It's dark in there, but he shows the light. It's not so scary after all. Hmmm . . . I'm uncomfortable with him looking inside. I guess because I'm afraid of what's there. I know he will find it. He knows me better than I know myself. Maybe because I'm afraid of what's there. If I don't look I don't have to see.

But he is relentless. He won't let me escape from myself. This is a good thing. I think. Why am I fearful? It's not him I fear. It's me. Why? Deeper. Deeper. I need to know. I keep pushing them away. They get too close to that person who lives inside. Who is she? There is rage. I just saw it. I'm afraid to let it escape. It should stay there. Bury it . . . deeper. *Deeper.* If it comes to the surface it won't be pretty. It squeezes out sometimes in secret moments. I cover it up the best I can and bury it again. It sleeps for long periods. I never know what suddenly jerks it awake. I don't like that. I push it back, deeper and deeper, but never deep enough. How do I make it come to the surface and kill it so it can't hide in me anymore? What is it anyway? I know I have to answer that or it will never die.

Michael scares me because he makes me look. He makes me see what I'm afraid of. His eyes are piercing. They look so deep inside of me that I have to look away. Not so much because he can see what lies beneath, but because I don't want to see. Even the good stuff. There are definitely two sides. I feel them with me always. It's work hiding Ms. Black. It's like raising a child, constantly scolding and punishing and hoping those lessons will stick and good will emerge. The good is there. I feel it sometimes overpowers the shadowy ghost that lurks from within, but then sometimes not.

I feel myself drifting now. I don't want to look anymore. Pretending all those *me's* don't exist again. Why do I do that? If I stay with it, I'll find out. Do I really want to know?

There he goes. He's looking into me again. Too close for comfort. Hmmm . . . what's that all about? Does he see the light? Maybe. He sketches in black and white. Is that all I am? No, there is gray. There is color too. Maybe too much color at times. I need to pull it in. I'd like to scream in color. That was a weird thought.

Man, am I complex. Don't think about it and it will go away.

Then there is the monster who appears in my dreams. I am glad he only comes in my dreams now. It's a dead nightmare, not a living one. That's better. I can control that. I can even kill the monster in my dreams. It's the waking monster that scares me, but I know how to bury him deep, deep inside my mind. Do I need to dig him up to bury him? Another strange thought.

I don't like this dark place. Why am I always going there? Take me to the light. Let there be shadows, that's okay. Shadows are behind you." – *Georgia Durante*

THANKSGIVING definitely proved to be an interesting one, but also a time that I made a major breakthrough. Working from life, as opposed to just taking photos of my subjects became an integral process that I'd use in numerous portraits over the course of the next few years. There was pressure in performing on the spot, knowing Georgia would be looking at my sketches once they were started and would also be giving me instant feedback. I wasn't home, or in my studio, where nobody saw "the magic happen". They just saw the finished product.

I practiced this some more as soon as I returned home in the form of portraits I did of several students of mine.

When I was named the MAEA's "Most Outstanding New Art Teacher of the Year" back in 2002 I also assumed the role of the MAEA's Secondary Division Director, which meant I had to create something for the organization, at least, I felt compelled to. So, I created the first ever "Artists Capturing Mentors" exhibition.

The idea behind the exhibition was for a teacher to paint a picture of a student, and the student would, in turn, paint a picture of their teacher. The concept was one I created to help other teachers spark a great relationship between themselves and a student they saw promise in. In 2002 I painted one of Rebecca Hill. In 2003, of Mollie Jones. And in 2004, Allisin Wagner. The unique thing that became the common thread in each of these works that began with Georgia and her poems was the idea to incorporate someone else's handwritten word in my art. So, Rebecca, Mollie, and Allisin all incorporated some poem or stream-of-conscious thing they wrote into the backgrounds of my paintings before I started them. They'd write it in charcoal. I'd seal it with fixative and begin each of their paintings from life, while also taking photographs of them to finish the works from. I even ended up doing a collaboration painting featuring Allisin for a future two-man exhibition in Red Bank, New Jersey with Michael Sprouse in 2004.

But, before all this, Georgia and I would do another domestic violence charity benefit in Chicago for *the Family Shelter Service*, auctioning off a painting of mine entitled, *In Bloom*. I'd give a short talk, as would Georgia, and being out and about with her, she introduced me to everyone. I listened to her as she did radio spots and learned from how well versed she was about her own story. It wouldn't be many years later until I could speak about my own story with the similar professionalism that just seemed to roll so easily off her tongue.

I'd return to Hollywood again for a Christmas party that same year at Georgia's house, this time flying solo, because my wife had to work. It was another interesting time, that's for sure. Henry Hill, the gangster turned rat that they based the movie *Goodfellas* on showed up at Georgia's party with his brother Michael. So did some *real* New York wiseguys, but these were guys still "in the life", not some *Witsec has-beens*. And then Hugh O'Brian showed up.

What a perfect, eclectic, volatile mix.

I immediately overheard the wiseguys telling Henry, "Listen pal, we're not earning any extra stripes for whackin' you out right here and now, nor do I feel like diggin' a hole, *however*, if anybody finds out *we were here—and you were here* and we *did nothin'*, well, that ain't gonna look so good. So, both you and your brother can get the fuck outta here now while you still can, or youse are *never fuckin' leaving*, if you know what I'm sayin' . . ."

Henry and his brother said their goodbyes and left the party immediately. As for Hugh O'Brian—*I re-introduced myself to him.*

Now, I certainly didn't want to embarrass myself or make a scene in Georgia's home, knowing he was a dear friend of hers, but *what's right is right*. So, when the opportunity finally presented itself to me, I quietly cornered him in Georgia's sunroom and whispered in his ear, "Remember me?"

He didn't appear to. Nor did I expect him to.

"I'm the kid who you auctioned off his painting, it never sold and then you never returned it."

He still didn't seem to know what I was talking about, as I'm sure was probably the case. Whether he did or not, how was I supposed to know? Either way, I felt used.

I also felt it was payback time.

"Listen," I whispered angrily, "I know you're just a fucking *antique*, and you probably don't give two fucks *about me*. But what you should be concerned with is whether or not I give two fucks enough *about you* to leave it alone, because at the end of the day *you stole my painting*. I know I'll probably never get it back. But I could take it out on *your ass*, or just embarrass you in front of your wife and everybody here. Do you want that?" I asked him, as I began boiling over inside with rage, seething through my teeth.

He took a moment to assess the situation and then quickly excused himself from me to his goodbyes, and then he left the party. The wiseguys that I overheard talking with Henry Hill must've also caught my exchange because they smiled over, raising a glass to me, as if to say, "Atta boy!"

Georgia was none the wiser. I was glad she didn't know what I said to him. I know she cared a lot for him. Probably in the way I care and have a deep respect for her.

But, I couldn't let that go. Me, I just saw Hugh O'Brian as someone who hijacked my painting. On the streets, someone could get whacked upside the head for a whole lot less.

To this very day, *I never saw my painting again.*

THIRTY-SIX

TEACHER OF THE YEAR

I turned thirty-three years old three days prior to April 13, 2004, when I was named Anne Arundel County's Public Schools "Teacher of the Year". While only in my ninth year teaching, I felt at that time, this was a testament to the fact that the Visual Arts were gaining traction as a key component in public education. I mean, after all, if they selected me as county "Teacher of the Year" they must feel I have a shot at becoming Maryland State Teacher of the Year. I thought this was a big thing for the arts. I talked in my acceptance speech (that I totally winged off the cuff) about how "there's been such a push for reading lately in the curriculum. People don't realize how verbal and visual language is so inter-connected, especially in art."

In *the Capital* newspaper, Staff Writer Kimberly Marselas wrote me up as a "professional portrait artist who spends his weekends traveling to gallery shows and painting actors, including some members of the cast of the hit HBO television show *the Sopranos*."

The media also interviewed several School Board members that said I "deserved the award," with one adding that "This came at a great time for the Southern High School community, with

Principal Paul Vandenberg dying earlier this year, and with police charging a student with bringing a gun to school. Southern needed it after everything that's happened," School Board Member Mr. McNelly said.

At the night's end, I got a check for $1,000, an additional $250 from the school system, and a lifetime of football coach, now Assistant Athletic Director Russ Meyers calling me "Teacher of the Year" no matter where I go or who he introduces me to.

Eric J. Smith, then Superintendent of Anne Arundel County Public Schools, addressed the audience by sharing how he felt that "teaching is a profession that defines the future for all of us." He then went on to quote Confucius: "If you think in terms of a year, plant a seed; if in terms of ten years, plant trees; if in terms of one hundred years, teach the people." From there he went on to explain how "any civilization relies on teachers—and an occasional awards ceremony, such as this one, is no more than a token of what they are owed."

As for me, I wasn't so sure how to feel about being "owed" such an honor, but it was one I was excited to have been awarded. I still thought it was too pretentious to write an acceptance speech beforehand since I didn't go into the evening expecting to win, nor did I want to jinx it if I did have a shot.

I will admit, though, there was nothing like hearing my name called, followed by a room full of cheers.

When I got back to Southern over the course of the next week it was back to work though for me. Michael Sprouse landed us our third two-man collaboration art show in Red Bank, New Jersey on April 25th we'd call *Revisitation* and the week after our show was *ArtQuest*, on the 29th for our kids at Southern.

Now, April is always the busiest time of anyone's lives in our Art Department. Tack on just being named "Teacher of the Year" and putting together final works for our *Revisitation* show, it definitely felt like there was no rest for the weary.

It was also a year I'd produce more portraits, not just of students and celebrity clientele, but also one of my wife, Lisa for our collaboration art exhibition. I'd title it, *The Zodiac*, and to me, it is still to this day one of my favorite paintings of all time—right up there with my early *Lascivia* painting. There's just something magical about the way I painted her portrait—from the intense luminosity of the natural lighting to the way the drips fade in and out of the blue sea of background to the way her eyes stare at you no matter where you are in the room, just like Leonardo da Vinci's *Mona Lisa*.

I also lined up some more commissions through Lisa's hair clientele at the salon she was working at in Marianne, whom I'd paint a portrait of in all her furs and jewels. Marianne was from Long Island, so we immediately hit it off and after Marianne's portrait unveiling as a surprise gift for her husband, we'd spend many dinners and nights over their beautiful home downing bottles of Grand Marnier and swapping stories with them. Marianne's husband was a successful stock broker and financial commentator on local Baltimore radio networks. I'd also end up donating prints of my artwork to help him support another local charity, which he became a Board Member of.

Another portrait done that particular year was for this wonderful woman named Karen—another client of Lisa's from the salon. This painting was of her two young boys. Looking back at the painting, it was one of the first one's I'd done that included objects and things fading in and out of the background to help further the narrative of the story between their two sons. One of their sons liked music so I painted sheet music through the background of the painting, much the same as the way I painted subway maps through my *Ticket to Ride, Carnevale* series and in my *John Gotti paintings* years later. I also included behind him a Grand Piano. In front of the Grand Piano I placed baseball bats and in the foreground, I faded a football field into the t-shirt of the other son since he liked sports.

Karen's husband was also a really great guy with an incredible sense of humor. He, like many of my painting clientele, liked the fact that I painted for actors from hit Mob shows like *the Sopranos*, and for actual guys *in the Mob*. I guess, to them, it gave them something else to talk about with anyone who saw my painting hanging in their home. It was an interesting niche clientele I was developing, and it made for great stories among "the civilians" as guys in "the life" would call them. So, when he showed up with my money while picking up his portrait, he gave it to me just as I requested—in a nondescript duffle bag.

When I invited him inside my home to pick up the work, he jokingly said, "Here it is—just like you asked, in small unmarked bills."

"That's good. Set it over there on the floor," playing up the part for him in order to give him a good laugh or story for later to share with his friends and family.

"You want to count it?" he asked.

"I'm sure it's all there. You wouldn't want me coming back for it." I responded with an ominous glare.

Then we both broke into laughter, I unveiled the painting to him, which he loved, and that was that. He appreciated the amount of work I poured into the painting and couldn't get over the attention to detail and the incorporation of all the hidden meaning I embedded into the work.

I'd embed that same work ethic into my students, along with my same "never quit, never say die" attitude. An incredible example of this would take the form of Pierrette Montone, who became one of the greatest student artists I've ever taught—only her story was born through failure.

This "failure" she experienced happened just two years prior in 2002 when she watched her best friend win ArtQuest as a sophomore, which also was a tremendous accomplishment of which no-one has ever done since.

Did she deserve it? Yes, I felt she did. Her work was phenomenal, and mature beyond her years. But the seniors were pissed! They didn't even come to school the next day. One of them didn't speak to me for two weeks after the show like it was my fault or something. My feeling was and always has been, "what the juror decides, the juror decides." This is a life lesson. There are no guarantees, and if a student is planning on going into the art business, or even thinking of going off to art school one day, it's a dog-eat-dog world out there. They better get used to rejection and get a tougher skin. That was my take on it. While I run ArtQuest and sponsor ArtQuest, I never offer up my own opinions on who should actually *win ArtQuest*.

This was a lesson I learned from visiting Towson High School's student art show shortly in the spring after Mark Coates took me around the state to visit their program.

The lesson being, "Don't get too involved in who wins, or the kids will think the show is rigged."

This is how one student from Towson High felt after inviting me out to see his work on exhibit at their annual student show. This was also a student I ended up privately tutoring. Now, Towson's show was held in the school's gymnasium, and while it was an impressive show from a work standpoint with paintings, photographs, sculptures and individual students on display all over the place, the thing that struck me as "odd" was as I walked in was that I was handed a program with a "list of prize winners".

"Prize winners?" I thought to myself, "Why announce the prize winners before the show even starts? What would keep kids around that didn't win anything?"

And I was right. John, the kid I had tutored, had a great display of work, but was already disappointed his name wasn't on the list of award recipients, so for him, the show was a bust. There was no juror present either, so the kids just figured the Art Teachers picked their "favorites" to win prizes, and he wasn't one of them. He certainly wasn't sticking around any longer than he had to that night. *Such a shame*.

"Where was the excitement in that?! Where was the showmanship? This," I felt, "was *how not* to run a show."

It made me want to hype up our own ArtQuest that much more. It was already well received by the public, and better attended than most sporting events, so why not keep it growing. That's when I decided to make an even bigger deal out of our "Community People's Choice Award" and announce that at the very end, just before the "Best of Show" award, giving the community and the student body a larger role.

This way, since the juror decided on the major prizes throughout the night, it's one more thing that could keep the public and students around until the end. And each year, my juror always stayed until the end, so they could not only address the crowd with a few words of inspiration behind why they chose the works they chose, but also to answer any questions the kids had. This made our show legit and separated us from the rest.

This was showmanship!

But that didn't matter to Pierrette Montone, or to the seniors who were pissed about a sophomore winning ArtQuest 2002 that spring. Life, Pierrette felt, for her as an artist—*was officially over.*

Her thinking was—since her best friend won ArtQuest in her sophomore year, she'd win it again next year and the year after that and her dreams of stardom would never become realized.

Now Pierrette was really active in the Art Department up until this point. She helped me start up our first ever National Art Honor Society Chapter No. 2129 in 2002. She also became a member of the Anne Arundel County Gifted and Talented Visual Arts Program, which I taught. I figured, even though she was disappointed that she didn't win anything at ArtQuest, I could still help her improve over the summer while teaching her in GT.

Then I got a call from Albert Montone—*Pierrette's father.* His phone call changed everything.

PIERRETTE'S DAD was this larger than life Italian guy that loved his family more than life itself. I taught his oldest daughter Annalise, who was more into Music and Theatre than Visual Arts when I taught her in art class, but she was also very talented, just not as gifted in art as Pierrette. Now, at this point in time, Pierrette was nowhere near as naturally gifted in art as her best friend who just won ArtQuest. But I also didn't realize just how much this was all negatively impacting Pierrette's life until her father clued me in. I remember the phone call like it was yesterday.

"Mr. Bell," Albert said, "my daughter is thinking of quitting art altogether. She's very upset, and I know she values your opinion of her. I don't know what you can do with this information, but I thought you should know and I have faith in you that you'll know what to do to help my daughter. I don't want her to give up."

I had no idea she was this far gone. It was upsetting to hear.

For us in the Art Department, when the show was over, the show was over. We all moved on. But to the kids, apparently not so much. As for Pierrette "quitting?" I thought to myself . . .

"Why?!"

So, when I had the opportunity that summer to talk with Pierrette on the expansive lawn at MICA while we were painting on location in Baltimore for the day, what began as a pep talk turned into a couple hours of deep conversation about life and art.

She listened as she drew, and expressed to me her insecurities about her work. She admitted that she knew she wasn't as good as her best friend. I spoke honestly with her about this too, and told her that was definitely the case "this year," I said. But it was up to her what happened this summer, next fall and through the spring and the following summer and the year after that . . .

A light bulb seemed to click on.

Nothing I could put my finger on, but just a gut feeling. I knew I reached her and knew she understood what she had to do. And that was—if she *really wanted it*, she'd have to *go and get it*.

Work for it! It was just that simple.

And she did.

She came back in 2003 with a vengeance. She outworked not only her best friend but everybody else in her path. She produced drawing after drawing and got immersed in the process of visual journaling and learning how to paint in oils on canvas with me.

I was busy working on my Master's Thesis on *Visual Journaling*, so, as I learned more, so did Pierrette. And, as I became better at oil painting, so did Pierrette. I'd work on my paintings in studio alongside the kids. And we pushed each other, as she produced one oil painting on canvas after the next, working larger with each piece and often in self-portraiture, just as I was. She definitely produced a larger volume of work than anyone else.

This led to her increased participation in numerous murals, one was a "Playhouse mural" collaboration with me for a local domestic violence charity, another completely on her own as a permanent installation in *Discovery Village*, which is a nonprofit group in Shady Side, Maryland designed to help children learn about the beauty, heritage, and ecosystem of the Chesapeake Bay.

For the Discovery Village mural, she studied the history of the estuary and created four six foot panels showing the bay from source to the ocean, with images showing its evolution from Ice Age to present day. I helped her initial drawings get approved by *Discovery Village* President Adam Hewison, and a few hundred hours later it was unveiled in front of some local press.

Pierrette went on to become the only student artist in the history of Southern High to repeat, winning "Best of Show" two years in a row at ArtQuest, in 2003 and 2004, where she also sold three 18" X 24" oil paintings on canvas for $1,200. She won 1st place in the "All-County" Anne Arundel County Senior Show in 2004 and earned a $32,000 scholarship to Corcoran School of the Arts and Design in Washington D.C., where she'd go on to graduate top 3% in her class. All because she wanted it—and she went after it.

I'll still never forget our conversation on the lawn at MICA that afternoon, the summer heading into her junior year as being a turning point in her life. There's nothing this girl can't accomplish if she puts her mind to it. This became a very fitting end to her tenure with me, and I was happy I won "Teacher of the Year" the year she went on to experience such similar great successes.

She later returned as a juror at ArtQuest, which became another tradition among former "Best of Show" champions that began with her.

THIRTY-SEVEN

REVISITATION

My reputation as "Teacher of the Year" was growing me a strong following in the education arena. And, in the art world, doing an ambitious four exhibitions in just over a year sparked an equally compelling interest in my work from collectors and gallery goers.

And then things got really weird.

I was contacted online through my website by a girl complimenting me on the work I created thus far for Georgia. She said she read Georgia's book and was inspired by her story. Now, this is nothing uncommon. I get tons of e-mails from my website and I do my best to respond to each and every one.

But this one girl in particular, who couldn't have been more than eighteen years of age, began showing up at my exhibitions. She first showed up for *the Milton Theatre Project*, which was the first two-man show I did with Michael Sprouse in Lewes, Delaware that showcased some of the paintings I did of Georgia.

Now, it wasn't the girl alone that weirded me out, it was the elderly gentleman that accompanied her. A man she referred to as "Daddy" but it seemed pretty clear to Michael and me by the way they were arm in arm throughout the duration of our opening that there was something more perverse going on. Then they showed up at our *Ireland Show,* and again, the night of our *Revisitation* opening at the POWYS Gallery in Red Bank.

While making small talk she told me that they were from somewhere in the southern part of Virginia. This would mean it's quite a hike driving all the way up to Red Bank, New Jersey! I mean, we're talking at least a six-hour drive. I know every artist has their fair share of groupies and gallery girls, as we call them, but this couple was just *really odd.*

The thing that stuck Michael and me as being so odd wasn't the fact they kept showing up for our openings, though, it was the fact that they never bought a thing! I mean, why drive all that way if you're never gonna buy anything? And, they never talked much. Just whispered back and forth to one another. Never even approached us to engage us in many conversations either.

"Maybe this was their date night," Michael Sprouse laughed, "and maybe they need to go a few states over in order to do it."

To make the *Revisitation* opening even stranger was the fact that the gallery owner hired *a bouncer* to watch the door.

Michael also agreed this wasn't standard gallery protocol.

"What do you know about the gallery owners?" I asked Michael, since it was him that got us hooked up with the show in Jersey in the first place.

"Nothing, other than they came into my gallery in Lewes, liked our work and wanted to give us a show. They seemed new to the gallery scene because they were asking me to help them with contracts for artists, stuff like that. I let them borrow one of mine to go off of," Michael explained.

"Well, while I appreciate the fact they were willing to pay for a hotel to put us up in and all, which wasn't customary either, but this whole bouncer thing is a little over the top, no?" I said.

The bouncer, who was this big black dude, maybe 6'5" or so, around 250 lbs. or more, nods me to come over and see him about half way through the opening to talk with him.

"What's up with those two?" motioning with his head over to *the odd couple* from southern Virginia standing by themselves in the corner of the expansive gallery space.

"Beats me. Michael and I were wondering the same thing. They've been to at least two other openings of ours," I explained.

"Listen," the bouncer said to me, "I know who you are."

"You do?" I asked, curious now.

"You did those paintings of Gotti and *the Sopranos* fellas? Love that shit, man. Great pieces," he said.

"Thanks, I appreciate it," I replied.

"Thing is, I think that's why they're here," nodding over to the odd couple. "They were acting strange, so my boss made a call. Ran the plates on their vehicle. Came back a *no hit*."

"*A no hit*?" Now I'm a little worried. "You think they're *Feds*?"

"Listen, man, wouldn't surprise me," he replied.

"They don't look like Feds. I mean, just figured they were –"

"You think *Feds* want you to pick them out of a hat? Listen, maybe they're not. Maybe it's a mistake. I'm just tellin' you out of respect. Just watch your back."

And with that, I slid over and updated Michael on the recent developments, and as we spent the rest of the evening making small talk with the gallery goers trying to make some sales and having some artful conversations. But, the night was a bust. No sales, just a lot of foot traffic from the locals, and of course from our "odd couple".

The next day we did the second opening during the day. No doorman-bouncer for this one, though. My family all came to the second-day opening. My mother and father, my Aunt Jeannie, my cousins Bonnie and Natalie, Lisa's mother and father and brother Marc, his wife Kellie and their kids. My Grandma and her sister, Aunt Ann even came. It was really nice they all made it. I was especially glad my Grandma got to see an exhibition of my work.

A FEW MONTHS LATER, after the gallery opened, they just as quickly shut their doors. Michael and I were disappointed with the sales, lack thereof, and this would end up being the last gallery exhibition we'd do together as a "two-man" tandem, although we'd still remain dear friends to this day.

We even had Thanksgiving one year with Michael, his partner George, me, Lisa and my mother-in-law Olga, who was hanging with us after one of our shows. Olga was a trooper. Between the steady flow of party-goers at Michael's place coming and going, doing shots and all she definitely saw more than most mother-in-law's eyes should see. But she'd also been with us to Brooklyn with Joey G and our crew, so she always knew she was in for *an experience* whenever she went somewhere with us. We loved having her there too, as did Michael. She's a sweetheart. Always treated me like one of her own sons.

Six months or so after the *Revisitation* show Michael sold $20,000 worth of paintings to fill some new restaurant with his work down in the Virginia Beach area. They also scheduled him to join everyone for the ribbon cutting ceremony where they'd also sell tickets, do a wine tasting and have Michael do a brief artist talk about the paintings.

He told me that the wife of the restaurant owner just happened to meet him through his gallery in Lewes and that she also knew who I was through a friend of hers in Long Island that also happened to be a portrait client of mine. Apparently, Michael's new client was over my client's house one evening, saw my portrait and because our styles are so similar she thought it was a Michael Sprouse painting. When they got to talking, my client went on to tell her that we did, in fact, know one another and were friends as well as artists that collaborated together.

"Small world," I thought. I was really happy for him.

And then I got the call from the restaurant opening, "Michael, it's me, Michael. You're not going to believe this shit?"

"What is it? You sound a little frazzled, what's the matter?" I asked.

"That couple. You know, the one with the freaky young girl and the old man. They showed up at this thing and they started asking all these strange questions to the owner. Stuff like, 'Did you know John Gotti?' Stuff like that. *Mob stuff.*"

"What the fuck?!" now I'm at a loss.

"I know, man," Michael said, "I'm a little freaked out! The owner looks pissed, and a little freaked out too. I assured him I didn't know the couple or why they showed up there, just that they had been to a couple of our shows. This restaurant owner and his backers are *your types of people*, if you know what I mean. What am I supposed to do?"

"You did good. Say no more. The less you say the better. You don't want them thinking anything about you, trust me."

FAST FORWARD TWO WEEKS—the restaurant's number was suddenly disconnected, as was the wife's phone, which was Michael's only point of contact.

The e-mail address associated with the girl *from the odd couple* all the sudden bounces back to us from Michael's gallery mailing list and was effectively *undeliverable*.

So, with all this happening, Michael asked a friend of his living nearby the new restaurant in Virginia Beach to drive by the place and see what was up. A few hours later he called me back.

"It's gone!" Michael exclaimed.

"What do you mean, gone?" I asked.

"Gone. Cleared out. Completely vacant."

"And your art?" I asked, now a little alarmed myself.

"My friend said it was all gone too," Michael said.

To this day we have no idea what happened to the restaurant, to Michael's artwork, or to "the odd couple".

We'd never see any of these people ever again.

THIRTY-EIGHT

VOICES OF VIOLENCE

S usan K. Carroll, Acting Manager of New Teacher Support and College and University Partnerships invited me to speak to around six hundred new teachers on August 18th, the summer following my "Teacher of the Year" crowning. As she introduced me to the packed audience that embraced me with a sea of applause I begin by asking them, "Is everyone ready for their first day of school?"

And then, peering out into the sea of hundreds of new faces smiling eagerly back at me for inspiration to kick off their new school year, I continued, "Well, here's a glimpse of who you will be meeting on your first day," pointing to a large slide projected behind me of Mollie, a girl from one of my art classes, along with the portrait I painted of Mollie juxtaposed next to a slide of a painting she, in turn, created of me.

It was from the *Artists Capturing Mentors* exhibition I created for the MAEA back in 2002 - 2003. So, I introduced everyone to Mollie, and I read a short story I wrote about her and one of her classmates named L.B.

I wrote the story like verses in a poem, and all from Mollie's point of view, as if it were her talking to the audience:

AUGUST 18, 2005
Michael Bell Keynote Address to New Teachers

"Pictures are filled with stories, and each of us has a story to tell. My story began just as my Mom's ended, suddenly and unexpectedly. I was just nine years old. She died just two years after Dad took his own life. I guess he was just so sad after him and Mom split up. I think about them all the time.

I would never have believed art could help heal wounds so deep until I saw for myself.

Pictures are filled with stories.

I would've been the last to try and help you understand how art can help heal wounds so deep, and how magically art opened doors and gave voice to my years of silence, but if seeing is believing, it is also understanding and unburdening the weight of responsibility. And I can tell you this, you're not alone.

L.B.'s story began years ago, just like mine, suddenly and unexpectedly. He was also just nine years old. Over this past year, we would spend a lot of time healing our wounds in Mr. Bell's art room. I guess he helped us feel like we belonged. We'd sit and watch him paint all the time.

His pictures are filled with stories.

We watched him paint right through the fall until one magical winter morning, around nine, L.B. finally broke his silence.

He hesitated at first and then softly asked, 'Who are those pictures of that you're painting? What are they about?'

Magically, his curiosity knocked and art opened the door.

Mr. Bell then handed him a new sketchbook and asked him to write out what he thinks the pictures are about.

The first line he wrote in his sketchbook read, 'Pictures are filled with stories.'

He wrote through the day and late into the night and the pure white snow was still falling. The next morning, as the snow began to settle, the sun broke free from the clouds and L.B. felt overcome with emotions.

Mr. Bell and I began reading L.B.'s visual journal.

It read, *'Pictures are filled with stories.'*

Georgia's story, L.B. figured out, must have begun many years ago, like his, suddenly and unexpectedly. It turns out she was born on the ninth day of July. She was a model turned stunt lady turned best-selling author.

He was right about the bruises in her paintings too.

'I've seen bruises like that before,' he wrote.

And just like Georgia must have felt, in the darkness all that time, filled with lies of shame, guilt and worthlessness, I sat and stared at her paintings for a while too, letting the light and all the colors fill me up, bringing me into the light, just as I imagined they did for Georgia and for L.B.

I thought about L.B.'s story too, how he told us he still remembered hearing the gunshots. How his sixteen-year-old sister Kathy was carried out on a stretcher so that he and the other little kids in the neighborhood would think she was still alive. He told us how they finally caught Kathy's ex-boyfriend near the state line. I guess he was just so angry he didn't want her to live without him.

L.B. thinks about her all the time.

Spring was about to fade into summer. I took up painting with Mr. Bell to get through it all, and one magical morning, around nine, Mr. Bell asked me about my paintings, and I finally broke my years of silence.

You see, pictures are filled with stories, and *each of us has a story to tell.*

One day, Mr. Bell decided to paint my story. It was an experience that will stay with me forever and one that I will share with others who must travel *from wounds to wisdom.*

And we'll never be the same again." – *Michael Bell*

ONCE THE STANDING OVATION from the crowd slowly waned, I reminded all these teachers in the crowd, "This is why it's so important to learn these kids' stories, and it's also just as important to continue to share them with others."

I'd go further to explain, "Stories like L.B.'s and Mollie's are forming all around us every day if you take the time to notice. So, be sure and take an active interest in your kids' lives."

Over ten years later, a young girl named Kamryn Tisdel entered my art studio.

Kamryn was a senior and also happened to be friends with some of the top photographers in my Advanced Placement photo class. She modeled for them on a pretty frequent basis and even became the subject of some students' Scholastic Art Gold Key winning photographs. I knew she looked familiar the first time I saw her, I just didn't know from where.

Then, one morning I just happened to be helping a student, showing them examples of early works of mine that included text in the paintings. Mollie's painting was one of the works I brought up on my computer. Then it clicked with me who she looked like. I immediately called Kamryn over to my computer to ask her if she recognized the girl in the painting. Turns out it was her mother's younger sister—her Aunt Mollie.

Pictures are filled with stories . . .

KAMRYN TISDEL
CLASS OF 2016

"Secrets to be told and homework to be done—it all took place in the art studio. When I think of Southern High School, I think about the safe haven that was room G101. It was a place full of creativity, inspiration, and friendship.

My two best friends were photography students and my last two years of high school were spent helping them with their photo projects and modeling for them when they needed me. But the more time I spent in the art room watching all of the hard work going on around me, the more I craved to be a part of it all.

One day, sitting in study hall, Mr. Bell called me over to his computer. He showed me this beautiful painting online of this girl when it struck me, 'Mr. Bell, I know her! The girl in your painting is my Aunt Mollie!'

I had seen this exact painting in her apartment many years ago. Mr. Bell went on to explain to me that she was, in fact, one of his students. After he showed me all the pieces she painted, and the sketches in her journal that were done in this very room, I was hooked. I immediately asked to join National Art Honor society and was granted a yes!

From that day on, I participated in festivals, art shows, and community service projects. I shed tears watching my best friends win awards for their art during our last ArtQuest and thought about how much I'd miss these moments.

When I think of Southern High now, I think of the art room and of all the memories that I will cherish forever. I think of my Aunt Mollie, and how she had lived these same moments. I think of the friendships, fun classes and of my favorite teacher. The teacher who never had the opportunity to teach me art, but who had the opportunity to teach me about life, dedication, and community. He taught me to give it all I've got and work hard. Lessons that will stay with me forever. I will always be grateful for the art community who made my high school years the best they could be. Room G101 will be missed, but we've taken our creativity with us to make room for whoever comes through there next."

THIRTY-NINE

AND THEN CAME THE PORN STARS

Days after sharing L.B. and Mollie's story, giving what every new teacher across all disciplines felt was one of the most inspirational and emotional keynotes they've ever heard, I was now sitting in the audience a few weeks later on the other end of a keynote to all art teachers in the county. I was hoping this woman's keynote would be something equally as motivational as the one I delivered a few days ago.

She began her keynote with, "Today I'm going to present you with *the most important teaching tool you could possibly have in your arsenal.*" With a bold statement like that, this has to be good. So, I got my sketchbook out, was eager to jot down this "most important teaching tool" that she made sound like we were about to receive the Holy Grail.

And then—*wait for it . . .*

"Your most important teaching tool is—*your Outcome!*"

Your Outcome? Really?!

The thing you write on your chalkboard that kids don't even read? *I shook my head.* But this woman was dead serious. Have we really sunk to this? Or was she really that clueless? This was unfortunately someone making the big bucks, *I laughed to myself.*

I'd liken this "Ah-ha" moment to the memorable scene from the 1983 holiday classic *A Christmas Story* when Ralphie finally receives his Little Orphan Annie decoder ring, only to find out it's just a "crummy commercial" telling him to "be sure to drink your Ovaltine!" I mean, *C'mon!!! My Outcome?!?*

Let me give you an example—*a singularly extreme example*, but also one that will show you why none of this really matters.

One of my sixteen-year-old students woke up one morning to find her father and his girlfriend brutally murdered in her home while her and her other siblings were sleeping. Her mother and younger sister were soon charged with the murders and arrested. She literally lost her entire family overnight. Now, she's a kid I absolutely love to pieces and so I spent the better part of the rest of her year making sure she felt safe in my room working out all this pain through a series of haunting portraits that only showed eyes dripping with color in each painting, as if wearing a mask . . . a mask to help her to make it through another day.

So, as my head's spinning hearing this lady talk about the importance of our "Outcomes" I'm thinking to myself, "Well, if this girl happens to come to class today and is totally distraught, or doesn't feel like working, or breaks down into tears in front of the whole class she'll be just fine—*because my Outcome is spot on!*"

What a bunch of bullshit!

This is how out of touch people really are. I soon realized this was the downside of being a "Teacher of the Year." I had spent so much time surrounded by a network of other *inspiring* "Teachers of the Year" throughout the state and nation, I guess I got spoiled for a moment. I forgot that not everybody "gets it" out there. Truth is, *most really don't*. So it all comes down to *you*.

Even back in 2005, when I was out there making a solid difference and a strong run at *Maryland State Teacher of the Year*, I was suddenly met with my first taste of newfound scrutiny. Apparently, someone sent a cowardly anonymous letter to the Superintendent of Schools saying something to the effect of, "Did you know your 'Teacher of the Year' spends his free time hanging out with Mobsters and Porn Stars?"

Obviously, this was someone looking to get me fired. Also, it was someone who didn't want it coming back on them, given the fact of *who* I actually spent my free time hanging out with. I mean, it's really not the smartest move in the world, right? I figured it couldn't possibly be someone local because everyone loves me here for all the good I do for their kids. When I finally got it out of them that the letter came from New York it didn't take me long to figure out which scumbag sent it. The only reason they even told me was because my lawyer threatened to sue for defamation of character if this went any further.

While the bogus letter didn't get me into any trouble, it did allow this particular Assistant Superintendent, who has long since retired, to show his true colors and suddenly have an issue with some of my paintings on my website. My lawyer quickly addressed this with, "You're seriously about to infringe on my client's freedom of speech if you're telling him what he can or can't put on his own personal website."

They agreed, but still "suggested" I take some stuff down. I didn't fight it. It wasn't the kind of battle I was looking to fight. I had too much other stuff going on to even want to deal with their censorship of my artwork, even though I knew they couldn't do much about it even if they wanted to, other than finding other ways to give me a hard time. So, I figured, I best keep the peace.

That same Assistant Superintendent even went as far as to say during our meeting, "I've looked at the work on your website, and your work is not to my liking."

My lawyer jumped in almost immediately, "I can assure you that your taste in art or whether or not you like my clients' art is not something he cares one way or the other about. *Freedom of speech*. We talked about this, did we not?" my lawyer shot back. "One would think you'd want to give your *Teacher of the Year* a modicum of respect?"

It amazed me how quickly people judged me, based on what? Some letter? Their misconceptions about my clientele? *Who knew?!*

What nobody did really know, however, was how this all started—*what my story was*. Nor did they care.

More "suits" and "yes men" just covering their asses. *I get it.* But therein lies the problem. *And it's a systemic one.*

For me, I didn't see the few "porn stars" I was commissioned to paint the same way this asshole apparently saw them.

I simply saw them as women. Women without a voice. Women who needed help. So, I empowered them through my artwork.

MY FIRST MAJOR PAINTING COMMISSION was actually for a porn star back in the late 90s. She went by the name "Janey". She ran an adult web hosting service for adult film stars that couldn't get hosted by a traditional host company. She and her husband ran the business off their own server out of their home where she also did webcam stuff, which is how they made a lot of their money, through that and selling subscriptions to pictures and videos Janey would put up on the website.

I did Janey's painting unveiling with my wife by my side at the AVN Adult Entertainment Industry Expo in the Meadowlands, New Jersey. We didn't know what to expect. While I saw the women as women, I wasn't blind or naïve about the industry or the types of people involved with it.

So, knowing we were going to be doing a *monetary exchange*, I decided, better to show up heavy (meaning: bring a gun tucked into your waistband), you know, *just in case*. After all, I wasn't about to exchange a painting for cash and then get hit over the head in the parking lot and robbed right afterwards. Call me paranoid. But, thankfully, I never needed to use it.

The transaction went smoothly and Janey was an absolute doll. I also think she liked my wife a whole lot more than she liked me though, asking us to come up to the room afterwards for a nightcap. I was just happy she loved her painting most of all. That means everything to me.

Through Janey I met Asia Carrera, who was living proof that just because you entered the pornography industry doesn't mean you're stupid. She was a classic pianist and her SAT scores were so high she got a full ride to Rutgers.

She turned to stripping to make extra cash, which became her gateway into the industry. Her IQ has been tested at over 150.

And then there was Zoe Zeman. She was an adult film star who befriended me through the other girls. I first ended up painting a series of small black and white paintings for her on paper, similar to the ones of Georgia, and later a larger than life sized vertical portrait of her nude, emerging from the canvas like a phoenix rising from the ashes. The palette was filled with warm yellows and Venetian reds. Zoe's hand-written poem she entitled, *The Walk*, was inscribed in charcoal throughout the background of the painting since this was something prevalent in many works of mine done during this time period. For her, these paintings became therapeutic, much as they were for Georgia.

The smaller paintings of Zoe were particularly hard to do, though, I mean, from an emotional standpoint because they were all re-creations of tragedy. She explained to me how she needed to somehow overcome an abusive cycle of rape she experienced as a young girl and that was the reason she went into the adult film industry in the first place.

Shocking as it may sound, she said this became the only place she felt truly safe having sex—under the bright lights and behind the lens of a camera with a crew of producers and assistants in the room to yell "cut" when she needed them to.

She explained to me how the first time she was raped it was multiple times at this shore house with a girlfriend of hers. What began as a typical party late-night took a horrible turn for the worse. She said they wound up on opposite sides of two separate twin beds across the room from one another in this seedy motel room after the party, both being raped by multiple guys. She said the only thing that helped her through this endless night of being raped over and over was to lock eyes with her girlfriend from across the other bed and never look elsewhere. They held each other in each other's gaze until it was finally over.

As I digested her horrific story I pondered whether it's legitimate to think of all problems as "solvable"? I wrote in my sketchbook, "We only judge the truth by the reality it creates."

I thought to myself, "If pictures serve as a form of visual language, they could also serve as visual persuasion for change. By examining someone else's life visually through artwork, we, as artists, could begin confronting the audience with questions."

My whole take on art became, "If we can begin thinking about ourselves through the paintings and identify with them, much the way Mollie and L.B. identified with the paintings I did of Georgia, it would spark a dialogue where we could talk openly about them (while still coming to grips with why we are experiencing empathy because of the paintings). Then, perhaps others could use my art in order to bring closure to things, as a means to bring feelings to the surface in order to get them out or dispel them forever. As a way to work through the pain."

MICHAEL SPROUSE AND I CREATED our second collaboration painting, which was a 22" X 28" acrylic painting on canvas entitled *Always Will* as the sequel to *Never Was*, which was auctioned off to benefit *the Milton Theatre Project*.

For this painting we used a Polaroid I had of Zoe juxtaposed against a vintage photograph of Jean Harlow, who was an actress from the 1930s who died tragically during the filming of *Saratoga* in 1937 at the young age of twenty-six. While these paintings merged together a very loose narrative, this was us, as artists, trying to figure out why fate led us to them . . . *or them to us*.

For Zoe, she said my paintings helped her heal. For me, though, especially the black and white ones, I felt like I was raping her all over again by bringing those events back to the surface visually. It's a difficult position to be in, as a male artist with my male gaze implied into the scenes, but she said it helped her. So, somehow, I was able to help her get over her pain through my art.

As for the *Mob Stars*, well, they became some of the most endearing men in my life. They certainly treated me a lot better and with far more respect than that particular Assistant Superintendent did, despite how great I consistently made him, our entire county and our state look on an annual basis.

This all made me deeply ponder that slanderous letter, "Why would someone write something like that against me if they *truly knew* the company I kept? Not particularly bright of them," I smiled to myself. I also thought about how demeaning that particular Assistant Superintendent was towards me.

But like I said, this can be a thankless profession filled with shallow bureaucrats climbing the corporate ladder on the backs of others—all of which are major contributors to the steadily eroding, broken system of public education in this country. Instead of finding out the story behind *who I was painting* or *why I was painting them*, they just looked to censor me, which, from an integrity standpoint, actually just made them ten times worse.

One morning, once all this finally died down, I awakened from a vivid dream about Georgia's ex-husband, the one that had been haunting her in her dreams every night for the past twenty years. He approached me in my dream from behind as I walked down this deserted city street late at night, his gun at my back.

He said to me, "You know why I'm here?" I nodded yes, but suggested, "Let's walk a little further first . . ."

When we got to the top of this hill all of the sudden the sun was starting to rise over the backdrop of a strange foreign town. Suddenly my father emerged from this two-story brick flat with two of his buddies from the bar.

I looked back at Georgia's ex as my Dad's pals quickly disarmed him, dropping him to his knees. They smiled at him and I said, "You should have killed me when you had the chance."

And with that, my father walked me inside as both his pals drew their guns and *Bang! Bang! Bang!* He lay dead in the street.

When I called my father to tell him about the dream he couldn't believe how I described everything, right down to the pattern and color of paisley carpeting in the two-story flat he grew up in as a child back in Ireland.

When I finally got around to calling Georgia about it, she asked, "When did you have this dream?"

"Not sure? A couple weeks ago, maybe . . . why?" I asked.

"It's a funny thing, *I haven't dreamed about him since . . .*"

FORTY

TICK, TICK, TICK . . .

It was time for change. And new directions in life for me meant *new directions in painting.* I felt like my hand was getting too close to the flame, so to speak. Marlene, whom I've been closest with since the beginning of my teaching career, walked past me one morning in the hallway, looked up at the clock and whispered, *"tick, tick, tick . . ."*

The only reason I even recalled this is because I documented it in my sketchbook. She was just busting my chops, but it was surreal, like she had followed me out of my own waking dream.

And while I felt the proverbial clock was ticking on some goals and dreams still left unaccomplished, I had been feeling blessed in the New Year with another lease on life and felt like my guardian angel was helping me with my own revival of sorts.

While I continued to ride out my *Teacher of the Year wave,* along with other esteemed colleagues in the race for Maryland State Teacher of the Year doing TV spots, as honored guests on the floor of the House and Senate, at Orioles games, and on cruises along the Chesapeake, *I was still riding out the wave with Georgia.*

From all our involvement with domestic violence charities across the country, where in 2005 we were both honored at the

Millenium Biltmore Hotel in Los Angeles as the Good Shepherd Domestic Violence Shelter Community Service Award recipients. We got to tour the shelter, along with pop singer Monét Lerner. The experience left me humbled, and while I left with a plaque and helped auction off some prints of my work to benefit the shelter that night, this would be a cause I'd continue to donate towards annually, in the form of creating hundreds of handmade sketchbooks with kids in my National Art Honor Society that we ship out just before Christmas.

Actresses Victoria Principal and Michelle Pfeiffer had already donated a swimming pool and apartments to the facility. And, while, financially, I couldn't do all that, they did have a Creative Arts class I was able to sit in on while touring the shelter, so I immediately thought *visual journaling* could help.

The fine arts teacher just had finished a project with them on the theme, "Walk a Mile in my Shoes", which consisted of their actual shoes turned into collages of photographs, text, clippings, all very emotionally charged autobiographical outpourings. So, sketchbooks I thought would be right up their alley as a place to deposit all that life threw their way. As a place to deposit all the anger and pain in *constructive*, as opposed to *destructive ways*.

She introduced me to this one little boy I'll never forget, whom she said couldn't be in a room where there wasn't an exit directly in front of him or directly behind him due to the fact that he was once locked in a closet while he watched his Dad set his Mom on fire.

These were the kinds of heartbreaking stories that were commonplace at this shelter, which housed some of the most extreme domestic violence cases in all of Los Angeles.

From the street, you wouldn't even know the shelter existed. It's so well hidden that once you're inside, you'd never believe how big the facility is. Professors from various institutions come to educate the mothers and their children there. There are two layers of fencing with barbed wire, security cameras and guard dogs roaming the grounds at all times. Once, one of the husbands found out his wife found refuge there and tossed poisoned meat over the fence to try and kill the guard dogs. This was when the second fence went up. These women literally never leave the facility until they are absolutely ready to return to society. Some of the women I met were there for years.

So, each year, my National Art Honor Society would make sketchbooks, each with personalized notes, often translated into Spanish since it's a large Spanish speaking population there. This became our annual "good deed" to these women and children.

I also did another auction in Chicago with Georgia that year, and was becoming more of a seasoned public speaker, following her lead. She was my mentor in this new world of activism and I was soaking it all up like a sponge.

I'd later do a portrait unveiling for her friend, Aida Bogosian, while bartering some jewelry from *Michael B. jewelry* for my wife, Lisa in exchange, and I would keep riding out this wave . . .

I was even asked to host my own talk radio show on a brand new network Alan Levy, creator, and CEO of *BlogTalk Radio*, was scheduled to launch later that September.

My show would be called *MBELLART Live!* And my co-hosts would be John Fiore from *the Sopranos* and Chicago's own Dominic Capone, who I hit it off with years ago at *the Golden Age of Gangsters Convention* in Chicago during the fall of 2004. We'd talk on the air about behind-the-scenes stuff that happened in our lives, in my painting studio, on and off the movie sets. We'd ask celebrities we knew to call in from time to time and we'd run merchandise giveaways, fine art print contests, stuff like that.

The Gangsters Convention was also when I first met Clem Caserta, who played Jimmy Whispers in Chazz Palminteri's film *A Bronx Tale*, opposite Robert De Niro. We went out on the town one night together and he gave me the single greatest advice anyone's ever given me in the entertainment industry.

He first asked me, "Kid, they fly you out to this thing?"

"Yeah," I said.

"They *pay you* to come out here?" he asked.

"They paid for my hotel and airfare," I said, "if that's what you mean," curious now where this was headed . . .

"No, I mean, did they *pay you*—anything else, beyond that? Because, *me*, I got an extra $1,500 on top of it all," he boasted.

"Yeah, but Clem, you're a movie star," I exclaimed, "You've been in *Goodfellas, Casino, A Bronx Tale*, people see you and they *know* who you are. Me, I'm an artist. It's different."

He pressed on, "You ever acted before?"

"Every day of my life," I quickly shot back with.

He laughed. He seemed to like that answer.

"That's a good one kid," he chuckled, "Listen, here's the thing, if they got nothin' invested in you, and I know, hotel and airfare are nice. At least it's somethin', but if they got something *really invested in you*, and mind you, it ain't about being cheap, this is just business . . ."

Now he's got my undivided attention . . .

"You see," he continued, "If they got somethin' invested in you, they're gonna want to get a *return* on their investment. Maybe they toss you a radio spot, a TV interview, somethin' to make sure they see a return on their investment. In turn, you're gonna do your part to make sure you talk them up too. You'll gladly do those radio spots, TV interviews, you name it! It gives *you exposure*, and it gives *them exposure*. It makes *everybody happy*. But if they got nothin' invested in you, they got no reason to promote you, or do anything else for you, for that matter."

"Makes sense," I said. "I get it. Thanks Clem."

Brilliant fucking guy.

I never did anything for nothin' ever again.

OVER THE NEXT COUPLE OF YEARS, doing my *MBELLART Live Radio show* with Dominic and John, we all became close friends. We did what I felt were inspiring broadcasts that went beyond the realm of traditional Q & A, and took our audiences into our private worlds, into our minds.

I also began re-engaging in painting again, a practice which had since escaped me for about a year. I had gotten too caught up in the aftermath of being "Teacher of the Year" and felt disenfranchised, even back then. I felt as though I had done my part, paid my dues . . . in the art world and beyond, but still felt completely alone in it all.

So, I began painting pictures of this Brooklyn photographer named Lauren Bentley, in order to re-engage myself in the process of painting again. She created these incredibly cinematic self-portraits and so I asked her if I could paint some of them, as a jumping off point for a new series of works I'd later call, *the Cinema of Truth*.

The series was pieced together more as a theme than an actual story, just choosing photographs of hers that I thought were interesting and went together based on content, but this also became an important step for me. It was my first venture into the art of storytelling. Hanging out with all these actors, I was falling in love with the art of storytelling.

And, the Gangsters Convention in Chicago wouldn't end up being my last trip to Chi-town. On February 10, 2007, I was invited to headline the world's 2nd annual *For the Love of Chocolate* event in Chicago. Over 3,000 patrons would get to indulge their senses and in the decadent world of live body painting with chocolate by yours truly.

And, yes, I followed Clem's advice and made sure I got paid, in addition to my airfare and hotel. Since I was headlining the event, I also agreed to donate a painting for their auction, which would end up being *Superbia*, a 30″ X 40″ oil painting on canvas that was to be auctioned off for $12,000 to benefit the organization's scholarship foundation for kids pursuing culinary arts who have no formal training.

Superbia also launched a new *Seven Deadly Sins in Chocolate* painting series, featuring Lauren Bentley, again, as my subject. This series would be me inching towards connecting my paintings as full-blown narrative stories, and these seven paintings would also become the sequel to my six *Cinema of Truth* paintings.

FORTY-ONE

OUR MIRACLE BABY

April 10, 2007 was the day of my 36th birthday, and my wife was nine months pregnant. Up until this point, over the course of our first eleven years of marriage, Lisa hadn't been able to get pregnant.

She sat by, watching her younger brother Marc and his wife Kellie go on to have three beautiful kids, one girl after the next with ease as we went through multiple *In-Vitro Fertilizations, Intrauterine Inseminations—nothing worked*. We figured it just wasn't in the cards. We even considered adopting. But, in the summer of 2005, we decided to say "fuck it!" We stopped trying to have kids and my wife took the plunge and went into business for herself, making that *her baby*.

I had been commuting back and forth to Southern High one hundred twenty-two miles roundtrip for the past eleven years, so it was time for us to take a chance and start over someplace new. We sold our townhouse in Bel Air, and invested a large chunk of the sale into developing Lisa's own cosmetics line. We rented a place literally a stone's throw from my school and Lisa started up her own company. Lisa literally grew up in her parent's salon in North Jersey, so the beauty business was right up her alley.

It was something, like art and teaching was for me, that was already in her blood, and it was something she was already great at doing. That summer she laid the groundwork for the creation of *NAVÉ Cosmetics*, named after her Nonna Navé, her father's mother in Italy. She spent a year in research and development before hiring a lawyer to create her own LLC, along with finding the right chemist and packaging company.

Once the line was complete, the warehouse was stocked, and by warehouse I mean *my father-in-law's basement*, we proceeded to put a down payment on renting a storefront to launch her new cosmetics line down the Jersey Shore in Beach Haven West, which is a popular vacation spot just west of Long Beach Island.

We found a partner through Lisa's father, who seemed like a sweet old woman who wanted one-third of the space to sell what she explained to us as being "high-end jewelry". With beauty and jewels, why not throw in my art? We envisioned this could become a cool, eclectic spot for us to embark on our new future together during the seasonal months and then expand from there. I incorporated "Galleria Red" as the storefront name and we headed to Jersey to bring our dreams to fruition.

And then, low and behold, just when we were a week away from opening up shop, she came out of the bathroom and hit me with, "Michael, you're not going to believe this one—*I'm pregnant!*"

It was *a miracle*, literally!

And *who knew*, with all the *In Vitro's* and *IUI's*, all it took was one drunken night in Jersey to do the trick!

We were ecstatic, though. We immediately had to pull the plug on the shop down the shore and Lisa would have to put her dreams on hold to ensure a safe and healthy pregnancy for our child. The thing was we had already signed a lease. On top of that, the day we arrived to set up shop, the old woman who told us by phone that she just wanted one-third of the place to sell some jewelry ended up taking over at least two-thirds of the store with these huge hideous display cases before we arrived. We took one look at the place and knew we had to get out of the lease.

Not just for the fact the place wasn't at all what we had envisioned or agreed to buy into, but for the stress I imagined Lisa was about to endure. I wasn't having it. Not with all we went through trying to have a child.

So, first I called the landlord. At first she didn't budge. So, I asked her if she *actually read* the article that came out in the newspapers about "the artist to *the Sopranos* and other Mob icons coming to Beach Haven?"

She immediately called me back and said that she didn't want any trouble and would have no problem letting us out of the lease, only the old woman had already changed the locks on her and she couldn't even get into her own building in order for us to get Lisa's cosmetics or my paintings back out of it! Talk about crazy!

So, after hearing that, I arranged a meeting with the old woman that evening to try and "work something out". I took my father-in-law, Bill, with me and asked Lisa to stay home and rest, that everything would be fine.

On the drive over the bridge from Manahawkin into LBI we slowly headed toward Beach Haven West and I insisted to Bill everything would be fine, just let me do the talking. I knew he felt bad partnering us up with this unconscionable woman in the first place, and now we were about to enter some uncharted waters. But for me, this was very familiar territory. It was a place I knew all too well. It would also prove to become a moment my father-in-law learned *exactly who I was* and *what I was capable of.*

The old woman was standing outside next to her son outside the storefront when we pulled up. He was extremely tall, but lanky. I let them wait and stew for a few moments, knowing they couldn't see inside my black Cadillac DTS through my blacked-out limo tinted windows. She seemed anxious, and her son began to look increasingly nervous with each passing minute as we sat idle in the car.

"You sure you don't want to wait here, Dad?" I asked my father-in-law.

"No, I still want to talk to her. I got you into this mess in the first place. Maybe I can straighten it out."

I knew just from a glance she wasn't going to listen to reason. After all, what kind of a person would change the locks on a place that wasn't even hers? I also figured she brought her son with her as "muscle" which made me laugh, knowing what I'd do to him if he pulled that card.

As I smiled to myself, playing out the events that were about to transpire in my head before getting out of the car, I caught my own reflection in the driver's side mirror unconsciously biting down on the inside of my left cheek, exactly the same way I'd seen my father always do over the course of many years as a kid before he'd erupt into a violent rage. It was always *his tell*. I always knew when he was about to fuck somebody up. This was the first time I saw it on me.

I got out of the car. My father-in-law had already begun trying to negotiate with the old woman but I could tell it wasn't going well. Her son stood by idling. So, I came around the car, approached her son with a menacing glare, clenched fist, and popped my trunk with the click of a button on my keychain.

"You've got one of two choices. I take out my paintings and my wife's merchandise that are inside the store, or I take out what's in the wheel well of my trunk. Either way, I'm not leaving without my paintings or my wife's stuff, *so think it through . . . you've got about ten seconds.*" I slowly reached inside my trunk.

Her son took one glance into my trunk, perhaps wondering what fate lied beneath my wheel well as he watched the anger brew in my face. After fumbling for the keys as quickly as he could he unlocked the door to the store against his mother's will.

"C'mon Bill. Let's load up the car," I commanded.

I quickly slammed my trunk shut, stormed right past them and went to work. After a few short trips back and forth to my car, a local police cruiser drove slowly past, curiously watching us load the last of the boxes of Lisa's cosmetics into my trunk.

The officer rolled down his window, "Is there a problem?"

I glared at both the old woman and her son to keep quiet as I ushered my father-in-law back into the car.

"Not anymore there's not," I smiled.

The officers nodded back and drove off, half-shaking their heads at the old woman and son standing there curbside.

We drove off quietly, but, before we hit home, I took Bill out to *Harvey Cedars Shellfish Company* on the other side of the Island for some Calamari Vera Cruz and some Clams on the Half Shell to celebrate getting Lisa's stuff back.

"I'm sorry I got you in the middle of all that, Dad."

"You know," Bill said proudly to me, "You really seemed like you knew what you were doing back there."

I smiled at him. "I'm just happy we got Lisa's stuff back."

Bill and I bonded that night. I knew a part of him loved that darker side of me. I knew he loved me like a son and I loved him right back just as much as I loved my own Dad.

OVER THE NEXT NINE MONTHS Lisa and I read lots of books about what to expect when you're expecting. Lisa also developed Gestational Diabetes during the course of her pregnancy so we had to eat super healthy and read every packaging label to keep her sugar intake down so she didn't have to go on insulin. She was taking shots in her finger in the meantime to check her sugar levels daily. This would become a practice we'd both go all in on. Eating healthy, exercising regularly, you name it we did it in order to ensure a healthy childbirth.

She was thrown two baby showers, one in North Jersey and one here in Maryland. It was a really glorious time for us. We were so excited.

And on the afternoon of my birthday, my kids at school treated me really great too, sending me on a ridiculous scavenger hunt around my studio to find one gift after the next. Silly stuff for me, and some gifts for the new baby, you know, stuff just to watch me squirm or melt my "tough guy" exterior. The kind of stuff that comes from having great relationships with each and every one of them, allowing them to feel comfortable just being themselves around me. They even surprised me with a big "It's a Boy" banner once Lisa and I found out the sex of the baby.

This is the kind of close-knit crew I teach on an annual basis. And, while I was at work, Lisa reluctantly was scheduled to go out to lunch with an old friend of hers from Bel Air that wanted to visit her before she had the baby. Lisa didn't want to go out, being she was due any day now, but her friend insisted, so she went off to lunch that afternoon to meet her along with my mother-in-law, who was staying with us in case Lisa happened to go into labor while I was at work.

Then, around 12:30 P.M. I got a frantic phone call from her girlfriend from *Chili's* in Annapolis. There was so much screaming and sirens filling the background that I could barely hear her, not to mention I was in the middle of teaching a class, so couple that with the noise of a large art studio in full swing, it was nearly impossible to hear anything at all. I immediately thought Lisa must have gone into labor!

Now, I was born on my mother's birthday, so I figured this was probably the case with our son now too. So, I stepped outside of my room so I can hear her friend better, given all the commotion in the background.

"She's been—*hit*? What do you mean *hit*?!" I exclaimed.

"A car lost control, crashed right through the window of the restaurant. Hit your wife and your mother-in-law! If we were one booth over we'd all be dead," her friend screamed. "You've got to get down here! NOW!"

Marlene just happened to stop by my room, so I immediately asked her cover my class and I bolted out the door, hopped in my car and raced in and out of traffic to get to Lisa and her Mom.

When I finally got there, it was a circus! Helicopters with news crews were hovering over the scene where the car still sat half-inside the restaurant, suspended in mid-air.

Reporters were everywhere snapping pictures as I arrived to find my mother-in-law being taken by stretcher into the ambulance, my wife blood splattered all over the shirt of her huge, pregnant belly like a Jackson Pollock painting.

Her first words to me were, "It's ok, it's not my blood—it's my mothers'!"

We embraced and I quickly hopped back in my car and followed her ambulance to the hospital.

My mother-in-law was being treated for a huge head wound and needed staples in her head. She had brain surgery once before to remove a tumor when Lisa was still in high school, so we were all terrified and praying she was going to make it through.

Lisa went to get an ultrasound and the baby seemed okay. As great as Lisa is in a crisis, this was pretty traumatizing for her. She still, to this day, won't sit near a window that sits along the street at any restaurant, but everything with the baby seemed okay, and with her focus being on making sure her mother was alright, the accident didn't induce labor like I thought it would.

We'd wait another eight days for Carmen to arrive, at 11:27 A.M., on April 18th after going nearly twenty-four hours straight in labor.

As for Carmen's official ASD and ADHD diagnosis at age eight, well, sure it crossed our minds if that accident had anything to do with it. Who knows? We never sued the restaurant or the old lady driving the car, even though we could have. Her girlfriend did, and she scored $10,000 out of the ordeal.

I was certainly furious enough to since nobody even helped my wife or her mother at the restaurant when the car crashed through that window, sending them both to the ground. But that's the kind of world we're living in now, unfortunately. Everybody else is just worried about being sued or suing. Not us, though. We figured it'd be good karma for our son not to since he seemed okay through the rest of her pregnancy, which we kept a close eye on over the next eight days until he arrived into the world. One thing I can say about our son Carmen, he was born a fighter, even before he came out of the womb.

FORTY-TWO

MARLENE

Meanwhile, one year later I'm back at Southern, and in the summer of 2008 I brought Marlene Kramer on board to co-teach the county's Gifted and Talented Program with me. She's been my right-hand-woman so to speak since first hiring her back in 2000.

Hiring a quality teacher isn't easy either. It's an art form in itself. But Marlene definitely lived up to her billing and is the single greatest hire I've ever made. Jean recently retired, so I was also back in hiring mode as the new Art Department Chair to try and fill her void. Then, an additional opening presented itself for Marlene to work with me in the GT Program, so I immediately made the case for her to join me. Suzanne Owens, my Coordinator of Art at that time, graciously agreed.

Now, I love Marlene. The kids all love her too. We both became very close over the years, literally doing practically everything together while building the program at Southern. We completed our Master's together at Towson; Marlene focused on *Printmaking* while I focused on *Visual Journaling*. We both painted side by side in Nora Sturges' classes and sat through weird, erotic art films like *the Pillow Book* in Michael Weiss' drawing classes together. Lisa and I were guests at Marlene's wedding in Key West when she got married to her husband Eric, and in the summer of 2007 she gave birth to her son Jacob, the same year Lisa and I gave birth to Carmen, only a few months later.

Fast forward a few years and we'd go through *National Board Certification* together in 2010. And, to begin the 2016—2017 school year things would come full circle in our department, with my 2008 hire Amanda Hagerman leaving us after eight years to pursue entrepreneurship, launching her own full-time jewelry business after suffering through a seven-year long salary freeze.

But, back to me and Marlene—in 2008, when I hired her to additionally co-teach the GT Program with me, it also became a turning point in our relationship. While I was close with Marlene already, in the fall of 2008, after coming off a successful week-long summer GT session it was the ten upcoming fall Saturday GT sessions we'd teach together that would bring us the closest.

You see, *great teaching* is also something of an art form.

Each day takes its shape the way any new work of art on your easel does. Some days you have to just listen to *the work* and allow it to dictate the direction of where a piece is headed, the same way you have to really listen to *your kids* while figuring your way through which direction each unit is headed. Some days you take charge and work through it, other days you change course.

I don't believe in "just making art for art's sake" either. Any artist that tells you they don't care what anyone thinks of their work is totally full of shit.

If this was the case, nobody would be trying to get shows, nobody would be sharing pictures of their work online to try and get *Insta-famous* by posting everything out—*that's just not reality.*

In reality, everyone wants to be appreciated. Everyone wants to be successful. Every artist wants their work seen. For me, it's always "Succeed or die trying. Leave it all on the field," as coaches would say. Through each and every day, every class, every painting, every drawing, we fight our way through it and work towards achieving our goals together.

Like NIKE says, we "just do it!"

If nothing else, we just keep showing up for the process and must be willing to work hard to understand what our process actually is, and then the final product should take care of itself. Everyone wants to be relevant. I don't care who you are. And I believe everyone matters. Everyone. And sometimes you have to face the unknown by staring it down. *Owning it.*

Sometimes we also have to embrace our limitations. If you pull off the mask you wear for everyone else, even for yourself at times, and just let go, you never know who might be there to catch you. Instead of trying to regain the illusion of control, once you let go, a funny thing happens . . . you suddenly realize that you clearly never had any control, to begin with.

ON FRIDAY THE 13TH, back in 2008, Marlene let go of hers, and I became closer to her than I ever was with her before. The afternoon began after a full day of teaching, as we were both now working late into the afternoon coming up with project samples for the Gifted and Talented Program. Typically, we'd meet after school, gather together materials for our Saturday projects and then call it a day. After all, *it was Friday.*

On this particular Friday, we decided to give the kids some ink wash drawings of metaphorical objects as our big "Saturday Challenge", which often ranged from innovative problems such as creating thirty works in ninety minutes, making a self-portrait using only one hundred marks, or feeling their way through a tactile drawing of objects hidden under sheets. I recalled how great Marlene was at contour drawings and ink wash paintings from our days together at Towson, so I took a shot and asked her if she had anywhere special to be that afternoon, and if she didn't, would she mind whipping up a sample work to show the class on Saturday?

She said "no problem," and she went right to work on it in my studio.

The problem at hand was to create a contour-ink wash of "objects that held symbolic meaning attached to them".

We figured this would be far more interesting for kids than drawing some random still-life devoid of any meaning just for the experience of creating something technically proficient. What we were after was something on a much grander scale; a work that was both high concept and high technical execution. So, we gathered a bunch of random stuff from the Drama Department and placed it in the center of my room to choose from.

Marlene took the lead, as if stepping into "our students' shoes", and proceeded to look for an object she could identify with to paint as the sample project.

She chose a pair of high heeled shoes from the pile of props, laid the shoes out on my hardwood studio floors in a random pose and started drawing. Before I knew it, the day had flown by and it was nearly 5:30 in the afternoon. The sun was going down in the sea of palladium windows along my back wall and Marlene was still going strong, totally immersed in what she was painting.

When I went over to see how she was making out, I reminded her, "this is just a sample work; you don't have to make it some Georgia O'Keefe masterpiece you know . . ."

And then she started crying.

Her tears began to flow, streaming down her face uncontrollably. And this was really uncharacteristic of her. Marlene's this bubbly, silly, fun-loving girl that makes everyone else smile. That's her personality. I couldn't figure it out.

So I carefully asked, out of genuine concern, "What's going on? What's the matter? Why are you working so hard on this particular piece? What's *really* going on?" These are some of the questions that the teacher in me, the friend in me, *the Artist in me* was trying to unravel from her. It had to be something with the shoes, I thought. *But what?*

"Do you know what I just realized?" she asked me. "Today is November 13th."

"Yeah, it's Friday the 13th too," I added.

"Exactly," she said, wiping the tears from her eyes. "As I'm trying to figure out why I picked up these high heeled shoes, and why I was spending so much time just staring at them as I'm drawing them it finally hit me. Fifteen years ago today, coincidentally or not, *on a Friday the 13th of all days, my mother left.* I still remember how I always played dress up and wore her high heeled shoes in the mirror as a young girl."

"Jesus, I'm so sorry," I said. Now tears started to stream down my face, right along with hers as I hugged her.

"The day she left I remember her asking me if I wanted to come with her. I was devastated. I said no, and then she left. She moved away to Florida, found a new boyfriend and from that day on, I took care of the day to day things Mom used to do. *I was now the mom.* I packed my Dad and my younger brother's lunches for work and for school. *You name it . . ."* she sobbed.

"Our relationship was difficult at the time," Mar explained, "because I didn't understand her choice of leaving. I've never even told my husband Eric this. I don't know why it all hit me the way it did today, but I knew there was a reason I was supposed to be here working on this—*painting these shoes, and telling you."*

I was floored. To this day, I share her story with my kids as they are trying to come up with reasons for painting a still-life, and how powerful it really could be if they came up with their own metaphorical object that has some symbolic significance.

I also remember this one kid named Evan. He brought in a *Heinz* ketchup bottle as his still-life for his homework assignment in my 2D Studio I drawing class. The kids in the class all laughed. Let me preface this by sharing the fact that this kid was a well-liked athlete, probably not going to be the next Van Gogh or anything, but the kids thought he didn't take the project seriously and was just goofing around with bringing in a Ketchup bottle, until it was time to share out "why".

The laughter and jeers subsided as his response turned the atmosphere of the room deadly serious. Evan shocked even me with his story behind this Ketchup bottle. I figured, like everybody else, maybe he did just grab something at random. But he didn't. He floored us with this incredible story about how his Grandfather passed away that year, and how he had the fondest memories of going out to lunch with his Grandfather.

How, as a kid, he always had this irrational fear of "bothering people" unnecessarily and how if a waiter at whatever restaurant they would be having lunch at would forget to bring Ketchup or anything for that matter, he'd just let it go. He'd never speak up for himself. Not until his Grandfather taught him not to be afraid to speak up, that whatever he thought was built up in his head as such a "big deal" really wasn't such a big deal at all, and pretty soon he started practicing. Practicing asking for things he needed. And sure enough, it wasn't such a big deal after all. Nothing usually is.

So, as jaws were dropping and kids were now scrambling in their heads to come up with a much better story behind why they brought in whatever object they brought in to draw or paint that day, Evan had them spellbound with his story of how a single Ketchup bottle symbolized standing up for himself, even if no-one else would, and it also reminded him of his Grandfather. Nobody laughed at anything Evan drew or painted ever again. No matter what it looked like. And he actually got pretty good at painting, much to even his surprise I think, but it was because there was a solid "why" behind his work. There was a reason for it to need to come into existence as a work of art. Everyone needs to find their why. It's one of the most important things in life, as an artist, or as anything or anyone in any business for that matter.

Now I knew *Marlene's why*.

Her father was her whole world. From that moment on we'd try to make sure and do whatever we could to help each other keep our own families together, at all costs. It became the thing both of us always feared the most—*losing our families*. Marlene, after her Mom leaving, and me, after nearly losing both my wife and my son in that traumatic crash on my birthday, just eight days before our son was born.

FORTY-THREE

TICKET TO RIDE

Hanging out with all these actors over the years helped me to learn to understand how to really "get into character" myself, but mostly for my paintings. While movies, Mob movies, in particular, had always been a big cultural influence on me ever since I first watched *the Godfather*, I was now beginning to look at my paintings not just as singular works anymore, but as a unique version of theater, with the drama unfolding scene by scene—painting by painting, as a compilation.

I was beginning to explore new directions in painting the way a Movie Director explores connections between the language of props, locations, camera angles and body language to create a symphony of sequential scenes to tell a story.

Ticket to Ride initially began as my first venture into the world of storytelling through a series of narrative paintings (serial paintings), each scene being able to stand on its own, but when placed in a particular, sequential viewing order it contributed towards a much larger tale.

The series began around the same time I finally realized who tried to get me fired during my race to become the "2005

Maryland State Teacher of the Year" with that cowardly letter anonymously mailed to the Superintendent. My initial reaction was—*send someone to pay them a visit.*

Most people entertain violent thoughts like this, especially in regards to someone who would go as far as to try and mess with your livelihood, so I figured—*now you've got my attention.* Only, unlike most, I also had the wherewithal to do something about it.

But my wife said not to do anything—at least, *not right now.*

"Don't waste your energy getting angry", she told me, "A slow kill is so much better. Let them walk around for the rest of their lives wondering *when* something's going to happen to them. And when the smoke clears, when many years pass, then decide if they're still worth it. If they are, do what comes naturally to you. The world will have forgotten about them by then."

If I had to compare my wife and me to the Corleone Family in *the Godfather*, Lisa would definitely be the cold, calculated Michael. Me, I'm Sonny. Smarter than most, but also a hothead.

Later that spring, Lisa wrote a poem to me, and it triggered the idea for my *Ticket to Ride* painting series. I would inscribe her words into the background of each canvas and use her as the inspiration behind my central character.

THE TRANSFER
By Lisa Bell

"Passing through life like a ticking time bomb.
Hoping to live out every dream imagined as a child.
Time is energy, good or bad,
but which one will tick for you?
Breezing through life's dimensions.
Feeling and seeing life's energies.
How do you know what to trust?
Thinking it will be a way to plug into
your hopes, dreams, and fears.
But all you ever found
was just another station."

So, with Lisa as my femme fatale for the series, and my model, we went back to New York City and took reference photos for the paintings—on the subway, out on the street, getting into a taxi, peering with me into the trunk of a taxi cab, in a hotel room, you name it, and we took photos for it, as if filming a movie.

I also printed out subway maps, pasting them into the background of each canvas before painting over them. In painting one, *The Transfer*, the subway maps literally document the beginning of her journey, *or descent*, if you will, that plays out like film stills in a movie, where she's staring out onto a deserted subway platform, contemplating the words she wrote in poem form in the back of her mind as she waits for her train. And, in this series of works, instead of them being "still frames", which capture a moment in time and freeze it, these moments were very much alive for the audience, revived through the accumulation of my experience with them, through layers of paint, text, mapping, drips—*layers upon layers of meaning*.

This would become my process of painting. *My signature style.*

This would also be my ticket to starring in roles for my own paintings, as well as for others to audition for future parts.

TICKET TO RIDE would usher in a new era for me in painting. I'd take all my own photographs, I'd go out on location, I'd do everything I had to do in order for my work to be authentic. I wanted to experience everything, like a movie I was starring in. I wanted to be there. Experience it all!

And, while working narratively, I also felt it was important not to alienate the audience. I think that's really, really important. It's not just about you and what you're trying to say. It's about making sure the audience can connect with it.

So, in painting two, *Room Service*, I wanted to invite the audience right up to the hotel room table where there sits imagery of a half-eaten breakfast, a cigarette still burning in a nearby ashtray next to a 9mm handgun, all larger-than-life, so that you, the audience, must assume the role of this hitman.

For painting three, *the Ring*, the story returns to the subway, and I started painting all these people coming and going in and out of the canvas, much like people do at a subway stop. I wanted to create the feel of movement since subways are so busy. Then, in the end, I decided to paint everyone out of the painting and just leave this payphone dangling off the hook near the tracks as the subway train races past us on the platform. Beneath the surface of the painting, the energy of the people coming and going are still there, and if you took an X-Ray to the painting you'd even see them, but on the surface, it's hauntingly vacant.

This would also become something important that I'd discover throughout the tireless patience and dedication it takes to complete a monumental series such as these nine works over the course of several years. Sometimes, I figured out, it's much more interesting to paint what happened *just before* or *just after* something happens, so the viewer can fill in the blanks and find a way to inject their own perspective and experiences into the scenes. If the scenes are too specific, it's not as easy.

Ticket to Ride became a series of very loose narratives. I'd continue leaving evidence of my painting process behind in each piece in the form of drips and text, maps, textures, you name it. These paintings were definitely coming alive.

Then I decided to introduce the iconic yellow taxi cab as the "third main character". While we explore the journey of two main characters from subway to hotel room to the streets of New York City, they both finally emerge from "underground", so to speak, in painting five, *Getaway Car*, as Lisa enters the back seat of a taxi, and the hitman peers back into the rear view mirror at her, as her driver. While this particular work was the first in the series to change the format, as I went to a "split-screen" to sustain movement throughout the narrative, something else happened in my studio one afternoon that changed the series for me forever.

One of my student artists bumped into the canvas as it was leaning up against my easel. Total accident, but the painting fell right into the corner of a wooden drawing horse sitting nearby. This tore a *huge rip* through the bottom right corner of the canvas.

In my head, I initially went, "Noooooooooo!!!! What am I going to do with this painting now? There's a huge rip in it!"

After taking a deep breath, I told myself, "There's gotta be a reason *why* this happened. And, it's up to me to figure it out."

I ended up pasting more subway maps onto the back of the painting so they'd show through the rip, and I even ended up ripping the canvas more. Once the maps were showing through from behind, I threaded a needle through the rips, loosely sewing thread in and out like a bad suture, symbolic of sewing up personal scars—wounds that will never heal quite perfectly.

Eventually, I also decided for paintings eight and nine that it might be interesting for my femme fetale's journey to come full circle. So, in painting eight, *Check In, Check Out*, I revisited the same hotel room where the hitman was in painting two, only the room is all cleaned up now, as if he was never there. Then, to end the series with painting nine, *the N and the R*, I revisited the same subway platform as in painting one, *the Transfer*, only from a new perspective, to pose questions to the audience "Did any of this even happen? Is it just all taking place in her mind? Or, maybe the events in each subsequent painting are about to happen and we just got a glimpse into what she is imagining in her mind?"

These are the kind of open-ended questions I was attempting to put out there for the audience, while also allowing them to assume whichever role they connected with, whether it's the femme fetale, the hitman, or the victim. It's up to the viewer.

I also learned to embrace mistakes in my work. Sometimes, even leave them in the canvases for the world to see, as evidence of the process. Painting people in, painting people out, ripping, tearing, and sometimes even setting my work on fire. Creating and destroying, re-working and re-discovering. These were familiar patterns in my life. Why not also embed them in my work. *Ticket to Ride* also became the first series I'd paste physical "things" into the works themselves, from actual subway maps to reeds I gathered from the Meadowlands that I glued into some of the works. This became a pattern I also continued in my next large narrative series, *Carnevale*, which I painted from 2011 – 2015.

ONCE TICKET TO RIDE WAS COMPLETED I did a photo shoot surrounded by these nine large 60" X 60" oil paintings on canvas over subway maps. Nine is a magical number, dating back to the renaissance. To me, at this point in time, it symbolized me having *nine lives*. It was my first truly narrative series to date, and one in which the viewing order of each painting mattered. While each painting could stand on its own, each also contributed toward a much greater narrative, from one painting to the next.

What did all this working so narratively do for me? Well, between spending so much time with the story behind the paintings and talking about them with fans and other celebrity guests on my *MBELLART Live Radio Show*, it prompted me to write my very own first screenplay, also entitled, *Ticket to Ride*.

John Fiore from *the Sopranos* told me the paintings were so cinematic that I should get into Screenwriting and Directing. This was my first dive back into writing since writing poetry as inspiration for my *Love Series* paintings back in college, and before that, my own comic book series I created at the young age of five.

Having never written a screenplay before, I asked John and Joey G how it works. Joe sent me a screenplay from one of his past episodes of *the Sopranos*.

Joe's advice was short and sweet, which is exactly how Joe is. He said, "Read the Screenplay, watch the Episode—*at the same time*. Then, go to work on your own."

John was more enthusiastic about it all, having just finished producing his own film and pumped me up with, "You're sooooo ready to write and direct!" he exclaimed.

I did eventually finish *Ticket to Ride*, registered it with the *Writer's Guild of America* and acquired a literary agent that owned a small Hollywood boutique agency after months of mailing off hundreds of queries.

Not much ever happened with it though. I had a couple offers that I didn't feel were strong enough to part with it, but who knows, maybe one day I'll see it as a full-length feature film.

Years later I'd get to have a candid conversation in Manhattan about *Ticket to Ride* with Eric Fischl, shortly after the opening of his *Portraits* show at *the Mary Boone Gallery* in 2012. Eric and I first became friendly after I reached out to him to ask if he'd mind critiquing Katie Emmitt's work, who was a student of mine that idolized him after I introduced her to his work, much the same way I was enamored with Eric's work after Nora introduced me to him back in my days at Towson. Eric would become one of my heroes in the art world and Katie would become my first National NAEA Rising Star Award Winner. Her work was phenomenal. Eric graciously agreed to critique her work, *which made Katie's whole world*, and I'd later return the favor by contributing content towards his *America: Now and Here* movement that he was pioneering at the time, which included a series of *Thirty Works* that were all based on the Declaration of our 30 Articles of Human Rights. In addition to this, he spotlighted a project I created that would later precipitate my *TED talk* and a nationwide movement of my own. This project I called *31 Nights*.

Eric said to me when we met how he "couldn't understand how I could do that, start all those paintings at once, or even paint for the clientele I painted for." He'd go on to explain to me, "I have to finish a painting before I'm going on to the next one. That painting dictates what happens next. I don't know how you do it. And my clientele, well, if they don't like something they might complain, but what happens when yours doesn't like something, given the nature of who you paint for?"

"I haven't had a complaint yet, so I couldn't tell ya'," was my response. "As far as they tell me, I'm the safest man on the planet."

Eric laughed.

It was like a dream come true meeting him that day. We talked about art and life, and he even got me a meeting with his art dealer, Mary Boone the next afternoon at her 5th Avenue location.

While I wanted to meet with Mary Boone in hopes of joining her stable of artists, she didn't seem to want to be bothered.

While she did take a moment to get up from behind her laptop to greet me and my wife, she just as quickly handed me a hardback copy of Eric's *Portraits* catalog of images from his exhibition, shook my hand and ushered us back out into the gallery. I took this gesture as some weird, dismissive consolation prize. It felt like the *HOBY Awards* all over again.

"Fuck her," I thought. "If I wanted a book I would've asked Eric for one myself." It still sits in plastic to this day.

Eric would later tell me he never had any success sharing friends with his gallery owners as potential artists, which I understood. I was just grateful to have met him, and that he took the time with me that he did, especially after coming off of a rough week, getting an incredibly unfair review of his Portraits show in the local New York newspapers. Chuck Close would go on to defend Eric on stage during his talk at the NAEA Convention in front of what is still, to this day, the largest crowd ever at a national art convention.

Eric's simply an incredibly generous guy, and one of the most brilliant minds and talented painters in the art world today. He's since returned to his easel with a powerful new body of figurative work surrounding the theme "Late America" for exhibition at the Skarstedt Gallery in New York. This new series began in 2016 as his personal response to the new political landscape of America following the Presidential election, and, he bravely revisits the iconic suburban settings and controversial subject matter he's best known for from back in the 1980s.

ISABEL DEL RIO
YAREAH INTERNATIONAL ARTS MAGAZINE

"Michael Bell is telling us it is more than a story of mobsters, solitudes and empty spaces to fill. It's, in fact, a story about the relationship among colors, characters and the narrative between shapes. Yes, we are not watching a film but we can feel the storytelling there, inside the underground and through the streets with methods the first renaissance painters used, such as when Giotto told us stories of *Saints and Sinners*. This time, Bell brings us a world of crimes, violence and deep silences, where voices shout through colors and stories.

It begins as I am watching *the N and the R*. The woman in the center of the painting is looking through the window. We can feel her tears and we can imagine the story. All the elements in the painting point at the woman and at a story to be revealed. We have the tickets to the right and the drips rushing to her, rushing to the narrative. We have a frame and we have some words too. What is your story, mysterious lady? We want to know more and we cannot wait for the next painting.

There's water again on the subway platform in *the Ring*. The woman is not there anymore but we can feel her presence. She is close, really close. Has she gone? There's a phone booth there. Someone has gone. We are on 40th Street waiting, still waiting for the man with the cigarettes and smoking gun from *Room Service*. We don't know his name but we know he is a tough guy.

We can see now her again on the streets, dressed in black. She has a mobile phone in her hand in *Never Look Back*. And, finally, here he is the bad guy in a dripping painting, *Getaway Car*. Then there's the cab left abandoned in *the Meadows*. The City is there, watching you, watching us. Tell me, what is the end of the story? We are watching violence. The man. The woman. We don't want to look but we cannot leave them. Finally, we have the end of the story, or do we? The woman looks through the window again. She is alone, but back on the same subway platform as in the beginning. Her story has come full circle."

FORTY-FOUR

STARS & CIGARS

Exactly one year to the date of our son being born, Noel Ashman, a New York City club owner, booked me to do a soft opening to launch the celebration of the completion of my *Ticket to Ride* series at his nightclub, The Plumm, located at 246 West 14th Street in Manhattan. Originally, the launch party was scheduled for April 17th, the day before Carmen's first birthday, but they had to move the date to the 18th to accommodate a larger than anticipated crowd, due to the fact some of my *Sopranos* pals were supposed to be stopping by, which of course included my main man at the time, Joey G.

It reminded me of when I had to break the news to Lisa about our having to return from our trip with Georgia in Lake Powell on the first anniversary of 9/11, instead of the originally scheduled day before. I knew it probably wouldn't go over well.

So, reluctantly I agreed, but we also both felt there was no way our son was spending his first birthday without us, so we waited until the morning of April 18th to celebrate his birthday with him before we rented a van and took the first three of my nine *Ticket to Ride* paintings up to Manhattan. My brother Will came along too, which was his first taste of what it is that I do.

He rode along with us with my art in the back of the van, and off we all went to Manhattan.

Joey G asked me if he could bring a couple women with him that were interested in meeting me that night to discuss partnering up for an Autism charity, *Bright Steps Forward*. It was a cause Joe became a spokesman for this particular year, and one I wasn't averse to helping out. While our son had just turned one year old, my cousin Natalie had triplets nine years prior—two girls and a boy. Her son, Donovan, was born with Autism. We didn't believe it was caused by genetics, but due to oxygen deprivation, being he was the last one out. I felt, at the time, if I learned a little bit more about Autism perhaps I could help my cousin in some way. Or, if nothing else, help gain my cousin access to the hyperbaric oxygen chamber therapy that Eileen de Oliveira said was helping her son Lucas. It wouldn't be until seven years later that I'd truly find out why I initially met Eileen.

So, as the evening rolled on and bottles continued to pop off in the VIP area, we toasted our son and I glad-handed a bunch of fans just outside of our roped off area with Joey G, Eileen, her friend Annette Cavaliere and my wife's friend Debbie from Jersey and her husband. Joe and I discussed the possibility of my doing a painting of Joe and Eileen's son Lucas to be unveiled five months later at a star-studded "Cigars and Stars" gala in Staten Island. Joe and I also finalized plans for a painting he commissioned me to do of him seated outside a Social Club for his new *Cugine* cigar line. My artwork would grace the boxes and the wrappers.

All in all, busy, but a productive night of networking. I was proud my *Ticket to Ride* series was first launched in New York City. That was important to me, being the paintings tell the fictional tale of murder and mayhem that originates in the subways of Manhattan. This would be how things went for me. Make the most of whatever opportunities come your way. This would be my first of many *tickets to ride.*

Five months later, on Tuesday, September 16th Eileen flew me out to Staten Island to do a red carpet unveiling and sale of my prints to benefit kids with Autism, Cerebral Palsy and traumatic brain injuries at a star-studded celebrity fundraiser called "Stars and Cigars" at *the Vanderbilt at South Beach.*

I was also asked to host one of a dozen tables headed by celebrities for the event that included: Master of Ceremonies Goumba Johnny, actor Nestor Serrano, *Sopranos* stars Dominic Chianese, Frank Vincent, Tony Darrow, Paul Borghese, Lenny Venito and Max Casella. Other notable stars who also headed up tables included actors Tony Plato, Yancy Butler, singer Cristina Fontanelli, New York Giants football stars Sam Madison, Harry Carson and Otis Anderson, Producer Sonny Grosso, boxing legendary trainer and analyst Teddy Atlas, New York Rangers legend Ron Greschner, "Mr. Baseball" Ed Randall, and comedians Adam Ferrara and Jay O. Sanders.

While I did explain in a red carpet interview before doing my portrait unveiling that "some of my followers chose to sit with me at my table", what I failed to mention to reporters was how much those followers paid to sit with me. This was a big part of why there were so many celebrities in attendance. I thought it was a brilliant way to fundraise. Not only could you guarantee attendance, but you could pay for which celebrity, actor, or in my case—*artist*—that you wanted to sit with.

It's how, for a while anyways, I became dubbed a "celebrity artist", which was a moniker I lived out for a few years while still seeking legitimacy in the art world beyond just the likes of having celebrity clientele.

My portrait unveiling, which was filmed in front of a crowd gathered outside the Vanderbilt, was a huge success and one I did alongside Joe, Frank Vincent and Dominic Chianese, which was a great honor—being that I grew up loving these guys in films like *the Godfather, Raging Bull,* and *Casino*—not to mention their iconic roles in HBO's hit series, *the Sopranos.*

The night raised a ton of money for the charity, I think around fifty-thousand in all and my painting made Eileen cry. She was so touched by it that she wanted it to hang in her Staten Island Headquarters. I also made the most out of networking throughout the evening.

This would prove to be just one of many more fundraisers I would do over the next few years for the cause. It also wouldn't be my last trip to the Vanderbilt on Staten Island.

EIGHT MONTHS LATER, on May 14, 2009, I was flown back out to the Vanderbilt courtesy of Nathan Wilson, CEO/Founder of Project Meridian Foundation (*PMF*), whose mission was to rescue and rehabilitate victims of human trafficking and sex trade. There, I joined Miss New York 2009 Ambre DeVirgilio, singer Danny Nova and *PMF* to auction off more of my art for the charity. I even got my students involved in this benefit too!

Years ago, while at Towson University, I created this series of drawings called *Thirty Works*. I began them in Michael Weiss' "Drawing on Meaning" class while completing my Master's. They were essentially speed drawings of a metaphorical object of our choosing, done at random time intervals called out to everyone in the class while drawing.

This would become a project Marlene and I would later challenge our GT students with annually. My *Thirty Works* were drawings of a single hollow-point bullet that I brought into the class. This was me beginning to *draw a line from my life to my art*, based on who my clientele was, and what I had gone through myself growing up around men in "the life".

Some drawings were better than others, depending on the time allotted for each work, and they were all done in various media, ranging from charcoal to pen and ink, to pastels to mixed-media speed paintings in tempera on paper. But, up until 2009, I hadn't done anything with the drawings. They literally just sat in a drawer in my studio—until I was asked to participate in this *Lunar on the Bay Charity Gala*.

Rewind back a few months to January 20, 2009. A colleague of mine was in D.C. to attend President Obama's first inauguration. "A New Birth of Freedom" was the phrase from the Gettysburg Address that served as the inaugural theme to commemorate the 200th anniversary of the birth year of Abraham Lincoln.

My colleague called me shortly after Obama's address and said construction workers breaking down the makeshift wooden ramp that President Obama walked across were going to scrap it in a nearby dumpster. He asked if I wanted any of it for my artwork.

I said, "Absolutely!" After all, this was a historic event! Our country's first African American President. So, he convinced the workers not to scrap all the wood and he brought some of it back home for me.

This, I thought, controversial as it may seem to some, would be a great thing to mount my *Thirty Works* on! I mean, how about that for a talking, or selling point even?! So, I cut the wood into thirty 6" X 6" pieces and I proceeded to rip, tear, cut and glue down pieces and parts of my thirty drawings of that single hollow-point bullet to the *Obama wood*.

Then I purchased long strands of black linked chains at the local hardware store, which I cut about two inches in length and proceeded to screw each short strand of chains into the top and bottom of each wooden square. From this, I created six individual strands containing five blocks of wood per strand, which made up thirty works overall. My drawings were mounted front and back, and if the strands of wood hung from the ceiling they would actually spin—just like a hollow-point bullet would—if fired out of the chamber of my 9mm Beretta handgun.

Brilliant, I thought to myself.

Now my drawings finally had a home, and the piece itself could be interpreted many different ways. One being, the fact that since the United States now had its first black President, there would most likely be threats to the President's life. The wood he walked across served as a metaphorical footprint others might try and take aim at.

So, I filmed a short ten-minute documentary of me piecing the works together and after that, I got my students involved in the cause. I asked if anyone in my classes wanted to contribute a work for the auction if so they could sign up for one of thirty Articles from the *Universal Declaration of Human Rights*.

I thought this would make for a great theme surrounding the Human Trafficking benefit, and I, of course, chose Article 30, given the fact that my piece actually contained thirty works, which reads:

"Nothing in this Declaration may be interpreted as implying for any State, group or person any right to engage in any activity or to perform any act aimed at the destruction of any of the rights and freedoms set forth herein."

The list filled up fast, and it generated not only great work to help benefit the silent auction in Staten Island, but it also generated some great conversations among the students and myself about why they chose the Article they chose and what significance it held to them. We even videotaped each student with their work explaining briefly why they chose the work they chose.

There seemed to be a great *power in the prompts*.

This would prove to be something I'd explore further as a way to help unleash my students' creativity and as a key to unlocking their art-making process. This led to the creation of what became one of my greatest and most innovative projects of all time—*31 Nights*.

FORTY-FIVE

31 NIGHTS

31 Nights originally began as a project I created to help my students find their signature style, much the same way I found mine. And, for other artists out there, this is literally the potential key to unlocking your own art-making process.

Looking back over the evolution of my style, it began long ago with my early 1998 *John Gotti, America* painting, where I painted subway maps into the work to document his journey. This evolved into me pasting actual New York City subway maps into the canvases of my *Ticket to Ride* paintings, along with reeds from the Meadowlands. This would return again in the form of me also painting New Jersey transit maps into my *Carnevale* paintings.

In 2013 I painted the map of Cicero into the background of Dominic Capone's portrait, tracing his infamous lineage back to the town his great-uncle once ruled. Then again, in my *Shadow of my Father* portrait for John A. Gotti everything came full circle, as I referenced my early *Gotti, America* painting as the inspiration behind the idea of bringing the New York City subway maps and twin towers back into this new painting. The mapping became something I began to do naturally in virtually every painting.

I'd do this again nearly a year later for a charcoal portrait I did for Peter Gotti of him and his iconic father in 2015, and then again, in 2016, I used my mapping technique in order to bridge a gap between two large panel paintings, created as a diptych, entitled, *John Gotti - REBEL.*

The top panel depicts John Gotti larger than life in the center of Little Italy, Manhattan, with the word REBEL across where his eyes are. This painting was for Johnny Gotti (Peter Gotti's eldest son), for his *REBEL INK Tattoo Parlor* that he opened in Ozone Park, Queens. The lower panel depicts a much younger John Gotti surrounded by friends and fellow inmates at Lewisburg Federal Penitentiary. I connected the two paintings with the use of an inverted New York City skyline, and the map of Howard Beach, Queens, bridging the two worlds Gotti Senior traveled between — one representing his family at home in Queens — to his "other family" at the Ravenite Social Club in Little Italy, Manhattan.

So, this *mapping technique* evolved into my "signature style". Now, how do you find yours?

This was a question I asked myself as far back as 2008 when I first began painting my *Ticket to Ride* series. I wanted the paintings to be cohesive, in addition to being narrative, so uncovering my own "signature" became something of great importance to me as an artist.

And then I stumbled upon the work of David J. Leeson, who was a staff photographer for the Dallas Morning News who went on to win the Pulitzer Prize for his photography portfolio of U.S. troops invading Iraq.

But it wasn't this Pulitzer Prize-winning portfolio of David Leeson's that sparked something in me. It was his personal portfolio of works, in particular, a series of self-portraits in 2007 he created called *31 in 24*.

They were, essentially, thirty-one extremely creative self-portraits taken using a tripod and self-timer which he documented as a short film over the course of a twenty-four hour period of time. In some shots, he covered himself in paint, in others reminiscent of his time in Iraq, coated in dirt, spitting sand.

What I loved about them was the risk-taking that was involved in making each of them, and how cohesive they were as an overall thematic series. I also absolutely fell in love with some of the titles behind each self-portrait, titles like *The Portal, The Beast, Lost You, Facing the Beast, Find Another Day*. The titles alone were so visual to me that I decided to do some self-portraits of my own as charcoal drawings in my sketchbook based on these titles, using them as "inspirational prompts". This "private conversation" I began having between David Leeson's work and my own would spark what would soon become one of the most groundbreaking projects I've ever created: *31 Nights*.

After doing some drawings, one per night, over the course of a week or so and noticing some familiar patterns I was creating naturally within each work, so I thought to myself, "*What if . . .*"

What if, instead of thirty works in twenty-four hours, I created a series of prompts around David's titles, tossing in a few new titles of my own, and spread the drawings out over the course of a month.

So, instead of thirty-one works in twenty-four hours, I created the groundwork for making thirty-one works, one per night, over the course of thirty-one nights.

"This was it!" I realized. "This was the key to unlocking our creative art-making process!"

After all, they say you can make or break a habit in just twenty-one days, imagine what artistic habits could be *formed* in thirty-one nights! This could be the way for my students, and other artists, to unlock their "signature style" while also getting really, really good at their craft!

All this was like some great epiphany. I soon realized the reason *why* so many students and fellow artists couldn't figure out the answer to what was becoming a very common question, "How come I don't have a signature style like yours?"

The reason was apparent to me now. It wasn't because they *didn't have one*. They just hadn't produced *enough work* to actually recognize the sea they're swimming in, to find familiar patterns that only show their face after producing lots and lots of work.

Think about it . . . In most high school art programs I've ever visited, most teachers push kids to produce maybe three to six works per semester—*at most*. It wasn't until a student either took AP Studio Art classes or until they were preparing to piece together their portfolios for college admissions that they would even create half as many works of art as they would produce while doing my *31 Nights* project. After all, how could anyone possibly be expected to find their signature style without producing enough work to actually be able to recognize it?!

31 Nights was the answer! I knew it immediately. It's like weightlifting on steroids, but for artists. It's an artist's training camp, where you can get so good in a month's time, you have no idea! After all, you're spending more time honing your craft, spending more time with your process, so naturally you'll start to understand why it is you do what you do.

In 2008, I challenged one of my students to try it. I figured, if it works for her, maybe I'll open it up to the entire class and see if they're up for the challenge. Her name is Katie Emmitt, and she was just a sophomore in high school at the time.

KATIE WOULD GO ON TO BECOME one of the most highly touted, greatest talents of my entire teaching career, and this is not something I throw out there lightly. When she first came into my drawing class, I've gotta be honest, she wasn't the greatest. Definitely not someone I'd pick out of the crowd and say, "Yep, this is going to be one of the greatest artists to ever walk through my doors." But Katie wanted to be an artist. She really wanted it and was willing to do whatever it took to improve, so when I posed this idea of her trying *31 Nights*, she embraced it.

I began by challenging her this, "Try one drawing, based on this list of titles I'm giving you, every night—over the course of thirty-one nights. I'll give you off on the weekends, but Monday through Friday I want one drawing every night. If you can give me twenty minutes you just might discover something good. Give me an hour every night—you just might become a rock star!"

She agreed to give me at least one solid hour every night.

"Listen," I went on to further instruct her, "whatever you do, just make sure you *give me that hour—every night*. Don't skip around time-wise. Don't give me twenty minutes one night, an hour another, two hours the next night . . . Literally, even if your drawing's not finished, stop at the one hour mark. Time yourself if you have to. This will be the only real way we can measure just how much better you've gotten over the course of the month."

She understood. She also asked me if she could turn the titles into mini-stories and make it like a girl's diary. This reminded me of my early *Love Series* works . . . how I used to work from poems I'd write as inspiration for the content that I'd later paint. So I said, "Sure, why not, just use yourself as the subject matter, and as much as you can, try working from a mirror—from direct observation. This will be the ultimate test of your skills."

I went on to show her David Leeson's photography, as well as my visual journal containing my first version of *31 Nights*, to give her some further inspiration. Katie worked really hard on these prompts, just as she said she would, with each self-portrait in charcoal accompanied with a diary entry next to each title.

She treated each title like a chapter in a much larger story. The diary entries I would read over the next month told the story of a teenage girl who gets pregnant and has to come to the decision whether to keep the baby or not. Each drawing was better than the next. But after entry four, *Facing the Beast*, which was a charcoal drawing of her sitting on a toilet reading the results of a pregnancy test, I felt compelled to ask her—

"Katie . . . *you're not . . . ?*"

"No, Mr. Bell! I'm not *pregnant*! It's just a made-up story."

I was relieved, but was curious why she chose to create this "fictional tale". As I dove deeper, and as I got to know Katie more, I learned that this *31 Nights* project was also her way of working through what she imagined life was like for her Mom, raising her as a single mother. I'd later learn that Katie never met her father.

It wasn't until she was graduating that she hit me with this: "Mr. Bell—you know people in *the Mob* and stuff, right?"

Some icebreaker, I chuckled to myself. "What do you need, Katie?" smiling at her. "Where's this going?" I asked.

Hesitantly, she finally hit me with a bombshell, "Could you help me find my Dad?"

My heart sunk.

Throughout Katie's career, I did my best to fill that void for her. During her senior year I'd help her fill out college scholarship applications, I'd help her apply for the NAEA's Rising Star Award, which is presented to just one student artist in the entire nation annually—an award which she'd go on to win, becoming my first of seven straight back-to-back national award winners. I accompanied her and her Mom to the NAEA Convention in Baltimore, and later, we'd go to her "Scholarship for Scholars" Awards Night, which she also won, and then to an exhibition she was selected for at the U.S. Department of Education.

You name it—I was there for her.

And so, I'd be there for her once again, this time to help her find her Dad. Finding him helped her bring some closure to that chapter of her life, but it wasn't a fairy tale ending by any means. Sometimes life plays out like that. But sometimes something remarkable emerges from the rubble.

As I look back over the arc of Katie's career with me—from sophomore year, barely able to render a realistic drawing in accurate proportions to where she ended up senior year—painting huge 48" X 96" hyper-realistic figurative scenes that Eric Fischl even marveled at . . . it's visibly astounding. So, how did she get there? By blowing through nine—*yes, nine*—visual journals in just two short years. That's what made her great.

Whatever she wanted, *she went after it.*

She's still, to this day, one of the best painters I've ever taught. And it all began with *31 Nights*. She would go on to try *31 Nights* in photography too, and I'd open this challenge up to all my future classes, in order to help them get better while finding their "signature style".

As for Katie, well, even when you've done more than most people would ever consider doing for a kid, sometimes "enough" is still not enough. I'll never forget Katie coming into my room on the afternoon she received her acceptance letter to Maryland College Institute of Art (MICA). All in all, she received around $550,000 in scholarship offers from numerous schools, but she really wanted to go to MICA, who offered her an impressive $103,000 in scholarship offers. *Only Katie was in tears.*

It still wasn't enough.

Mom couldn't afford to send her there, even with that impressive offer. So, I called the liaison at MICA, explained the situation, asked what else could she apply for, and after several days of everyone working on it with her, we were able to earn her another seventeen thousand, capping her out at $120,000 overall from MICA, just enough for Mom to swing it without having to put her house up for sale.

It was the best news in the world, and the best thing she could have possibly done with her life. If anyone was meant for art school it was Katie, and I was glad to have been a part of the journey that helped her get there.

As for her evolution of Katie's style, at the time we didn't fully understand why she began painting her friends as if they were trapped in the box-like structure of square canvases, which began junior year. This evolved into a college portfolio at MICA, in which she began boxing herself nude into clear cubes in these larger-than-life sized figurative scenes. This somehow got Katie into making a connection between figures and sacred geometry.

She later started up her own business, *Katie Emmitt Hoops*, dedicating her craft to creating the most customized hula hoops on the planet. You see, in sacred geometry, the circle represents the spiritual realms. So, all of this—this evolution of her process, which began with boxing herself into her paintings to encircling herself in drawings using sacred geometry, to her forming a hula hoop business using a handmade circle—was really the same conversation that began while in high school under my tutelage, ever-evolving over time, much the same as my signature style has.

So, does *31 Nights* work? For both drawing and photography students? Absolutely! Is it *hard*? Yes, but is it worth it? *Undeniably.*

There certainly is power in those prompts! *Want more proof?*

In 2014, we had our first major breakthrough at the Scholastic Art and Writing Awards with record-breaking sixty-seven Region-At-Large awards, and thirty-four of sixty-seven award-winning works—eleven of twenty-three gold keys, and three out of five National Medal-winning works were all *31 Nights* projects.

This has become such a groundbreaking way for allowing kids the creative freedom to explore whatever they want to within their own work while finding their "signature style" that I had to develop more than one version of *31 Nights* for kids coming back the following year that didn't want to repeat the same one again.

I've since developed five different versions of *31 Nights*, each catering to a different need, and a different way of working, which allows you to pick and choose which of the five versions you want to tackle after trying the first version to further develop your arsenal of skills as an artist and storyteller.

Just prior to Katie's graduation in 2010, I had the pleasure of being asked to represent our faculty and speak in front of a packed house one evening as our county celebrated our school's recent National Blue Ribbon status.

It was there, in front of our entire school, community and dignitaries that I was sure to address the impact our visual arts program has had on the education of our students, touting the fact that, "at Southern High, our most creative and talented artists are also our highest academic achievers."

I also made sure all the big brass in there knew "It's *quality teachers* that make *quality programs*, not the other way around."

Right now, somewhere out there, the next great artists are just getting started on their *31 Nights*. Their talents—just beginning to show, just the same as they did for Katie, by pouring their imagination, dedication, and hard work into each and every drawing and photograph they take. Their drive—just beginning to push them from obscurity into the spotlight among their peers. And their connection to those that came before them—legends like Katie, Louis, Tyler, Cat, Zoe, Shanna, Hannah, Sienna and countless others who have thrived before them *is undeniable.*

Remember, when you're on the verge of greatness, it's always the road behind you that's gotten you there. When I asked Katie to reflect on her journey, here is what she had to say:

KATIE EMMITT
CLASS OF 2010

"In my very first round of *31 Nights*, I was struggling with what it must have been like to be my Mom—to be a single, divorced female, and how at that time I didn't want my life to end up like hers. I found myself focusing, as most teenage girls I knew did, on the negative way too much.

I was thinking about how I didn't know my father, how my Mom did a lot of dating, how I didn't have that archetypal 'American family' type of lifestyle. I was also wondering how difficult it must have been for my Mom to work so hard to support me, why she was tough on me when it came to school and grades, and how it must have been trying to raise me to be the best I could be.

I worked this out through a project Mr. Bell gave me called *31 Nights*. *31 Nights* was essentially a series of thirty-one self-portraits, each based on a unique title *as a prompt*. I chose to make mine like diary entries where I assumed the role of my Mom, exploring her life from my point of view, one drawing at a time.

This was where I began working through things that most teenage girls have to experience at some point—*through my artwork*.

In high school, I was always thinking about worst-case scenarios, trying to put myself in the shoes of so many different women. Women who got pregnant unexpectedly. Women who don't feel that they can be themselves. Women who feel burdened by their own skin.

I was dealing with all of those American societal pressures that are loaded onto our young women—you have to be pretty, you have to be skinny, you have to be smart, you have to go to college, you have to get a good job, you have to have a boyfriend, you have to be 'normal'.

And what was coming out in my work was all the feelings I had about those expectations—*mainly that I thought they were complete bullshit*—but also that I wasn't entirely immune to them either, as much as I wanted to be.

When I first started to draw, all of Mr. Bell's visual journaling projects were really how I got a lot better and really fast! I mean, if you commit to spending time doing something—*anything*—every day for at least an hour or so, you're going to improve quickly . . .

31 Nights was no exception. I did several different versions of this project over the course of a few years, and when I look back at them, I can really see my style beginning to develop. The project itself wasn't just about the fine-tuning of artistic skills, but also the development of themes and content.

Although I always liked to treat them as an opportunity to create a storyline over anything else, I think that they were essential for my development as an artist mainly because I really learned how to follow through on an idea or plan. I made a commitment to work every single day on it, so I had to see it through.

As I look back on my career, even over the course of my college years, I always improved the most and created my best work when I committed to working every day. I absolutely believe that the work ethic instilled in me still stems from his *31 Nights* projects and in all those visual journals I did for Mr. Bell that began six or seven years ago.

Those journals also jump-started my affinity for self-portraiture, which I do almost exclusively today in my own work. I believe they really were a way to pull myself deeper into a situation—to visually create and experience it on different levels, which definitely stems from my empathetic tendencies and desire to see the world in as many perspectives as possible.

Today, strangely enough, although I still typically use myself as a model, I don't always see the final drawing as 'me'—I see it as 'her'. They are personal works but on a somewhat removed level. I feel that my body is just a kind of stand-in for the typical woman and what she might experience.

It's a way for me to put myself in the work, but also to create something that other women can relate to on a broader scope.

What began with *31 Nights* of me exploring what a woman might experience in her daily life—like societal expectations of how she must act or behave, several years later has evolved into what women experience spiritually and what they are capable of physically, mentally, and emotionally—celebrating the beauty and strength of women.

To this day, when I need to work through something, I go straight for my visual journal to write and draw. Most of my ideas for larger works of art come directly out of that process. And I have to thank Mr. Bell for instilling this in me." – *Katie Emmitt*

In 2004 I was invited to exhibit in the world's first Golden Age of Gangsters Convention organized by Harry Lawrence in Chicago. I'd showcase my Mob Art with *Sopranos* pals Joey G and John Fiore. It's where I'd meet Mafia Princess Antoinette Giancana, actor Clem Caserta from *A Bronx Tale*, Big Frank D'Amico and Chicago's own Dominic Capone.

2004 was also the year I was named one of twenty-four Maryland State Teachers of the Year.

Celebrating Teacher of the Year honors with an embrace from Konrad M. Wayson, and a special portrait unveiling for Dr. Nancy S. Grasmick, Maryland State Superintendent.

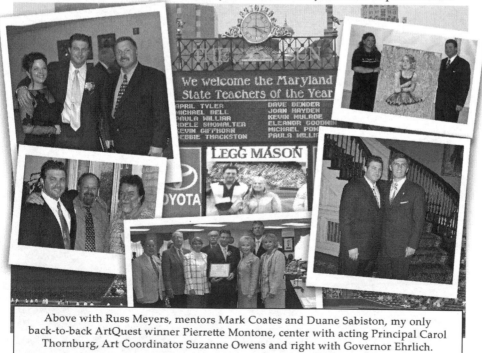

Above with Russ Meyers, mentors Mark Coates and Duane Sabiston, my only back-to-back ArtQuest winner Pierrette Montone, center with acting Principal Carol Thornburg, Art Coordinator Suzanne Owens and right with Governor Ehrlich.

This was the crazy crash scene on my birthday, April 10th, 2007. Our son was born eight days later. We have no idea whether this accident that injured my wife, her mom and a friend contributed to Carmen's Autism or not. One year later, on our son's birthday, my *Ticket to Ride* series was launched in NYC.

WE DON'T NEED TO DREAM A NIGHTMARE.
IT IS POSSIBLE TO ENJOY A PLEASANT DREAM

My *Ticket to Ride* launch party led to a 2009 *Stars & Cigars* Autism benefit with Annette Cavaliere, Bright Steps Forward Founder Eileen de Oliveira, *Sopranos* pals Joseph R. Gannascoli, Frank Vincent and Dominic Chianese, and three years later a friendship with Kathrine Narducci of *A Bronx Tale*. This was all long before our son's official Autism diagnosis in 2015.

I created more artwork for Joey G and his *Cugine* Cigar line, then was off to the U.S. Department of Education to deliver a 2009 national presentation for U.S. Secretary of Education Arne Duncan on *Arts, Innovation & Design*. My team from Southern received National Blue Ribbon Schools honors with Dr. Darla Strouse, and Principals Jason Dykstra and Maryalice Todd.

This Red Box is my *Relics of Childhood*. It was a re-creation of the tragedy surrounding the stillbirth of my sister, Amanda. Many years later, my brother Will was born, named after my Grandfather. We'd never miss one of his games.

Marlene and I working the crowd at ArtQuest, which now boasts over 1,000 in attendance, making it one of the largest student art shows in the nation. We award over $2,500 in prize money in over 60 different categories annually.

Marlene and I went to Grad School together in 2005, both of us had kids in 2007, and we went through National Board Certification together in 2010. From left: dear friend, Councilman Jerry Walker, (below us) with Marlene and Coordinator Suzanne Owens, my family (center), my 1st National Art Award Winner Katie Emmitt (right), and ArtQuest 2016 winners with juror Seton Hurson Rossini.

31 NIGHTS

The only work really worth doing – the only work you can do convincingly – is the work that focuses on things you really care about.

I began presenting my *31 Nights* project nationwide, and contributed art for longtime hero in the art world Eric Fischl's *AMERICA: NOW AND HERE* project. The media also began to take notice. Below is Eric and I swapping stories with Dorothy Dunn and Jude Harzer at the 2012 NAEA Convention.

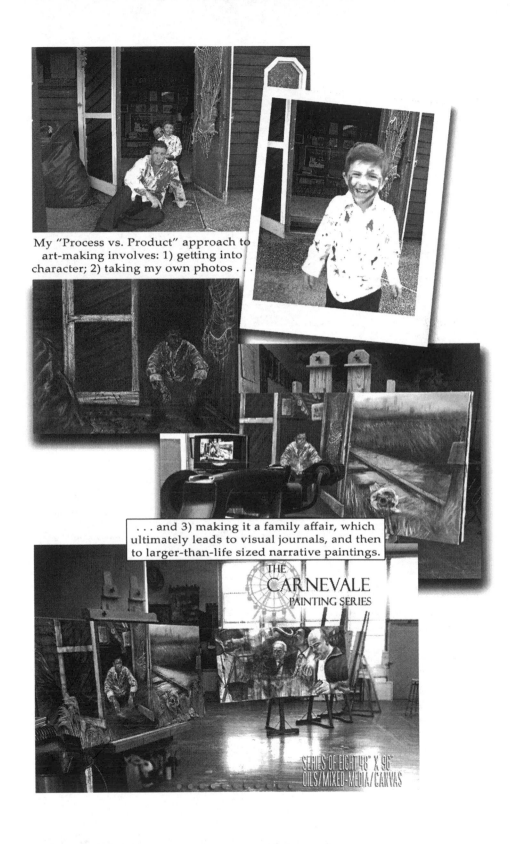

My "Process vs. Product" approach to art-making involves: 1) getting into character; 2) taking my own photos . . .

. . . and 3) making it a family affair, which ultimately leads to visual journals, and then to larger-than-life sized narrative paintings.

THE
CARNEVALE
PAINTING SERIES

SERIES OF EIGHT 48" X 96"
OILS/MIXED-MEDIA/CANVAS

Dominic Capone visited me one summer to pose for my *Carnevale* paintings.
I also incorporated my son, my father-in law Bill, and my niece Teresa in these.

Portrait unveiling for Toni Marie Ricci on the set of *Mob Wives* in 2013.

I also played the role of a spy on *CBS's the Amazing Race,* and made another cameo portrait unveiling for Dominic on set of *the Capones.*

In a back alley smoking ACID 1400 cc's in Chicago while on the set of *the Capones* with former Cicero Police Sergeant John DiCosolo and Dominic.

This painting, one of seven in a series for Toni Marie Ricci, of Peter J. Gotti walking his brother John A. Gotti (Junior) to freedom with attorney Charles Carnesi led to my cover art painting for John's book, *Shadow of my Father.*

In 2013 I received these national awards: the NAEA's NAHS Sponsor of the Year, my 4th back-to-back National Rising Star Award winner, Cat Allen, in Fort Worth, TX, the CollegeBoard's William U. Harris Award in Brooklyn, NY and the Washington Post's Agnes Meyer Most Outstanding Teacher of the Year Award in D.C.

Above, being honored on the floor of the House in Annapolis; right with Congressman Steny Hoyer and below with then Superintendent Kevin Maxwell, Principal Marc Procaccini, Assistant Superintendents Chris Truffer and George Arlotto.

May 14th was the night of the Washington Post's Agnes Meyer Awards. I wanted it to be a memorable night to celebrate my third national award with my colleagues, but it was also four days after my Grandma Violet passed away at the age of 95 and I was heartbroken.

FORTY-SIX

THE WASHINGTON POST AWARDS

Over the past few years I've earned several honors that are not only distinguished but separate my career from the rest of the pack. 2013 was definitely a year to be remembered.

May 14th, in particular, for several reasons . . .

For one, this was the night of *The Washington Post Agnes Meyer Outstanding Teacher Awards*. It capped off what should have been one of the pinnacle moments in the history of my career in education. In a field I've often heard described as a thankless profession devoted to "selfless service towards someone else's success" it's pretty remarkable to be recognized at all, let alone be honored not once, not twice, but with three national awards in just one year! This was something no-one in the country had done in my field and I knew it was unprecedented.

The accolades train began in February when I was awarded the College Board's 2013 national *William U. Harris Award of Excellence* in Brooklyn for demonstrating extraordinary leadership across the nation in the field of education. I traveled by train with an entourage consisting at that time of Principal Marc Procaccini, Anne Arundel County Superintendent of Schools Kevin Maxwell,

Associate Superintendent George Arlotto and Regional Assistant Superintendent Chris Truffer. Deb Curdts, our Advanced Placement Test Coordinator, wrote the incredible piece about me for the submission and also met us there. I was humbled by what she wrote about me, and Dr. Maxwell treated me to a first class experience, but after all, it was Valentine's Day!

This became the running joke of the weekend from teachers back home, "So, how did Maxwell treat you on Valentine's?"

My principal at that time shared a kinship with me also due to my "dual life". While just a college kid, Procaccini once roomed with a well-known Mob associate in Miami who was a member of *the Untouchables* car-theft ring. So, naturally, we hit it off.

After I got back from Brooklyn, I was then honored on the floor of the House of Delegates in Annapolis that March. Chris Truffer attended this one with me too. Afterwards, we all enjoyed cocktails with Bob Costa, a Republican Delegate from District 33B in his suite.

In April, my success continued. I was awarded the NAEA's *National Art Honor Society Sponsor of the Year* in Fort Worth, Texas, another award given to just one selected educator in the entire country, of all the National Honor Society Chapter Sponsors in America. That meant a lot to me because I truly pour my heart and soul into my NAHS chapter, and give kids real-world experiences with causes I was personally vested in. Kids gained wisdom from acting and doing, all the while, learning about empathy from participating in meaningful service projects. Our membership has also soared over the years from a couple dozen kids in 2002 to eighty-five in 2016.

This particular year, in 2013, I also flew my fourth back-to-back NAEA National Rising Star Award Winner in art, Cat Allen, to Texas celebrate her achievements. Her father was in poor health at the time. He's since passed away, so I know it meant a lot to Cat to win this award, among others she earned that particular year, so her Dad could see her so accomplished at such a young age. I taught Cat since she was first accepted into the county's Gifted and Talented Program back in 7th grade.

This was another trend that emerged among a few of my national award winners. The more time I seemed to have with them, the more they seemed to soar.

These NAEA Rising Star Awards have also proven to be a vehicle in itself for me to take my students places, from one year to the next, beginning with Katie. I flew my second Rising Star Winner, Louis Fratino and his family out to Seattle to receive his award in 2011, which he already attested to the fact that this alone inspired him to pursue his *Fulbright* in college, which is viewed as one of the most prestigious visiting scholar programs in the United States. Ashely Lim, whom I taught in the GT Program earned her Rising Star award in 2012 in New York City in collaboration with her regular classroom teacher, Jim Dell, from North County High. They both joined me by train to celebrate her accomplishments that year in Manhattan. Cat Allen, whom I just mentioned, received hers in 2013 in Fort Worth, Texas. Zoe Kasprzyk—in San Diego, California in 2014. Shanna Dunlap, my first photographer to ever win this prestigious award, was awarded hers with me in New Orleans in 2015. And Sienna Broglie, who won the 2015 Scholastic Art National Gold and Silver Medals in the category of Painting, also become my 2016 NAEA Rising Star—my seventh back-to-back winner.

But, recapping May 14, 2013—*it was literally the trifecta.*

First, was the College Board's national William U. Harris Award of Excellence, then came the NAEA's National Art Honor Society Sponsor of the Year Award, and lastly—*the Washington Post* Agnes Meyer Outstanding Teacher Award.

THIS HONOR was described by Katharine Weymouth, Publisher of *the Washington Post*, as "a way to spotlight teachers who, through their work, exemplified Meyer's steadfast commitment to education and, most importantly, our local D.C. area students."

This was a great honor, and one I truly felt humbled to receive. I respected the Washington Post and was always inspired by the story of Jaime Escalante that was made into the famous

1988 film *Stand and Deliver*, which was written by Jay Mathews, a famed longtime educational reporter for *the Post*, who later gave me great feedback and a book blurb for this memoir. So, this was an award and an evening I planned to truly try and enjoy and savor for once in my life.

It had been nearly a decade since I was awarded Anne Arundel County Public Schools "Teacher of the Year" back in 2004, becoming one of just twenty-four Maryland State Teachers of the Year in 2005, and a Maryland State Department of Education (MSDE) *Teachers of Promise Mentor* to each new exciting crop of undergrads from local colleges in Maryland deemed "the best of the best" coming out of their respective schools each year.

I was only in my ninth year teaching back when I was first crowned "Teacher of the Year," so the night was a like a blur to me. I remember kissing my wife, heading up to the podium to deliver my speech immediately following the 2004 Private Schools Teacher of the Year.

I started my speech off with something to the effect of, "Wow, that was some really well-prepared speech from the Private Schools Teacher of the Year that just went before me . . ."

My wife even joked to friends at our table, "I have no idea what he's going to say. He's had at least two or three scotches and didn't prepare a speech!"

But, all in all, things went well. This would be my first taste of public speaking. I'd become much better at over the years. But, I was only thirty-three years old and new to the public speaking game at that time. I still had a lot to learn and felt I still had a lot more to accomplish, but at the same time, I also felt blessed to be recognized with such an honor. I was a long way from the inspiring keynotes, workshops and *TED talks* I give across the country today.

In 2005 my talents were recognized yet again for the work I was doing on Visual Journaling. I just completed my Master's Thesis with Dr. Jane Bates at Towson University and I was asked to co-present with her at my first ever national NAEA Convention in Boston that year along with her colleague, professor Ray

Martens. I would deliver this presentation again that same year to our Maryland State Superintendent of Schools, Dr. Nancy S. Grasmick. I would also be commissioned to paint Nancy's commemorative portrait that would hang in the headquarters bearing her name, the Nancy S. Grasmick Building of Education in Baltimore. We did a huge unveiling party for Nancy just before Nancy's retirement, coordinated by Dr. Darla Strouse, Executive Director at MSDE (*who is, incidentally, one of the sweetest and most dedicated women on the planet*).

Nancy liked my painting so much she took it off the wall and it went home with her when she retired and left office.

A couple years later, with the help of my continuous annual involvement with Dr. Strouse, Southern High became honored by the U.S. Department of Education as a National Blue Ribbon School. I helped write our initial proposal with then Signature Program Director Marilyn Harmon, Principal Jason Dykstra (who got the whole train rolling and did such amazing things during his short time at Southern), and later, Principal Maryalice Todd, whom I also worked closely with when she joined Southern as new principal when Jason moved up the corporate ladder. Jason's wife Eleni would end up becoming Coordinator of Art once Sue Owens retired. Eleni and I work well together to this day.

The process of becoming a National Blue Ribbon School took well over a year to complete, and in 2009 I would be selected as one of just two secondary educators by then U.S. Secretary of Education Arne Duncan to deliver a presentation about our accomplishments, specifically on "Arts, Innovation and Design" in Washington D.C. at the National Blue Ribbon Schools Convention. I would continue working closely with Dr. Strouse, delivering Keynotes for her to new teachers annually. I even painted a portrait of her grandchildren in 2015 for the cover of a heartwarming children's book she's been writing. Like I said, she's an incredible woman with many talents.

So, as I began getting myself psyched back up to try and enjoy my trip to Washington D.C. to receive my *Washington Post Agnes Meyer Most Outstanding Teacher Award* in May of 2013, I selected a dozen or so colleagues to celebrate this monumental occasion with me at *the Washington Post*. I got dressed to the nines, with one of my son's favorite crimson red silk ties he picked out for me, along with a matching silk kerchief to go in my favorite deep blue double-breasted suit chest pocket and off we headed to *Washington Post Headquarters*.

While I couldn't take everyone with me, since there was a limit on the number of people I could invite, I did my best to choose wisely. I invited Mr. Truffer, Assistant Superintendent to celebrate with us, since he'd been part of my journey for quite a while now, traveling with me from my National Blue Ribbon presentation to my award in Brooklyn, NY to the floor of the House in Annapolis, now back to Washington D.C.

I also invited Marlene, the rest of our Art Department, and a team from Southern that included my principal, a vice-principal, and a few other teachers that either supported me, *didn't need anything from me*, or ones I felt had potential.

There were a lot of people that I wished I could have invited in addition to those that I brought, but I was glad the people who were able to come out on my behalf came to support me. It's funny how people react to stuff like this. I overheard my wife being asked, "Why did Michael bring so-and-so?"

"Michael always has a reason behind everything he does," Lisa explained. "If he asked someone to be here, there was a reason. Maybe he felt this was something they could shoot for one day, who knows? But there definitely was a reason."

Now, I've never looked the part of a teacher, or an artist, for that matter. I'm okay with that. Marc Procaccini, who nominated me for this award wrote, "He looks like a figure straight out of a New York Mafia Social Club." He meant it lovingly. *I promise.*

I was okay with that though, because those "men of respect" were a certain breed of men I was much more familiar with. It certainly wasn't *teachers* growing up that ever helped me get anywhere in life. It was always the ones that outsiders would label as the "bad guys" that would always seem to do the most good by me over the course of my life.

Love me or hate me, I never cared, I liked being me. And I will never apologize for who I am or for who I may associate with. I felt exactly the same as John Gotti, Sr. once famously expressed, "All I wanted was to be who I became . . ."

So, on May 14th, I arranged for my parents to visit us the night of the awards so they could babysit Carmen, who had just turned six years old at the time. This way, my wife and I could go out and enjoy ourselves and then celebrate with my parents later that evening when we got back.

And, like I said earlier, this was all supposed to be what I felt was probably the pinnacle of my career. I felt like I deserved to enjoy it. This is what I told myself anyways as I stared into the mirror and took a deep breath, smiling to myself as I unconsciously slipped on one of the many masks I've donned for many years and headed out the door to receive my award. A mask that conceals what's really going on inside. One that could get me through the night.

But, on a night I planned to try my best to be entirely present, I couldn't help fading into the woodwork and viewing everything from a distance as I listened to Katharine Weymouth, Publisher of *the Washington Post*, call me up to the podium to read off my accolades as I stood beside her on stage.

You see, I don't remember May 14, 2013, as some poignant date in my storied career because it was the night I received *the Washington Post Agnes Meyer Award.*

I remember it as the last night I'd speak to my parents again for what sadly turned into *years* . . .

KATHARINE WEYMOUTH
PUBLISHER OF THE WASHINGTON POST

"While Southern High School may be the smallest public school in Anne Arundel County, Maryland, art teacher Michael Bell thinks big. And I mean REALLY BIG! You see it in his own art, the large-scale cinematic paintings for which he is well-known, and again, the big ambitions for his students.

A colleague has said, 'He can take students with raw talent and inspire them to create works that rival renowned professional artists. On the other end of the spectrum, he can take a student that despises art and instill in them appreciation and productive habits of mind.' A fellow art teacher says he has, 'a magic about him that can motivate budding art students to work harder than they normally would. He empowers them to believe in themselves, to trust their abilities, and push themselves to achieve amazing results.'

Mr. Bell takes this smaller school and makes it bigger by plugging into the wider community. He encourages community service. Students have created sketchbooks for victims of domestic violence. They have volunteered to face paint at local events. Their works hang in local shops and murals grace local walls. And the community responds each year as Southern hosts ArtQuest, an exhibition Mr. Bell launched as a showcase for his students' work. There are multiple juried categories and the show attracts sponsors and over A THOUSAND visitors.

So what does all this big thinking do for his kids? Big things! All students in AP Drawing and 2D Design took the AP exam and all students scored a 3 or better surpassing everyone in the entire county. For three consecutive years, Mr. Bell's students have won the NAEA's Rising Star Award, which goes out to one student each year in the country. Stacy Smith, Assistant Principal at Southern said that while Michael Bell clearly has the talent to do things with his art that could take him to places of recognition that artists truly dream of, he has chosen to stay in the classroom, and we are all grateful for that."

FORTY-SEVEN

I'D RATHER BE PAINTING

Just four days prior to *the Washington Post Awards*, my Grandmother, Violet passed away. It was May 10, 2013, she was ninety-five years old and my heart was completely broken.

This, along with the events surrounding my Grandma's death became major bones of contention between me and my family the night of my awards. So much so, it precipitated an argument between my parents and me that escalated into something that changed things forever.

What my mother will probably never understand is just how much I loved my Grandma, how she was quietly my rock, my inspiration. In many ways, she was like a second mother to me. I mean, this was a woman I even lived with for a while, in the basement of her quaint little two-bedroom home in Lyndhurst, New Jersey, just before making my move into Manhattan to try and make it as an artist back in the early 90s. She was one of the reasons I started painting, and why I pursued Art into art in the first place.

What I learned on May 14th, just four nights after my Grandma passed away, is the thing that matters most is also the thing we have the least control over—*where we come from*. Who brings us into the world and how we go out of it.

We are our stories. We can use them as inspiration, use them as an excuse, or use them as fuel.

So, on May 14th, as I'm being applauded at *the Washington Post Awards* while standing on stage next to Katharine Weymouth, peering out into the crowd, surrounded by respected colleagues, esteemed reporters and photographers I felt completely empty. I saw my face plastered on a huge banner and on TV screens throughout *the Post* headquarters, and as I'm being honored as one of the year's great ambassadors representing the nation's "best of the best teachers" in the Washington D.C. area it all felt bittersweet.

It wasn't just because of my Grandma's passing. After all, she lived a long life, still sharp as a tack right up until the end at the age of ninety-five. She was able to see my career blossom, as both an artist and educator. She even got to meet her great grandson and spend quality time with him, which is a blessing most people never could say. She was able to see some of my larger art exhibitions, and loved the company I kept, no matter how infamous. She was an old school gal and loved her neighborhood. She'd even send me clippings from the newspaper whenever guys like John Gotti made headlines. She loved who I hung out with and no matter what, she never judged me. Even when I turned bad for a time. She always knew my heart.

But it wasn't just her death that was stinging me so much, despite the fact that she had just passed away four days prior.

It was *how she died* that was really haunting me.

That winter she slipped and fell on some ice taking her garbage cans out to the curb. A stranger happened to walk by hours later and found her laying there on the sidewalk freezing to death with a broken hip and she was then rushed to the hospital. I couldn't image how she felt out there all alone, freezing cold, in such terrible pain, unable to call out for help. Not being able to have been there to "catch her before she fell," like I take pride in doing for so many of the kids in my classes.

This was all that I could think about.

She rehabbed it at a nearby facility in Passaic where she needed 24-7 care and was now remanded to a wheelchair. This is where she'd stay for the months leading up to her death. The last time Lisa, Carmen and I visited her was on March 29th. She was scheduled to be released from the rehab facility soon and there were on-going debates happening behind the scenes between my mother and her sister, who lived in Texas, as to what the next step would be upon my Grandma's release. No-one could seem to decide where she would go next, only that the doctors said she couldn't live alone any longer. Finally, my Aunt decided she would be moving to Texas. The news broke my heart.

I knew it would be a one-way trip.

March 29th would be our very last card game. I knew it wasn't a good idea for her to take a flight across the country in her condition, but I also wasn't in a position to dictate what was going to happen to her. I sure as hell tried, but my pleas fell on deaf ears.

She should have been able to go back to her home in Lyndhurst where she belonged, at least for a little while until everyone figured something else out. After all, this woman literally spent her whole life in that house, even some twenty-five years by herself since my Grandfather's death. My Grandfather literally died in that house. I knew she didn't want to leave it behind. But, no matter what I thought, her going back home was not to be.

The day she was released from Passaic, my Aunt picked her up at the rehab facility and almost immediately flew her out to Texas, barely given enough time to have a brief lunch with one of Grandma's old friends from her Church. She never even got to go home, go through her belongings and take with her anything she may have felt was important or sentimental.

I was furious.

"How could she not have been allowed to go back to the only place she called home for over seventy years of her life?" I thought to myself. "Who does that?! How does something like this happen?!"

So, as I received my award at *the Washington Post*, I couldn't shake the horrific vision of my Grandmother laying there in the freezing cold out on the street in front of her home as being the last memory she'd have of the place she called home for her entire life. I'm sure it probably wasn't like that. I'm hoping it wasn't, at least. But, it was tearing me up inside. Why did she have to fly out so soon? What was the sense of urgency?! Why not give it a week, or a few days at least to let her rest and gather up some personal belongings. Some memories even?

But all this was not to be, and shortly after arriving in Texas, her health took a turn for the worse. It actually started that day on the plane. She was bleeding internally and shortly after arriving in Texas she was in hospice.

It wouldn't be long now.

I talked to her on the phone one last time before she passed away. It was the first time in my life I heard my Grandmother cry. We both tried to hold back our tears and stay strong, even though I could hear her crying on the other end of the telephone, same as me. It broke my heart to hear her so sad.

Afterwards, I remember standing in my backyard staring out at the Chesapeake Bay feeling completely lost, much like I felt that hot summer day I started writing this memoir after receiving our son's Autism diagnosis, and then again, after receiving that call July 20, 2015 from Louie about Angelina, summoning me to Philly where we'd spend the next two grueling weeks.

My Grandma said she wanted me to have her car. It was the only thing she ever owned besides her home, but the title was back at her house in Lyndhurst, and she'd have to sign it over to me. She didn't know how she'd get it done in time. I told her not to worry, that I'd take care of it. She knew I would because she also knew if she gave me her car I would never sell it on her.

It's a White '77 Cutlass Oldsmobile with a light blue vinyl top. The bumper sticker on her back fender reads: *I'd rather be painting*.

It's exactly how I felt as I stood on the stage at *the Washington Post* while being honored.

I would've rather been painting somewhere alongside my Grandma at one of those serene spots she used to paint at so many years ago, in front of some empty red barn, or by some abandoned railroad tracks near Kingsland station in Lyndhurst. Perhaps someday we will, when I join her in the afterlife.

When I arrived home that night from *the Post*, my emotions had already gotten the best of me, and anybody who really knows me knows my temper can erupt as explosive as any volcano. Toss a few drinks into the equation and my sadness turned to rage.

I immediately went into the bag my mother brought with her before we left for D.C. that was sitting on the bar in my front foyer. She had just returned from Lyndhurst and gathered some stuff for me from my Grandma's house.

I slowly opened it.

It was filled with old pictures, cards, letters—everything I'd ever written to my Grandma over the course of my lifetime, every picture of Carmen we'd sent to her over the years, newspaper clippings . . . *everything—all given back to me.*

It's pretty devastating. All your memories just recycled back to you like that. This was something I hadn't experienced in my life until that point in time. It stung deeper than words, and I completely lost it. This turned into what became one of the biggest blow-outs I'd ever had between me and my parents. I take the full blame for what happened next.

I screamed at my mother for not taking my Grandma in, for allowing her sister to fly her out to Texas in the first place, even though deep down I knew none of this was my mother's fault. I blasted her for how I thought Grandma was treated, about how I imagined her last memories to be lying in the freezing cold streets of Lyndhurst for hours until a stranger finally helped her.

It was wrong of me, I know, and it probably wasn't my place to yell at her for any of this. In hindsight, I realize there was a lot more to the story than the fragments of it I was feeding off of, but there was no going back now. *Things started getting really ugly.*

My father jumped in, coming to my mother's aid with, "Watch how you talk to your mother!"

At this point, my take on everything was "How could you let this all happen to this woman?"

By this late in the night, in my condition, *nobody, and I mean nobody—not even the Pope*, was gonna tell me how to talk in my own home.

So, I told them if they didn't like what I had to say or how I said it they could "get out!"

And they did.

They stormed right out, not looking back and drove away, and that was the last memory I have surrounding my last of three national teaching award "crownings" that year. That and a pile of recycled memories sitting on the bar near my front door.

Strange thing was, neither of us reached out to one another afterwards. It became this weird standoff and neither party would break or bend.

No, "man, that really got out of hand, let's sit down and talk now . . ." *Nothing.*

We didn't talk again for the entire two months leading up to my Grandmother's funeral in Lyndhurst. I even had to find out when and where my own Grandmother's funeral was taking place from my Aunt in Texas, of all people.

This would be how I'll always remember *the 2013 Washington Post Agnes Meyer Most Outstanding Teacher Awards.*

VIOLET VALLERY
JANUARY 19, 2008

"When you were little you liked it when you had a pencil in your hand and you used to scribble. And so I said to you, 'If you're going to do that, you might as well draw a picture.' And so I drew you a picture, I think of a rabbit, and you wanted to do the same thing so I said you have to trace it. Trace your pencil over the picture and see if you could do it by yourself. And you did it even better than I showed you.

As you progressed, you were interested in all things that had to do with paintings and paintbrushes and stuff like that, and you liked to see me do my little sketches. And then we talked you into entering the art show because you started to do little figure paintings, telling stories and doing these action pictures. And you liked Superman. Superman was your idol. You drew pictures of Superman. You dressed like Superman. And when you went to the art show everybody was really interested, and so I said, 'You have to keep drawing because people are going to come and look at your stuff.' And then came all these little girls—maybe they were thirteen, and you were only about four or five—they were standing around you and saying, 'Oh my, look at him! Isn't he good! Isn't he good?!' And you never looked up. You just kept on drawing.

The next year at the art show I was teaching you how to do a triangle and cubes, how to show the depth of it through shading, and the moon—anything circular. Then this man came up to you. He was interested in talking to you about getting art lessons. I said, 'See that, everybody is interested in you.' And that was the year you won 1st prize.

And then, taking you into New York City every Thanksgiving, we always went to *Tavern on the Green*, watched the figure skaters at Rockefeller Center, and one time you almost got blown away by the wind. You had to hang on to a lamp post! I wish I had a picture of that. We went to the museums too and I let you sit on the steps and look at all the tall buildings to try to teach you what perspective is about. You learned a lot about art then, and then you kind of took off on your own after that . . . although you did try to write books."

FORTY-EIGHT

HILLSIDE

I hope to God our son never has to go through what I had to the day of my Grandmother's funeral. It was scarring. The kind of scars that don't heal. The kind that don't build character. The kind you try and hide, but know deep down everyone can see. When I look in the mirror at mine, they remind me how sometimes you never know how strong you are until being strong is the only choice you have.

It took two months to the exact date of our blow-out to bring my Grandmother home from Texas back to Lyndhurst, to her final resting place. July 14th was her funeral. My parents and I still hadn't spoken.

My Grandma was cremated in Texas, so it was her ashes that were eventually brought back to North Jersey to be buried beside my Grandfather, beneath a headstone they would now share in Hillside Cemetery in Lyndhurst overlooking the beautiful New York City skyline. It's where I want my final resting place to be one day too.

My wife and I dropped Carmen off at her parents' home down the Jersey Shore before we headed north for the funeral. I certainly didn't want our son to see me cry, or to see me in the kind of pain I was forecasting to be in. It's why we didn't take him to Angelina's funeral either. I told my in-laws, Bill and Olga, that it would be best for them just to stay home too and not go to Vi's funeral, despite knowing her for over fifty years.

"Just be there for us by watching our son," I asked of them.

They graciously agreed, asked us to send their love and Lisa and I headed North up the Garden State Parkway.

We were the first ones to arrive at Hillside Cemetery. I pulled my car alongside the path where the headstone is, and we got out. It was eerily quiet. Like the calm before the storm. The silence was deafening. The heat and humidity made things even worse. I wore a dark suit and a dark purplish-gray silk shirt underneath—*for Violet*.

I slowly approached the headstone, the name "VALLERY" inscribed across the top, and the image of a book opened to a two-page spread that reads "William E. 1911—1981" at left, my Grandmother's blank slate not yet inscribed to its right. In front of the headstone lay a green tarp, the perfect shade of a card table at Atlantic City, with my Grandma's remains in a vessel beneath it. I said a few prayers for my grandparents before my parents arrived twenty minutes later with my younger brother, Will.

All I could think about was what's going to happen next? Were we going to make amends? Was there even going to be a Priest?! When were all the relatives showing up to pay their respects? All these questions swirled through my head . . .

My Grandma had two sisters, both of whom passed away before her, but I do remember attending their funerals, so I assumed everyone would also, in turn, be attending my Grandma's. Her sister Helen passed away first. She was the middle child. She had five kids with my Uncle Vincent, Sr., the oldest being Vincent, Jr., who was the one that ended up part of that double-murder trial that made him so infamous. He also had another brother, Billy, who also died young, and three sisters who I was close with growing up—Helen Lucas, Alana Onorato, and Donna Salvano. They all had lots of kids and we do have a substantial sized family on my mother's side.

So where was everyone?

My Grandmother's eldest sister, Aunt Ann, lived to see 100 years old before she passed away. She and my Grandma were very close. Aunt Ann's daughter was my Aunt Jeannie. She is my Godmother. I'm still close with her to this day. She and my Godfather Uncle Billy had three girls—Natalie, Bonnie, and Elissa. They were also all really good to me growing up. I'd consider them the closest of all my cousins. I used to stay with them at their home in North Brunswick, New Jersey every summer and swim in their pool with their neighbors' kids while everyone partied.

And when I say party, *I mean party!* My Aunt Jeannie used to throw these big bashes every summer. They were *always* partying over there. Tons of people coming and going. My cousin Elissa used to let me stay up late and watch *Cinemax Late Night*. Her biker friends were all pretty cool too. Once they took me to the movies to see *Jaws 3 in 3D* when it first came out. When they wanted a smoke, they'd pull over along the Garden State Parkway, never smoking with me in the car. I always thought that was pretty cool of them. I loved hanging out with my cousins growing up. And at my Aunt Jeannie's in the summertime you could also cut the cigar smoke with a knife filtering out of her garage, from the old timers gambling and drinking at card tables set up everywhere. The kids just swam in the pool 'til the late night hours and there were always lots of people around. *Always lots of family*. At weddings, funerals, *you name it . . .*

So, this is why it bothered me that no-one seemed to be coming to my Grandmother's graveside. Where was everyone?

It turned out being just my Aunt Ginger, her husband John, and my cousin Erik who flew out from Texas with his young daughter. That was it. No relatives. No flowers. Not even a Priest! Just some groundskeeper standing idly nearby with a shovel in hand waiting to fill the hole and till the ground over the box containing my Grandmother's ashes. And, when my parents finally arrived, they walked right past me . . . *as if I was never born.*

My brother was caught between a rock and a hard place, and I didn't want to bring him into the middle of any of this, so we said hi, I gave him a hug and let him go back to standing beside Mom and Dad. He was never that close with my Grandmother, not like I was, because by the time my brother was born I was nearly seventeen years old and my parents were older. So, no more trips back and forth to North Jersey for them with Will. My Godmother had since retired in Toms River down the Jersey Shore, and my cousins were also all either married or moved away, so Will didn't grow up around the North Jersey crew that I grew up around. We were raised as two very different people. But I love my brother. I didn't want him to get involved in the madness that was "my life" anyway, certainly not get him in the middle of all of this nonsense.

If anything, I always tried to shield him from who I "really was". I never told him about my being in trouble as a kid while he was growing up because I never wanted him to think it was okay to go down that same destructive route. Lisa and I even moved back to Bel Air until he graduated high school just to make sure he was always safe and we attended every one of his football games, which became a tradition we'd keep up even when he played college football at East Stroudsburg University in Pennsylvania. Coincidentally or not, we both attended Pennsylvania colleges that were both nicknamed "Warriors".

When Will graduated college with a teaching degree in Phys. Ed., just like our father, I put a call into Skip Lee, the Phys. Ed. Coordinator in our county at that time, who just happened to be the Anne Arundel County Public Schools' Teacher of the Year the year after I won the prestigious award. I was on the judging panel that voted Skip in as "Teacher of the Year", which led Skip on a fast-track to becoming the Phys. Ed. Coordinator, and later to becoming Director of Curriculum at the Board of Ed.

Skip eagerly agreed to look at my brother's resume, and help my brother land a job in the county. My brother's first teaching assignment was at one of the roughest middle schools, while also serving as an Assistant Football Coach at Meade High School. After a few years of paying his dues, Will finally earned himself a Head-Coaching position and a full-time Phys. Ed. teaching job at

Severna Park High, where he is just at the beginning stages of building his program from the ground up, much the same way as I built up my Art program over the past twenty years. He was truly my father's son, following in his footsteps as a Head Football Coach. Everyone is really proud of him, especially me. It took a lot of hard work for him to get to where he is. I love that he's building his own legacy and his own story. He's always meant more to me than he'll probably ever know. I still see him as that little kid that used to fall asleep on my chest at night when I was in high school, and who I used to roll around in the grass with.

So there we were, just nine of us, standing around this green tarp in front of my Grandparents' headstone, not one of us knowing what to say or what to do.

It was humiliating.

Eventually, my father looked around and finally said, "We should all say the Lord's Prayer or something."

So we all did.

To this day, I have a really hard time saying *the Lord's Prayer.*

DOUGLAS ELLMORE, JR.
CLASS OF 2008

"Mr. Bell has been more than a teacher. He truly has been a mentor. I have known him since the 6ᵗʰ grade as part of the Gifted and Talented Art Program, where he taught me from 6ᵗʰ—8ᵗʰ grade. I was then his student in high school, and then his colleague when he hired me for my first teaching position in 2014, as an art teacher at my alma mater, Southern High. Mr. Bell can attest that growing up I was a reserved person, quiet and shy. I tended to have a thick wall around me when I was growing up. That didn't ever stop Mr. Bell from making me feel welcomed, or understood. Especially during a time I was grappling with a loss in the family.

I had lost my Grandmother my junior year of high school. I was at school, I was coping, but I had just lost my Gran. She was my mother's mother and she lived right across from us since we lived on a family farm. During the weekdays growing up, she watched us before and after school 'til my parents came home. She helped dress us, she fed us, she taught us how to fold bed sheets, and how to keep a clean room. She took us to the doctors when we were sick, and sometimes tucked us into bed. She was essentially a second mother, and my sisters and I had a very loving and close relationship with her. Not many people can say they were close to their Grandmother or Grandfather. She was a role model for me and showed me and my sisters what a caring, compassionate human being looks like.

My Gran died of pancreatic cancer. She had been a part of an experimental treatment and was fighting it with all that she had. I had decided to do a painting series on family dynamics shortly after she had been diagnosed. I worked with personifying simple objects, teacups, and other dishware, as a family unit. Through my art, I had already begun asking the questions: what happens when a family member passes away, what could or would happen to that family? Without ever really realizing it, I had been mentally and emotionally trying to prepare myself for the kind of loss that would be felt in the wake of Gran's passing. While I hoped she would get better, I knew on a very real level that what she was going through was serious.

When she finally passed, I, like the rest of my family was devastated. *Shattered.* I remember talking one on one with Mr. Bell about it. He brought me back to my art and pointed out how sometimes our artwork is prophetic. It can show us things, or help us realize things that we may not understand or recognize on the surface. And it made me feel better. It made me realize that I shouldn't feel ashamed or guilty for being a step ahead of other family members and friends in coping with the loss. I had been processing and working through that moment before I knew it would actually come. I had created a space for myself in my art. And because of that, I was just that little bit more prepared to cope with the fact that I lost my second mother. And I realized, I needed to, more than ever, be there for my family.

The following year, I still struggled with the new normal. Now, Mr. Bell has all of his students keep a visual journal. To others, it may just look like a drawing pad or a sketchbook, but in Mr. Bell's class, it was more than that. It wasn't just a sketchbook, but a home for your thoughts, ideas, and stories, as well as a place to practice your visual art skills and techniques. He encouraged us to creatively express ourselves in our journals and reminded us that it was our space. It wasn't often that I got deeply personal in my visual journal, but that year I wrote, documented, and vented. There was one entry where I was trying to understand why my family wouldn't visit and be social at my Gran's and PopPop's house. I felt as if we were avoiding it. I wanted to visit that space that held so many memories, but I wasn't able to go alone, so I waited until my family was ready.

Instead of skimming over that entry—ignoring it, instead of simply quietly showing support, Mr. Bell responded. He wrote an encouraging message back and reminded me that he understood what I was experiencing and was there for me if I needed someone to listen."

FORTY-NINE

THE BOXER

My mother, Alma, was always *Daddy's girl* more than anything else. I know her relationship with my Grandma wasn't the same close relationship I had, quite the opposite even, but I also know death constantly surrounded my mother and it was probably difficult for her to process the final resting place of both her parents now.

We both made a lot of mistakes on May 14, 2013, and we compounded them by letting too much time pass before making amends. It only made things worse. It's a story that needs to be told though, in order for you to understand how passionately we all loved each other, *fought with* each other and *fought for* each other. It's a story that also created an even tighter bond between me and my in-laws, because despite everything, they never judged me. Never had a bad word to say about my parents, despite our not talking. Always just loved me like a son and were there for me. I'm hoping things will be better between me and my family one day. It's another unfinished chapter for now, though.

I never understood why my mother hated Lyndhurst so much. Maybe I'll never know. It definitely became some strange, unspoken point of contention between us over the years, the fact that I loved it there so much. I know my Mom had such a terrible experience with her teachers there, so much so that many years later when I was still a child she took me with her, storming back into her high school guidance counselor's office to let her have it.

"Remember me? You once told me how I wasn't *college material*. Well, I have degree, a husband, and I am a teacher now. I feel bad for all the others who were misguided by you, or who weren't as strong as me and might have heeded your advice!"

Maybe that was why Lyndhurst was a place she never wanted to talk about unless it was a conversation about her father. They were really close and she loved talking about my Grandpa. But when he died, she seemed to slip back into depression, just like she had after the stillbirth of my sister, Amanda.

It wasn't until many years later, around 2010 to be exact, that she started researching her genealogy online. While she grew up knowing Grandma's parents came over from Poland, Grandpa's history was a mystery. This opened up some dialogue between us about Lyndhurst. While researching, she also made contact with one of Grandpa's relatives, and together they found immigration and travel records for his Dad, *Arcangelo Dalla Valeria*. She learned his place of birth was Roncà, Italy, situated in the Province of Verona, in the Italian region Veneto, fifty miles west of Venice.

Apparently, his Dad already had relatives living in the United States from *the other side* (Italy), in both Florida and in New Jersey. So, when he married Julia Zabora, from New York, he must have shortened his name from Angelo Dalla Valeria to Andrew Vallery, Americanizing it, as was often the custom back then in order to try and get gainful employment. You can see his name change in U.S. Census Records several times over the years.

Amidst our discussions about our ancestry, I asked my mother to journal out whatever she could remember about Grandpa, and about her childhood, growing up the daughter of this mysterious man that never spoke much about his own upbringing, not even to my Grandma.

Whenever I used to ask her about Grandpa she said, "I only know what your Grandfather would tell me." *Which was nothing.*

So, when asking my mother about my Grandfather, *the Boxer,* this is what she lovingly recalled, in her own words:

NOVEMBER 4, 2010
Alma Vallery Bell

"Dad grew up with his mother and stepfather in Bergen County, NJ. He was from a large family and said that his father and two of his brothers died when he was young. He was a lightweight boxer and traveled out west and fought when he was a teenager. I think he was wild when he was younger. I don't believe that he graduated from high school. Few working people did in those years. Dad got married to Violet Golis and lived in an apartment in Lyndhurst, NJ until they bought the house that he lived in until his death in 1981. My mother says they used to go out New York City often.

Dad was likable, stubborn, opinionated, and usually right more than wrong. He had a lot of common sense and disliked people who had their noses up in the air. I remember baking birthday cakes for Dad when I was married and always being with him on his birthday. We shared the same sign of the zodiac in *Aries.* We also shared mystery novels and cigarettes at times. He sat at the head of the table in a wooden chair with arms. That was his chair and his alone.

He loved hamburgers and was a meat and potatoes man. I remember he always had a plate of raw onions with oil and vinegar next to his dinner plate that he shared with me (I always sat on his right at the table). He always wore dress pants and dress shoes and socks. I don't ever remember him in jeans or sneakers. He did wear suspenders and bow ties when he got dressed up. I remember him belonging to *the Kiwanis Club.*

Lots of family outings when I was very young. We went to county fairs every year . . . went to my Uncle's house in Highland Lakes, NJ a lot and went swimming and fly fishing . . . on day trips swimming at Lake Hopatcong, NJ, picnics at lakes, visits to his cousins in CT (they owned and operated a trucking company), trips to Ocean Beach, NJ visiting my parents friends, visiting *Ideal*

Farms in North Haledon, NJ, going to the dairy for homemade ice cream, visiting Branch Brook Park to see the cherry blossoms, going for pony rides—those are the fun times I remember. Dad also marched in the local parades which we always attended and sometimes participated in.

Dad got up around 1:30 A.M. and after making himself something to eat, he would go outside and leave in his milk truck to deliver milk at 2 A.M. He went to his customers on an every other day basis, Lyndhurst, Rutherford and maybe North Arlington.

The huge refrigerated truck from *Ideal Farms* in North Haledon would back into our driveway and deliver the milk in crates that were ordered. Dad would store the milk iced down and in the morning he would load the milk he needed to deliver onto his truck. We had a stone driveway because the Ideal truck was too heavy to accommodate any other type of driveway. He usually had a helper that he paid to help him in the mornings. Sometimes they were not very dependable; some were troublemakers that Dad was trying to help out. Bud worked for him for a long time and he and his family lived across the street from us. I am friends to this day with Bud's wife, Peggy.

I went out and helped Dad do his route when I was allowed to and we always stopped around 6 A.M. on Ridge Road across from Lincoln School for a hamburger. I would sit at the counter and eat while Dad talked to his friends. We returned home before my mother was up. Dad was usually around when I went to school and sometimes he gave me a ride in his milk truck even when I was in high school. I walked to school from Kindergarten—6th grade at Franklin School; then went to 7th and 8th grade at Lincoln School; and then Lyndhurst High. My sister attended River Road School for Kindergarten and Roosevelt School—8th grade then Lyndhurst High. It is interesting that we did not attend the same school until my sister's senior year of high school.

Dad would go up in the attic and work on his books and then go out to '*collect*.' Then he would be back at his desk in the attic counting his money; working on his books, and getting his orders ready and getting organized for the next day. Dad would also sit at the kitchen table and count his money and he always let me help him count and he'd tease me to '*hold some back.*' He saved silver dollars, fifty cent pieces, and two-dollar bills. He kept his money wrapped in rubber bands.

Always enjoyed Dad's company—we talked a lot. I listened to his many stories and helped him with his work whenever I could. When he got older, he moved his desk from the attic to the basement.

He always listened to country music. A radio was always on. He read mystery paperbacks; watched sports on TV, which we got around 1950. The TV was in the living room and it was for adults only. While in elementary school I could pick one show to watch. I remember watching *The Howdy Doody Show, Lawrence Welk, The Dinah Shore Show, Arthur Godfrey*, and on Sunday a one hour Disney show with the song *When You Wish Upon a Star* together.

Dad had a temper which I rarely saw. He got mad at my sister a lot and once I witnessed him shaking her so hard that her head broke the glass on our bedroom window while I was pulling on his leg telling him to stop and my mother was trying to pull me away from them! I don't remember my Dad ever yelling at me. I remember having fun with him.

But when Dad got mad at someone you knew it. Usually, he was quiet and kept to himself. We had to be quiet when he was sleeping during the day. My sister and I got punished at night if we were not sleeping (talking in bed) and my mother would sit us in the chairs against the wall in the kitchen. We would have to stay there until Dad woke up to go to work at 2 A.M. so that he would see that we were bad. Sometimes he let us go back to bed and other times we had to sit there until he came back home at 6 A.M.

I used to go with Dad in the afternoon (when I was in elementary school) in the car to run errands—went along River Road to Kearny; across the Passaic River to Nutley and Belleville and we usually stopped for burgers while he did whatever he did and I sat at the counter or in the car. I was young and obedient and never asked questions but we talked, sang songs, and ate together and kept to ourselves about what we did. We loved *White Castle* hamburgers and *Stewart's Root Beer*.

We didn't go to church together as a family. Dad would ride by *Sacred Heart* on Ridge Road and make the sign of the cross — *that was it for him*. I went to Sunday school and church at St. Thomas on Stuyvesant Avenue with my mother and sister.

When I was in high school, Dad was strict and he told me who I could and could not be friends with; *it was maddening*. In high school, I skipped school whenever the Catholics had a holy day and watched TV at my friend Marian's house. Did this for several years until the principal told my dad in passing how religious I was. They had a good laugh over it but I did stop doing it after that. Dad thought it was pretty cool but not to tell mom.

Dad taught me how to drive a stick shift- a yellow and black Plymouth if I remember correctly. We called it the Yellow Bird and you could see it coming! When Dad drove, he owned the road and often drove down the middle and on the left side.

Walt was his best friend and they talked all the time. He was also friends with the owner of the candy store on River Road and he often bought me ice cream while he visited him in his store and in his apartment upstairs.

Dad had a lot of friends. He knew everyone in town and was good to his customers. Some had money problems and he'd still give them milk and butter. Lots of people owed him money and he never saw it.

In the summertime, my mother, sister and I went on vacations together. We spent weeks at a time in a beach house in Ocean Beach, NJ. We also went camping across the USA and also took summer trips to New England. We spent a lot of time swimming and fishing at Highland Lakes when we stayed with Dad's brother and his wife.

Dad belonged to *the Kiwanis* and Mom belonged *to the Elks*. They got dressed up often and attended meetings and social events. When I was little we did a lot of things together as a family; county fairs, Sunday dinners with relatives, trips to Connecticut visiting Dad's relatives, and as I got older, I remember going with Dad to visit his mother on a regular basis. My mother would stay home.

His Dad died when he was young. His mother, Julia, got remarried to George Horstman, so Grandma Horstman is what we called her. His brother Walter worked for Lackawanna Railroad and lived in Highland Lakes. His sister Effie lived in Hackensack. I remember visiting Aunt Effie and Uncle Andy often. They were really nice. Uncle Walter, Aunt Marie, and Aunt Effie did not have any children. His brother Arthur, a milkman too, also lived in Lyndhurst. Dad was close with Effie and Walter but not with Arthur who lived less than a mile from us. Arthur and he became competitors in the milk business. I met Uncle Arthur's kids when a friend in high school asked me if they were related to me. His sister Edna lived across the street from us but he never spoke to her and I never knew she was a relative until I was sixty years old! My Uncle Arthur had three children that I met when I was in high school but never really connected with. Edna had a son that went to school in Lyndhurst but I have yet to meet him. He lives in Texas.

While Dad visited his mother, his brother Walter, his sister Effie, and his cousins Eugene and Edna regularly, as we got older, the trips to Connecticut lessened. He also enjoyed his brother-in-law Al who was a mechanic in East Rutherford, NJ. We had many visits with him and his family and attended dinners at their church as well. Dad and Uncle Al talked a lot over a beer while we visited and spent the day. Dad built a fireplace in our backyard and we had lots of cookouts with relatives and friends of my parents. He met my future in-laws after I got engaged and we had a party out back. He got along well with my future husband, Alex, and his parents, John and Jessie Evelyn.

After attending college for three years in Tennessee I got married in Lyndhurst and moved to Maryland where I taught first grade and attended Towson State University. My sister was married and lived in California at this time.

Dad didn't care for my sister's husband, and rightfully so. *He had good insight.*

During my second year of marriage, my sister and her baby arrived at Dad's house after her husband left her at the Newark Airport. Mom and Dad had a hard time having them live there, so Alex and I offered to help out. We found a house to rent and my sister and her baby, Erik, moved in with us for several years. This created less stress for my parents but what an experience for us!

In 1969, we purchased our first house. My parents came down to help us paint, clean and set it up. My sister and her son were still living with us. My parents visited us often; he liked Maryland. He helped me with my garden and also took day trips with us. Several years later my sister got a job and her own apartment and they moved out on their own. My parents often drove down to visit. Dad got along well with my husband Alex. He'd sit on the front steps directing Alex as to 'how to mix and pour concrete' while Alex poured his front sidewalk for him.

Our son Michael was born in 1971 and his grandparents on both sides of the family adored him. We traveled a lot to upstate NY and northern NJ visiting them. Dad stayed with us by himself in the summers for a vacation from Mom. We enjoyed having him as much as Mom enjoyed having him with us.

He had a terrible time with his arthritis and one summer we took him for acupuncture at *the Baltimore Washington Acupuncture Center* for treatment. Michael was around two years old and he loved to walk around with Grandpa's cane. Michael came with me to the treatments. Dad was reluctant to go at first but as his arthritis improved he became more mobile and was so excited that he could lift his arm high enough to comb his hair. Dad had a head of hair on him and was always combing it. I remember combing his hair when I was little.

During the 1970s Dad's business went downhill. People could buy milk in the stores, his customers died off and he actually couldn't afford to work anymore. My mother had to get an office job when she was in her fifties. Dad was always the breadwinner and didn't like my mother going to work, but Dad never paid into

Social Security so Mom working was a necessity that they had to adjust to. Dad missed working and seeing people.

He knew everybody in town and was now home all the time. His friend Walt lived up the block and they would get together sometimes. I remember taking Dad to the Luray Caverns in Virginia and also to a dinosaur exhibit which he and Michael enjoyed. He enjoyed Michael's company and spunk. We all went to the Strasburg Railroad in Pennsylvania and Dad took Michael in the railroad museum there, just the two of them. Fond memories . . .

In 1979 we picked out a lot and had a house built in Bel Air, Maryland. Dad liked our new house and I remember him helping Alex shovel out the driveway one winter.

1981 is a year I will never forget. The sun was shining, I was on the tractor mowing the lawn and Alex was trimming. We got a phone call from my mother saying, 'Dad is sick in bed and won't go to the doctors—would you talk to him because he'll listen to you?' I spoke to Dad and he said that he would go to doctors if I took him. I was told that he was stopped while driving on the wrong side of the road on River Road near home. He cursed out the cop and had his license taken away and then suddenly got 'sick.' It was never clear if he had a stroke or heart attack but he never recovered from that incident. I got in my Volkswagen and four hours later was sitting with Dad in his bedroom. He was happy to see me and said he would let me take him to the doctor. He was weak and did not look good. We talked and he sat up and I held him up with both arms.

He said, 'Vi, I'm going home.'

Dad died right then and there in my arms with the most peaceful and serene look on his face that I still can see to this day."

– Alma Vallery Bell

FIFTY

THE AFTERMATH

Later that afternoon, when we got back to my Grandmother's house after the burial all hell broke loose again. I had to sign paperwork to get the title for my Grandmother's car from my Aunt Ginger.

At this point, I didn't even have a clue whether Vi's car would even start, let alone make it from North Jersey all the way back down to Maryland where we were living now.

Inside her house was trashed, as everyone was picking through the bones, going through the remains of my Grandmother's belongings, deciding what was of value to keep and what to bag up and set out under her carport for trash.

By the time I reached Grandma's carport my father grabbed me and said, "Let's go! You and me. Right now! Let's get this over with."

If it wasn't for my little brother stepping in we probably would have fought right then and there. It felt like the whole neighborhood was watching us from behind their curtains.

It was a shame all this was going down, because prior to this, the last memory I had of me and my father outside at my Grandma's carport was after a drunken night we spent together in

New York City at *Pazza Notte*, knocking back two-for-one martinis. He and I ended up missing the New Jersey Transit stop on our way back home to Lyndhurst and wound up many, many miles out somewhere in Clifton. When we realized we missed our stop, we got out, staggered our way to a nearby Diner about a half a mile along the highway and then called for a cab after grabbing a late night meal. By the time we made it back to my Grandma's we didn't want to wake her up so we sat outside drinking by the carport smoking cigars until the sun came up.

That was a good night. *A great memory.*

This memory, I figured, was going to haunt me forever if things went any further.

"Is this how history is gonna repeat itself?" I yelled to my father. "Shame on you if you're gonna let it happen!"

This pissed him off something fierce. Now I thought he definitely was gonna hit me! But I didn't care. He had to hear it. Even if it meant him takin' a crack at me.

It wouldn't be the first time I took a punch from him, and, I can take a punch. *So, I pressed on . . .*

You see, when I was around twelve or thirteen, my PopPop, who was my Grandfather on my father's side, got into a similarly heated argument with my Dad and they literally never spoke again. My father had to read about his own father passing away in the newspaper.

So sad.

A lot of what I do with my art, what my pictures are all about, is embedded with all these things. It's also why I am the way I am, and why I'll do anything not to let history repeat itself with my father or with my own son. It's why I've always painted it out, and why here, I'm writing it out.

To give you a little backstory on my PopPop, I have to preface everything by saying he absolutely hated it here—*in America, I mean*. While he came here for my MomMom, in search of a "better life" he actually liked the simple life he had in Belfast. And he hated it even worse just before the blowout he had with my Dad that ended their relationship forever.

My MomMom had just passed away around six months or so before my Dad's big blowout with PopPop. She was a sweetie pie. A tiny, little soft-spoken woman with a thick Irish accent. She always had this electric smile across her face. She had charm. She used to make pies whenever we visited them. That's what I remember about her the most—her vicious sweet tooth. On every pie she made the crust was caked with sugar. They were absolutely delicious. Her passing away made my PopPop extremely lonely.

During better times, the thing I remember most about my PopPop was this beautiful garden he had in Syracuse, filled with gorgeous rose bushes everywhere. While he still didn't have much money, he kept his garden immaculate, and his lawn looked as if it was worth a million bucks. He certainly had his pride. He even mowed his lawn down so low in one section of the backyard so he had his very own putting green. My MomMom and PopPop were both always good to me, but I never saw them much. Holidays mostly. My PopPop always arm wrestled me whenever I'd see him. He had these gigantic disproportionate forearms like Popeye and was strong as a bull, despite his wiry frame. He was real tough on my Dad when he was younger. In turn, my Dad was tough on me.

With me, though, PopPop used to sit around, play cards with me, smoke Camel cigarettes and tell war stories about how he'd take on three Teamsters at a time down the docks, come home all bruised and bloodied fighting for work each day, and when my Dad would ask him why he was going back he'd just laugh.

"You should see the other guys, Sonny," he'd say. "You gotta fight. Stand up for yourself. Nobody's gonna hand it to ya'. Besides, it took three of them to take me on. They walked outta there knowin' they were in a fight! Tomorrow they'll try picking on someone else that'll put up less of a fight," he'd boast.

And he was right. But he still hated it here in America. In Belfast, Northern Ireland, in the small town of Legoniel, my PopPop was at least *a somebody*. He knew everybody there, and everybody knew him. In America, he was *a nobody*.

Here he had to literally start all over. Can you imagine that? Starting over in a new country where you knew no-one, could barely understand the language—at the age of forty-two?!

Coincidentally, just like my Grandfather on my mother's side here in Lyndhurst, he also owned his own milk business back in Ireland. He had a decent life. It was simple, but it was all he knew. And when they decided to come to America he really didn't want any part of it. But he went along for the ride. It was my MomMom that wanted to go. So my Dad had to part ways with his close friends, and with his cousins Harold and Jim.

Harold was my Dad's older cousin. He was also, coincidentally or not, a fighter. He used to box for money and used to sleep over my Dad's house down the street for a couple days at a time until his bruises healed from his fights so his mother, my Dad's Aunt Sissy, wouldn't find out. She didn't like him fighting, but, according to my Dad—all he did was fight.

"Harold would pick a fight with somebody on the streets just to stay in shape," my Dad explained. "That's just how he was."

He also used to come to my Dad's aid whenever my Dad fought or was outnumbered. And, in turn, my Dad would come to his younger cousin Jim's aid. My Dad learned to fight from Harold. And, this was the pecking order.

Jim was like the brother my Dad never had, growing up like me, as an only child, until my brother arrived when I was nearly seventeen. His cousin Jim, whom I finally got to meet in June of the following summer while he was visiting America for the first time, told me all about all the fights my Dad used to get in when they were kids. He hated seeing my Dad leave for America because he said: "Now I had nobody around to protect me!" He also told me that my Dad could've probably gone pro as a football player over there. He was that good of an athlete, even as a kid.

But nevertheless, my PopPop moved their family to America "for a better life", and after arriving at Ellis Island, where his name, my MomMom's and my Father's names are inscribed on a huge wall beneath the Statue of Liberty, they settled upstate in the outskirts of Syracuse, New York.

Years later, just prior to my MomMom's passing, life dealt him a raw deal. His house burnt down, along with everything in it. No-one was hurt, as they were away on vacation when it happened, but it was a total loss. Might've been that one of my Dad's cousins fell asleep with a cigarette burning. Could've been electrical. Nobody knew what happened. All we did know was that they had no insurance, and they lost everything, so my mother and father moved them to Maryland to a small apartment complex.

My MomMom passed away shortly after they moved.

PopPop got a girlfriend that moved in shortly thereafter, which my Dad definitely didn't approve of. My Dad felt it was too soon after MomMom's passing. I remember going over there one day, seeing my Dad pissed off that the two single beds from his bedroom were suddenly both pushed together. Add to the mix she was also Irish, but from *Southern Ireland* as opposed to *Northern Ireland*, which in my Dad's family was like shacking up with your mortal enemy!

This all led to a major blow-out, and now my Dad and I we were having our own blow-out in my Grandmother's carport.

I pressed on, reminding him who's always been there for him just as much as he's always been there for me.

I reminded him how he felt the day he read about his own father passing away in the newspaper. How PopPop never got to meet his other Grandson. How he, too, would miss out on the best years of his own Grandson's life, and all over what?!

I asked him if he remembered it was me who was handed a box and given an address where to "find your Grandfather's things and to not come home without them" after he passed away.

How I took it upon myself years later to try and track down where his Dad might be buried so he could try and make peace with his own demons. Only this mission was unfortunately never to be realized when the trail went cold after a couple years of searching.

How could he not see he was letting history repeat itself?! How dare he?! Now it was *me* getting pissed!

At this point, it was growing late in the afternoon and after a few long hours of yelling at one another, my father's anger had turned inward and his face actually seemed to change, forming over it a special kind of anguish I never want to see on his face ever again. It broke my heart to see it.

He said, as he started shaking, "I don't like this . . ."

I was actually afraid he was having a heart attack. I knew he was sincere and didn't really want any of this to be happening either. Deep down my father is a really good man, one I've always looked up to and someone I always wanted to be like, right up until May 14th.

I wanted our relationship to be salvaged, though. There was no point in fighting on anymore, so we stopped, and went our separate ways for the night.

There was a church service for Grandma the next day.

So, Lisa and I left to stay with her longtime friend Christine and her husband Kurt that lived nearby. Ginger, her husband John, my cousin Erik and his daughter were going to stay at my Grandma's house. My parents headed off to my Aunt Jeannie's and my brother was off to Pennsylvania to his fiancé's.

As my wife drove us to Christine's house, my brother passed us along Route 46. As he did, he smiled at me, shaking his head as he suddenly noticed the huge new tattoo scrolled along my entire right forearm dangling out the passenger's side window.

It read, "**VIOLET**" in beautiful script, accompanied by a large black and gray solitary flower.

FIFTY-ONE

THE PSYCHIC

Vi's funeral turned into a two-day affair. There was a service for her the day after the burial of her ashes at her Church, *St. Thomas* on Stuyvesant Avenue in Lyndhurst, just up the street from her house.

Prior to pulling up to the church, I got a message on my cell phone from this girl named Andrea, whom I simply knew growing up as one of the girls who lived next door to Vi. She was close in age to me, only a few years younger. I first heard from her back in May after hearing of my Grandmother's passing:

"Michael,

I am writing to you in sympathy for the loss of your Grandmother, Mrs. Vallery. I'm not quite sure if you would remember me, but I am Andrea, the oldest daughter of Pete and Dorothy's three girls that lived next door to your Grandmother. Your Grandmother always spoke of you and your art. She had told me about how you have painted celebrities, and to look you up on the internet to see your work and accomplishments. Michael, your work is amazing. You have been blessed with talent, your Grandmother was very proud of you and I am glad to know you as well. I have wanted to reach out to you myself in the past to let you know you have a familiar fan in New Jersey. Unfortunately, it took me 'til now. I send my condolences to you and your family. Mrs. Vallery will be missed. She was the very nice lady who lived next door she was a part of my life for the last thirty-five years—I will always remember her." – *Andrea*

Now, Andrea was a girl that would always see me whenever I visited my Grandmother as a kid, but just to say hi. She always struck me as shy, but a sweet kid from a nice family. Her father, Pete always kept his house immaculate, everything in its proper place.

Whenever we'd visit my Grandma, she'd immediately put me and my father to work to try and keep her house up to par. We'd power-wash her white vinyl siding, trim her overgrown trees, stuff like that. Lisa would always try and help my mother tidy up the house inside, cleaning the bathrooms until they were spotless, the stove, countertops, stuff like that, but as the years went on and people visited her less and less her house became overwhelming for her.

And, while her house was probably one of the tiniest houses in the neighborhood, her property was one of the largest. I often imagined putting an in-ground pool in one day, if I were to move back there and keep the house in the family.

As I arrived at the church, Andrea texted me that she wasn't going to be able to make it to the funeral service but wanted to meet me briefly, if only for a few minutes before the service started to tell me something.

"It's something very important," she texted.

So, I met Andrea on the corner of Stuyvesant and Page Avenue while the rest of the family, as some relatives, my Godmother, and their family, my Grandmother's sisters' kids and their children all began filing into the church.

"At least some of our relatives showed up for Vi today," I thought to myself. I was happy about that at least.

As soon as Andrea arrived she told me not to get freaked out.

I smiled back with, "Andrea, after the past couple months I've had, I think it would take a lot to freak me out at this point, so fire away."

She anxiously proceeded to tell me how ever since one of her own Grandparents passed away she's been getting these "visits" from *the departed*.

She said they come and go, and often she doesn't understand the messages, but in my case, it came in form of my Grandmother visiting her last night, and it came in the form of three numbers. It's funny, even as I write this numbers have always played a role in my life as well. I see them all the time. You might even pick up on some familiar number patterns in certain numbers while reading this book.

She shared with me how my Grandmother asked her to reach out to me with these "three significant connections" and that "Your Grandmother wanted you to know that you were very special to her and that she will always be with you."

As we stood outside the Church watching everyone filing in, my wife watching on from afar, she shared this with me from her journal:

1) The #10, a family connection

2) Take care of precious "Car"—male?

3) #480 (heart) Lyndhurst? NJ and also something with the word Todd (and the color pink) and a smile of "thank-you."

"The last one with the word Todd was to be told to you, but it was from an outside voice (not your Grandmother)," Andrea said.

Well, the number 10 could've been many, many things. After, all, it was no secret I'm born on the 10th. *April 10th*. A birthday I also curiously share with my mother, my second cousin Bonnie, and my first childhood friend, Danny Johns. I'm not sure what made me think of Danny on this day. I hadn't thought of that kid in years. I often imagined his life and mine as these parallel lives, and that either of us could've ended up going down one path or the other. Danny and I came into the world together, and when we were around six or seven years old, almost went out together.

My mother and I were visiting Aunt Jean, as I called her (Danny's mom), at their new rental house. Aunt Jean was recently divorced from a volatile relationship with an abusive husband who had this ferocious temper. She and Danny moved around a lot from place to place after they split, and this new rental house out in the middle of nowhere was spooky as hell. It definitely felt haunted! It was really old—one of those farmhouse-types that was built around the late 1800s. I remember it also had one of those claw-foot tubs in the bathroom upstairs too. That's one of the things that stuck in my memory about the place.

Later that afternoon Danny and I raided his mother's cabinet for about a half-dozen or so bottles filled with chewable vitamins, *Spiderman* and *Flinstones* mostly, and we hid under the kitchen table while my mother and Aunt Jean sat in the other room talking—all the while, *downing pill after pill.*

We must have watched too many of those commercials for Superhero vitamins, I guess. *You know,* the ones where if you ate your vitamins you could get super powers? Well, we figured, "Why take two a day for the next ten years when we could just take them all right now and have superpowers *instantly!*"

My mom and Aunt Jean eventually found us under the kitchen table and we were rushed to the hospital. The only thing I really remember from that point on was sitting back-to-back with Danny as they pumped our stomachs, occasionally hearing the nurse make the occasional wisecrack, stuff like, "Oh look, here's Fred! Wait, there's Wilma! Ooooh, another Spiderman!" Shit like that. At least someone had a sense of humor about what happened. My mother sure didn't find anything funny about it— an overdose at the young age of six or so.

"That'll look great on my permanent records!" she probably figured.

Later in life, I'd lose touch with Danny. His Mom eventually left the state and moved to Rehoboth Beach for a while. We used to visit them in the summertime and park at his Grandma Almond's house, which was only about a block or two from the ocean. Later Danny would move to Florida, get mixed up with heavier stuff and would die tragically from a drug overdose. Some thought it was a suicide. I refuse to believe that about Danny because he left behind a young daughter I know he loved dearly. His mom, Aunt Jean, came to the last solo exhibition I had in Delaware shortly before she, too, passed away. She was always really good to me like that. A really sweet lady.

So, as I tried to sift through the possible significance of the number ten, there are more dates I pondered over—the 10th was also my father's birthday—November 10th. It was also the day my Grandmother passed away, which was on May 10th. It was also on the 10th that John Gotti, Sr. passed away, June 10, 2002, to be exact. Lisa and I were also married on August 10th.

Beyond all that, the number 10 also held significance to me due to a portrait I painted for Carol Todd, mother of Amanda Todd, the Canadian teen that tragically committed suicide after years of bullying on October 10, 2012. Her story made international headlines due to the haunting YouTube video that garnished millions of hits, foreshadowing her own death just one month prior. My painting also went on to make international headlines in *the Huffington Post* and assisted in bringing awareness to bullying and suicide prevention in a "real world" way.

I figured the last part Andrea told me about "Todd" and "thank you" must have been Amanda Todd's spirit thanking me for her painting, and for raising awareness in the wake of her tragedy. I even got my National Art Honor Society involved in the actual painting of her portrait, and hundreds of kids from throughout the school, some I didn't even know, lined up outside my studio to paint their hands purple and stamp them into the canvas' background as we painted. Now, every year on October 10th everyone wears purple in honor of Amanda Todd and World Mental Health Day. So, the number ten had a lot of different forms of significance. The greatest being the link to my marriage, to my mother and father, and to my grandmother's passing.

As for me "taking care of that precious Car", well that made sense on two fronts, both of which I figured there was probably no way of Andrea knowing. The first being my Grandmother did want me to take care of her "car." Her 1977 Oldsmobile, to be exact. As far as I knew, Andrea would have no way of knowing that, or that my wife and I had a son named Carmen.

"Take care of that precious Car –" was my thinking.

You see, Andrea moved when she got married and whenever we visited my Grandmother I never ran into her. It's been years. And, my Grandma never really left the house except to take out the trash and recycling or drive to the grocery store, all of which she still did right up until she fell. Yes, she still drove, at 95 years of age. So, now I was intrigued.

As for the last thing? "Always remember **480**—her heart, New Jersey."

To that, I really had no clue, but I thanked Andrea for blessing me with these messages from my Grandmother, and that I'd think on it and if anything ever came to me I'd let her know. And with that, I headed into the church to meet up with my wife for Vi's send-off.

As I made my way into the first row of the pew inside the church, I whispered to Lisa what Andrea had said. I told her I could figure pretty much everything except the number 480. Was it a highway? Someplace along Route 4 or Route 80? I couldn't figure it out. *But Lisa knew right away.*

"It's the building!" she said. "*Sorrento's!* Where we first met. Where your Grandma got her hair done for the past thirty-five years. My Dad's Beauty Parlor. The address is 480 Stuyvesant Avenue!"

The hair stood up on my skin.

I smiled. Mustered up the courage to wipe my tears long enough to do Grandma's reading. Tears flowed heavy once again after the service. I wanted to get it all out before leaving for home and getting our son.

The Priest did a nice job with everything. Quite a few people showed up, which I was glad to see. Some relatives I hadn't seen in years. Her church promised us they'd always leave a place to put flowers in "Vi's seat" on holidays.

I WAS THE LAST ONE OUT of the church. It was eerily quiet now. I snapped a photo with my cell phone from the middle of the last aisle before I left. Part of me knew it might be the last time I might ever step foot in the church I was baptized in, where we laid my Grandma to rest. The other part of me was the artist in me wanting to document everything with my third eye and use them as reference photos for future art. I would end up using a few of the photos that I took at my Grandma's graveside and in her Church for a mini-series of drawings that framed up how I felt in the aftermath of these past few months. I called this *31 Nights*.

I remember being emotionally moved from a painting I saw over the course of my studies called *The Funeral: A Band of Men (2 Women) Abandonment*. It was painted in 1980 by one of my heroes of the art world, Eric Fischl. I didn't know much about the painting back then, but it stuck in my head, even at my Grandma's own funeral. It wasn't until much later, after re-creating my own funeral experience that I came to find out that Fischl also included himself in his painting, as a young boy at his mother's funeral. He was depicting the awkwardness of the ritual. It was unnervingly similar to my own experience.

Once back at Grandma's house, I went inside to gather a few of her things—some of her paintings and drawings, whichever ones my mother and her sister would allow me to leave with. I also grabbed my Grandfather's chair, which was something of a keepsake. It always reminded me of him, since he always sat in this one chair that was different from all the rest at the head of the table. It wasn't part of any set. It was unique in that way. It was "his chair" as my Mom always said, so I wanted it to stay with us.

I also wanted some of my Grandma's antique skeleton keys she had hanging on walls and on nightstands throughout her house to give to Lisa to one day pass down to Carmen. Lisa was always a *witchy woman*. I think it spans back to her Italian roots. The myth is that a skeleton key can unlock any door. Lisa always loved those keys and thought they were good luck, so I wanted her to have them.

Once we were packed up, I took the car around the block to Vi's local mechanic. As it turned out, the car looked good. Being a '77 Olds with only 57,000 miles on the car, it was still in good running condition, but it hadn't been driven in a while and he wasn't sure how it would hold up on the highway for such a long trip, so we called AAA. It cost $600 to transport it via tow since we were beyond the allowable mileage under my coverage. My mother just happened to have $600 with her and agreed to let me borrow it. With that, we all made peace, I kissed my parents goodbye and off I went.

With only about an hour to go in the drive, I asked the driver to pull over and unhitch my Grandma's ride. I figured the old gal could make it for the last hour of our home stretch. Plus, I wanted some time to myself with her in her car for the last little bit of our journey back home. It felt good to be behind the wheel of her '77 Olds. The car still smelled like her old garage. With my arm dangling outside the window, the summer breeze whipping against my skin, I gazed into the rearview mirror into the back seat at what was now filled with her belongings before the sun went down. I kept her small, wooden painting easel, several of her original oil paintings on canvases of some of the most serene places you'd ever want to visit, scenes of expansive green pastures, old farmhouses, and historic railroads.

A few months later, my father-in-law, Bill called me from Lyndhurst when he was checking on his building. Apparently, my Aunt sold my Grandma's house and whoever bought it knocked it down to put something new in its place.

I was sick to my stomach.

This was the house my Grandfather died in.

I promised myself this—One day, I'll make enough money to buy it back, whatever it costs—*and burn it to the ground.* This is who I was becoming.

A man driven to create and to destroy.

I was an interesting dichotomy in the making, not just for me as a man, but for me as an artist. All of this began impacting my artwork and my personal relationships. I began burning pages from my sketchbooks to kill memories I didn't want anymore, which escalated into destroying some of my own paintings.

After all the dust settled from the funeral, I put a check in the mail for the $600 my parents gave me to get Vi's car back home, eventually unpacked everything and laid out the entire collection of my Grandma's paintings in the spare bedroom. I had some of her pen and ink drawings from her sketchbooks matted and custom framed over the next week and proceeded to hang some of them throughout our home.

Then I received another message from Andrea.

She said she woke up to another dream of my Grandmother just as Justin Timberlake's song *Mirrors* was blasting from her alarm clock. She said she wouldn't have thought anything of the song except for the fact that it was also playing, coincidentally or not when she turned on her car just after I left her and headed into the church the day of my Grandmother's service. She thought maybe the lyrics meant something.

So, with that, I went to my laptop to play the *YouTube* video of the song and read along with the lyrics. And just as I did, there was this loud blaring vibration coming from the front of my house. It sounded like the base blowing out a speaker at a rock concert!

My son came running into the back bedroom where I was watching the Justin Timberlake video yelling, "Daddy, Daddy, come quick! The jukebox just turned on all by itself! It just turned on by itself!! Come quick!!!"

So I raced to the front bar area of my home where sure enough, our jukebox lifted an old 45 LP onto the record player, with no-one playing it, no credits even available on it that would allow it to play. There was no viable explanation for how it even turned itself on.

What was the track it was playing so mysteriously by itself?
Track #201.
My Grandmother's area code.
The old area code for Bergen County, New Jersey.
I miss you, Vi . . .

FIFTY-TWO

PAINTING JOHN GOTTI

On December 16, 1985, John Gotti became the most powerful gangster in America, with the dramatic assassination of then-Gambino boss Paul Castellano outside *Sparks Steak House* on 46th Street in between Second and Third Avenue in midtown Manhattan.

The hit on Castellano was like something even the best screenwriters couldn't have scripted out for a movie. It made headlines around the world and, in turn, made John Gotti *Public Enemy Number One* to the FBI.

Twenty-nine years later—*to the very date*—I was commissioned to paint the portrait that would become the iconic cover art for his son, John Gotti, Jr.'s groundbreaking memoir, *Shadow of my Father*.

It's these eerie synchronistic coincidences that would surface again and again throughout the course of my painting career. And, since everyone always asks, "How did you end up painting John Gotti?" I figured I'd share with you exactly how it happened.

The most recent painting commission came to fruition like this . . .

DECEMBER 16, 2014

"Hello Michael, this is Peter Gotti. Please contact me as soon as you possibly can, I have a time sensitive project that I need to come to decision on immediately. Thanks, Michael."

Later that day I got a text and then a second phone call from a man named Big Steve telling me to expect another call shortly from Peter, son of the late Dapper Don—John Gotti, Sr. And, like clockwork, an hour or so later came the next call from Peter Gotti, outlining what needed to be done—an "epic painting" that he and his family felt "only I could do." One that, if done just right, would become the cover art for his brother, John Junior's book, *Shadow of my Father.*

Soon after that, came the phone call from the man himself—*John A. Gotti—Junior.*

Now, let me preface everything by saying I'm used to deadlines. I'm used to the Hollywood-style hurry-up-and-wait game. When I got the call to do the painting for my buddy Dominic Capone's reality television series *The Capones*, which aired back in 2013, I literally had 48 hours to complete the painting in time for it to dry and ship to Chicago. Talk about pulling an all-nighter! And that's just one of just many instances where I've had to produce creativity on-the-spot. But I always deliver. *Always have. Always will.*

I was once explained, "In life, there are three kinds of people: those who want, those who have, and those who deliver."

I was definitely of *the latter*.

But this job was different, for a couple reasons. For starters, I had the flu. And I had it bad! I was literally laid up on the couch when I got the first call with a fever, chills . . . the works! Second, most of my painting supplies were at my work studio, and my home wasn't the place I usually completed these types of epic works, with the exception of the one I created for Dominic, which also happened right here at home in the same front bar/foyer area I was about to quarantine myself to for John Junior's painting. Third—*it was Christmas*—one week before Christmas to be exact!

And, when commissioned to do a job for the former reputed head of the most powerful crime family in America, it goes without saying that it's a job that needs to be done "just right".

When I asked how soon it needed to be done, I was initially thinking probably a couple months, at best. The reason being, typically I'm booked to do portraits at least six months out. I've got a pretty steady wait list. Not for book covers, but for portraits for family members, loved ones, for wedding or anniversary gifts, that sort of stuff. Plus, I'd been also keeping busy on the public speaking circuit as of late, and was gearing up for a huge keynote and workshops out in Utah for the Utah Art Education Association and doing an hour long artist talk for SUU for their "Arts and Insights" television program in February. So, while I was still preparing for that, it was also just before Christmas, which is always my busy time, finishing up last minute touches on commissions from months prior.

According to John Junior and Peter Gotti, the turnaround time on this particular job was aggressive, which I'm used to. Most clients want everything yesterday. They wanted an answer on whether I'd agree to do the painting or not immediately.

"We're looking at a January 1ˢᵗ kind of deadline," John said to me. I took a deep breath, didn't show any hesitation, and simply responded with the kind of confidence I knew a man like John Gotti Junior would most appreciate and I simply said, "Okay, I understand John. I'll get it done for you by then. As only I can. I'll put everything else aside and get started right away."

You've gotta understand — *this was unprecedented* — John coming out with his memoir against vehement protests from even his own mother, Victoria Gotti, Sr., who at first feared if he wrote this book that the Government would come after him again, seeking out more indictments.

Now, for those of you not familiar with John Junior's story, he beat four — yes FOUR — federal racketeering trials. All back-to-back in as many as five straight years, spanning from 2004 - 2009. And while his father, John Gotti, Sr. was made famous for beating three back-to-back cases and dubbed "The Teflon Don" by the media, it was John Junior, who truly earned the moniker "The Teflon Son." John Junior kept silent for decades—about everything. But after beating his fourth trial with another hung jury, John also felt *enough was enough.* He was going to publish his memoir no matter what the risk and set the record straight once and for all about his family.

He was brave like his father that way, and from the first moment I met him, he also struck me as extremely intelligent like his father. Definitely not anything like the media portrayed him or any of his family out to be. He has an extremely high IQ, the kind you'd find in a top trial attorney. John is also very personable, extremely engaging and always eloquent with his words.

Peter Gotti described the differences between his brother and his iconic father, John Gotti, Sr. at dinner once with me as, "My father was more Chief Crazy Horse while my brother is more like Chief Joseph," likening his family to two of the greatest Native American warrior leaders.

This happened to be another prophetic "coincidence." You see, I painted a series of seven oil paintings on paper over a year prior for ex-Mob wife Toni Marie Ricci entitled *Seven Scars,* which told the tale of her life overcoming great odds, trials, and tribulations. I related the paintings to my *Voices of Violence* series that I painted for Georgia Durante back in 2002, as a visual vehicle to help her heal "wounds" or "scars" that ran so deep.

One of the paintings, *Scars - Scene 5,* depicted John Gotti Junior emerging from court victoriously to freedom heading towards a waiting car, accompanied by his brother Peter and his lawyer Charlie Carnesi on either side. In the top right corner sat Toni Marie Ricci, on the witness stand juxtaposed against twelve empty juror chairs and barbed wire stretching across the scene. John Gotti Junior happened to be Godfather to Toni Marie's son Michael, and Toni Marie testified on John Junior's behalf at his last trial, refuting testimony given by her ex-husband. Her cousin was also Frank DeCicco, underboss to the late John Gotti. DeCicco was blown up by a car bomb back in 1986, and brother was also a former Gambino soldier, so she, too, understood "the life."

In the lower left corner of the painting, I included a "WELCOME HOME" sign and three figureheads of Crazy Horse, Chief Joseph, and Sitting Bull. Across the center of the painting, just beyond where John is about to walk through into the waiting car I included crime scene tape, which instead reads "DO NOT CROSS", which I did symbolically for three reasons.

Number one, it served as a finish line for John, crossing it like a marathon runner would break the finishing line tape of an endless race. Two, it was a line the Government did not want him to actually cross, and three—it could also be interpreted another way, to literally mean "DO NOT CROSS" John Gotti Junior.

This is why I included the Native Americans in this particular piece. It was also no secret John Gotti Junior had a fascination with them. In an interview he agreed to do on camera for *60 Minutes*, breaking his silence for the first time after beating his fourth trial back in 2010, he talked with host Steve Kroft about having "an Indian room" in his home, which had statues of some of the great Native American warriors. He talked about "understanding their plight".

After all, his family had been through what most families could never withstand—trials, deaths, incarceration, unspeakable tragedies. And yet, he was still standing, still fighting the good fight. But it wasn't until Peter told me what he told me, in reference to the likening of his father and brother to the famous Indian Chiefs that it struck me just how "in tune" my paintings really were. And, as I got to know John Junior better over the course of bringing his painting to life for his *Shadow of my Father* book, I came to understand why Peter said what he said.

After researching further, I found out that in his final years, Chief Joseph spoke eloquently against the injustices of U.S. Government policies and racial discrimination against Indigenous peoples and he held out hope that America's promise of freedom and equality would one day be fulfilled for Native Americans.

John's fight was also against the injustices he'd faced against our own U.S. Government, and against the *Federal Bureau of Prisons*. Little did I know, I'd end up doing a big painting unveiling one year after the making of this epic painting, December 27, 2015, just two days after Christmas.

Lisa and I drove into the City from my father-in-law's house to meet John in Tribeca at *Da Mikele*, another restaurant his longtime friend and lawyer Tony D'Aiuto is also part-owner of. Along with John Gotti Junior was his son, also named John, Jr., (he's a highly celebrated MMA fighter), John's lawyer Charlie Carnesi, author Peter Lance (who wrote the foreword for John Junior's book), John's younger brother Peter Gotti and sister Angel.

As John began opening his gift wrapped painting I had framed for him prior to driving up over the holidays, Peter also opened up a charcoal drawing I did for him of he and his iconic father. Angel supplied me with the photograph of them to work from months prior. And then, just as they both began tearing open their gifts, actor Mickey Rourke, of all people—one of my idols growing up—shows up! He even joined us for a group photo and some great conversation between John and me at the bar.

It's funny, I always loved Mickey Rourke as an actor, and since I brought several hand-signed prints of John's *Shadow of my Father* painting with me for John, Angel, and Peter to pass out to family members when they got back home as Christmas presents, I decided to give one to Mickey Rourke too. While I would have loved getting his autograph, being he was one of my idols, the funny part came when he said, "Your signature's on this, right?" He wanted mine. He also got John to sign it. He'd go on to tell me how John Gotti, Sr. saved his ass once when he lost his temper and beat up on a made Genovese soldier.

"That's the Chief right there," he smiled to me, tapping on John Gotti, Sr.'s image in the print I just gave him, and then he patted me on my stomach and headed outside to grab a cigarette before re-joining his dinner party.

Now, it's hardly customary to have a painting be the cover for a book, especially one's memoir. So, in case you're still wondering "Why a painting?" for this book cover, it turns out it was for a couple of reasons. First, John said everyone was advising him to go with a photo for the book cover. There was this one photograph of him holding an umbrella for his iconic father as he entered a waiting car that was a possible cover image. Then there was one of his Dad standing by his car as John Junior was being dropped off at Military School as a younger boy. But John was defiant about using a photograph for the cover.

"C'mon John, everyone uses a photo for a book cover," his lawyers and close advisors reminded him.

But, John shot back with, "I dare to be different!"

He wanted something so unique, so mesmerizing that it would not only capture the relationship between him and his father that no singular photograph could accurately capture but one that would weave its own tale through the work of art itself.

Secondly, he also felt that the photos that made it into the final list of possible choices didn't say all that needed to be said about what the relationship between him and his father was truly about.

So, we talked some more and he agreed to send me some photographs of his father, in addition to photographs of himself that nobody else had. Personal family photographs that I thought that would capture their personalities in action and make a more original cover. But, he also freely admitted that he really didn't know what he wanted the cover to look like—just that he'd "know it when he saw it."

Meaning—it was up to me to decipher this code and present him with a winner.

This was something I'd been training for my entire life though. I always figured it out and knew I would eventually with this one too. After all, I had painted many pictures of his iconic father, John Gotti, Sr. dating back to the early 90s, some of which John's sister Angel owned, so I was already familiar with painting him and felt confident in my ability to do so.

I also understood their plight, having been through what I'd been through in my own life, and given the fact that it was simply something in my blood too, having a relative who was at the center of what is still, to this day, the longest gangland double murder trial in the history of the State of New Jersey, I could inject some authenticity into the piece that nobody else could but me. I could essentially practice what I was preaching to all those other artists and student artists of mine out there, which was "to draw that line from my life to my art that is straight and clear".

The interesting thing about this particular job was that it felt like it had been over two decades in the making. Did I literally "draw Gotti", and all of the other colorful characters into my life by "literally drawing them"? These are the kinds of questions that randomly encircle my head as I begin getting into the zone as I begin my process of painting. One never knows the real answer. All I can see is how things were coming full circle.

So, it began—the process behind my painting of John Gotti for his book, *Shadow of my Father*.

The first thing I do when coming up with an idea for a painting, beyond talking with everyone involved, like John and his brother Peter, is to hit my sketchbook and journal out initial ideas. At first, I came up with this sketch of his father in the foreground with John Junior in the background and a flat New York City skyline behind them as a silhouette. Then, I did my research on the places where John spent most of his time. At his home in Howard Beach. At *the Bergin Hunt and Fish Club* in Ozone Park. At *the Ravenite* in Manhattan.

This made me reflect on how every time I'd drive back to Lyndhurst ever since 9/11 how the skyline just didn't look the same anymore. Even with the new "Freedom Towers" that were erected to replace the iconic Twin Towers at 1 World Trade Center that everyone born prior to 9/11 freely associated with New York City. *It still wasn't the same.*

This made me think of just how much the city actually changed since John Gotti was sent to prison for life, prior to 9/11.

I wondered if the Twin Towers would still be there if John Gotti wasn't sent away. If the U.S. government exhausted the same resources towards actually keeping active surveillance on terrorists instead of making careers for themselves on the Gotti name, which certainly created more opportunity for advancement in the careers of the likes of the Giuliani's of the world. My wife, Lisa, and I talked about this as I was bouncing ideas back and forth off her for John Junior's painting. She's always been my best critic because she's brutally honest.

Lisa also understands *"the life"*.

It was then that I decided to return to my roots. Return to the first *John Gotti, America* painting that I did as a response piece to how I felt after he was convicted. The painting shows his face in profile smiling at left above lower Manhattan with the Statue of Liberty at right, the American Flag blowing in the background as it fades into the colors of the Italian flag in red, white and green in the top right corner of the painting. I incorporated subway lines throughout the piece too, mapping his travels underground as a symbolic tribute to a "hoodlum's hoodlum" who was definitely a "street boss" as opposed to a white collar criminal.

This gave me the idea to incorporate them in more detail for Junior's painting—but as actual bloodlines that went from the City up and into John, Sr.'s necktie, which I created as the pattern of our American Flag—*Red, White, and Blue*.

This brought me back to my *Ticket to Ride* paintings, with each painting bearing a map pasted into it, from New York City Subway maps to New Jersey Transit maps, serving as clues to locations behind possible crimes, from one painting to the next, eventually leading you from the streets of Manhattan into the marshes of the Meadowlands in North Jersey.

I incorporated this same "mapping technique" into Dominic Capone's painting back in 2013. I'd do this again in my *Carnevale* painting series and again in my two recent 2016 *Bonnie & Clyde* paintings for a client in North Jersey.

I even used myself and Kelly Carroll, a Scholastic Art award-winning photographer as a model to help represent the infamous couple over the backdrop of the New York City skyline.

I'd do this again in late 2016 with a two-panel painting entitled, *John Gotti—REBEL*, created for Peter's son, Johnny Gotti for his *REBEL INK* Tattoo Parlor. This was then when it really hit me, though while painting John's *Shadow of my Father* painting.

It's the thing that most artists are always seeking to find like it's the Holy Grail—when you recognize the sea you're actually swimming in. When you recognize "your own signature style". This was mine. The mapping. The narrative elements. The realism. All combined together as one unique *signature style.*

It was also then when I told my wife, "I know I need to make this painting as realistic as possible since it's not just any painting, but I also need it to be 'one of mine' if that makes sense? Only something I'd do. Embed things into the work that would immediately cause anyone who looks at it to say—*that's a Michael Bell painting.* No doubt about it!"

So, I went back to the drawing board, scrapped the early flatter New York City skyline idea and returned to that early *Gotti, America* painting for inspiration, only this time around, with my skills peaked, it would become a more hyper-realistic rendition of the piece with both father and son. I created the City from a more interesting three-dimensional vantage point as opposed to a flat skyline view and painted both John Gotti, Sr. and Junior as "colossuses over Manhattan", as described by one New York Daily News reporter, emerging from the very city buildings that they spent their life walking and earning on below.

To incorporate the element of "a shadow" to reference the title, and to further drive that point home, I placed John Junior behind his father at left with a shadow of the top of the Empire State Building hitting his body and neckline. I even brought back the Twin Towers at the far right of the painting in the distance to make commentary on the fact the City totally changed since Gotti was put away. One last little fun fact that John Junior doesn't even know—the tie I used as a reference for John Junior's was *my own.*

I chose this one thing to hide into the piece as a small little secret "just for me". I didn't want it to be a tie he wore through his own trials. I wanted to bring him some new energy. I also chose a green tie I owned because I felt green would be a great symbol for many, many things that could be read into the work, and the direction of the stripes on the tie I purposely angled the way I did in order to help enhance the design element of moving the viewer's eye around the piece. Everything in the painting is there for a specific reason. Right down to the way Gotti, Sr. has his hand inside his coat jacket, as if to be reaching in to draw a gun. Like he still, even in death, has something up his sleeve, *ever confident, ever prevailing*.

And so, the painting progressed. I worked through the night. *And into the next night*. Peter and John continued to check in on me with the familiar pattern of conversations that went like this, "Man, that flu is a nasty bitch! Call you again in a half hour . . ."

They showed no mercy.

Tirelessly, I painted for the next few nights, working hard to complete it not just in record time, but in time for me to actually be able to enjoy Christmas with my family.

It wasn't without some bumps in the road, but I was in the zone and it was happening effortlessly for the most part once the intricate details of the City were finally completed. Then I started working on the really fun stuff, which were the faces of both Gotti, Sr. and Junior.

I love rendering faces. Portraits are my specialty and I knew I could get their expressions just right to capture the moment for the cover painting. It's the most intimate and intricate part of a work that needs to be done just right. One brushstroke too long and a smile becomes a grimace. A look of confidence becomes suspicion. Anything can change with one shadow too large or too small, one marking too dark or too light.

This was my realm, though.

And I always know when a painting's done. *When it's just right*. That's instinctual for me. Always has been. I don't need anyone to tell me. It's when I become the audience.

I was also excited to share my progress, which I would, shortly after Christmas. As it turned out, the flu ripped through the rest of my family, first with my son catching it. We had to take him to the E.R. the day after Christmas. And then Lisa caught it from him after that.

The next night, Peter Gotti called me again and told me a story . . .

It started off funny enough with, "Jesus Mike, you sound worse than you did the last time I talked to you."

I laughed and jabbed back with, "Well you guys should stop calling me every hour on the hour then!"

Peter and I had a good laugh about him and John calling me constantly for updates. Partly they were just excited. I also imagined John probably didn't know what to expect out of me with the painting, but they were both encouraging me nevertheless, making sure I felt as though they had all the confidence in the world in me. And, just four days after Christmas, I was finished with John Gotti's masterpiece.

DECEMBER 29, 2014

"Mike, you way waaaaaay outdid any expectations. To me, this is your best work," exclaimed Peter. "We are at a table with five people and they all feel the same. Mike, I can't thank you enough. John will call himself tomorrow."

That very next day I was out at dinner with my wife at a *Houlihan's* restaurant in Maryland when John called. I quickly hustled outside so I could talk and also hear John's voice over the loud backdrop of the bar nearby the front lobby. Once I got outside I could hear the sounds of clapping fill the background.

"Michael—that's the sound of APPLAUSE," John yelled.

I could hear the smile in his voice.

"That's the sound of—YOU NAILED IT! *Beautiful job!*" John went further to exclaim. "I honestly didn't know what to expect when you said you finished it but it's unbelievable. I'm here with a room full of guys who all said 'You gotta go with a photo for the cover.' Now they're all saying—'John, you gotta go with *the painting* for the cover!' You absolutely outdid yourself. I'll be in touch again real soon."

With that, I breathed in a triumphant sigh of relief. It was such a satisfying feeling to even outdo John and his family's initial expectations and I quickly headed back inside the restaurant to share the news with Lisa and enjoy a few drinks and dinner.

My painting would go on to make the cover of the New York Daily News with a huge spread on Junior's release of his new book *Shadow of my Father* which was now everywhere. The headline read: "My Secret Life with Gotti."

This was fitting. It felt like this could have been directly pertaining to my life with John as well. In February, Peter and I talked about this journey—and about the past. He also shared with me something I never knew . . .

FEBRUARY 25, 2015

"Mike," Peter said, "I'm sending you a text. Let me know if you remember this?"

Peter texted me the picture of a letter I wrote to his iconic father while he was in prison for nearly two decades prior.

"Holy shit you still have that letter?" I couldn't believe it. "Talk about reminiscing."

"We save everything, but what was most impressive is the fact that *my father saved it*," Peter explained.

"That means a lot. I appreciate you sharing that with me. I've been in your corner for decades, my friend," I said.

"It was among his belongings that he mailed home to us just before he turned terminal, it was sent home from Marion, a lot of years ago," Peter recalls.

"That's beautiful brother. Simply beautiful," I said.

"Hey Mike, if you ever have moments like we all do, know that in this corner we appreciate anything and everything that comes from genuine people, and you are genuine."

"Thank you, Peter that means a lot. And I always will be. Always in your corner. I've had my moments too."

This little moment between Peter and I capped off a journey that came full circle, and one that definitely drew a line from my life to my art that was straight and clear. I looked up to his father, like most people did, because of his Robinhood-like ways, defying the Government, defying whatever he needed to defy in order to always live for exactly what he stood for.

Never wavering.

Not against any circumstances, no matter how horrific or deplorable. Never showing weakness. Never giving in.

These are the things John Gotti stood for to me.

It wasn't about his criminal activity or all the stuff the tabloids glamorize. While he was a gangster, for sure, and the way he dressed and carried himself definitely gave off a certain allure, for me, it was the fact that he lived his life the way he wanted to live it no matter what the cost. Always projecting an undiminished display of strength, no matter what the circumstances were. This is what I admired about him the most.

I saw these traits exemplified in both his sons, John Junior and Peter. It was the way they all carried themselves—*like winners*. It was also the way they treated me, my wife and my son—like members of their own family, with such class and warmth.

So, while I knew my painting skills, and the fact that I had painted their father many times before was one of the reasons for going with me for this cover art commission, what I didn't realize until Peter shared that text message with me was *that other reason*.

Peter explained to me how his father was only allowed to keep a few things in his cell when he was declared terminal with cancer. One of those things he kept, to my surprise—*was my letter*. This was that "other reason" Peter later confessed to me as to why their family decided they had to go with me for John's book cover painting. It was this connection we all shared. *This bond.*

As for the letter I wrote to their father in prison—I'd share it with you, but I feel some things should stay private, out of respect for the family. It's the way John, Sr. would've wanted it. So that's how I'll leave it. *Between us . . . between me and his family.*

FIFTY-THREE

MIRRORS

April 21, 2016 was the night of our 19th annual ArtQuest at Southern High. It was also a night that would cap off an incredible career for Sienna Broglie, who joined the legends of all former "Best of Show" winners she's looked up to over the course of her own remarkable career. Sienna's was a journey that first began as a student artist of mine in the Gifted and Talented Program back in 7th grade. This is a girl I literally got to watch grow up. She went on to earn some of the most prestigious awards in the nation, from Scholastic Art National Medals, to the nation's NAEA Rising Star. She scored perfect scores on her AP Studio Art exams junior and senior year, and earned close to a half a million in scholarship offers that spring.

A few states away, that very same night at Gallery 130 on the campus of Ole Miss, a former 2012 student of mine from Tommy Taylor's class, Paige Shryock, was exhibiting her artwork for her senior BFA Thesis show. Paige asked me to collaborate with her on a piece for this exhibition, which became an engaging showing of her photographs, mixed with several multi-media voiceovers you could listen to through headsets below certain works.

The collaboration Paige and I worked on was entitled, *Mirrors, Everlasting Dualities*. She went on to explain the concept behind her show to me:

"Throughout our lives, people, conversations, and events leave a mark on us eternally. As time passes, we hold on to these little moments with emotions that range from passion, uneasiness, tension, grief, resentment, and nostalgia. Three distinct relationships are featured in this exhibition conveying romantic, family, and the relationship we have with one's self. Using these three categories, I investigated the ways in which relationships ultimately shape our identities and who we become.

Each image in this exhibition is created using self-portraits in varied domestic and non-domestic locations while paired with an ordinary representative object. Through the use of self-portraiture, I present the complicated relationship that one has with themselves and individuals in their lives. The text is sourced from anonymous digital submissions and then embedded on the body to create tattoos which illustrate the permanent effect that relationships have on us. By using both black and white and color imagery the photographs depict the conflict between new and old memories. In addition to imagery, there is an audio component created from these digital submissions that allow viewers to feel completely emerged emotionally and physically into the individual personal stories presented.

Everlasting Dualities is a narrative about that struggle between holding on and letting go of the past." – *Paige Shryock*

AS I SAT HERE WRITING OUT the last chapters of this book, I realized just how much this was not only about my own narrative, but also my own personal struggle between holding on and letting go of my past.

You see, as I was writing this chapter, it was July 30th, exactly one year to the day my best friend Louie and I said goodbye to Angelina, his eleven-year-old daughter, who passed away at 10:08 P.M. this very evening one year ago.

As I finished this chapter, I toasted her memory and then spent the rest of the evening with our son watching the fights.

My everlasting dualities continued.

Paulie Malignaggi was fighting on TV. He is a kid originally born in Italy fighting now out of Bensonhurst, a tough Italian neighborhood in Brooklyn, NY. Interestingly enough, this may also be his very last fight. It was followed up by a Carl Frampton main event. Frampton's kid from Belfast, in Northern Ireland where my father grew up, who was trying to make history by becoming the first Northern Ireland fighter to win world titles in two weight divisions. More *everlasting dualities.*

The day began as I was awakened by a string of group text messages, initiated by Louie, thanking me for my support of Angelina and for sticking by her side in her final days, just one year ago. For me, it was ten days I'll never forget.

It was also just over one year since our son's Autism diagnosis. A lot has changed in a year. We've fought, in and out of the ring, alongside him. Through his battles at school, battles at home, battles with friendships and learning his place in the world. We even battle learning our place in his.

I texted Louie back with: "I love you, Louie. Today I finished a 480-some page book about my art and life, in the studio, and in and out of the classroom. I reflected on all our years together too and wrote about them, like the time we got stuck in the mud when it rained and we stayed up all night just talking through the downpour back in my college years.

I wrote about Angelina too and what those ten days were like at the hospital, along with the miracles we witnessed there letting us know there is an afterlife. I know your Dad is there enjoying his time spent there with her.

I know you'll never get over this. Just know—neither will I, and neither will a lot of people whose lives she changed through what she battled through. Know she will never be forgotten, nor will those lottery tickets we bought with the fateful number 10-08 from those receipts that ended up being more prophetic than we knew. I love you and I'm with you. Your brother always, *Michael.*"

I THINK OF THIS BOOK as the ultimate collaboration, so it's fitting that I'm coming to the end of my book with collaboration between Paige and me. For my part of the collaboration, I sent Paige a poem that I wrote for the start of the 2015—2016 school year. This poem served as a prompt for my classes on day one, asking them to answer, "When I look in the mirror I see . . ."

This was an alternative means to get to know my kids on day one, other than playing "If you really knew me you would know". For this game, my students had to write about what they saw in the mirror, while also responding to the prompt with a visual for homework as a "one-night project".

One-night projects were something Paige was also familiar with, having studied under me her senior year in high school. I was always trying new ideas. And, towards the end of her year, after having passed her AP 2D Photography Portfolio with flying colors, after winning the Maryland State Federation of Women's Club contest with an amazing self-portrait, and after ArtQuest was all over, Paige decided to undertake a challenge I posed to my classes every year. It was one last challenge to go above and beyond in order to discover something new, even when it doesn't matter. I call this project "24".

For twenty-four hours you try and stay up for as long as you can and document your life, through photographs, drawings, writing, screen captures of text messages, collecting evidence of what you ate from food wrappers, receipts, and stuff like that. Paige documented everything right down to brushing her teeth before finally crashing. She also discovered something interesting in the form of diptychs after sifting through all the evidence of her twenty-four hours "art-ing". This is something I noticed with her work for her BFA Thesis: *Everlasting Dualities*.

For her Thesis Show I sent her an .mp3 clip of my voice reading her my poem, which she created a self-portrait based off of, featuring her staring into a shattered mirror, from a bird's eye view peering down on her from above.

She inter-mixed her own voiceover with mine, reading lines from my poem along with me as gallery-goers tuned in via the privacy of the various headsets stationed nearby her narrative photographs on display. This show would also close out Paige's chapter on a stellar college career. My poem reads:

MIRRORS
By Michael Bell
"When I look into the mirror I see
not what the rest of the world thinks I would be.
Broken in fragments, floating in seas
of grasses and marshes where crime scenes lead.
Broken, shattered fragments of birthday cards
sealed for my sister, each year to discard.

Locked closets, closed drawers,
rites of passage, cuts, and lures . . .
Casting lines, waging wars,
paddling on without oars . . .
To your shores, where I find you
staring into the broken glass
A shattered oval, shards surround you
at your feet, the naked grass.
My eyes drift to the departing ship
Your image fades into its last . . .

When I look in the mirror you think I would see
all the tremendous success that appears around me.
My journey to fame and making a name,
but it's hurricanes and rain, tornadoes and trains.
Darkness and shadows, destruction I see,
and scars to remind me who I was born to be.
But that's not what you will see . . ."

PAIGE SHRYOCK
CLASS OF 2012

"Everyone knows the artist Michael Bell as the award-winning, celebrity painting star that he is. While I know and love these identities like everyone, Michael Bell 'the Educator' will always be my favorite.

Growing up with a teacher mother, from an early age I saw the dedication that many overlooked when thinking of the profession of education. Through the years I saw that being a teacher meant educating your students in every part of their life and ultimately being the hope and guidance they may not be receiving at home.

While I knew this, this idea became a part of me when I was a senior in high school. Mr. Bell taught me an infinite amount of life lessons in the short time I was in his class. After expressing to him my extreme interest in photography upon showing the few works I did have, Mr. Bell allowed me to do an independent study with him in order to fit in Advance Placement Photography into my busy senior year schedule. This would be the first of many times Mr. Bell believed in me more than I believed in myself.

I can still remember the encouragement he gave me after my first critique. With overwhelming feelings, literally shaking from the nerves of showing dark depictions of the internal struggles seventeen-year-old me was experiencing, Mr. Bell reassured me that my photograph was incredible and to take negative and positive criticism the same. Throughout my time with Mr. Bell, I worried about opinions of me for my subject for being too emotional heavy. Mr. Bell encouraged me to continue producing photographs in this style because if it was therapeutic for me, someone else would also find peace in my message.

This fear of creating from my inner voice was something Mr. Bell awakened from me. I was always asked how I could push my concept further, to the point where I would exceed my own standards for myself. Through encouraging this experimentation in my work, I didn't see it then, but Mr. Bell was helping me gain the confidence to stand on my own two feet, creating a voice for myself as an artist.

Being the first child in my family to go to college, Mr. Bell helped me every step of the way. Whether it was guidance on where to apply, last minute recommendation letters, or helping me build a strong portfolio for scholarship interviews, Mr. Bell helped genuinely without hesitation. When I was stuck between my top college choices, Mr. Bell encouraged me to pick the option that terrified me the most.

Truly being the most petrifying decision of my life, I look back with such gratitude for Mr. Bell. I know I wouldn't be the person I am if it wasn't for his impact on my life. As I prepare my thesis exhibition in Imaging Arts at the University of Mississippi, I think back to the start of my journey when I was just a student at Southern High School 'interested' in photography.

I think about life after college and I know I eventually want to teach young adults who have a passion for art but don't know exactly how to express it. While I will hold that position of mentor, I want to continue to build myself as an artist in front of my students.

Seeing Mr. Bell work on his narrative series works was the biggest inspiration to me. I learned the arts can be more than just a hobby to those who truly have the hard work, dedication, and passion. I've come a long way from the timid, insecure girl I was when I asked for the opportunity to be a student of his, but I can only thank Mr. Bell for inspiring me to be the confident, innovative artist I grow to be more like every day."

FIFTY-FOUR

THE TRIANGLE OF SUCCESS

The only success I've ever known has been built from the ground up, like any dynamic pyramid. My crew of five 2014 National Medalists built their success on the heels of success stories like Paige Shryock and the many others that came before them. And, while this 2014 crew became my only crew prior to writing this that got to take a large field trip to Carnegie Hall, our success with Scholastic Art continued, with eighty-four Region-At-Large winners in 2015 and another National Medalist in painter Sienna Broglie. In 2016, our kids rocked it again with a whopping one hundred fourteen Region-At-Large winners. I also had two more National Medalists in senior photographer Nicholas Orsini and sophomore painter Caterina Grandi (another future National Art Honor Society Officer and GT student).

Among the one hundred fourteen Region-at-Large winners emerged two other incredible photographers, Alex Talbott and Kelly Carroll. They both overcame an incredible amount of adversity to achieve the kind of success they experienced as seniors. Both, interestingly enough, also submitted work to Scholastic Art as juniors the previous year in 2015.

Both came up short of winning anything—*not even an Honorable Mention*. Their senior year, I urged them to step back up to the plate and submit again for the 2016 competition. Both were reluctant but I knew their work was strong. They both took risks within the content of their work, and they both were artists not afraid to *go there*—Alex with her risqué self-portraits that tackled issues surrounding teen rebellion, alcoholism, and teen sexuality. Kelly tackled an even more personal world of loss which began with an amazing self-portrait she started the year with as a response to my prompt, "When I look in the mirror I see . . ."

Alex would go on to be awarded two Gold Keys, 2 Silver Keys, and four Honorable Mentions. Kelly Carroll would go on to be awarded 3 Gold Keys, 5 Silver Keys, and 3 Honorable Mentions as she pushed the envelope and the heartstrings of emotion with her work. Kelly would also become the artist to create the commemorative photograph for our school's Senior Awards Night and for the Graduation Program Cover for the class of 2016.

These are all opportunities I made available to Kelly and helped her to achieve. She's grown tremendously as a photographer and as an incredible young woman over the past couple of years. But, unless you really pried, you'd never know her story.

Now, a few years back, our Administration began doing something called "walk-throughs". While they used to just "stop by" my room to shoot the shit with me because "they knew me", our new crop of administrators seemed to need to document everything they did, right down to stopping by your room. These "walk-throughs" typically lasted about five to ten minutes, and there wasn't much talking. Clipboards and notetaking mostly, on a sheet developed as a "checklist" to help them document what they see taking place in the classroom.

Once the walk-through is complete, they exit, slip this checklist in your mailbox documenting that they stopped by your room, sharing what they observed or did not observe (*yes, there's a box for that too*), along with any feedback they may feel is necessary to provide for you.

Back in the day, and I'm not even talking *that far back*, our administration knew, with as many years of experience that I had at Southern High, there was great value in stopping by and talking with a guy like me. They also actually enjoyed getting "the skinny" from my perspective on what was happening in our building, and back then, those administrators seemed to like getting to know the kids. *But times were still a-changin'.*

These days, administrators were being shuffled from school to school so often there weren't too many left that really even knew me anymore, let alone our Department, unless they read the newspaper, since we were making headlines all the time. This was on purpose, of course—all carefully orchestrated by *yours truly* by reaching out to contacts I've developed in the media over many, many years. Whenever something exciting was going on in our Department or with our teachers or kids, I'd let them know about it. I wanted to keep our South County community "in the know" too and keep a strong presence out there, so we'd never become a Department that was expendable. And let me tell you, if you're not tooting your Department's horn out there or letting people know what you're doing, *they're never gonna know*. Don't rely on your district or supervisors to be your PR train. Get behind the wheel yourself and become your own best Public Relations Department. It's also a very integral part of becoming indispensable.

ONE FALL MORNING in October, long before the numerous Scholastic Awards Kelly and the others would win later that spring, our new Administration decided to do one of these "walk-throughs" with Alex and Kelly's AP 2D Photography class.

Now getting back to what I like to call "the Triangle of Success", it's about: *School—Home—Community*. When the triangle is connected it looks like this: The School communicates effectively with Home. Home trusts the School. The Community supports the child in other areas, whether it's through community centers, at church, by whatever means.

Everybody is essentially working to surround the child at the center of this "triangle". But, what happens when the triangle is non-existent or broken? What happens when there's also no box to check to accurately portray what the educational process is supposed to look like? *I'm about to show you . . .*

Take Kelly Carroll, for instance. Here's a girl that if you saw her amazingly cinematic photographs taken primarily of herself (as narrative self-portraits), she looks confident, powerful, in total control in almost every one of them.

In one future Scholastic Art award-winning photograph, she's gazing off into the distance in the middle of the forest surrounded by trees in a scene that could be snatched right out of a Hollywood big budget film. She's wearing a long trench coat with a huge fur collar. She's standing with both hands in her pockets, long hair flowing in the breeze of what appears to be a crisp winter day, just before dusk. The photograph is softly filtered in bluish tints. It looks like it's just about to snow, and everything is very blue-ish in tone, like the calm before the storm.

And then there's another shot of Kelly in her bedroom, which looks more like a college dorm room, on purpose in order to contribute toward the meaning behind the scene, with a large purple and gold tapestry hanging behind her head, a lava lamp pulsating on a nightstand nearby. As she sits up in bed, wearing just a deep purple Yale sweatshirt, bare legs hanging outside the sheets and blankets she stares intensely at you, the viewer, while answering an old fashioned black rotary telephone.

"Who's on the other end?" it makes you wonder. *I knew.*

I also knew Kelly was in the midst of contemplating a very uncertain future at this point in her life, and a very unclear path as to how she would even make it through the school year, let alone make it into college.

You see, nowadays our children grow up in a world where adulthood is not synonymous with age. More often it's circumstances far beyond our control that afford us the title of reaching "adulthood". Sometimes it all happens far too young.

It did for me.

And then, in some of the most emotional photographs I've ever seen Kelly take. In the first one she's standing in the empty kitchen of an abandoned house. She shot it in black and white, standing in silhouette, staring at the dirt spread throughout the floor, the appliances all gone, ripped out . . . *the place—gutted.*

In a second photograph, presented as a diptych, Kelly is balled up on the floor of a deserted bathroom, as a silhouette with the last light from the sunset filtering through a nearby window just beyond where she's sitting for what could have been hours, given the passage of time represented by the setting sun. She clutched onto both knees, in a near fetal position, her head titled back in repose, her expression—powerfully emotional. *But why?*

Well, what our current Administration did not know about Kelly when they stopped by my room one October morning for a five to ten-minute "walk-through" was *Kelly's story.*

I could tell they were waiting as patiently as they could with their clipboard and checklist for my class to start. Waiting for something to happen. *Anything.* Yet, nothing was. I hadn't delivered any "measurable outcomes" or given any "warm ups". My kids were just sitting there, taking my cue from a brief glance over at them not to disrupt me as I sat down across the room right next to Kelly, who had her head planted inside her folded arms on her desk. At a glance, it could have been interpreted by most as "just a tired kid still half-asleep this early in the morning".

But this felt different.

Eventually, Alex Talbott and some of the other kids proceeded to disperse over to their respective computer stations to begin some photo manipulations while they, too, waited for me to "officially get the class started".

While I didn't know exactly what was wrong with Kelly yet, I knew today she seemed different. Something just felt "off" about her and I couldn't bring myself to start the class until I figured out why. Despite her reassuring me, "I'm fine Mr. Bell, really, I'm good," and notwithstanding the pink elephant in the room in the form of our Administration waiting for me to actually teach something *I stayed there with her.*

I could tell Administration was getting anxious, especially after five minutes ticked by, but for whatever reason, call it paternal instincts or me just having a sixth sense when it came to all of my kids—*I knew Kelly*, and her head still planted down on that desk was for more than just "I'm tired".

So, I continued prodding her gently, at this point not giving a shit whether our Administration decided to stay or go, or whether they'd check this box or that one on my walk-through.

My goal was to make Kelly comfortable enough to tell me what was really going on. Then class could begin.

It's all I cared about.

Now, let me preface this by saying Kelly's always been a model student. She's highly intelligent and extremely consistent when it came to completing all of her assignments on time, no matter what class it was. And while this was the first period of the day, and she's had a day or two here and there where she had been tired from working late the night before and wanted to put her head down, today seemed different to me.

And, while I could've easily pawned this all off as "she's just tired", and covered my ass with Administration and started the class, for some reason this felt more important—getting to the bottom of what my gut was telling me.

And the clock was still ticking . . .

Ten minutes passed.

On her computer screen in the bottom right corner, it read 7:27 A.M., 10/13/2015. It was a Tuesday, October 13th, a date I'd soon learn was the reason for her silence.

She finally lifted her head up and quietly said to me, "Today's the two-year anniversary of both my parents being killed."

I would later stop by Administration to explain the entire magnitude of the situation from that morning. I explained why I didn't start class and what was really going on with Kelly. I also alerted our Guidance Department so they could let Kelly's other teachers know what the situation was today, to help keep an eye on her, make sure she was okay. Did I have to do any of this? *Of course not.* But, for me, going the extra mile is all that matters.

While staring at the photograph of Kelly standing in the kitchen of that abandoned house, and of her balled-up on that cold, tiled empty bathroom floor, I realized—*that was her home.* Before her parents were killed tragically in a car accident this was where she lived. She broke back in to take these photographs, to document a new portrait of her world. *What once was. What always will be.* A portrait of a void that will never be filled in her heart. This was how Kelly was beginning to experience every October 13th, at least it was until I stepped in, on the second anniversary of her parent's death in a tragic accident.

What's supposed to matter most in education, above all else, is our kids. Not "checking a box". Having survived, thrived even, through ten different administrations in my career at Southern, every couple years began feeling like you had to re-audition for a role you already earned . . . over and over again. Re-proving your Department's worth. Never resting on your laurels. Never allowing yourself, or members of your department to become expendable. Always finding ways to become a valuable asset . . . all that sort of stuff. But when it came to days like today with Kelly, she was all that mattered to me—making her day a little better. Helping her, even when she tried hiding the fact that she needed my help as best she could.

LATER THAT FALL, our new principal sat in on one of my classes in action for an entire class period to formally observe me. That was when I believe it all clicked for him. He finally understood *why* I get the kind of results I do.

"I get it," he said to me, in our Post-Observation meeting. "There's no statistic or data point that could accurately paint the kind of picture in words that could describe *the kind of magic* I truly felt while observing your class in action. It's not something I can put a number on. It was just something I felt as I observed. I get it now."

I was glad he finally felt what all our kids feel while in my studio on any given day. It was a great moment we shared, between this new principal and me. It was great of him to drop his guard and share that with me too. I appreciated him more for that than I'm sure he'll ever know. While he and I didn't always see eye to eye, he was a genuinely good guy, and I was glad he got to experience seeing my class in action.

Bill Parcells, when coaching the New York Giants to the *Super Bowl* was once asked, "What's the one measurable quality you could give us that would define what makes players like a Lawrence Taylor and all those Hall-of-Fame types that you seem to keep producing year after year all have in common?"

His answer, "I'll tell you—the one thing they all have in common is that *immeasurable quality* that you can't put any kind of measure on. They all have that certain something that you don't know exactly what it is, but you just know it when you see it. That's what they all have in common!"

He wasn't being a smart-ass either, it's just reality. Some things you can't measure. Take my studio, for instance—*it has a pulse!* Anybody who's been in it will tell you the same. It looks and feels like there's some *serious fun* going on in there!

It's not something you could put a checklist to and replicate elsewhere because it's the relationships I've built with these kids and the stories surrounding the legacy of all those who came before them that makes our studio have that "immeasurable quality" that *makes champions*.

Our nation has to do better than this. After all, how do kids really learn? They've always learned best by being outdoors, in small groups, learning by doing—*by experiencing*.

And what do we do with our nation's children? Overload class sizes, force them to sit still for long periods of time, never go outside, stay in rooms—many of which don't even have windows, and we teach them how to be *compliant*.

Due to our son's Autism and ADHD, he physically can't sit still, or stay in one place for very long. Is it his fault if he can't be compliant in that way?

Do you think I want him to be in a class with a teacher that forces him to try to do things he's not physically capable of?

Am I "okay" with sitting back and watching other kids try and bully him because he's different while no one does anything about it? Don't you think I'd just as quickly take anyone to task looking to harm our son or diminish his pursuit of a quality education?

You bet your ass! *Anyone in our path.* But that's not what I want to waste my time and energy on.

What I really want is what *everyone truly wants*—for all teachers and administrators to truly care for their kids in immeasurable ways, like I do. To go above and beyond the call of duty. Build the kind of relationships that makes heroes emerge from the shadows and taps into the hidden talents lurking all around us. *Is that so much to ask?*

Do you think the current direction for education is going to do it for our nation's youth? I believe we need more *John Keating's, Jaime Escalante's, LouAnne Johnson's and Erin Gruwell's* in the world. I also believe you get what you pay for, and teachers deserve the kind of quality pay that encourages quality teacher retention and a reason for our youth to even want to go into this profession anymore in the first place.

As artists, I believe we also have to re-assess the direction of our artwork and our place in the world. My longtime hero in the art world, Eric Fischl asks, "What does art do that makes it necessary and special?"

Eric believes it opens us up to "connection, to intimacy and empathy. It gives us language and forms that penetrate into the unexpressed but felt realities of our lives."

He has always believed that art brings order to our chaos and makes us feel so not alone. I believe we need more *Eric Fischl's, more Chuck Close's, Sabrina Ward Harrison's, Dan Eldon's, David Leeson's and Journal Fodder Junkies* in the art world.

Now is the time.

And as Eric has said, "Give people what they need, not what they think they want, and not what the art market dictates."

SO, WHAT DID I DO with the information Kelly had given me that Tuesday morning on October 13th? After a considerable amount of one-on-one, I suggested that instead of every year allowing this particular date to become one she dreads, one that will paralyze her and depress her, why not make it a day of remembrance. A day of celebration—*not regret.*

"Why not figure out something to do as an annual tradition," I said to her, "something just for your parents."

I went on to tell her that I was sure they were looking down on her, that they are with her still, in spirit. I explained how when my Grandmother passed, as a child, she used to always take me into New York City around Thanksgiving every year. How we used to go to *Tavern on the Green* for lunch, even if she couldn't afford it. We spent the day together looking at the big city buildings, studying the architecture, or going to a museum, always stopping by *the Plaza* to see the portrait of Elouise.

I explained to Kelly, "This is what we ended up doing the year after my Grandmother passed, as our new annual family tradition. We'd visit my Grandparents in *Hillside Cemetery*, put a wreath on their grave, visit *Lyndhurst Pastry Shop* and then take our son Carmen into New York City the day before Thanksgiving to see the floats get inflated on the Upper West Side of Manhattan. We'd stay in the City for the night, in remembrance of my Grandma, Violet. A tribute, if you will, in her honor. So she can smile down and know we're thinking of her, doing something positive with all this pain we feel. A tradition maybe our son will carry on with his family long after we're gone. And you'll see the signs they're with you. For me, with my Grandma, *it was feathers.*"

Kelly smiled an understanding smile at me and said she would. Said she'd devote some time to thinking up something positive to do for her parents, and for herself, in remembrance. Do I know how the rest of Kelly's day would have gone had I not noticed the slightest little thing seeming off about her that morning? Had I cared more about covering the curriculum than I cared about whom I was actually teaching the curriculum too? *Who knows?*

Maybe her day would've gone on just fine. But maybe it would have been a disaster. The point is, I noticed because of the relationship I had established with her. *Because I care.* For me, Kelly was what was most important the morning I got my first walk-through from our new Administration. It's always been that way for me, though. I'm sharing this all with you in hopes it will become that way for you too. Later that day, as I was working on Kelly's recommendation letter for college, I received an e-mail from Kelly. It read:

> "Hey Mr. Bell,
> I really appreciate you taking the time to write me a recommendation letter. You have been there for me through my whole journey of getting back on my feet after my parents died and I feel like you are really the only teacher in the school that really understands who I am and what I have been through. If there's any teacher that knows who I am it's definitely you. I am so grateful to have you as a teacher, thank you. – *Kelly C.*"

That's what great teaching is really all about. It's not about data points and over-testing our youth. It's about getting to know your kids' stories. Whether you're a CEO getting to know your executives, a principal getting to know their teachers and students, a bus driver getting to know the kids on the bus, or an artist truly knowing and understanding their clientele . . .

A lot of problems are solved before they even happen simply because a positive relationship is in place. Eventually, the data everyone is so desperately worried about nowadays in order to validate their jobs will take care of itself. It will follow, trust me. *People*—that's what really matters. *First and foremost.*

It's about making emotional connections.

It's literally the difference between reading hundreds of love stories and actually falling in love. However, we, as humans, tend to repeat the familiar. This is the difficulty, as John Keating would tell you, "in maintaining your beliefs in the face of others."

This involves having the courage to swim against the stream, and not conform to society's idea of who you should be. When our "triangle for success" is connected, children are surrounded by the love and care they need to in order to become successful. When the triangle is disconnected: "Home blames the School—School blames the Home—and the Community (this could be your church, youth centers, etc.) . . . they blame everybody."

We have to re-connect everyone.

Rebuild trust between all three. It's the only way. So, right now, wherever you are in your career—know it's never too late to re-examine existing relationships (or non-existing ones) and change them for the better—forever.

And parents, you aren't off the hook either. Inspire your children to take control over the small piece of the pie they can control, which is usually a really small piece, and do something positive with that. When it comes to parenting, Reginal Clark put it pretty spot on back in 1983 when saying, "It is not family composition, but a parental disposition that makes the biggest difference in the achievement of our youngsters."

Now let's talk data, since it's become more and more prevalent and pervasive in the educational system, and since it's not going away, you need to know how to choose "the right kind of data" to inform your instruction. Notice I said, "inform instruction"—not *drive instruction*. I don't believe data should *drive anything.* I believe relationships should be the driver. Motivation and inspiration—those should be the passengers. But when it comes to stats, you have to start somewhere. *And it always starts with one.*

Whether it's helping a kid earn their first perfect score on an Advanced Placement Exam, or whether it's your first kid you help get into college, maybe for you as an artist it's finally landing that first gallery show. Whatever the case may be—*it always starts with one.*

Since taking over as Art Department Chair in 2008, we had a 46% increase in students taking AP Studio Art classes, a 60% increase in students taking AP Art History since Marlene took over teaching the course, and an increase in staffing from three to five full-time art teachers over just a couple short years of hard work and promoting. Our student artists became not only rock star artists; they were also becoming our school's highest academic achievers, earning over ten million in scholarship offers the past five years alone.

Our Scholastic Award Winners grew from our 1st Scholastic Gold Key winner in Leigh Rogers in 2011 to six awards in 2012 to thirteen awards in 2013 to sixty-seven in 2014, eighty-four in 2015 and one hundred fourteen in 2016, in addition to three years producing back-to-back National Medalists and seven years back-to-back NAEA Rising Star Award Winners. Suddenly, as if overnight, the smallest school in our public school system, with just shy of 1,100 kids had the largest and most prestigious Art Department not just in our county or in the state, *but in the nation*.

In May of 2016, shortly before yet another graduation, I asked Kelly Carroll to dress up and attend the school's evening Senior Awards Ceremony. I told her the principal was going to honor her and ask her to come up on the stage to receive recognition for creating the Senior Awards Program and Graduation Program Cover Art. I was glad she agreed to do the photography for the cover art, and that she agreed to attend the ceremony. I secretly invited Kelly's sister, Katie, who I taught many years ago, and any extended family of Aunts and Uncles she wanted to bring.

After asking Kelly to come up on the stage to join Scholastic Art National Medalist Nicholas Orsini and National Rising Star Award Winner Sienna Broglie under the guise of being recognized for her "Cover Art Photography," I began sharing Kelly's story and her amazing list of accomplishments with the packed house in attendance that evening. It was a moment that left not one dry eye in the building, and one I hope Kelly will always remember *for the rest of her life . . .*

MICHAEL BELL
2016 SENIOR AWARDS SPEECH

"Kelly Carroll has had tremendous success in art this year, earning 11 Scholastic Art Regional Awards in Photography, including 3 Gold, 5 Silver and 3 Honorable Mentions. She's earned scholarships totaling: $168,000. She even created the cover art photograph for tonight's awards ceremony and for this year's Graduation Program Cover. But, beyond all this, Kelly is so special not just for her accolades, but for what she's had to go through to get where she is today. Her creativity comes with a lot of courage. The kind of courage I couldn't even put into words. So here it is, in Kelly's own words, from a very personal essay about her journey that she graciously shared with me. *Buckle up . . .*

'Childhood usually ends when someone celebrates their sweet sixteen, bar mitzvah or confirmation. My childhood ended as I walked down a cold hospital hallway, where my mother and father died within the time span of two months shortly before my sixteenth birthday. My life took a complete 360-degree turn in a direction that I didn't see coming. I had to adapt to something that I wasn't ready for—*adulthood.*

I didn't realize how strange the adult world works. I didn't realize how this tragedy would make me better but it did. I guess now more than ever I wanted to make my parents proud so I kept pushing myself and something wonderful came out of a tragedy—*my success.'*

And more of this success Kelly Carroll certainly shall see. Kelly has committed to attend Johnson and Wales in Providence."

FIFTY-FIVE

BECOME LEGENDARY

Each of us has a story to tell, and success is often created mentally first. The Olympic Games have always been a place that's often remembered for the faces that emerged into the spotlight from out of the crowd.

Much like the faces that emerged in the 2016 Olympic Games, it's *their stories* that made them legendary. The Mayor of Virginia Beach said of 2012 Olympic Star Gabby Douglas—"I can't help but admire someone so young and talented—someone who overcame so many challenges and yet kept up such a grueling training regimen."

Bob Bowman, lifelong trainer of Michael Phelps has said of him—"I've always tried to find ways to give him adversity and have him overcome it. The higher the level of pressure, the better Michael performs. As expectations rise, he becomes more relaxed. That's what makes him the greatest."

Usain Bolt, the famous Jamaican Olympian once said it best— "I don't want to just win. I want to give the kind of performance that makes you remember where you were when you saw it."

In the 2016 Olympic Games, Usain Bolt did just that, ending his historic career with a world-record setting performance and his 9th Olympic Gold Medal. "I've proven to the world I'm the greatest," said Bolt. "I can't prove anything else."

As for me, the thing I hear most from other people in my profession about me is always: "Michael Bell knows how to make people better than they are." And after another year filled with incredible highs and lows, I also felt as though I had nothing left to prove.

So, in the summer of 2016, I began contemplating my return to Southern for yet another year working for a public educational system I wasn't as passionate about or as trusting of anymore.

I felt like a castaway, lost at sea.

I even went on interviews for other higher paying leadership positions at the Board of Education, thinking that might be the way to go. After spending years in the trenches watching other colleagues with far less talent and experience rise to new heights in supervisory roles with much higher pay, why not me? I'm more qualified than anyone who could interview for most *any position.* No-one's done what I've done. But despite being one of the most highly decorated teachers in the history of my county and state, perhaps in the nation . . . *I was passed over.*

This became another incredible blessing in disguise, though, and the best thing that could have ever *not* happened for me. Then, in the midst of massive teacher turnover at Southern that went from half-a-dozen or so in 2015 to over a dozen in 2016, including three art teachers in my own department jumping ship, an interesting turn of events happened—our Principal was given a promotion, and I decided to stay at Southern. I ended the year hiring three exciting new art teachers: Mary Kate Bergh (former partner in crime with Joan Beckner from Southern Middle School, Emily Ragan (my 2016 student teaching intern), and Sam Peck.

MY FIRST WEEK BACK in the fall of 2016 with my twelfth new principal, an energized new team of three highly touted new art teachers, my longtime work companion Marlene Kramer and a renewed spirit, I decided to begin the year with what else . . .

A self-portrait and a story.

I decided to share Lilly Nugent's story with everyone. Lilly and I grew very close over her three years with me. She had loads of talent and lots of promise early in her high school career, and she was a very popular 2015 graduate that most of the kids knew.

Lilly also had a complicated and tumultuous relationship with her mother which I could relate to that severely impacted her school work in adverse ways. I showed my classes a picture of one of Lilly's early self-portraits that included Lilly's hand over her face in the foreground; Mom's pill bottles in the background in front of a faceless, pregnant mother holding a child amidst the chaos of a hand-written diary entry scrolling through the background.

I explained to the class how lucky I was that I took a photograph of this drawing when Lilly first completed it, because when Lilly's mother found it in her bedroom she wrote all over it and crumbled it up, ruining it with, "This is all about your mother, the one that ruined your life!"

Lilly ended up dropping AP Drawing with me during her senior year. It just all became too much for her. Despite her dropping the class I kept all of her unfinished paintings and drawings, and we still remain close to this day. On my desk the last day of school she placed this note:

LILLY NUGENT
CLASS OF 2015

"As I sit here holding an old photograph of my mother between my teeth I think of how much this used to be about her and I feel sick with defeat. I felt as though I was following a passion in which one is supposed to find themselves, only to realize I'd lose myself even more than I already had.

I can't stand that every day I might be disappointing you and the other people surrounding me as the vortex of time sucks more and more of the little artistry I have left in me. I can't stand that my whole life I've loved doodling on napkins and in the corner of my math papers, yet recently that empty space has terrified me.

I'm ashamed I let the insecurities I tried so desperately to work through in my art manifest and begin to cramp my own style. But the truth is I'm terribly lost in the pursuit of my own identity and the art I was trying to produce was for someone who had long found theirs. The fact is I have no idea if my sweet mother is to blame. I just know that I actually love the fact that my life hasn't been unbearably normal. I've spent this whole sector of my life acting as though those who encounter normalcy when they get home from school are *the lucky ones*. But I actually love my man-made insecurities and constant need to be liked by all whom I encounter. I love that I'm so horrified to disappoint that I just shut down completely. I can't bring myself to apologize though, because I may have never realized what I'm telling you now if all this hadn't happened.

I miss art.

I miss my ability to mirror myself on a blank page and love who I see. And that's the reason I've always loved art. I can never look in the mirror and love who I actually see there, but I can look at the four pencil lines in my first works and love who I see in my artwork.

And Mr. Bell, *I miss myself.*

I realized today as I opened my sketchbook just how much I actually wanted to *draw her again.* I can't remember the last time I felt that. I may just be caught up in the spirit of this journey coming to an end or I may have finally regained the passion I lacked throughout the year.

All I know is these words would never be pouring from me if it weren't for you. The fact that I know you hear that all the time says it all. I don't think I'll ever have the pleasure of meeting someone like you again. This experience wouldn't be possible anywhere else. I don't use the word blessed often, but I am blessed to have been a part of your life. Thank you for being one of the most selfless people I've ever met. Thank you for giving me hope and a sense of family when I felt I had none. I'm sorry this year didn't go as planned. Much love, and thank you."

– Lilly Nugent

Beneath this heartfelt letter was a beautiful self-portrait of Lilly done in pencil with the words, "P.S. – I promise to love art as long as we both shall live".

I held Lilly's drawing up to the class. They were amazed by the realism, by the hauntingly timeless way she was able to capture the essence of all she was at that moment in time through one incredible pencil drawing.

With Lilly's story and drawing as their inspiration, off the class went—to begin *their first self-portrait* of the new school year.

Off to become legendary . . .

As I reflected on all this while the class began working, I realized that one of the greatest fears we all have is just truly "being ourselves". Facing ourselves, and all we encounter in life head on. This is a lesson I want my kids to learn from being in here with me. And, while they may or may not all become the next "National NAEA Rising Star" or the next "Scholastic Art National Medalist" they're all so incredibly important to me in countless, immeasurable ways. To me, they all matter so much to me, more than they know.

I've come to realize just how often people will come and go in and out of our lives; how they will do things directly and indirectly to us. How the world can be so cruel. We can either waste our days reacting to it all or we can begin fighting for the next glorious chapters that lie directly in front of us. And, while we have little control over much in our lives, what we can control is *what we dream, what we create,* and in doing so, we can take fearless steps towards building *what we will become.*

And artists, like fighters—have no place to hide.

Much like boxers, musicians, writers, entrepreneurs—we're all cut from a similar cloth—we're all born from a similar temperament. *We're all individuals in the extreme.* You don't "make it" and suddenly feel like a rock star. The "rock star" is how you have to feel already. *That's creating success mentally first.*

And when the bell rings, we're also left alone to fight our way through each new work, through each new class and through each new year, having only ourselves to fall back on. There's no need to look outside ourselves to find the key to unlocking doorways to success. You simply have to look within, because each of us has a story to tell.

We have to keep finding ways to *draw that line from your life to your art that is straight and clear*. Be bold. Be brave. Be relentless. This is the kind of self-belief you have to have if you want to become legendary.

I realize now more than ever—the destination *is the journey*. It's not some magical place you get to and say, "That's it, I've finally made it!" It's about the precious moments we are living in right now. And like my dear friend Peter J. Gotti has told me time and time again, "Tomorrow is promised to no-one."

FIFTY-SIX

BATTLE IS MY COMPANION

As I completed this memoir exactly one year to the date of beginning them, it was now a few weeks before kicking off the 2016 - 2017 school year. It was also one week before my twentieth wedding anniversary on August 10th. That particular week I was also scheduled to drive up to New York City to unveil my new 4' X 16' two-panel, *John Gotti: REBEL* paintings for Peter Gotti's oldest son, Johnny.

Life felt good again.

I was back to painting. Boxing was going great for me and our son Carmen. Summer also helped ease some of the stress that comes along with raising a child battling Autism and ADHD while surviving a public school system that we're quickly learning is tragically ill-equipped with the kind of talent or the wherewithal to best service his needs.

I lined up two keynote addresses and workshops on *Visual Journaling* and *31 Nights* in Nashville, Tennessee, and Tucson, Arizona in October and November. While I was busy with all this, John and Peter Gotti were busy spending time this summer in Ohio on the movie set of *The Life and Death of John Gotti*, based on John's book that I painted the cover art for a year and a half ago.

It was a glorious time for everyone.

And then the bottom dropped out of everything, just two days before Peter was scheduled to return home to Queens to be at my painting unveiling for his eldest son Johnny at his *Rebel Ink Tattoo Parlor.* Johnny was ambushed and arrested in an unannounced raid on his father's home, and on Johnny's business.

According to Peter, their family's Howard Beach home was destroyed by the NYPD during the raid, using battering rams to break the house to pieces. It broke my heart to also hear how his seventy-four-year-old mother was manhandled and how his small children were terrorized during the raid when all law enforcement had to do was knock on the door and everyone would have quietly stepped aside. But that wouldn't have made any headlines. Apparently, it took a dozen cops inside the house and another dozen outside standing around doing nothing to make it look like something out of a movie scene for the press. Tragically enough, this was definitely not the Gotti's first rodeo with law enforcement, but it was the first time they were able to gain access to the iconic Gotti, Sr.'s Howard Beach home.

Peter's son was remanded to Rikers Island, immediately labeled as a "high profile" inmate and was put in twenty-three-hour-a-day isolation for the next seven months. Johnny was arrested the same day that more than forty alleged mobsters were indicted in a massive *unrelated* East Coast sweep from New York to Florida. But with the name "Gotti" being more newsworthy, the "coincidental timing" on his arrest would help give more media attention to the Feds' massive "Mob bust".

As I prayed for Peter and his family, a familiar theme kept resurfacing: *fathers and their sons.* That's the only story that really matters now.

I'd continue to check in on Peter to see how his son and family were holding up he'd always be quick to remind me, "Enjoy every second you have together with your wife and son, because tomorrow is promised to no-one."

I always promise him I will, and that I pray every day for his son. I try and encourage Peter that life can go the other way too.

"Battle is my companion," Peter strongly replies. "I have spent too much time in it, one way or another."

I concurred.

"When everything went down last year with Angelina," I explained to Peter, "I spent the whole year writing this book. Stories surrounding my art, my career in education, our son and his battle with Autism, and stories about countless other kids I've tried to help along the course of my life. Maybe one day I'll publish it."

I felt at the time I began writing this, it was worth it to finally get my story out, if anything, so our son will know his story and my real heart one day too. Hard as it may have been, it's helped me—journaling it all out. I know this is something Peter did while bedside visiting his Dad those six months in Marion. So, I urged Peter, "Try journaling for your son and date each entry. One day they'll be more important to your son than you know."

"Michael, I can't agree more. I'm going to start tonight," Peter replied. "Like I always thought, sometimes even a slight nudge from a loved one can be a catalyst for great things ahead."

I smiled to myself, knowing Peter would soon put pen to paper again, and I hoped it would prove to be just as therapeutic.

ONE MONTH FLEW BY, and in September I was surprised and honored with a plaque from our new principal, my eleventh now in twenty-two years. She was awarding me "September's Staff Member of the Month".

It's funny how things always seem to keep coming full circle for me. My career began as Southern High's first ever "Teacher of the Month" back in 2000. This was long before my becoming honored as the Anne Arundel County Public Schools 2004—2005 Teacher of the Year, long before earning National Board Certification, and long before all my National Teacher of the Year accolades, National Rising Star Award Winners, and National Scholastic Medalists. Our enthusiastic new Principal shared this about me with our entire faculty one afternoon:

"September's 2016 staff member of the month goes to a staff member that is passionate about his content area and his programs here at Southern High School and is overall a positive influence on both students and staff. He is always willing to lend an ear or offer positive encouragement and feedback.

Additionally, he assisted with two professional development sessions with our staff during opening week for teachers. He added three new to Southern High teachers to his department after a tenuous year of a long-term substitute and two departing teachers. He had our cafeteria looking great while showcasing his art program at 9th grade orientation, back to school night, and during the opening of school. In the summer months, he assisted with the MATI conference, which is a statewide organization of arts educators; and he organized and presented another session of the Gifted and Talented Visual Arts Program for AACPS middle and high school students. Congratulations to Mr. Michael Bell!" – *Katie Feuerherd, Principal, Southern High*

ON OCTOBER 20ᵀᴴ, I arrived by plane to Nashville, Tennessee for my first of two keynote appearances this month, while our son geared up to take part in his first huge Autism benefit downtown Annapolis. It killed me to miss it, but I was excited for him.

His new celebrity began following the blog I wrote for *Autism Speaks* that went viral. Then, we attended a charity football game at the Naval Academy to benefit *the Bowen Foundation for Autism.* We initially went to watch Tony Acevedo, owner of our boxing gym, play in the annual game and cheer him on. But, one thing led to another, and Lil' C landed his first big moment in the spotlight as a "celebrity spokesman" for the Bowen Foundation.

So, after delivering an inspiring keynote following Deborah Reeve, Executive Director of NAEA, to a sea of amazing art educators from throughout the state of Tennessee, I remembered to text Peter Gotti when I got to my hotel to wish his son Peter, Jr.

a happy birthday. I told him, "While I'm busy here in Nashville inspiring the masses our son is back home tonight with my wife as featured star of an Autism fundraiser downtown Annapolis."

"Good luck brother," Peter congratulated me, "and send a message to Lil' C that we're there with him. These are rare moments in a lifetime that form priceless memories for a child."

This is the interesting dichotomy that also keeps resurfacing again and again throughout my life. This is something that nobody will ever truly understand about my life or my art, or why I paint what I paint or *who* I paint *for*.

Some people think I glorify the so-called gangsters I've spent my life surrounded by.

People have even had the balls say to me, without truly knowing me, "How can you rise to the highest levels of education and be hanging out with fighters and killers?"

The answer is profoundly simple. I've had to fight since the day I was born. So has my wife. And, so has our son. More than most people ever will know, or ever have to experience. And these so-called "fighters and killers" have been the only constant in my life that have been there for me and fought alongside me.

It certainly wasn't the teachers I grew up having in school, or the *muckety-mucks* in the very public education system that I've spent two decades making look so good that have ever come to my aid, or gone out of their way to do right by my son when he was badly in need . . . It's only been those so-called "gangsters".

You see, throughout my life, I've seen the people that were supposed to do right by me—and I'm talking about those same teachers, coaches, bosses, even some members of my own family in some instances—*abandon me when I needed them the most.*

The ones that truly embraced me and have become endearing to me and to our child are the very ones the public has quickly rushed to label as "gangsters and killers", without even knowing them either. Well, I know them. *And I love them dearly.*

Here's a small token why . . .

TUESDAY MORNING, October 18ᵗʰ, just two days before my son's Autism benefit and just before my flight to Nashville, Peter's brother John Gotti Junior reached out to me bright and early around eight in the morning after receiving word about the benefit we were hosting around our son.

"What can I do to help? Whatever you need brother, just let me know." John offered.

I explained that I was having several "Gotti prints" made for Carmen to feature in this silent auction. From my early *John Gotti, America* painting, to the *Safety Social Club* painting and the courtroom scene drawings that I did back in the day for his sister Angel. Since John offered, I thought it'd be a huge hit to offer a fine art print of his *John Gotti, Shadow of my Father* book cover painting, along with a hand-signed book from the man himself.

"Send the info to Big Steve and I'll drop off an autographed book today and have it overnighted to you, for your son. Give my love to the family and hope to see you soon. Anytime, anywhere you need me brother, whatever I can do to help," was John's reply, without hesitation.

"John Gotti did that *for me?*" Carmen said when I told him. "Awwww, tell Uncle John thanks for me, Dad."

Every John Gotti print sold.

As did the autographed book from John Junior.

The gangster art prints were so popular at the auction that Teresa Giudice's lawyer, James J. Leonard, from the television show *the Real Housewives of New Jersey*, private messaged me wanting to know the opening bid for the *Gotti, Shadow of my Father* book and print combo after seeing something posted about it online. I texted back and forth with my wife on the bidding, and James J. Leonard won them. What a great guy!

As a thank you to him for supporting our son, I even made James a special hand-signed 16" X 20" print to accompany the autographed book from both John and me on the opening page. The charity raised $15,000 that night in a few short hours. The incredibly generous local bar owner that hosted the event at his *Armadillo's* restaurant was a huge part of that contribution.

So, as I sat in my Nashville hotel room, anxiously waiting to hear how the night ended for Carmen, Lisa sent me pictures of him posing with his fist raised next to various supporters. It warmed my heart that one of his teachers showed up. Lisa told me that she even took him out for ice cream to give him a break from the loud music that was putting him on sensory overload.

Carmen's night in the limelight also included him being announced and honored in front of the entire crowd gathered and he took lots of photos in front of my art and with John's book, donning his favorite suit from his first communion. Bryan Levy, President of the Bowen Foundation for Autism was so good to our son that night. I can't thank him for all he did to make Carmen feel special. It was hard being so many miles away from him. I was overwhelmed with emotion, and when Lisa texted me around 1 A.M. with pictures of him from throughout the night, I immediately went to my laptop in order to insert them into the end of my slideshow for the next day's TAEA keynote address.

NOVEMBER 10th, ON MY FATHER'S BIRTHDAY, my plane touched down in Tucson, Arizona where I was brought out to deliver my next back-to-back keynote to the Arizona Art Education Association and give hands-on workshops on my innovative *31 Nights* project that is steadily sweeping the nation. While there, I shared all these amazing stories, taking everyone through a roller-coaster ride of emotions—from laughter to tears as I inspired them to create a movement among themselves.

And then, just as I was concluding my keynote, I received a text message with a selfie from 2012 graduate Paige Shryock, taken from inside my classroom art studio standing in front of my painting easel. You see, Paige was substituting for me while I was out in Arizona. Talk about a journey coming full circle! I shared the pic of Paige standing in my studio with the crowd on hand at the conclusion of my workshop. You see, *it's all about this—* experiences beyond the norm.

It's about transcendence, or in Italian—trascendenza.

Trascendenza is also a word I had my tattoo artist Ty Pallotta scribe on one of two books that were positioned beneath one of the lion's large paws in my *Daniel in the Lion's Den* forearm sleeve over the course of a twelve-hour straight session just over one year ago. Back then it was about *my need* to transcend. Now I've come to realize it's more about how I've survived by making very distinct, yet unconventional and sometimes extremely dangerous choices, leading me down dark paths and unstable bridges, often destroying them behind me just as quickly as I crossed. Sometimes in *metaphorical ways*. Sometimes in *violent ways*.

For me, this ride of life has always been about knowing how long to stay on, when to get off and when to re-assess our paths. I'm re-assessing mine now. Anyone in my way better step aside, because I'm coming with a vengeance.

Like Apollo Creed said in his last conversation with Rocky Balboa in *Rocky IV*, I'm also born with a killer instinct that you can't "turn off and on". I also have to be right in the middle of the action because I am a warrior. And like Apollo said, "Without some challenge . . . without some war to fight . . . then the warrior might as well be dead."

As I finished up in Tucson, Lisa sent me a text with a pic of a painting our son Carmen brought home from his art class in school. It's a large, colorful collage on light blue painted paper with various patterns making up the sun in oranges, reds, greens and yellows. At the top in BOLD green letters, he painted into the sky the word: **BRAVE**. *It brought a tear to my eyes.*

Especially after hearing about the particularly difficult couple of weeks he had at school standing up to bullies and trying his best to hold it all together. We've since hired one of the best advocates in the State of Maryland and are fighting hard to ensure our son's needs are being met, no matter what battles we have to go through. I've even enlisted the help of longtime friend Jerry Walker, our County Councilman now running for State Delegate.

We later learned Carmen made that painting as his way of dealing with having to sit directly across from one of those bullies in his art class, all the while, still staying "brave".

This was his way of communicating it to us through his art. When Lisa asked him to tell her more about the painting he simply said proudly, "I did it because I'm brave—*like a fighter*."

Just like Peter Gotti said, "Battle is my companion." And if he's gonna fight, we're gonna fight. *Any way we can.*

FEBRUARY 9TH, I WAS BACK AT WORK reading through various contests shared with all Art Teachers throughout the county, when I read about a *2017 Artists Without Limits Exhibit*, sponsored by The Anne Arundel County Commission on Disability Issues and the Arts Council of Anne Arundel County. Entries for the show had to reflect the theme of "My World." I immediately thought of Carmen and his *BRAVE* painting.

I thought to myself, "You know what, I've spend every fabric of my being helping kids in my classes enter every contest that's out there—and they win—*a lot!* Why not submit my own son for a change, even though technically he's not a kid in my class."

I checked the rules, and any individual artist could submit. I figured, if no-one at his school ever picks his work for any shows or anything, not even as a courtesy to me being an art teacher in the county, *I'm at least gonna give him that shot,* just like I do for my own students and see what happens.

And you know what? *He won!* His very first art award! Carmen was honored at the Arundel Center downtown Annapolis and received a signed Executive Citation from the County Executive, which mirrors the likes of the many Citations I have framed hanging on my studio walls. He was sooooooo excited!!!

So, for you parents out there fighting for your children, especially parents of amazing special needs children—don't ever back down. Do your research, hire the best advocate you can afford, and do whatever it takes to ensure your child's safety and well-being. We will continue to fight for our son's happiness and success. Even if it means taking legal action against the very public school system I've devoted my life to making look so good, if it comes down to that. *I'll never back down.*

Neither should you with whatever your situation is. My wife and I are committed to devoting all our energy to ensuring our son is provided with the best opportunities to receive a great education. I'll give this fight the same level of imagination, dedication and hard work I've given to my students, to the community, and to my craft over the course of my storied career.

We will find that key to help guide and channel his energy in the right directions, help him uncover his hidden gifts and true purpose in life, just like I found mine. Will there eventually be another teacher like me come out from the shadows and into his life to help guide his journey and help him find his true purpose?

Only time will tell.

AS I SAT ON THE PLANE awaiting my departure for home after an inspiring week in Arizona, I glanced out from my window seat to take a photo for our son of the gorgeous sunrise over the Santa Catalina Mountains. Just as I was about to snap the picture, something immediately snatched my attention away. On the runway sat three taxiway signs set up, one next to another, in front of a backdrop of F-22 Raptors.

The letters on the taxiway spelled out: **D-A-D** in big bold letters. *I smiled to myself.* It felt like the Universe was talking to me again. Just like that last fateful night Angelina passed away at the Children's Hospital in Philadelphia when I glanced over to see that *Coca Cola* can staring back at me with the word *DAD* written along its' side.

"I'm coming home, son," I smiled to myself.

I'm coming home . . .

This was my very last card game with my Grandma, and the last time Lisa did her hair. Below is my *31 Nights* drawing of St. Thomas' Church the day of Vi's funeral, and me with my father-in-law, Bill, at *Harvey Cedars Shellfish Company* on Long Beach Island the day we got Lisa's Navé Cosmetics back. That's Lisa's Nonna Navé in Italy (bottom right).

My Grandfather, the Boxer, with my Mom (above) in Lyndhurst. Below is my Dad (center, age 10) the day he departed for America from Northern Ireland. (from left) is Leta Deering, my Dad's Uncle Earl, Aunt Agnes McNeill, his Mom Jessie Evelyn, his Dad John, his Aunt May and cousin Andre (right).

My Dad wouldn't see his cousin Jim again until Jim's first trip to America in June, 2014. Where'd they go? To an Irish Pub, of course!

Lisa's Uncle Amore and wife Maria's first visit to America in 2009.
(top left) Lisa's Aunt Carmina, Aunt Connie and Lisa's Dad, Bill.
(below) Lisa's Mom, Olga with Carmen, age 2 and Maria. Top (right)
with Lisa's brother Marc, Bill and Amore. (center) Lisa with her
brothers Peter and Marc, circa 1974. Below, with Lisa's brother, Pete.

Lisa with her Dad on a family trip to Italy, at St. Peter's Square in Rome, 1981.
This was the last time Bill saw his brother, Amore, until the 2009 visit (above).

Lots of memories were left behind in my Grandma's house in Lyndhurst. We keep my Grandparents' memory alive through art and boxing. We honor them every Thanksgiving by taking Carmen into New York City to see the floats.

My 2015 painting unveiling in NYC with Lisa, Angel Gotti, Peter J. Gotti, Charles Carnesi, Peter Lance, John A. Gotti, Mickey Rourke & John Gotti, Jr.

Storytelling became my new artform, from delivering my first *TEDx* talk in New Jersey to giving keynotes across the country to packing the crowds into my sessions at NAEA National Conventions with artistic accomplices Eric Scott, David Modler and Sam Peck. I ended up hiring Sam in 2016.

From Carmen's Baptism with his Godparents Marc and Kellie, to Carmen's first Holy Communion with the Molinaro and Bell families.

Family comes in many forms. Carmen's "other family," with the generosity of his "Uncle John" helped him raise money for *the Bowen Foundation for Autism* through auction of John's book and prints of my John Gotti artwork.

Each of us has a story to tell. I was proud to share the accomplishments of my 2016 national award recipients, and Kelly's story with everyone at her Senior Awards.

Kelly also served as the model for these narrative 24" X 48" "Bonnie and Clyde" oil paintings for one of my fabulous New York City painting clients.

Carmen painted this award winning picture in art class after standing up for himself against bullies in school. John Gotti, Jr. mailed us out these "Lions only" hoodies shortly after, with his iconic father's quote inscribed on the back.

3 years into his boxing training, Lil' C (age 9) is on his quest to become a Golden Gloves champion, still fighting at the boxing gym with these lions in his corner.

My artwork for John Gotti's book was showcased throughout the City. Peter Gotti was also excited to own a work with him and his iconic father.

My 2016 two-panel *John Gotti - REBEL* diptych, each 48" X 48" for Peter Gotti's son, Johnny was to be unveiled two days after his arrest. I promised his father Peter they'd stay on my easel until he comes home. Above is me and Peter, hours after Johnny's last visit with me the day before his sentencing. *Another unfinished chapter . . . Fathers and their Sons . . .*

AFTERWORD

THE CHALLENGES OF CHANGE

December 27, 2016 was the second back-to-back year we drove to New York City at Christmas time to visit John Gotti Junior. The first visit was to do the epic painting unveiling for his *Shadow of my Father* book cover. This time, it was more of a low-key affair that began accompanying John and his lovely wife Kim to dinner for some great Italian food and some laughs. John put us up at a hotel nearby his home (and *never* lets you pay, by the way, just the kind of guy he is) and we went out from there. Lisa and Kim sat together at dinner so they could chat and Lil' C sat between John and me, donning a fresh black sports coat, looking all grown up.

John immediately took a liking to him.

They talked non-stop. It was heartwarming to see how genuinely warm he was with our son, and it was also quite comical. Especially because Lil' C, probably due to his ASD, is quite candid. There's never much of a filter, and you never know what's going to come out of his mouth.

Things like . . . "Uncle John—your Dad was the king of New York, right? So where did all his money go?"

My wife and I were mortified.

John just laughed.

"To the lawyers, mostly, C," he chuckled. "Where does all your money go?"

"I buy trains," he replied very matter-of-factly. "And boxing gloves. I try and use my Dad's money, though, most of the time." It was the funniest conversation ever!

We met up with his brother Peter later that night at the Carltun after dinner where we'd smoke cigars and John and Peter would take turns shooting pool against C until the wee hours of the morning.

He had such a blast hanging out late night with the men at the Carltun. Guys like singer Johnny Avino, and actors from John's new film, *The Life and Death of John Gotti*. Everyone made him feel right at home, like one of the guys. Just like everyone did for him at the boxing gym.

When he asked Big Steve, "Man, what time does this place close?"

"About three hours ago," Big Steve retorted, smiling to C. "But no-one leaves while John's still here."

C's eyes got wide, probably imagining the opportunity to pull an all-nighter.

When we finally did pack it in around 3 A.M. I walked Peter over to our car where I handed him a Christmas present I had waiting for him. I told him not to open it until he got home.

Naturally, he couldn't wait and immediately called me, in tears. "It's beautiful. I'm speechless . . ."

"I knew I couldn't bring your son Johnny home to you," I explained, "but at least I could bring him home to you through my art. Through a picture where he looks strong. And every time you look at it, you'll see his strength. *Heart of a lion.*"

The highly realistic charcoal drawing of his son I rendered from a photograph Johnny once told me was his favorite, staring out boldly into the viewer's eyes, his heavily muscled and tattooed arms folded across his chest in a proud, self-reflective pose. I also incorporated the mapping into the work, bringing the neighborhood of Howard Beach through his face, neck and shoulders, much the same as I did with a drawing I did for Peter in the form of the charcoal drawing I created of him and his father last Christmas. The same mapping I incorporated into Johnny's two-panel *REBEL* painting of his iconic Grandfather, John Gotti, Sr., that still sits on my easel to this day, with one panel overlooking Little Italy in Manhattan, the other panel of him in Lewisburg federal prison with his friends. Sometimes pictures really can be very prophetic. I promised Peter the paintings will stay on my easel until his son comes home for them himself.

MARCH 1, 2017 I took a train to New York City on route to deliver national presentations at my ninth National Art Education Association national convention. The theme of the convention was entitled: *The Challenge of Change.*

I was flooded with thoughts on my way to the City. First, because it was my wife's birthday, so Carmen and I surprised her the night before and took her out to dinner to celebrate before I left. Secondly, because Peter Gotti had promised to write me the Foreword for this book and hand it to me in person while I was in the city. I knew he had a lot on his plate, with his son's sentencing the next day, on March 2nd, so I was grateful to him for finishing it.

When I arrived at my hotel and touched base with him and John, Peter hit me with: "If you feel up to visiting my son with me it's 125 White Street. I can meet you in front of the Roxy Hotel at 7:20 P.M. Great place to have coffee if you get there early."

"I'd be happy to go with you tonight," I replied.

"Love you, buddy. No jewelry, t-shirt or sweatshirt. *Don't forget your ID.*"

Later that evening I put my cash and jewelry in a safe, slipped on a comfortable track suit and caught the Q train from 57th and 7th Avenue down to Canal Street. I walked a few brisk blocks to the Roxy, where I was greeted with the fireworks of flashbulbs to the sights of Carl Weathers (*Apollo from the Rocky films*) arriving, followed by Ray Liotta from *Goodfellas*, and then came J-Lo, all of them there for the NBC Season 2 premiere of *Shades of Blue.*

I smiled to myself, "Man, Lil' C would've loved to meet Apollo Creed."

Fifteen minutes passed as I waited patiently for Peter Gotti to finally arrive. When he finally did, I greeted him with a hug and kiss on the cheek, but was quick to notice *he was beside himself*.

"What's the matter, pal? You okay?" I asked.

"What's the last thing I told you before you left your hotel?"

"No cash, no jewelry, bring your ID," I replied.

"That last thing—*bingo*. You're not gonna fucking believe this, but I always keep my ID in my visor of my car. In a rush to get down here to see my son, I fucking left it in the visor when I parked to catch the subway in from Queens. Can you believe that? They're not gonna let me in to see my son. And it's too late. Too late to go back and get it. We'll miss visiting hours. And it's his last night before his sentencing . . ."

"But they *know you*. You've been in there to see him how many times?" I figured.

"It doesn't matter." Peter shot back with, totally distraught.

"We can at least try," was the only hopeful response I could muster.

And we did try. But to no avail. Even the guards who knew Peter on a first name basis wouldn't even do anything to help him without that ID.

"It's gotta be you then," Peter said to me. "I can't deny the kid his last visit. You go for me, in my place."

"I'd be honored to."

And just like that, off I went, inside the MDC in lower Manhattan. A hop, skip and a jump away from the bright lights of the paparazzi with their cameras outside *the Roxy*. A few miles away from the sea of 7,000 Art Educators from across the entire United States getting their first taste of inspiration at the NAEA Convention's pre-conference workshops with my *Journal Fodder Junkie pals* David Modler, Eric Scott and Sam Peck, who came by train with me to New York City just a few short hours ago.

And now, here I am, getting strip searched at the MDC before heading through three different levels of security to get to Peter's twenty-three-year-old son, John J. Gotti, Jr., who not only bears his iconic Grandfather's name, but all of the sudden—*his burdens*. Buried at the furthest end of the facility with other high-profile inmates and potential escape risks, I found Johnny waiting for me as I entered a room set aside for us.

"Michael Bell—Holy shit! It's so great so see you, cuz!"

He greeted me with a huge smile and big hug before we both sat down across a table from each other and began to talk about this and that for what ended up being the better part of over a couple of hours. I explained to him how devastated his father was that he couldn't get in here to see him, how he was outside waiting, hoping I got in safely. I explained in great depth just how deeply his father loved him and never wanted this life for him, but that he was also committed to being in his corner until he's home. Same thing goes for me, and my painting, that still sits on my easel in my studio.

"You know, when they handcuffed me at the house," Johnny explained, "that's the very first thing I thought of . . . I said to myself, *man*—Michael Bell is supposed to be up here to unveil those paintings day after tomorrow and now *THIS happened*."

"The paintings will be here for you when you get home, don't you worry brother."

"Thank you, brother. It's just so crazy how things came so full circle. Do you know, I still have the letter and pictures you drew for my Grandfather that he kept in the safe back home? *I have those*. And now, here I am, with the pictures you did for me printed out hanging up in *my cell*. How fucked up is that?"

"It's pretty fucked up, that's for sure," I laughed with him.

Time flew, us talking in there, swapping stories. When it was time to leave, we hugged again, and I felt good about our visit. He looked strong. Positive about the journey he was about to go on.

As I emerged back out of the MDC Peter was right where I left him, standing curbside waiting anxiously to know how the visit went. I assured him he looked great. Told him that I gave his son exactly what he needed—some good laughs and some trips down memory lane.

I told Peter how we compared tattoos, swapped stories about our families, about Johnny's Grandfather, about the state of things in the old neighborhood. We also talked about my paintings, about his little brother Dante, how he wanted to be a positive role model for him when he got out, just like I felt about my little brother when I was a troubled kid around his age. We talked about my son and how he's doing with boxing and how it's our *father-son bonding*, going to the boxing gym together. He told me how he hated missing his cousin John's MMA fight, but how proud he was that he won the Triton Welterweight title (*his cousin is John A. Gotti's son, also another John Jr.*). He told me he's going on this journey as a lion, just like his Grandfather and his Uncle John, and will come out of it a better man. *Lots of positive stuff.*

I also shared with Johnny how his cousin John, the MMA fighter, sent my son one of his "Lions Only" hoodies and that everything has been about lions with my son since that day on. Even Carmen's gamer tag in X-BOX is now a roaring lion!

"Even in a Cage, a Lion is Still a Lion," Johnny said to me, smiling proudly. "That's the quote on the back of the hoodie!"

"You know it, brother," I smiled back. "Do you know, that's what your Uncle John inscribed in the books he overnighted a few months ago for our son's first Autism benefit. Same quote."

"That's really cool of him."

"He and your father are great men. They've been fighting for you, more than you could ever know. And that quote means different things to different people. For John's son, it's the steel octagon cage of the MMA ring. For my son, it's his Autism. For you, it's these bars. But they can never take your heart. They can never change the person you truly are *inside* if you don't let them. So stay strong and I'll write you, just like I wrote your Grandfather," I assured Johnny as we smiled and hugged.

Peter smiled as I shared the conversations I had with his son as we walked and talked before we finally found a spot to cop-a-squat on a downtown neighborhood stoop.

"Sometimes God puts people in the right places at the right time," Peter reflected.

SUNDAY MORNING, MARCH 5ᵀᴴ I met Peter Gotti one last time before heading back home by train, having to be back at work Monday morning. We met at the Time Warner Building at Columbus Circle. Winner of the Keith Thurman—Danny Garcia fight from the other night had to buy brunch. That was our bet from the night before. I took Garcia, so naturally, to break my balls as soon as the fight ended I got a text message from Peter:

"You're a rare dinosaur, called Brunchasaurus Rex." That meant—*brunch was officially on me*. Even my wife broke my balls the next morning with a "Good morning Rex" text message.

But it's all good. Brunch was worth its weight in gold, because after we sat down Peter handed me the Foreword for this book. He asked me to skim through it as we ate. He assured me he read every page of my book, making copious notes and marking the book up like crazy all the way through it as he familiarized himself with the "other sides" of the dear friend he had grown to love like a brother over the past couple of years.

And before heading back to my hotel we ended up having a really interesting conversation surrounding my book, and the kids I teach. Now, any of you reading this book may know Peter and John's father, John J. Gotti, Sr. as the notorious "Boss of Bosses," head of the Gambino crime family and principal target of the FBI for well over a decade back in the 80s and early 90s. You may be familiar with him from seeing all the newspaper and magazine articles, since the paparazzi followed him around like he was a movie star. And, as his legend grew, he steadily rose to become this Robinhood-like figure that landed him on the cover of *Time Magazine* at the age of just forty-six.

But what you don't know—what one of the last things we talked about the morning we met for breakfast as Peter handed me the physical hand-written version of the Foreword for this book—was how he "wished that he could've been one of those kids he read about in my classes."

That moved me beyond words.

"If I could've had someone like you," he went on, "a teacher as dedicated as you—someone who truly cared about 'entering my world' during my teenage years, it might have changed the course of my own destiny, maybe even my oldest son's."

He'd go on to explain to me how he lived through three of his father's high-profile trials while still just a child in the 1980s, and how he was only sixteen years old when his father was arrested for his fourth and final trial in 1992, where he was convicted and sent away for life in a maximum security prison without parole.

That being said, for the two years leading up to his father's trial, the only contact he had with him was seeing him through a plate glass window on visits. Can you imagine that? Being just a teenager and not being able to physically touch your own father ever again?

After he was sent away, Peter explained to me, for the next nine years or so he still had no physical contact with him, nor did anyone else, as he was under the harshest twenty-three-hour solitary confinement known to man.

"It wasn't up until around the last six months I was finally able to touch him again, as I sat with him for two hours each day journaling everything I could while at his bedside, when he was terminal, battling cancer."

I understood even more how "battle became Peter's companion," and how the arc of his iconic father's journey became the map of a terrible country he surely never wanted to revisit until he had no other choice to. This time it was to fight for his son, just prior to writing my Foreword. What a beautiful man.

Fathers and their sons.

These are the challenges of change.

Peter's challenges have recently proved to become even more complicated. Less than a month later, on the day his son was scheduled to go upstate to serve out an eight year sentence handed down by the State of New York, the Feds swooped in and grabbed Johnny up, dragging him into a five-year-old case.

"We tried to move on with our lives," Peter told me, "but God wants us to fight, so fight we will."

I told him to keep smiling, like his old man would — *and fight*. My son noticed my reaction to the news and asked me why I was so sad. I explained how I couldn't imagine spending even one day away from him, let alone what Peter is forced to go through with his son, just the same as "Uncle John" has had to endure through his four trials, and through their father's trials before that . . .

My son hugged me and said, "He'll be okay, Daddy. We're all fighters. Send Uncle Peter my favorite song (*Future, Last Breath from the Rocky Balboa movie Creed*). That will keep him fighting."

So I did. This will, unfortunately, remain an *unfinished chapter*.

As for the rest of my story, while my journey certainly has come full circle, I hope it will also inspire you to tap into "your why" and be that change you want to see in the world. I also hope it inspires you to share "your story".

Because each of us has a story to tell.

Just know, at the end of the day, I've given it to you straight, from someone at the top of their game who is still in the trenches, still in the classroom, still behind my easel. Still helping kids rack up millions in scholarships annually. Still there to catch any kids I can before they fall. All the while, still finding the time to fly back and forth across the country to share my inspirational stories with others, deliver *TED talks*, put on more gallery exhibitions and create more commissioned paintings for these powerful and endearing men that have been labeled *America's most infamous*.

So, as an artist still driven to create and destroy; and as a national award-winning educator who never rests on his laurels; as a husband to an incredibly beautiful and supportive wife and mother; and as a fighter and devoted father to a truly brilliant and charismatic son — I leave this book with each of you as fuel to go and do something truly epic with your journey. It's up to you.

The time is now . . .

And, in the words of John A. Gotti himself, from the words his father shared with him:

"At the end of the day, all we have are memories.
Make as many as you can . . ."

INDEX

Note: Artworks are by Michael Bell unless otherwise noted.

ABOUT THE AUTHOR

Michael Bell is a renowned American Artist, most famous for his gangster series paintings and his infamous portrait painting clientele, which includes John Gotti, Dominic Capone and numerous actors from *the Sopranos, Goodfellas, A Bronx Tale* and more. He's also a father, fighter, boxing enthusiast, anti-bullying and Autism activist.

Bell has also excelled in the field of education, playing a vital role in pioneering a worldwide Visual Journaling movement. Bell is a National Board Certified Teacher and a 3-time national award-winning public school "Teacher of the Year" that has been honored with: *the Los Angeles Good Shepherd Shelter* Community Service Award, *the College Board's* William U. Harris Award of Excellence, *the NAEA's* National Art Honor Society Sponsor of the Year, *the Washington Post's* Agnes Meyer Outstanding Teacher Award and the Dr. James E. Douthat Outstanding Achievement Award from Lycoming College. Bell is also a 7-time NAEA Rising Star Award-Winning Art Educator (2010 – 2016) and a 3-time Scholastic Art National Medalist Educator (2014 – 2016).

Bell has a BFA from Lycoming College and an M.Ed in Art Education from Towson University.

MBELLART PRODUCTIONS

To Commission Original Artwork by Michael Bell
or for Public Speaking/Workshop Inquiries visit:
www.MBELLART.com

∞

View Michael Bell's Visual Journaling Website:
www.VISUALJOURNALING.com | #visualjournaling

∞

View Michael Bell's 31 Nights Website:
www.31nights.com | #31nights

∞

FOLLOW Michael Bell on Social Media:
TWITTER.com/mbellart
INSTAGRAM.com/mbellart
FACEBOOK.com/mbellartlive

∞

FOLLOW Lil' C's journey at:
www.CARMENBELL.com
TWITTER.com/LilContender
INSTAGRAM.com/ LilContender
FACEBOOK.com/ LilContender